St. John of the Cross

Ascent
of
Mount Carmel

Translated and edited by
E. Allison Peers

Dover Publications, Inc.
Mineola, New York

Bibliographical Note

This Dover edition, first published in 2008, is an unabridged republication of *Ascent of Mount Carmel* from *The Complete Works of Saint John of the Cross (Volume I),* originally published by The Newman Bookshop, Westminster, Maryland, in 1946.

Library of Congress Cataloging-in-Publication Data

John of the Cross, Saint, 1542–1591.
    [Subida del Monte Carmelo. Enlish]
    Ascent of Mount Carmel / St. John of the Cross ; translated and edited by E. Allison Peers.
       p. cm.
    Originally published: Westminster, Md. : Newman Bookshop, 1946, in series: The complete works of Saint John of the Cross ; v. 1.
    ISBN-13: 978-0-486-46837-2
    ISBN-10: 0-486-46837-2
    1. Mysticism—Catholic Church. I. Peers, E. Allison (Edgar Allison), 1891–1952. II. Title.

BV5082.3.J64213 2008
248.2'2—dc22

                                2008029625

Manufactured in the United States of America
Dover Publications, Inc., 31 East 2nd Street, Mineola, N.Y. 11501

CONTENTS

ASCENT OF MOUNT CARMEL

BOOK I

CONTENTS

BOOK II

CONTENTS

BOOK III

CONTENTS

CONTENTS

AN OUTLINE OF THE LIFE OF S. JOHN OF THE CROSS

1542. Birth of Juan de Yepes at Fontiveros (Hontiveros), near Ávila.

> The day generally ascribed to this event is June 24 (S. John Baptist's Day). No documentary evidence for it, however, exists, the parish registers having been destroyed by a fire in 1546. The chief evidence is an inscription, dated 1689, on the font of the parish church at Fontiveros.

? c. 1549. Death of Juan's father. 'After some years' (? c. 1551) the mother removes, with her family, to Arévalo, and later to Medina del Campo.

? c. 1552–6. Juan goes to school at the Colegio de los Niños de la Doctrina, Medina.

c. 1556–7. Don Antonio Álvarez de Toledo takes him into a Hospital to which he has retired, with the idea of his (Juan's) training for Holy Orders under his patronage.

? c. 1557–61. Juan attends the School of the Society of Jesus at Medina.

c. 1562. Leaves the Hospital and the patronage of Álvarez de Toledo.

1563. Takes the Carmelite habit in the Monastery of Santa Ana, Medina del Campo, as Juan de San Matías (or de Santo Matía).

> The day is considered by most biographers to have been that of S. Matthias (February 24), but P. Silverio postulates a day in August or September.

1564. Professes in the same monastery—probably in August or September and certainly not earlier than May 21 and not later than October.

1564 (November).   Enters the University of Salamanca as an *artista*.   Takes a three-year course in Arts (1564–7).

1567.   Receives priest's orders (probably in the summer).

1567 (? early in September).   Meets S. Teresa at Medina del Campo.   Juan is thinking of transferring to the Carthusian Order.   S. Teresa asks him to join her Discalced Reform and the projected first foundation for monks.   He agrees to do so, provided the foundation is soon made.

1567 (November).   Returns to the University of Salamanca, where he takes a year's course in theology.

1568.   Spends parts of the Long Vacation at Duruelo, Medina and Ávila.

1568 (November 28).   Takes the vows of the Reform at Duruelo as S. John of the Cross, together with Antonio de Heredia (Antonio de Jesús), Prior of the Calced Carmelites at Medina, and José de Cristo, another Carmelite from Medina.

1570 (June 11).   The Duruelo monastery is transferred to Mancera.

1570 (October).   Founds the second monastery of the Reform at Pastrana.

1571 (? January ? April).   Goes to Alcalá de Henares where he founds the third (a collegiate) monastery of the Reform and directs the Carmelite nuns.

> 1571 (October).   S. Teresa becomes Prioress of the Convent of the Incarnation, Ávila, and holds this office till 1573.

1572 (shortly after April 23).   Recalled to Pastrana.

1572.   Goes to Ávila as confessor to the Convent of the Incarnation.

> The month generally given is May, but P. Silverio thinks (and I entirely agree with him) that it must have been considerably later.   It was, however, certainly before September 27.

1572–7.   Remains at Ávila.

> This is the period of open hostility between the Calced and Discalced Carmelites.

1575. A General Chapter of the Carmelites determines on the suppression of all houses of the Reform but two. S. Teresa writes to Philip II, asking that the Discalced may be made into a separate province. Envoys with petitions to the same effect are sent by the Discalced to the Vatican.

1577 (October). The election of a new prioress at Ávila leads to a display of intolerance against the Discalced on the part of the Provincial of the Calced Carmelites.

1577 (night of December 3–4). S. John of the Cross is carried off to Toledo by the Calced as a prisoner, with Fray Germano de Santo Matía. He is imprisoned in the Calced Carmelite monastery at Toledo.

1577–8. Composes in prison 17 (or perhaps 30) stanzas of the 'Spiritual Canticle' (i.e., as far as the stanza : 'Daughters of Jewry') ; the poem with the refrain 'Although 'tis night' ; and the stanzas beginning 'In principio erat verbum.' He may also have composed the paraphrase of the psalm *Super flumina* and the poem 'Dark Night.' (*Note:* All these poems, in verse form, will be found in Vol. II of this edition.)

1578 (*c.* March 11). Fray Germano de Santo Matía is no longer a prisoner.

1578 (night of August 15). S. John of the Cross has a vision of Our Lady, instructing him to escape.

1578. Escapes to the Convent of the Carmelite nuns (San José) in Toledo, and is thence taken to his house by D. Pedro González de Mendoza, Canon of Toledo.

     This occurred either on the night of August 16 or on a later night within the Octave of the Assumption.

1578 (October 9). Present at a Chapter General of the Discalced at Almodóvar. Is sent to Monte Calvario as Vicar, in the absence in Rome of the Prior.

     1578 (October 16). A Papal Decree submits the Discalced Carmelites to the Calced.

1578 (end of October). Stays for 'a few days' at Beas de Segura, near Monte Calvario. Confesses the nuns at the Carmelite Convent of Beas.

1578–9. Remains at Monte Calvario as Vicar. For a part of this time (probably from the beginning of 1579), goes weekly to the convent of Beas to hear confessions. During this period, begins his commentary entitled *The Ascent of Mount Carmel* (Cf. pp. 1–334, below) and also the *Spiritual Canticle* (translated in Vol. II).

1579 (June 14). Founds a house of the Reform at Baeza.

1579–81. Resides at Baeza as Rector of the Carmelite house. Visits the Beas convent occasionally (sometimes every fortnight). Writes more of the prose works begun at Monte Calvario and the rest of the stanzas of the *Spiritual Canticle* except the last five, possibly with the commentaries to the stanzas.

    1580 (June 22). The Discalced Reform is recognized by a bull of Gregory XIII.

    1581 (March 3). ' Chapter of the Separation ' (of Calced and Discalced) at Alcalá. P. Gracián is elected provincial by a majority of one.

1581 (March 3). Attends the Alcalá Chapter.
    Appointed Prior of the Granada Monastery of Los Mártires.

1582 (January 20). Arrives at Los Mártires.
    1582 (October 15). Death of S. Teresa.

1582–8. Prior at Granada. Resides there continuously till 1584 and intermittently afterwards. Visits the Beas convent occasionally. Writes the last five stanzas of the ' Spiritual Canticle ' during one of these visits. At Los Mártires, finishes the *Ascent of Mount Carmel* and composes his remaining prose treatises. The *Living Flame of Love* is written in 1585, in fifteen days, at the request of Doña Ana de Peñalosa.

    1583 (May 1). Provincial Chapter of Almodóvar.
    1585. Chapter of Lisbon (May 10 ; continued at Pastrana on October 17) divides the one Discalced province into four vicariates. S. John of the Cross becomes Vicar-Provincial of Andalusia. P. Gracián's provincialate comes to an end. P. Doria succeeds him.

1585–7. S. John of the Cross Vicar-Provincial of Andalusia. Numerous foundations, notably : San José de Málaga, February 17, 1585 ; Córdoba, May 18, 1586 ;

Manchuela de Jaén, October 1586 ; Caravaca, December 18, 1586 ; Bujalance, June 24, 1587.

1587 (June 27). P. Doria obtains the new Constitution of the Reform by a brief of Sixtus V.

1587 (April). Chapter of Valladolid. S. John of the Cross is re-elected Prior of Granada.

1588 (May). P. Gracián is deprived of his offices in the Order.[1]

1588 (June 19). Opening of the first Chapter General of the Reform, which S. John of the Cross attends. P. Doria becomes Vicar-General. Consulta[2] formed. S. John of the Cross is elected the first of the *consiliarios*.

1588 (August 10). Is made Prior of the Monastery of Segovia, which becomes the central house of the Reform and the headquarters of the Consulta. (In the absence of the Vicar-General, he would govern both the Consulta and the house). He remains Prior till February 1589.

1590 (June). Re-elected first *consiliario* at the Chapter of Madrid.

1591 (June). Deprived of his offices and elected Provincial of Mexico. (*N.B.* This appointment was revoked.)

1591 (end of July). Goes to La Peñuela.

1591 (September 12). Attacked by fever. (September 22) Leaves La Peñuela for Úbeda. (December 14) Dies at Úbeda.

.   .   .   .   .   .

January 25, 1675. Beatified by Clement X.

December 26, 1726. Canonized by Benedict XIII.

August 24, 1926. Declared Doctor of the Church Universal by Pius XI.

---

[1] [Cf. E. Allison Peers, *Studies of the Spanish Mystics*, Vol. II, p. 156.]
[2] [*Ibid.*]

THE COMPLETE WORKS OF SAINT JOHN OF THE CROSS

ASCENT OF MOUNT CARMEL

INTRODUCTION

As will be seen from the biographical outline which we have given of the life of S. John of the Cross, this was the first of the Saint's treatises to be written ; it was begun at El Calvario, and, after various intervals, due to the author's preoccupation with the business of government and the direction and care of souls, was completed at Granada.

The treatise presents a remarkable outline of Christian perfection from the point at which the soul first seeks to rise from the earth and soar upward towards union with God. It is a work which shows every sign of careful planning and great attention to detail ; as an ascetic treatise it is noteworthy for its detailed psychological analysis ; as a contribution to mystical theology, for the skill with which it treats the most complicated and delicate questions concerning the Mystic Way.

Both the great Carmelite reformers pay close attention to the early stages of the mystical life, beyond which many never pass, and both give the primacy to prayer as a means of attaining perfection. To S. Teresa prayer is the greatest of all blessings of this life, the channel through which all the favours of God pass to the soul, the beginning of every virtue and the plainly marked highroad which leads to the summit of Mount Carmel. She can hardly conceive of a person in full spiritual health whose life is not one of prayer. Her coadjutor in the Carmelite Reform writes in the same spirit. Prayer, for S. John of the Cross as for S. Teresa, is no mere exercise made up of petition and meditation, but a complete spiritual life which brings in its train all the virtues, increases all the

soul's potentialities and may ultimately lead to ' deification '
or transformation in God through love. It may be said that
the exposition of the life of prayer, from its lowest stages to its
highest, is the common aim of these two Saints, which each
pursues and accomplishes in a peculiarly individual manner.

S. John of the Cross assumes his reader to be familiar with
the rudiments of the spiritual life and therefore omits
detailed description of the most elementary of the exercises
incumbent upon all Christians. The plan of the *Ascent of
Mount Carmel* (which, properly speaking, embraces its sequel,
the *Dark Night*), follows the lines of the poem with the latter
title (p. 10). Into two stanzas of five lines each, S. John of
the Cross has condensed all the instruction which he develops
in this treatise. In order to reach the Union of Light, the
soul must pass through the Dark Night—that is to say,
through a series of purifications, during which it is walking,
as it were, through a tunnel of impenetrable obscurity and
from which it emerges to bask in the sunshine of grace and to
enjoy the Divine intimacy.

Through this obscurity the thread which guides the soul
is that of ' emptiness ' or ' negation.' Only by voiding ourselves of all that is not God can we attain to the possession of
God, for two contraries cannot co-exist in one individual and
creature-love is darkness, while God is light, so that from
any human heart one of the two cannot fail to drive out
the other.[1]

Now the soul, according to the Saint's psychology, is
made up of interior and exterior senses and of the faculties.
All these must be free from creature impurities in order to
be prepared for Divine union. The necessary self-emptying
may be accomplished in two ways : by our own efforts,
with the habitual aid of grace, and by the action of God
exclusively, in which the individual has no part whatsoever.
Following this order, the Ascent is divided into two parts,
which deal respectively with the ' Active ' night and the
' Passive.' Each of these parts consists of several books.
Since the soul must be purified in its entirety, the Active
Night is logically divided into the Night of Sense and the
Night of the Spirit ; a similar division is observed in treating
of the Passive Night. One book is devoted to the Active
Night of Sense ; two are needed for the Active Night of the
Spirit. Unhappily, however, the treatise was never finished ;

---

[1] *Ascent*, Bk. III, Chap. ii.

not only was its author unable to take us out of the night into the day, as he certainly intended to do, but he has not even space to describe the Passive Night in all the fullness of its symbolism.

A brief glance at the outstanding parts of the *Ascent of Mount Carmel* will give some idea of its nature. The first obstacle which the pilgrim soul encounters is the senses, upon which S. John of the Cross expends his analytical skill in Book I. Like any academic professor (and it will be recalled that he had undergone a complete university course at Salamanca), he outlines and defines his subject, goes over the necessary preliminary ground before expounding it, and treats it, in turn, under each of its natural divisions. He tells us, that is to say, what he understands by the ' dark night ' ; describes its causes and its stages ; explains how necessary it is to union with God ; enumerates the perils which beset the soul that enters it ; and shows how all desires must be expelled, ' however small they be,' if the soul is to travel through it safely. Finally he gives a complete synthesis of the procedure that must be adopted by the pilgrim in relation to this part of his journey : the force of this is intensified by those striking maxims and distichs which make Chapter xiii of Book I so memorable.

The first thirteen chapters of the *Ascent* are perhaps the easiest to understand (though they are anything but easy to put into practice) in the entire works of S. John of the Cross. They are all a commentary on the very first line of the poem. The last two chapters of the first book glance at the remaining lines, rather than expound them, and the Saint takes us on at once to Book II, which expounds the second stanza and enters upon the Night of the Spirit.

Here the Saint treats of the proximate means to union with God—namely, faith. He uses the same careful method of exposition, showing clearly how faith is to the soul as a dark night, and how, nevertheless, it is the safest of guides. A parenthetical chapter (v) attempts to give some idea of the nature of union, so that the reader may recognize from afar the goal to which he is proceeding. The author then goes on to describe how the three theological virtues—faith, hope and charity—must ' void and dispose for union ' the three faculties of the soul—understanding, memory and will.

He shows how narrow is the way that leads to life and how nothing that belongs to the understanding can guide the soul to union. His illustrations and arguments are far more complicated and subtle than are those of the first book, and give the reader some idea of his knowledge, not only of philosophy and theology, but also of individual souls. Without this last qualification he could never have written those penetrating chapters on the impediments to union—above all, the passages on visions, locutions and revelations,—nor must we overlook his description (Chapter xiii) of the three signs that the soul is ready to pass from meditation to contemplation. It may be doubted if in its own field this second book has ever been surpassed. There is no mystic who gives a more powerful impression than S. John of the Cross of an absolute mastery of his subject. No mistiness, vagueness or indecision clouds his writing : he is as clear-cut and definite as can be.

In his third book S. John of the Cross goes on to describe the obstacles to union which come from the memory and the will. As we have observed elsewhere, he considered the memory as a distinct and separate faculty of the soul. Having written, however, at such length of the understanding, he found it possible to treat more briefly of that other faculty, which is so closely related to it.[1] Fourteen chapters (ii–xv) describe the dark night to be traversed by the memory ; thirty (xvi–xlv) the passage of the will, impelled by love.[2] The latter part is the more strikingly developed. Four passions—joy, hope, sorrow and fear—invade the will, and may either encompass the soul's perdition, or, if rightly directed, lead it to virtue and union. Once more S. John of the Cross employs his profound familiarity with the human soul to turn it away from peril and guide it into the path of safety. Much that he says, in dealing with passions so familiar to us all, is not only purely ascetic, but is even commonplace to the instructed Christian. Yet these are but parts of a greater whole.

Of particular interest, both intrinsically and as giving a picture of the Saint's own times, are the chapters on ceremonies and aids to devotion—the use of rosaries, medals, pilgrimages, etc. It must be remembered, of course, that he spent most of his active life in the south of Spain, where exaggerations of all kinds, even to-day, are more frequent than in the more sober north. In any case there is less need,

---

[1] *Ascent*, Bk. III, Chap. iii, § 1.
[2] Cf. *Ascent*, Bk. III, Chap. xvi, §§ 1–2.

in this lukewarm age, to warn Christians against the abuse of these means of grace, and more need, perhaps, to urge them to employ aids that will stimulate and quicken their devotion.

In the seventeenth chapter of this third book, S. John of the Cross enumerates the ' six kinds of good ' which can give rise to rejoicing and sets down his intention of treating each of them in its turn. He carries out his purpose, but, on entering his last division, subdivides it at considerable length and subsequently breaks off with some brusqueness while dealing with one of these sub-heads, just as he is introducing another subject of particular interest historically—namely, pulpit methods considered from the standpoint of the preacher. In all probability we shall never know what he had to say about the hearers of sermons, or what were his considered judgements on confessors and penitents—though of these he has left us examples elsewhere in this treatise, as well as in others.

We cannot estimate of how much the sudden curtailment of the *Ascent of Mount Carmel* has robbed us. Orderly as was the mind of S. John of the Cross, he was easily carried away in his expositions, which are apt to be unequal. No one would have suspected, for example, that, after going into such length in treating the first line of his first stanza, he would make such short work of the remaining four. Nor can we disregard the significance of his warning that much of what he had written on the understanding was applicable also to the memory and the will. He may, therefore, have been nearer the end of his theme than is generally supposed. Yet it is equally possible that much more of the author's typical subtlety of analysis was in store for his readers. Any truncation, when the author is a S. John of the Cross, must be considered irreparable.

THE MANUSCRIPTS

Unfortunately there is no autograph of this treatise extant, though there are a number of early copies, some of which have been made with great care. Others, for various reasons, abbreviate the original considerably. The MSS. belonging to both classes will be enumerated.

Alba de Tormes. The Discalced Carmelite monastery of Alba de Tormes has a codex which contains the four principal treatises of S. John of the Cross (*Ascent, Dark Night,*

Spiritual Canticle and *Living Flame*). This codex belonged from a very early date (perhaps from a date not much later than that of the Saint's death) to the family of the Duke of Alba, which was greatly devoted to the Discalced Carmelite Reform and to S. Teresa, its foundress. It remained in the family until the beginning of the eighteenth century, when it came into the hands of a learned Carmelite, Fray Alonso de la Madre de Dios, who presented it to the Alba monastery on April 15, 1705. The details of this history are given by Fray Alonso himself in a note of this date.

For over half a century the MS. was believed to be an autograph, partly, no doubt, on account of its luxurious binding and the respect paid to the noble house whence it came. In February 1761, however, it was examined carefully by P. Manuel de Santa María, who, by his Superior's orders, was assisting P. Andrés de la Encarnación in his search for manuscripts of the Saint's writings. P. Manuel soon discovered that the opinion commonly held was erroneous,—greatly, it would seem, to the disillusionment of his contemporaries. Among the various reasons which he gives in a statement supporting his conclusions is that in two places the author is described as ' santo '—a proof not only that the MS. is not an autograph but also that the copyist had no intention of representing it as such.

Although this copy is carefully made and richly bound— which suggests that it was a gift from the Reform to the house of Alba—it contains many errors, of a kind which indicate that the copyist, well educated as he was, knew little of ascetic or mystical theology. A number of omissions, especially towards the end of the book, give the impression that the copy was finished with haste and not compared with the original on its completion. There is no reason, however, to suppose that the errors and omissions are ever intentional ; indeed, they are of such a kind as to suggest that the copyist had not the skill necessary for successful adulteration.

MS. 6624. This copy is in the National Library of Spain (Madrid)[1], and contains the same works as that of Alba de Tormes. It was made in 1755, under the direction of P. Andrés de la Encarnación, from a manuscript, now lost, which was venerated by the Benedictines of Burgos : this information is found at the end of the volume. P. Andrés had evidently a good opinion of the Burgos MS., as he placed

[1] [Abbreviated ' N.L.M.' in this edition.]

this copy in the archives of the Discalced Reform, whence it passed to the National Library early in the nineteenth century.

As far as the *Ascent* is concerned, this MS. is very similar to that of Alba. With a few notable exceptions, such as the omission of the second half of Book I, Chapter iv, the errors and omissions are so similar as to suggest a definite relationship between the two—perhaps a common source.

MS. 13498. This MS., which gives us the *Ascent* and the *Dark Night*, also came from the Archives of the Reform and is now in the National Library. The handwriting might be as early as the end of the sixteenth century. The author did not attempt to make a literal transcription of the *Ascent*, but summarized where he thought advisable, reducing the number of chapters and abbreviating many of them—this last not so much by the method of paraphrase as by the free omission of phrases and sentences.

MS. 2201. This, as far as the *Ascent* is concerned, is an almost literal transcription of the last MS., in a seventeenth-century hand ; it was bound in the eighteenth century, when a number of other treatises were added to it, together with some poems by S. John of the Cross and others. The variants as between this MS. and 13498 are numerous, but of small importance and seem mainly to have been due to carelessness.

MS. 18160. This dates from the end of the sixteenth century and contains the four treatises named above, copied in different hands and evidently intended to form one volume. Only the first four chapters of the *Ascent* are given, together with the title and the first three lines of the fifth chapter. The transcription is poorly done.

MS. 13507. An unimportant copy, containing only a few odd chapters of the *Ascent* and others from the remaining works of S. John of the Cross and other writers.

Pamplona. A codex in an excellent state of preservation is venerated by the Discalced Carmelite Nuns of Pamplona. It was copied, at the end of the sixteenth century, by a Barcelona Carmelite, Madre Magdalena de la Asunción, and contains a short summary of the four treatises enumerated above, various poems by S. John of the Cross and some miscellaneous writings. The *Ascent* is abbreviated to the same extent as in 13498 and 2201 and by the same methods ; many chapters, too, are omitted in their entirety.

Alcaudete. This MS., which contains the *Ascent* only, was copied by S. John of the Cross's close friend and companion,

P. Juan Evangelista, as a comparison with manuscripts (N.L.M., 12738) written in his well-known and very distinctive hand, puts beyond all doubt. P. Juan knew the Saint before entering the Order ; was professed by him at Granada in 1583 ; accompanied him on many of his journeys ; saw him write most of his books ; and, as his close friend and confessor, was consulted repeatedly by his biographers. It is natural that he should also have acted as the Saint's copyist, and, in the absence of autographs, we should expect no manuscripts to be more trustworthy than copies made by him. Examination of this MS. shows that it is in fact highly reliable. It corrects none of those unwieldy periods in which the Saint's work abounds, and which the *editio princeps* often thought well to emend, nor, like the early editions and even some manuscripts, does it omit whole paragraphs and substitute others for them. Further, as this copy was being made solely for the use of the Order, no passages are omitted or altered in it because they might be erroneously interpreted as illuministic. It is true that P. Juan Evangelista is not, from the technical standpoint, a perfect copyist, but, frequent as are his slips, they are always easy to recognize.

The Alcaudete MS. was found in the Carmelite convent in that town by P. Andrés de la Encarnación, who first made use of it for his edition. When the convent was abandoned during the religious persecutions of the early nineteenth century, the MS. was lost. Recently, however, it was re-discovered by P. Silverio de Santa Teresa in a second-hand bookshop and forms a most important contribution to that scholar's edition, which normally follows it. It bears many signs of frequent use ; eleven folios are missing from the body of the MS. (corresponding approximately to Book III, Chapters xxii to xxvi) and several more from its conclusion.

In the footnotes to the *Ascent*, the following abbreviations are used :

    A = MS. of the Carmelite Friars of Alba.
    Alc. = Alcaudete MS.
    B = MS. of the Benedictines of Burgos.
    C = National Library, Madrid, MS. 13498.
    D = National Library, Madrid, MS. 2201.
    P = MS. of the Carmelite Nuns of Pamplona.
    E.p. = *Editio princeps* (Alcalá, 1618).

ASCENT OF MOUNT CARMEL

Treats of how the soul may prepare itself in order to attain in a short time to Divine union. Gives very profitable counsels and instruction, both to beginners and to proficients, that they may know how to disencumber themselves of all that is temporal and not to encumber themselves with the spiritual,[1] and to remain in complete detachment and liberty of spirit, as is necessary for Divine union.[2]

ARGUMENT

All the doctrine whereof I intend to treat[3] in this *Ascent of Mount Carmel* is included in the following stanzas, and in them is also described the manner of ascending to the summit of the Mount, which is the high estate of perfection which we here call union of the soul with God. And because I must continually base upon them that which I shall say, I have desired to set them down here together, to the end that all the substance of that which is to be written may be seen and comprehended together ; although it will be fitting to set down each stanza separately before expounding it, and likewise the lines of each stanza, according as the matter and the exposition require. The poem, then, runs as follows :[4]

[1] A omits : ' and not . . . spiritual.'
[2] So Alc. On his own account P. Juan Evangelista adds : ' composed by P. Fray Juan de la Cruz, Discalced Carmelite.' Other codices, like Alc., give the name of the author. E.p. alone reads : ' *Ascent of Mount Carmel*, composed by the Venerable Father Fr. Juan de la Cruz, first Discalced friar of the Reform of Our Lady of Carmel founded by the virgin Saint Teresa.'
[3] So Alc., e.p.—A, B read : ' All the doctrine which is to be treated.'
[4] [*Lit.* : ' It says, then, thus.'] Only Alc. has these words.

STANZAS[1]

Wherein the soul sings of the happy chance which it had in passing through the dark night of faith, in detachment and purgation of itself, to union with the Beloved.[2]

1. On a dark night, Kindled[3] in love with yearnings—oh, happy chance!—
I went forth without being observed, My house being now at rest.[4]

2. In darkness and secure, By the secret ladder, disguised— oh, happy chance!—
In darkness and in concealment, My house being now at rest.

3. In the happy night, In secret, when none saw me,
Nor I beheld aught, Without light or guide, save that which burned in my heart.

4. This light guided me More surely than the light of noonday,
To the place where he (well I knew who!) was awaiting me— A place where none appeared.

5. Oh, night that guided me, Oh, night more lovely than the dawn,
Oh, night that joined Beloved with lover, Lover transformed in the Beloved !

6. Upon my flowery breast, Kept wholly for himself alone,
There he stayed sleeping, and I·caressed him, And the fanning of the cedars made a breeze.

7. The breeze blew from the turret As I parted his locks ;
With his gentle hand he wounded my neck And caused all my senses to be suspended.

8. I remained, lost in oblivion ;[5] My face I reclined on the Beloved.
All ceased and I abandoned myself, Leaving my cares forgotten among the lilies.

---

[1] For a verse translation in the metre of the original, see Vol. II.
[2] Several editions read : ' to union of love.' E.p., Alc., A, B have all the reading of the text above.
[3] [The adjectives are feminine throughout.]
[4] [The word translated 'at rest' is a past participle : more literally, 'stilled.']
[5] [*Lit.* : ' I remained and forgot.']

PROLOGUE

1. In order to expound and describe this dark night, through which the soul passes in order to attain to the Divine light of the perfect union of the love of God, as far as is possible in this life, it would be necessary to have illumination of knowledge and experience other and far greater than mine ; for this darkness and these trials, both spiritual and temporal,[1] through which happy souls are wont to pass in order to be able to attain to this high estate of perfection, are so numerous and so profound that neither does human knowledge suffice for the understanding of them, nor experience for the description of them ; for only he that passes this way can understand it, and even he cannot describe it.

2. Therefore, in order to say a little about this dark night, I shall trust neither to experience nor to knowledge, since both may fail and deceive ; but, while not omitting to make such use as I can of these two things, I shall avail myself, in all that, with the Divine favour, I have to say, or at the least, in that which is most important and dark to the understanding, of Divine Scripture ; for, if we guide ourselves by this, we shall be unable to stray, since He Who speaks therein is the Holy Spirit. And if in aught I stray, whether through my imperfect understanding of that which is said in it or of matters unconnected with it, it is not my intention[2] to depart from the sound sense and doctrine of our Holy Mother the Catholic Church ; for in such a case I submit and resign myself wholly, not only to her command,[3] but to whatever better judgement she may pronounce concerning it.

[1] E.p. : ' both spiritual and corporal.' The correction was no doubt made because ' corporal ' is the usual antithesis of ' spiritual ' ; all the MSS., however, have ' temporal.'

[2] E.p. modifies : ' Since both may fail and deceive ; but to Divine Scripture, for, if we guide ourselves by this, we cannot stray, since He Who speaks therein is the Holy Spirit. Nevertheless I shall make use of these two things—knowledge and experience—whereof I speak. And if in aught I stray, it is not my intention, etc.'

[3] E.p. : ' to her light and command.' A, B : ' to her opinion.' There are slight variations in these last few lines in different MSS. We follow Alc., with which A and B agree very closely.

3. For this cause I have been moved,[1] not by any possibility that I see in myself of accomplishing so arduous a task, but by the confidence which I have in the Lord that He will help me to say something to relieve the great necessity which is experienced by many souls, who, when they set out upon the road of virtue, and Our Lord desires to bring them into this dark night that they may pass through it to Divine union, make no progress. At times this is because they have no desire to enter it or to allow themselves to be led into it ; at other times, because they understand not themselves and lack competent and alert directors[2] who will guide them to the summit. And so it is sad to see many souls to whom God gives both favour and capacity for making progress (and who, if they would take courage, could attain to this high estate), remaining in an elementary stage[3] of communion with God, for want of will, or knowledge, or because there is none who will lead them in the right path or teach them how to get away from[4] these beginnings. And at length, although Our Lord grants them such favour as to make them to go onward without this hindrance or that, they arrive at their goal exceeding late, and with greater labour, yet with less merit, because they have not conformed themselves to God, and allowed themselves to be brought freely[5] into the pure and sure road of union. For, although it is true that God is leading them, and that He can lead them without their own help, they will not allow themselves to be led ; and thus they make less progress, because they resist Him Who is leading them, and they have less merit, because they apply not their will, and on this account they suffer more. For there are souls who, instead of committing themselves to God and making use of His help, rather hinder God by the indiscretion of their actions or by their resistance ; like children who, when their mothers desire to carry them in their arms, kick and cry, insisting upon being allowed to walk, with the result that they can make no progress ; and, if they advance at all, it is only at the pace of a child.

4. Wherefore, to the end that all, whether beginners or proficients, may know how to commit themselves to God's

[1] A, B : ' In order to write this I have been moved.'
[2] [Lit. ' and wideawake guides.']   E.p. reads ' skilled,' and B ' prepared,' for ' alert.'   [3] [Lit., ' a low manner.']
[4] So e.p.   [P. Silverio's text, following Alc., reads : ' disengage themselves from.']   [5] E.p. omits ' freely.'

guidance, when His Majesty desires to lead them onward, we shall give instruction and counsel, by His help, so that they may be able to understand His will, or, at the least, allow Him to lead them. For some confessors and spiritual fathers,[1] having no light and experience concerning these roads, are wont to hinder and harm such souls rather than to help them along the road ;[2] they are like the builders of Babel, who, when told to furnish suitable material, gave and applied other very different material, because they understood not the language, and thus nothing was done. Wherefore, it is a difficult and troublesome thing at such seasons[3] for a soul not to understand itself or to find none who understands it. For it will come to pass that God will lead the soul[4] by a most lofty path of dark contemplation and aridity, wherein it seems to be lost, and, being thus full of darkness and trials, afflictions and temptations, will meet one who will speak to it like Job's comforters, and say that[5] it is suffering from melancholy or low spirits, or morbidity of temperament, or that it may have some hidden sin, and that it is for this reason that God has forsaken it. Such comforters are wont to infer immediately that that soul must have been very evil, since such things as these are befalling it.

5. And there will likewise be those who tell the soul to retrace its steps, since it is finding neither pleasure nor consolation in the things of God as it did aforetime. And in this way they double the trials of the poor soul ; for it may well be that the greatest affliction which it is feeling is that of the knowledge of its own miseries, thinking that it sees itself, more clearly than daylight, to be full of evils and sins, for God gives it that light of knowledge[6] in that night of contemplation, as we shall presently show. And when the soul finds someone whose opinion agrees with its own, and who says that these things must be due to its own fault, its affliction and trouble increase infinitely and are wont to become more grievous than death. And, not content with this, such confessors, thinking that these things proceed from sin, make these souls go over their lives and cause them to make many general confessions and crucify them afresh ; not

---

[1] Alc. omits : ' confessors and.'
[2] E.p. omits : ' along the road.'
[3] ' Reasons ' is a copyist's or printer's error. E.p. has ' occasions.'
[4] E.p. : ' For it will happen that God will lead it.'
[5] E.p. : ' who will say to it what Job's comforters said to Job, that it, etc.'   [6] E.p. : ' for God gives it to understand this.'

understanding that this may quite well not be the time for any of such things, and that their penitents should be left to the purgation which God gives them, and be comforted and encouraged to desire it until God be pleased to dispose otherwise ; for until that time, no matter what the souls themselves may do and their confessors may say, there is no remedy for them.

6. This, with the Divine favour, we shall consider hereafter, and also how the soul should conduct itself at such a time, and how the confessor must treat it, and what signs there will be whereby it may be known if this is the purgation of the soul ; and, in such case, whether it be of sense or of spirit (which is the dark night whereof we speak), and how it may be known if it be melancholy or some other imperfection with respect to sense or to spirit. For there may be some souls who will think, or whose confessors will think, that God is leading them along this road of the dark night of spiritual purgation, whereas they may possibly be suffering only from some of the imperfections aforementioned. And, again, there are many souls who think that they have no aptitude for prayer, when they have very much ; and there are others[1] who think that they have much when they have hardly any.

7. There are other souls who labour and weary themselves to a piteous extent, and yet go backward, seeking profit in that which is not profitable, but is rather a hindrance ; and there are still others who, by remaining at rest and in quietness, continue to make great progress. There are others who are hindered and disturbed and make no progress, because of the very consolations and favours that God is granting them in order that they may make progress. And there are many other things on this road that befall those who follow it, both joys and afflictions, both hopes and griefs : some proceeding from the spirit of perfection and others from imperfection. Of all these, with the Divine favour, we shall endeavour to say something, so that each soul[2] who reads this may be able to see something of the road that he ought to follow, if he aspires to attain to the summit of this Mount.

8. And since this instruction relates to the dark night through which the soul must go to God, let not the reader

---

[1] E.p. : ' and others, on the contrary.'
[2] E.p. : ' each one.'

marvel if it seem to him somewhat dark also. This, I believe, will be so at the beginning when he begins to read ; but, as he passes on, he will find himself understanding the first part better, since one part will explain another. And then, if he read it a second time, I believe it will seem clearer to him and the instruction will appear sounder.[1] And if any persons find themselves disagreeing with this instruction,[2] it will be due to my ignorance and poor style ; for in itself the matter is good and of the first importance. But I think that, even were it written in a more excellent and perfect manner than it is, only the minority would profit by it,[3] for we shall not here set down things that are very moral and delectable[4] for all spiritual persons who desire to travel toward God by pleasant and delectable ways,[5] but solid and substantial instruction, as well suited to one kind of person as to another if they desire to pass to the detachment of spirit which is here treated.

9. Nor is my principal intent to address all, but rather certain persons of our sacred Order of Mount Carmel of the primitive observance, both friars and nuns—since they have desired me to do so—to whom God is granting the favour of setting them on the road to this Mount ; who, as they are already detached from the temporal things of this world, will better understand the instruction concerning detachment of spirit.

---

[1] E.p. : ' will appear more certain.'

[2] So Alc. [and P. Silverio]. The other codices and editions have ' reading ' [i.e., ' that which they read '].

[3] E.p. : ' than it is, it would not be appreciated by many.'

[4] Needless to say, the Saint does not here mean that he will not write in conformity with moral standards—no writer is more particular in this respect—nor that he will deal with no delectable matters at all, but rather that he will go to the very roots of moral teaching and expound the ' solid and substantial instruction,' which not only forms its basis but also leads the soul toward the most intimate union with God in love.

[5] E.p. : ' for spiritual persons who desire to travel, by [ways] that are pleasant, to God.' There are various other readings in these lines—all of them, however, differing from the text extremely slightly.

BOOK THE FIRST

Wherein is described the nature of the dark night and how necessary it is to pass through it to Divine union; and in particular this book describes the dark night of sense, and desire, and the evils which these work in the soul.[1]

CHAPTER I

Sets down the first stanza.—Describes the differences between two nights through which spiritual persons pass, according to the two parts of man, the lower and the higher. Expounds the stanza which follows.

STANZA THE FIRST[2]

**On a dark night, Kindled in love with yearnings—oh, happy chance!—
I went forth without being observed, My house being now at rest.**

1. In this first stanza[3] the soul sings of the happy fortune and chance which it experienced in going forth from all things that are without,[4] and from the desires[5] and imperfections[6] that are in the sensual[7] part of man because of the disordered state of his reason. For the understanding of this it must be known that, for a soul to attain to the state of perfection, it has ordinarily first[8] to pass through two

---

[1] The codices give neither title nor sub-title : both were inserted in e.p. ['Desire' is to be taken as the direct object of 'describes'; 'these' refers to 'sense' and 'desire', not to the dark night.]

[2] So e.p., A, D. Omitted from Alc., B, C.

[3] Alc. : 'In this happy stanza.'

[4] E.p. omits : 'that are without.'

[5] [*Lit.*, 'appetites,' but this word is uniformly translated 'desires,' as the Spanish context frequently will not admit the use of the stronger word in English.]   [6] A, B : 'and affections.'

[7] [The word translated 'sensual' is sometimes, as here, *sensual*, and sometimes, as at the beginning of §4, *sensitivo* (in e.p.). The meaning in either case is simply 'of sense'.]

[8] E.p. omits 'first.'

principal kinds of night, which spiritual persons call pur-
gations or purifications of the soul ; and here we call them
nights, for in both of them the soul journeys, as it were, by
night, in darkness.

2. The first night or[1] purgation is of the sensual part of
the soul, which is treated in the present stanza and will be
treated in the first part of this book. And the second is of
the spiritual part ; of this speaks the second stanza, which
follows ; and of this we shall treat likewise, in the second
and the third part,[2] with respect to the activity of the soul ;
and in the fourth part, with respect to its passivity.

3.[3] And this first night pertains to beginners, occurring
at the time when God begins to bring them into the state
of contemplation ; in this night the spirit likewise has a
part, as we shall say in due course. And the second night,
or purification, pertains to those who are already proficient,
occurring at the time when God desires to set them in the
state of union with God. And this latter night is a more
obscure and dark and terrible purgation, as we shall say
afterwards.

EXPOSITION OF THE STANZA

4. Briefly, then, the soul means by this stanza that it
went forth (being led by God) for love of Him alone, enkindled in love of Him, upon a dark night, which is the
privation and purgation of all its sensual desires, with
respect to all outward things of the world and to those
which were delectable to its flesh, and likewise with respect
to the desires of its will. This all comes to pass in this
purgation of sense ; wherefore the soul says that it went
forth while its house was still at rest[4] ; which house is its
sensual part, the desires being at rest and asleep in it, and it
in them. For there is no going forth from the pains and

[1] So Alc. The other authorities read ' and ' for ' or.'

[2] So Alc. The other authorities read : ' and of this we shall treat
likewise, in the second part with respect to the activity [of the soul]
[*these last three words are not contained in the Spanish of any authority*],
and in the third and the fourth part with respect to its passivity.' E.p.
follows this division. Alc., however, seems to correspond more closely
with the Saint's intentions ; for he did not divide each of his ' books '
into ' parts ' and appears therefore to indicate by ' part ' what we know
as ' book.' Now Book I is in fact devoted to the active purgation of
sense, as are Books II and III to the active purgation of the spirit. For
the ' fourth book,' see Introduction, pp. lviii–ix above.

[3] This paragraph is omitted from e.p.

[4] [On the phrase ' at rest,' c^r. p. 10, n. 2, above.]

afflictions of the secret places of the desires until these be mortified and put to sleep. And this, the soul says, was a happy chance for it—namely, its going forth without being observed : that is, without any desire of its flesh or any other thing being able to hinder it. And likewise, because it went out by night—which signifies the privation of all these things wrought in it by God, which privation was night for it.

5. And it was a happy chance that God should lead it into this night, from which there came to it so much good ;[1] for of itself the soul would not have succeeded in entering therein, because no man of himself can succeed in voiding himself of all his desires in order to come to God.[2]

6. This is, in brief, the exposition of the stanza ; and we shall now have to go through it, line by line, setting down one line after another, and expounding that which is to our purpose.[3] And the same method is followed in the other stanzas, as I said in the Prologue[4]—namely, that each stanza will be set down and expounded, and afterwards each line.[5]

CHAPTER II

Explains the nature of this dark night through which the soul says that it has passed on the road to union.[6]

On a dark night

1. We may say that there are three reasons[7] for which this journey[8] made by the soul to union with God is called night. The first has to do with the point from which the soul goes forth, for it has gradually to deprive itself of desire for all the worldly things which it possessed, by denying them to itself ;[9] the which denial and deprivation are, as it were, night to all the senses[10] of man. The second reason

---

[1] A, e.p. : ' from which there comes so much good.'
[2] E.p. : ' to go to God.'
[3] The rest of the paragraph is omitted from e.p., possibly because it was already in the ' Argument ' above (p. 9).
[4] i.e., in the ' Argument.'
[5] A : ' each line separately.'
[6] So A, Alc., C, D. B, e.p. read : ' to union with God.' A, B, C, D, e.p. add further : ' Sets down the causes thereof.'
[7] Alc., D : ' three things.'
[8] [More exactly, this ' passage ' or ' transition ' (*tránsito*).]
[9] [*Lit.*, ' in negation of them.']
[10] E.p. : ' for all the desires and senses.'

has to do with the mean,[1] or the road along which the soul must travel to this union—that is, faith, which is likewise[2] as dark as night to the understanding. The third has to do with the point to which it travels,—namely God, Who, equally, is dark night to the soul in this life.[3] These three nights must pass through the soul,—or rather, the soul must pass through them—in order that it may come to Divine union with God.[4]

2. In the book of the holy Tobias these three kinds of night were shadowed forth by the three nights which, as the angel commanded, were to pass ere the youth Tobias should be united with his bride. In the first he commanded him to burn the heart of the fish in the fire, which signifies the heart that is affectioned to, and set upon, the things of the world ; which, in order that one may begin to journey toward God, must be burned and purified from all that is creature, in the fire of the love of God. And in this purgation the devil flees away, for he has power over the soul only when it is attached to things[5] corporal and temporal.

3. On the second night the angel told him that he would be admitted into the company of the holy patriarchs, who are the fathers of the faith. For, passing through the first night, which is the privation of all objects of sense, the soul at once enters into the second night, being alone in faith to the exclusion, not of charity, but of other knowledge acquired by the understanding, as we shall say hereafter,[6] which is a thing that pertains not to sense.

4. On the third night the angel told him that he would obtain blessing, which is God ; Who, by means of the second night, which is faith, continually communicates Himself to the soul in such a secret and intimate manner that He becomes another night to the soul, inasmuch as this said communication is far darker than those others, as we shall say presently. And, when this third night is past, which is the complete realization of the communication of God in the spirit, which is ordinarily wrought in great darkness of the soul, there then follows its union with

---

[1] E.p. : ' the manner.' [By ' the mean ' is meant the middle, or main part, of the journey.] [2] E.p. omits ' likewise.'

[3] E.p. glosses the text by substituting : ' Who, since He is incomprehensible and infinitely transcendent, may also be called dark night.'

[4] E.p. shortens this sentence : ' Through these three nights the soul must pass in order to come to Divine union with God.'

[5] E.p. : ' to the pleasures of things.'

[6] The words ' to the exclusion . . . hereafter ' are found only in Alc.

the Bride, which is the Wisdom of God. Even so the angel said likewise to Tobias that, when the third night was past, he should be united with his bride in the fear of the Lord ; for, when this fear of God is perfect, love is perfect, and this comes to pass when the transformation of the soul is wrought through its love.[1]

5. These three parts of the night are all one night ; but like night itself, it has three parts.[2] For the first part, which is that of sense, is comparable to the beginning of night, the point at which things begin to fade from sight. And the second part, which is faith, is comparable to midnight, which is total darkness. And the third part is like the close of night, which is God, the which part is now near to the light of day. And, that we may understand this the better, we shall treat of each of these reasons separately as we proceed.[3]

CHAPTER III

Speaks of the first cause of this night, which is that of the privation of the desire in all things, and gives the reason for which it is called night.[4]

1. We here describe as night the privation of every kind of pleasure which belongs to the desire ; for even as night is naught but the privation of light, and, consequently, of all objects that can be seen by means of light, whereby the visual faculty[5] remains unoccupied and in darkness, even so likewise the mortification of desire may be called night to the soul. For, when the soul is deprived of the pleasure of its desire in all things, it remains, as it were, unoccupied and in darkness. For even as the visual faculty, by means of light, is nourished and fed by objects which can be seen, and which, when the light is quenched, are not seen,[6] even so, by means of the desire, the soul is nourished and fed by all

---

[1] E.p. reads : ' for, when this is perfect, the love of God is so likewise, and this comes to pass when the transformation of the soul is wrought through its love for God.'

[2] E.p. reads : ' And, that we may the better understand it, we shall treat of each one of these reasons separately as we proceed. And it will be noted that these three nights are all one night, which has three parts.'

[3] E.p. omits this sentence, which it has prefixed to the beginning of the paragraph. Alc. alone reads ' reasons ' ; the other authorities have ' things.' [4] Alc. alone has the words ' and . . . night.'

[5] A adds : ' as to all things.'

[6] E.p. has : ' and, when the light is quenched, this ceases.'

things wherein it can take pleasure according to its faculties ; and, when this also is quenched, or rather, mortified,[1]
the soul ceases to be fed upon the pleasure of all things,
and thus, with respect to its desire, it remains unoccupied
and in darkness.

2. Let us take an example from each of the faculties.
When the soul deprives its desire of the pleasure of all
that can delight the sense of hearing, the soul remains unoccupied and in darkness with respect to this faculty. And
when it deprives itself of the pleasure of all that can please
the sense of sight, it remains unoccupied and in darkness
with respect to this faculty also.[2] And when it deprives itself
of the pleasure of all the sweetness of perfumes which can
give it pleasure through the sense of smell, it remains equally
unoccupied and in darkness according to this faculty. And
if it also denies itself the pleasure of all food that can satisfy
the palate, the soul likewise remains unoccupied and in
darkness. And finally, when the soul mortifies itself with
respect to all the delights and pleasures that it can receive
from the sense of touch, it remains, in the same way, unoccupied and in darkness with respect to this faculty. So
that the soul that has denied and thrust away from itself the
pleasures which come from all these things, and has mortified
its desire with respect to them, may be said to be, as it were,
in the darkness of night, which is naught else than an
emptiness within itself of all things.

3. The reason for this is that, as the philosophers say, the
soul, as soon as God infuses it into the body, is like a smooth,
blank board[3] upon which nothing is painted ; and, save
for that which it experiences through the senses, nothing is
communicated to it, in the course of nature, from any other
source. And thus, for as long as it is in the body, it is like
one who is in a dark prison and who knows nothing, save
what he is able to see through the windows of the said prison ;
and, if he saw nothing through them, he would see nothing
in any other way. And thus the soul, save for that which is
communicated to it through the senses, which are the
windows of its prison, could acquire nothing, in the course of
nature, in any other way.

---

[1] E.p. : ' and when this is mortified.'
[2] E.p. omits the next ten lines, continuing thus : ' And the same may
be said of the other senses. So that the soul that has denied, etc.'
[3] [' Blank board ' : Sp., *tabla rasa* ; Lat., *tabula rasa*.]

4, Wherefore, if the soul rejects and denies that which it can receive through the senses, we can quite well say that it remains, as it were, dark and empty ; since, as appears from what has been said, no light can enter it, in the course of nature, by any other means of illumination than those aforementioned.[1] For, although it is true that the soul cannot help hearing and seeing and smelling and tasting and touching, this is of no import, nor, if the soul denies and rejects the object, is it hindered more than if it saw it not, heard it not, etc. Just so a man who desires to shut his eyes will remain in darkness, like[2] the blind man who has not the faculty of sight. And to this purpose David says these words : *Pauper sum ego, et in laboribus a juventute mea.*[3] Which signifies : I am poor and in labours from my youth. He calls himself poor, although it is clear that he was rich, because his will was not set upon riches, and thus it was as though he were really poor. But if he had been really poor and had not been so in his will, he would not have been truly poor, for his soul, as far as its desire was concerned, would have been rich and replete. For this reason we call this detachment the night of the soul, for we are not treating here of the lack of things, since this implies no detachment on the part of the soul if it has a desire for them ; but we are treating of the detachment from them of the taste and desire, for it is this that leaves the soul free and void of them, although it may have them ; for it is not the things of this world that either occupy the soul or cause it harm, since they enter it not, but rather the will and desire for them, for it is these that dwell within it.

5. This first kind of night, as we shall say hereafter, belongs to the soul according to its sensual part,[4] which is one of the two parts, whereof we spoke above, through which the soul must pass in order to attain to union.[5]

6. Let us now say how meet it is for the soul to go forth from its house into this dark night of sense, in order to travel to union with God.

---

[1] E.p. omits : ' than those aforementioned.'
[2] E.p. has ' as much as ' for ' like.'
[3] Psalm lxxxvii, 16 [A.V. lxxxviii, 15].   E.p. omits the Latin text and the words ' Which signifies.'
[4] E.p. omits the rest of this paragraph.
[5] Only Alc. gives : ' in order to attain to union.'

CHAPTER IV

Wherein is declared how necessary it is for the soul truly to pass through this dark night of sense, which is mortification of desire, in order that it may journey to union with God.[1]

1. The reason for which it is necessary for the soul, in order to attain to Divine union with God, to pass through this dark night of mortification of the desires and denial of pleasures in all things, is because all the affections which it has for creatures are pure darkness in the eyes of God, and, when the soul is clothed in these affections, it has no capacity for being enlightened and possessed by the pure and simple light of God,[2] if it cast them not first from it ; for light cannot agree with darkness ; since, as S. John says : *Tenebræ eam non comprehenderunt.*[3] That is : The darkness could not receive the light.

2. The reason is that two contraries (even as philosophy teaches us) cannot coexist in one person ; and that darkness, which is affection for the creatures, and light, which is God, are contrary to each other, and have no likeness or accord between one another, even as S. Paul explained to the Corinthians, saying : *Quæ conventio luci ad tenebras ?*[4] That is to say : What communion can there be between light and darkness ? Hence it is that the light of Divine union cannot dwell in the soul if these affections first flee not away from it.

3. In order that we may the better prove what has been said, it must be known that the affection and attachment which the soul has for creatures renders the soul like to these creatures ; and the greater is its affection, the closer is the equality and likeness between them ; for love creates a likeness between that which loves and that which is loved. For which reason David, speaking of those who set their affections upon idols, said thus : *Similes illis fiant qui faciunt ea : et omnes qui confidunt in eis.*[5] Which signifies : Let them that set their heart upon them be like to them. And thus,

---

[1] A adds : ' This is proved by comparisons of passages and figures from Sacred Scripture, etc.'

[2] E.p. : ' for being possessed in the pure and simple light of God.'

[3] S. John i, 5. Neither this nor any of the other Latin texts in this chapter is found in e.p.

[4] 2 Corinthians vi, 14.   [5] Psalm cxiv, 8 [A.V. cxv, 8].

he that loves a creature becomes as low as is that creature, and, in some ways, lower ; for love not only makes the lover equal to the object of his love, but even subjects him to it. Wherefore in the same way it comes to pass that the soul that loves anything else[1] becomes incapable of pure union with God and transformation in Him.   For the low estate of the creature is much less capable of union with the high estate of the Creator than is darkness with light.   For all things of earth and heaven, compared with God, are nothing, as Jeremiah says in these words : *Aspexi terram, et ecce vacua erat, et nihil ; et cœlos, et non erat lux in eis.*[2]   I beheld the earth, he says, and it was void, and it was nothing ; and the heavens, and saw that they had no light.   In saying that he beheld the earth void, he means that all its creatures were nothing, and that the earth was nothing likewise.   And, in saying that he beheld the heavens and saw no light in them, he says that all the luminaries of heaven, compared with God, are pure darkness.   So that in this sense all the creatures are nothing ; and their affections, we may say, are less than nothing, since they are an impediment to transformation in God and the loss thereof, even as darkness is not only nothing but less than nothing, since it is loss of light.   And even as he that is in darkness comprehends not the light, so the soul that sets its affections upon[3] creatures will be unable to comprehend God ; and, until it be purged, it will neither be able to possess Him here below, through pure transformation of love, nor yonder in clear vision.   And, for greater clarity, we will now speak in greater detail.

4. All the being of creation, then, compared with the infinite Being of God, is nothing.   And therefore the soul that sets its affections upon the being of creation is likewise nothing in the eyes of God, and less than nothing ; for, as we have said, love makes equality and similitude, and even sets the lover below the object of his love.   And therefore such a soul will in no wise be able to attain to union with the infinite Being of God ; for that which is not can have no agreement with that which is.   And, coming down in detail to certain examples,[4] all the beauty of the creatures, compared with the infinite beauty of God, is the height of

---

[1] The editions add, for a better understanding of the phrase, ' apart from God.'

[2] Jeremiah iv, 23.   [3] A, B, e.p. : ' that has affection for.'

[4] The words ' And . . . examples ' are found in Alc. only.

deformity,[1] even as Solomon says in the Proverbs : *Fallax gratia, et vana est pulchritudo.*[2] Favour is deceitful and beauty is vain. And thus the soul that is affectioned to the beauty of any creature is as the height of deformity[3] in the eyes of God. And therefore this soul that is deformed will be unable to become transformed in beauty, which is God, since deformity cannot attain to beauty ; and all the grace and beauty of the creatures, compared with the grace of God, is the height of misery[4] and of unattractiveness. Wherefore the soul that is ravished by the graces and beauties of the creatures has only supreme[5] misery and unattractiveness in the eyes of God ; and thus it cannot be capable of the infinite grace and loveliness of God ; for that which has no grace is far removed from that which is infinitely gracious ; and all the goodness of the creatures of the world, in comparison with the infinite goodness of God, may be described as wickedness. For there is naught good, save only God.[6] And therefore the soul that sets its heart upon the good things of the world is supremely[7] evil in the eyes of God. And, even as wickedness comprehends not goodness, even so such a soul cannot be united with God,[8] Who is supreme goodness. All the wisdom of the world and human ability, compared with the infinite wisdom of God, are pure and supreme ignorance,[9] even as Saint Paul writes *ad Corinthios*, saying : *Sapientia hujus mundi stultitia est apud Deum.*[10] The wisdom of this world is foolishness in the eyes of God.

5. Wherefore any soul that makes account of all its knowledge and ability in order to come to union with the wisdom of God is supremely ignorant in the eyes of God and will remain far removed from that wisdom ; for ignorance knows not what wisdom is, even as S. Paul says that this

---

[1] [The words often translated ' deformity,' ' deformed,' or ' vileness,' ' vile,' are the ordinary contraries of ' beauty,' ' beautiful,' and might be rendered, more literally but less elegantly, ' ugliness,' ' ugly.']

[2] Proverbs xxxi, 30.

[3] E.p. softens this phrase to : ' has its share of deformity.'

[4] [For ' grace . . . misery ' the Spanish has ' gracia . . . desgracia.' The latter word, however, does not, as might be supposed, correspond to English ' disgrace.']

[5] E.p. omits ' supreme ' ; the Spanish word [having a more literally superlative force than the English] can hardly be applied, save in a restricted sense, to what is finite. [6] S. Luke xviii, 19.

[7] This again is omitted from e.p.

[8] E.p. adds : ' in perfect union.'

[9] B abbreviates greatly here and then omits the remainder of the chapter. [10] 1 Corinthians iii, 19,

wisdom seems foolishness to God ; since, in the eyes of
God,[1] those who consider themselves to be persons with a
certain amount of knowledge are very ignorant, since the
Apostle, writing to the Romans, says of them : *Dicentes enim
se esse sapientes, stulti facti sunt.* That is : Considering themselves to be wise, they became foolish.[2] And those alone
gain the wisdom of God who are like ignorant children,
and, laying aside their knowledge, walk in His service with
love. This manner of wisdom S. Paul taught likewise *ad
Corinthios : Si quis videtur inter vos sapiens esse in hoc sæculo,
stultus fiat ut sit sapiens. Sapientia enim hujus mundi stultitia est
apud Deum.*[3] That is : If any among you seemeth to be
wise, let him become ignorant that he may be wise ; for the
wisdom of this world is foolishness with respect to God.
So that, in order to come to union with the wisdom of God,
the soul has to proceed rather by unknowing than by knowing ; and all the dominion and liberty of the world, compared with the liberty and dominion of the spirit of God, is
the most abject[4] slavery, affliction and captivity.

6. Wherefore the soul that is enamoured of prelacy,[5] or
of any other such office, and longs for liberty of desire, is
considered and treated, in the sight of God, not as a son, but
as a base slave and captive,[6] since it has not been willing to
accept His holy doctrine, wherein He teaches us that he
who would be greater must be less, and he who would be
less must be greater.[7] And therefore such a soul will be
unable to attain to that true liberty of spirit which is en-
compassed in His Divine union. For slavery can have no
part with liberty ; and liberty cannot dwell in a heart that
is subject to desires, for this is the heart of a slave ; but it
dwells in the free man, because he has the heart of a son.
It was for this reason that Sarah bade her husband Abraham
cast out the bondwoman and her son, saying that the son of
the bondwoman should not be heir with the son of the
free woman.[8]

7. And all the delights and pleasures of the will in all the
things of the world, in comparison with all those delights

---

[1] E.p. abbreviates : ' knows not what wisdom is, and, in the eyes of
God. . . .'   [2] Romans i, 22.   [3] 1 Corinthians iii, 18–19.
 [4] [*Lit.*, ' is supreme.']
 [5] [The word is applicable to any kind of preferential position.]
 [6] E.p. reads : ' not as a dear son, but as a base person, a captive of its
passions,' etc.
 [7] E.p. : ' . . . doctrine which teaches us that he who would be greater
must be less.'   [8] Genesis xxi, 10,

which are God, are supreme affliction, torment and bitterness. And thus he that sets his heart upon them is considered, in the sight of God, as worthy of supreme affliction, torment and bitterness ; and thus he will be unable to attain to the delights of the embrace of union with God, since he is worthy of affliction and bitterness.[1] All the wealth and glory of all the creatures, in comparison with the wealth which is God, is supreme poverty and wretchedness. Thus the soul that loves and possesses creature wealth is supremely poor and wretched in the sight of God, and for this reason will be unable to attain to that wealth and glory which is the state of transformation in God ;[2] since that which is miserable and poor is supremely far removed from that which is supremely rich and glorious.

8. And therefore Divine Wisdom, grieving for such as these, who make themselves vile, low, miserable and poor, because they love this world which seems to them so rich and beautiful, addresses an exclamation to them in the Proverbs, saying : *O viri, ad vos clamito, et vox mea ad filios hominum. Intelligite, parvuli, astutiam, et insipientes, animadvertite. Audite quia de rebus magnis locutura sum.* And farther on he continues : *Mecum sunt divitiæ, et gloria, opes superbæ et justitia. Melior est fructus meus auro, et lapide pretioso, et genimina mea argento electo. In viis justitiæ ambulo, in medio semitarum judicii, ut ditem diligentes me, et thesauros eorum repleam.*[3] Which signifies : Unto you, O men, I call, and my voice is to the sons of men. Attend,[4] little ones, to subtlety and sagacity ; ye that are foolish, pay heed. Hear, for I have to speak of great things. With me are riches and glory, high riches and righteousness. Better is the fruit that ye will find in me than gold and precious stones ; and my generation—namely, that which ye will engender of me in your souls—is better than choice silver. I go in the ways of righteousness, in the midst of the paths of judgement, that I may enrich those that love me and fill[5] their treasures perfectly.—Herein Divine Wisdom speaks to all those that set their hearts and affections upon anything of the world, according as we have already said. And she

[1] E.p. omits : ' since . . . bitterness.'
[2] The remainder of the paragraph is found only in A and e.p.
[3] Proverbs viii, 4–6, 18–21.
[4] So A, Alc. E.p. : ' Understand.' The other authorities omit this passage.
[5] A, Alc. both have ' fulfil ' [*cumplir*] but in the archaic Spanish sense of ' swell,' which is the reading of e.p. and later editions. [For the rendering of the text cf. A.V. : ' I will fill their treasures.']

calls them ' little ones,' because they make themselves like to
that which they love, which is little.   And therefore she tells
them to be wise and to take note that she is treating of great
things and not of things that are little like themselves.
That the great riches and the glory that they love are with
her and in her, and not where they think.   And that high
riches and justice dwell in her ; for, although they think
the things of this world to be such, she tells them to take
note that her things are better, saying that the fruit that
they will find in them will be better for them than gold and
precious stones ; and that that which she engenders in souls
is better than the choice silver which they love ; by which is
understood any kind of affection that can be possessed in this
life.

CHAPTER V

*Wherein the aforementioned subject is treated and continued, and
it is shown by passages and figures from Holy Scripture how
necessary it is for the soul to journey to God through this
dark night of the mortification of desire in all things.*

1. From what has been said it may be seen to some extent
how great a distance there is between all that the creatures
are in themselves and that which God is in Himself, and how
souls[1] that set their affections upon any of these creatures
are at an equal distance from God ; for, as we have said,
love produces equality and similarity.   This distance was
clearly realized by S. Augustine, who said in the *Soliloquies*,
speaking with God :[2] Miserable man that I am, when will
my littleness and imperfection agree with Thy uprightness ?
Thou indeed art good, and I am evil ; Thou art merciful,
and I am unholy ; Thou art holy, I am miserable ; Thou
art just, I am unjust ; Thou art light, I am blind ; Thou,
life, I, death ; Thou, medicine, I, sick ; Thou, supreme
truth, I, utter vanity.[3] All this is said by this Saint.[4]
2. Wherefore, it is supreme ignorance for the soul to think
that it will be able to pass to this high estate of union with

---

[1] E.p. : ' We have already spoken of the distance that there is between
the creatures and God, and how souls,' etc.

[2] A, B omit : ' speaking with God.'

[3] A, B, C : ' universal vanity.' D : ' supreme vanity.'

[4] *Soliloq.*, chap. ii (Migne : *Patr. lat.*, vol. xl, p. 866). E.p. adds : ' The
which this Saint says concerning the inclination of man for the creatures.'

God if first it void not the desire of all things, natural and supernatural, which may hinder it, according as we shall declare hereafter ;[1] for there is the greatest possible distance between these things and that which comes to pass in this estate, which is naught else than transformation in God. For this reason Our Lord, when instructing us in this way, said through S. Luke : *Qui non renuntiat omnibus quæ possidet, non potest meus esse discipulus.*[2] This signifies : He that renounces not all things that he possesses with his will cannot be My disciple. And this is evident ; for the doctrine that the Son of God came to teach[3] was contempt for all things, so that a man might receive as a reward the spirit of God in himself. For, as long as the soul rejects not all things, it has no capacity to receive the spirit of God in pure transformation.

3. Of this we have a figure in Exodus, wherein we read that God[4] gave not the children of Israel the food from Heaven, which was manna, until the flour which they had brought from Egypt failed them. By this is signified that first of all it is meet to renounce all things, for this angels' food is not fitting for the palate that would find delight in the food of men. And not only does the soul become incapable of receiving the Divine Spirit when it stays and pastures on other strange pleasures, but those souls greatly offend the Divine Majesty who desire spiritual food and are not content with God alone, but desire rather to intermingle desire and affection for other things. This can likewise be seen in this same book of Holy Scripture,[5] wherein it is said that, not content with that simplest of food, they desired and craved fleshly food.[6] And that Our Lord was grievously offended that they should desire to intermingle a food that

---

[1] So Alc. The other authorities have merely : ' which may pertain to it,' and e.p. adds to this : ' through self-love.' Even when softened by Diego de Jesús this phrase of the Saint did not escape denunciation, and it was the first of the ' propositions ' condemned in his writings (cf. p. lxiv, above). It was defended by P. Basilio Ponce de León in his *Reply* (p. lxv), and more extensively by P. Nicolás de Jesús María (*Elucidatio*, Pt. II, Chap. i). In reality little defence is needed other than that contained in the last chapters of the *Ascent of Mount Carmel*, which clearly show the harm caused by supernatural favours, when these are abused, to the memory, the understanding and the will. Who, after all, can doubt that we may abuse ' things supernatural ' and by such abuse hinder the soul's union with God ?

[2] S. Luke xiv, 33.   [3] A, e.p. : ' to teach the world.'
[4] E.p. : ' that God's Majesty.'
[5] E.p. alters this to : ' in the same Scripture.' [It does not, in fact, occur in the same book.]   [6] Numbers xi, 4.

was so base and so coarse with one that was so noble [1] and
so simple ; which, though it was so, had within itself the
sweetness and substance[2] of all foods.   Wherefore, while
they yet had the morsels in their mouths, as David says likewise : *Ira Dei descendit super eos.*[3]   The wrath of God came
down upon them, sending fire from Heaven and consuming
many thousands of them ;   for God held it an unworthy
thing that they should have a desire for other food when He
had given them food from Heaven.

4. Oh, did spiritual persons but know how much good
and what great abundance of spirit they lose through not
seeking to raise up their desires above childish things, and
how they would find in this simple spiritual food the sweetness of all things, if they desired not to taste those things !
But such food gives them no pleasure, for the reason why
the children of Israel received not the sweetness of all foods
that was contained in the manna was that they would not
reserve their desire for it alone.   So that they failed to find in
the manna all the sweetness and strength that they could
wish, not because it was not contained in the manna, but
because they desired some other thing.   Thus he that will
love some other thing together[4] with God of a certainty
makes little account of God, for he weighs in the balance
against God that which, as we have said, is far distant from
God.

5. It is well known by experience that, when the will of a
man is affectioned to one thing, he prizes it more than any
other ;   although some other thing may be much better, he
takes less pleasure in it.   And if he wishes to take pleasure in
both, he is bound to do injustice to the more important,
since he makes an equality between them.[5]   Now, inasmuch
as there is naught that equals God, the soul that loves some
other thing together with Him, or clings to it, wrongs Him
greatly.   And if this is so, what would it be doing if it loved
anything more than God ?

6. It is this, too, that was denoted by the command of God
to Moses[6] that he should ascend the Mount to speak with

---

[1] [*Lit.*, ' so high.']   [2] E.p. omits : ' and substance.'
[3] Psalm lxxvii, 31 [A.V. lxxviii, 31].
[4] E.p. omits ' together.'
[5] E.p. substitutes for the last clause : ' because of the unjust equality
that he makes between them.'
[6] A, B : ' This likewise is that which God intended to teach when He
commanded Moses,' etc.

Him : He commanded him not only to ascend it alone,
leaving the children of Israel below, but not even to allow
the beasts to feed over against the Mount.[1] By this He signified that the soul that is to ascend this mount of perfection,
to commune with God, must not only renounce all things
and leave them below,[2] but must not even allow the desires,
which are the beasts, to pasture over against this mount—
that is, upon other things which are not purely God, in Whom
every desire ceases : that is, in the state of perfection. Thus
he that journeys on the road and makes the ascent to God
must needs be habitually careful to quell and mortify the
desires ; and the greater the speed wherewith a soul does
this, the sooner will it reach the end of its journey. But until
these be quelled, it cannot reach the end, however much it
practise the virtues, since it is unable to attain to perfection
in them ; for this perfection consists in voiding and
stripping and purifying the soul of every desire. Of this
we have another very[3] striking figure in Genesis, where we
read that, when the patriarch Jacob desired to ascend
Mount Bethel, in order to build an altar there to God whereon
he should offer Him[4] sacrifice, he first commanded all his
people to do three things : one was that they should cast
away from them all strange gods ; the second, that they
should purify themselves ; the third, that they should change
their garments.[5]

7. By these three things it is signified that any soul that
would ascend this mount in order to make of itself an altar
whereon it may offer to God the sacrifice of pure love and
praise and pure reverence, must, before ascending to the
summit of the mount, have done these three things aforementioned perfectly. First, it must have cast away all
strange gods—namely, all strange affections and attachments ; secondly, it must be purified from the remnants
which the desires aforementioned have left in the soul, by
means of the dark night of sense whereof we are speaking,
habitually[6] denying them and repenting itself ; and thirdly,
in order to reach the summit of this high mount, it must
have changed its garments, which, through its observance

---

[1] E.p. : ' within sight of the Mount.' A, B : ' near the Mount.'
[2] E.p. omits : ' and leave them below.'
[3] E.p. omits ' very.'
[4] The codices have : ' whereon he offered Him.' The editions change
this to : ' whereon to offer Him.'   [5] Genesis xxxv, 2.
[6] A, B have ' in due order ' for ' habitually.'

of the first two things, God will change for it, from old to
new, by giving the soul a new understanding of God in God,
the old[1] human understanding being cast aside ; and a new
love of God in God, the will being now detached from all its
old desires and human pleasures, and the soul being brought
into a new state of knowledge and profound delight,[2] all
other old images and forms of knowledge being cast away,
and all that belongs to the old man, which is the aptitude
of the natural self, being quelled, and the soul being clothed
with a new supernatural aptitude according to all its faculties. So that its operation, which before was human, has
become Divine, which is that that is attained in the state of
union, wherein the soul becomes naught else than an altar
whereon God is adored in praise and love, and God alone is
upon it. For this cause God commanded that the altar
whereon the Ark of the Covenant was to be laid[3] should be
hollow within ;[4] so that the soul may understand how
completely empty of all things God desires it to be, that it
may be an altar worthy of the presence of His Majesty. On
this altar it was likewise forbidden that there should be any
strange fire, or that its own fire should ever fail ; and so
essential was this that, because Nadab and Abihu, who were
the sons of the High Priest Aaron, offered strange fire upon
His altar, Our Lord was wroth and slew them there before the
altar.[5] By this we are to understand that the love of God
must never fail in the soul, so that the soul may be a worthy
altar, and also that no other love must be mingled with it.

8. God permits not that any other thing should dwell
together with Him. Wherefore we may read in the First Book
of the Kings that, when the Philistines put the Ark of the
Covenant into the temple where their idol was, the idol was
cast down upon the ground at the dawn of each day,[6] and
broken to pieces ; and He only permits and wills that there
should be one desire where He is, which is to keep the law
of God perfectly, and to bear upon oneself the Cross of
Christ. And thus naught else is said in the Divine Scripture

---

[1] A reads : ' the new.'
[2] [More literally : ' and abysmal delight.']   Alc. omits these words by
a copyist's oversight. A, B, C give them ; D has : ' and habitual delight.'
The Saint certainly wrote *abisal*, a word which had passed out of use when
the *editio princeps* was made, in 1616.
[3] E.p. : ' whereon sacrifices were to be offered.'   The reading is nearer
to Scripture than that of the codices.   [4] Exodus xxvii, 8.
[5] Leviticus x, 1–2. E.p. reads : ' before the same altar.'
[6] A, B : ' of each morning.'

to have been commanded by God to be put in the Ark,
where the manna was, save the book of the Law,[1] and the
rod of Moses, which signifies the Cross.[2] For the soul that
aspires to naught else than the keeping of the law of the
Lord perfectly and the bearing of the Cross of Christ will be
a true Ark, containing within itself the true manna, which
is God,[3] when that soul attains to a perfect possession in
itself of this law and this rod, without any other thing
soever.

CHAPTER VI

*Wherein are treated two serious evils caused in the soul by the
desires, the one evil being privative and the other positive.*[4]

1. In order that what we have said may be the more
clearly and fully understood, it will be well here to set down
and state how[5] these desires are the cause of two serious
evils in the soul : the one is that they deprive it of the spirit
of God, and the other is that the soul wherein they dwell is
wearied, tormented, darkened, defiled and weakened, according to that which is said in Jeremiah, Chapter II : *Duo mala
fecit Populus meus : dereliquerunt fontem aquæ vivæ, et foderunt
sibi cisternas, dissipatas, quæ continere non valent aquas.* Which
signifies : They have forsaken Me, Who am the fountain of
living water, and they have hewed them out broken cisterns,
that can hold no water.[6] Those two evils—namely, the
privative and the positive—may be caused by any disordered
act of the desire. And, first of all, speaking of the privative,
it is clear[7] from the very fact that the soul becomes affectioned to a thing which comes under the head of creature,
that the more the desire for that thing fills the soul,[8] the
less capacity has the soul for God ; inasmuch as two contraries,
according to the philosophers, cannot coexist in one person ;[9]

---

[1] Deuteronomy xxxi, 26.   [2] Numbers xvii, 10.
[3] E.p. ends the chapter here.
[4] E.p. adds : ' This is proved by passages from Scripture.'
[5] E.p. : 'it will be well here to state how.'   [6] Jeremiah ii, 13.
[7] So Alc.—A, B, e.p. read : ' These two evils are caused by one act of
the desire. For it is clear,' etc.
[8] [*Lit.*, ' the greater the bulk that that desire has in the soul.']
[9] E.p. modifies : ' . . . it has for God ; for, as we said in Chapter iv,
two contraries cannot coexist in one person ; and affection for God and
affection for creatures are contraries and so cannot coexist in one person.'
A, B omit ' according to the philosophers ' and ' as we said in the fourth
chapter.'

and further, since, as we said in the fourth chapter, affection for God and affection for creatures are contraries, and thus there cannot be contained within one will affection for creatures and affection for God.[1] For what has the creature to do with the Creator? What has sensual to do with spiritual? Visible with invisible? Temporal with eternal? Food that is heavenly, spiritual and pure with food that is of sense alone and is purely sensual? Christlike detachment with attachment to aught soever?

2. Wherefore, as in natural generation no form can be introduced unless the preceding, contrary form is first expelled from the subject, which form, while present, is an impediment to the other by reason of the contrariety which the two have between each other; even so, for as long as the soul is subjected to the sensual spirit,[2] the spirit which is pure and spiritual cannot enter it. Wherefore our Saviour said through S. Matthew : *Non est bonum sumere panem filiorum, et mittere canibus.*[3] That is : It is not meet to take the children's bread and to cast it to dogs. And elsewhere, too, he says through the same Evangelist[4] : *Nolite sanctum dare canibus.*[5] Which signifies : Give not that which is holy unto the dogs. In these passages Our Lord compares those who deny their creature desires, and prepare themselves to receive the spirit of God in purity, to the children of God ; and those who would have their desire feed upon the creatures, to dogs. For it is given to children to eat with their father at table and from his dish, which is to feed upon his spirit, and to dogs are given the crumbs which fall from the table.

3. From this we are to learn that all creatures are crumbs that have fallen from the table of God. Wherefore he that feeds ever upon[6] the creatures is rightly called a dog, and therefore the bread is taken from the children, because they desire not to rise from feeding upon the crumbs, which are the creatures, to the table of the uncreated spirit of their Father. Therefore, like dogs, they are ever hungering, and justly so, because the crumbs serve to whet their appetite rather than to satisfy their hunger. And thus David says of them : *Famen patientur ut canes, et circuibunt civitatem. Si vero*

---

[1] Cf. p. 34, n. 9.   [2] E.p. : 'sensual and animal spirit.'
[3] S. Matthew xv, 26.
[4] So AJc. A, B : *Et alibi.* E.p. : 'and elsewhere.'
[5] S. Matthew vii, 6.   [6] [*Lit.*, ' he that goes feeding upon.']

non fuerint saturati, et murmurabunt.[1] Which signifies : They shall suffer hunger like dogs and shall go round about the city, and, when they see not themselves satisfied, they shall murmur. For this is the property of one that has desires, that he is ever discontented and dissatisfied, like one that suffers hunger ; for what has the hunger which all the creatures suffer to do with the fullness which is caused by the spirit of God ? Wherefore this fullness that is uncreated[2] cannot enter the soul, if there be not first cast out that other created hunger which belongs to the desire of the soul ; for, as we have said,[3] two contraries cannot dwell in one person, the which contraries in this case[4] are hunger and fullness.

4. From what has been said it will be seen how much greater is the work of God[5] in the cleansing and the purging of a soul from these contrarieties than in the creating of that soul from nothing. For these contrarieties, these contrary desires and affections, are more completely opposed to God and offer Him greater resistance than does nothingness ;[6] for nothingness resists not at all.[7] And let this suffice with respect to the first of the important evils which are inflicted upon the soul by the desires—namely, resistance to the spirit of God—since much has been said of this above.

5. Let us now speak of the second effect which they cause in the soul. This is of many kinds, because the desires weary the soul and torment and darken it, and defile it and weaken it. Of these five things we shall speak separately, in their turn.

6. With regard to the first, it is clear that the desires weary and fatigue the soul ; for they are like restless and discontented children, who are ever demanding this or that from their mother, and are never satisfied. And even as one that digs because he covets a treasure is wearied and fatigued, even so is the soul wearied and fatigued in order to attain that which its desires demand of it ; and although in the end it may attain it, it is still weary, because it is never satisfied ;

---

[1] Psalm lviii, 15–16 [A. V., lix,14–15].

[2] E.p. : ' this fullness of God.'

[3] E.p. : ' . . . cast out from it this hunger of the desire; for, as has been said,' etc.

[4] E.p. omits : ' in this case.'

[5] [*Lit.,* ' how much more God does.'] E.p. adds : ' in a certain way.'

[6] E.p. : ' . . . affections seem to hinder (*estorbar*) God more than does nothingness.'

[7] E.p. : ' for nothingness resists not His Majesty at all, and creature desire does resist Him.'

for, after all, the cisterns which it is digging are broken, and cannot hold water to satisfy thirst. And thus, as Isaiah says : *Lassus adhuc sitit, et anima ejus vacua est.*[1] Which signifies : His desire is empty. And the soul that has desires is wearied and fatigued ; for it is like a man that is sick of a fever, who finds himself no better until the fever leaves him, and whose thirst increases with every moment. For, as is said in the Book of Job : *Cum satiatus fuerit, arctabitur, æstuabit, et omnis dolor irruet super eum.*[2] Which signifies : When he has satisfied his desire, he will be the more oppressed and straitened ; the heat of desire hath increased in his soul and thus all grief will fall upon him. The soul is wearied and fatigued by its desires, because it is wounded and moved and disturbed by them as is water by the winds ; in just the same way they disturb it, allowing it not to rest in any place or in any thing soever. And of such a soul says Isaiah : *Cor impii quasi mare fervens.*[3] The heart of the wicked man is like the sea when-it rages. And he is a wicked man that subjects not his desires. The soul that would fain satisfy its desires grows wearied and fatigued ; for it is like one that, being an hungered, opens his mouth that he may sate himself with wind, when, instead of being satisfied, his craving becomes greater, for the wind is no food for him. To this purpose said Jeremiah :[4] *In desiderio animæ suæ attraxit ventum amoris sui.*[5] As though he were to say : In the desire of his will he snuffed up the wind of his affection. And later he tries to describe the aridity wherein such a soul remains, and warns it, saying : *Prohibe pedem tuum a nuditate, et guttur tuum a siti.*[6] Which signifies : Withhold thy foot (that is, thy thought) from detachment and thy throat from thirst (that is to say, thy will from the indulgence of the desire which causes greater drought) ;[7] and, even as the lover is wearied and fatigued upon the day of his hopes, when his attempt has proved to be vain, so the soul is wearied and fatigued by all its desires and by indulgence in them, since they all cause it greater emptiness and hunger ; for, as they commonly say, desire is like the fire, which increases as wood

[1] Isaiah xxix, 8. The editions supply the translation of the first part of the Latin text, which the Saint and the codices omitted : ' After being wearied and fatigued, he still thirsteth,' etc.
[2] Job xx, 22.   [3] Isaiah lvii, 20.
[4] E.p. : ' And thus Jeremiah says of such a soul.'
[5] Jeremiah ii, 24.   [6] Jeremiah ii, 25.
[7] E.p. reads ' dryness ' for ' drought ' and omits several lines, continuing : ' Desire is like the fire,' etc.

is thrown upon it, and which, when it has consumed the wood, must needs burn away.

7. And desire is in yet worse condition here ; for the fire goes down when the wood is consumed, but desire, though it increases when fuel is added to it, decreases not correspondingly when the fuel is consumed ; on the contrary, instead of going down, as does the fire when its fuel is consumed, it fails from weariness, for its hunger is increased and its food diminished. And of this Isaiah speaks, saying : *Declinabit ad dexteram, et esuriet : et comedet ad sinistram, et non saturabitur.*[1] This signifies : He shall turn to the right hand, and shall be hungry ; and he shall eat on the left hand, and shall not be filled. For they that mortify not their desires, when they ' turn ', justly see the fullness of the sweetness of spirit of those who are at the right hand of God, which fullness is not granted to themselves ; and justly, too, when they eat on the left hand,[2] by which is meant the satisfaction of their desire with some creature comfort, they are not filled. For, leaving that which alone can satisfy, they feed on that which causes them greater hunger. It is clear, then, that the desires weary and fatigue the soul.

CHAPTER VII

Wherein is shown how the desires torment the soul.   This is proved likewise by comparisons and quotations.[3]

1. The second kind of positive evil which the desires cause the soul is in their tormenting and afflicting of it, after the manner of one who is in torment through being bound with cords from which he has no relief until he be freed. And of these David says : *Funes peccatorum circumplexi sunt me.*[4] The cords of my sins, which are my desires, have constrained

---

[1] Isaiah ix, 20.

[2] Thus Alc. [with ' run ' for ' eat ']. A, B, e.p. read : '. . . . when they turn from the way of God (which is the right hand) are justly hungered, for they merit not the fullness of the sweetness of spirit. And justly, too, when they eat on the left hand,' etc. [While agreeing with P. Silverio that Alc. gives the better reading, I prefer ' eat ' to ' run ' : it is nearer the Scriptural passage and the two Spanish words, *comen* and *corren*, could easily be confused in MS.]

[3] Thus Alc. and e.p.   A, B read : ' This is proved by comparisons and quotations from the Sacred Scripture.'

[4] Psalm cxviii, 61 [A.V., cxix, 61].

me round about. And in the same way wherein one that lies naked upon thorns and briars is tormented and afflicted, even so is the soul tormented and afflicted when it rests upon its desires. For they take hold upon it and wound it and distress it and cause it pain, even as do thorns. Of these David says likewise : *Circumdederunt me sicut apes : et exarserunt sicut ignis in spinis.*[1] Which signifies : They compassed me about like bees,[2] wounding me with their stings, and they were enkindled against me, like fire among thorns ; for in the desires, which are the thorns, the fire of anguish and torment increases. And even as the husbandman, coveting the harvest for which he hopes, afflicts and torments the ox in the plough, even so does concupiscence afflict the soul in its desire to attain that for which it longs. This can be clearly seen in that desire which Delilah had to know whence Samson derived his strength that was so great, for the Scripture says that it fatigued and tormented her so much that it caused her to swoon, almost to the point of death, and she said : *Defecit anima ejus, et ad mortem usque lassata est.*[3]

2. The more intense is the desire, the greater is the torment which it causes the soul. So that the torment increases with the desire ; and the greater are the desires which possess the soul, the greater are its torments ; for in such a soul is fulfilled, even in this life, that which is said in the Apocalypse concerning Babylon,[4] in these words : *Quantum glorificavit se, et in deliciis fuit, tantum date illi tormentum, et luctum.*[5] That is : As much as she has desired to exalt and fulfil her desires, so much give her of torment and anguish. And even as one that falls into the hands of his enemies is tormented and afflicted, even so is the soul tormented and afflicted that is led away by its desires. Of this there is a figure in the Book of the Judges, wherein it may be read that that strong man, Samson, who at one time was strong[6] and free and a judge of Israel, fell into the power of his enemies, and they took his strength from him, and put out his eyes, and bound him in a mill, to grind corn,[7] wherein they tormented and afflicted him greatly ;[8] and thus it happens

---

[1] Psalm cxvii, 12 [A.V., cxviii, 12].
[2] A, B : ' like stinging bees.'
[3] Judges xvi, 16.
[4] E.p. omits : ' concerning Babylon.'
[5] Revelation xviii, 7.
[6] E.p. : ' . . . figure in that strong man, Samson, who at one time was so strong,' etc.
[7] [*Lit.*, ' bound him to grind in a mill.']
[8] Judges xvi, 21.

to the soul in which these its enemies, the desires, live and rule ; for the first thing that they do is to weaken the soul and blind it, as we shall say below ; and then they afflict and torment it, binding it to the mill of concupiscence ; and the bonds with which it is bound are its own desires.

3. Wherefore God, having compassion on these that with such great labour, and at such cost to themselves, go about endeavouring to satisfy the hunger and thirst of their desire in the creatures, says to them through Isaiah : *Omnes sitientes, venite ad aquas ; et qui non habetis argentum, properate, emite, et comedite : venite, emite absque argento, vinum, et lac. Quare appenditis argentum non in panibus, et laborem vestrum non in saturitate ?*[1] As though He were to say : All ye that have thirst of desire, come to the waters, and all ye that have no silver of your own will and desires, make haste ; buy from Me and eat ; come and buy from Me wine and milk (that ·is, spiritual sweetness and peace), without the silver of your own will, and without giving Me any labour in exchange for it, as ye give for your desires.[2] Wherefore do ye give the silver of your will[3] for that which is not bread—that is, of the Divine Spirit—and set the labour of your desires upon that which cannot satisfy you ? Come, hearkening to Me, and ye shall eat the good that ye desire and your soul shall delight itself in fatness.

4. This attaining to fatness is a going forth from all pleasures of the creatures ; for the creatures torment but the Spirit of God refreshes. And thus He calls us through S. Matthew, saying : *Venite ad me omnes, qui laboratis, et onerati estis, et ego reficiam vos, et invenietis requiem animabus vestris.*[4] As though He were to say : All ye that go about tormented, afflicted and burdened with the burden of your cares and desires, go forth from them, come to Me, and I will refresh you and ye shall find for your souls the rest which your desires take from you, wherefore they are a heavy burden, for David says of them : *Sicut onus grave gravatæ sunt super me.*[5]

---

[1] Isaiah lv, 1–2.
[2] A, B repeat : ' wine and milk—that is, peace and sweetness.'
[3] E.p. : ' of your own will.'
[4] S. Matthew xi, 28–9.   [5] Psalm xxxvii, 5 [A.V., xxxviii, 4].

CHAPTER VIII

Wherein is shown how the desires darken and blind the soul.[1]

1. The third evil that the desires cause in the soul is that they blind and darken it.   Even as vapours darken the air and allow not the bright sun to shine ; or as a mirror that is clouded over cannot receive within itself a clear image ; or as water defiled by mud reflects not the visage of one that looks therein ; even so the soul that is clouded by the desires is darkened in the understanding and allows neither[2] the sun of natural reason nor that of the supernatural Wisdom of God to shine upon it and illumine it clearly.   And thus David, speaking to this purpose, says : *Comprehenderunt me iniquitates meæ, et non potui, ut viderem.*[3]   Which signifies : Mine iniquities[4] have taken hold upon me, and I could have no power to see.

2. And at this time, when the soul is darkened in the understanding, it is stultified also in the will, and the memory becomes dull and disordered in its due operation.   For, as these faculties in their operations depend upon the understanding, it is clear that, when the understanding is embarrassed, they will become disordered and troubled.   And thus David says : *Anima mea turbata est valde.*[5]   That is : My soul is sorely troubled.   Which is as much as to say, ' disordered in its faculties.'   For, as we say, the understanding has no more capacity for receiving enlightenment from the wisdom of God than has the air, when it is dark, for receiving enlightenment from the sun ; neither has the will any power to embrace God within itself in pure love, even as the mirror that is clouded with vapour has no power to reflect clearly within itself any visage,[6] and even less power has the memory which is clouded by the darkness of desire to take clearly upon itself the form of the image of God, just as the muddied water cannot show forth clearly the visage of one that looks at himself therein.[7]

[1] A, B, e.p. add : ' This is proved by quotations from the Sacred Scripture.'
[2] [*Lit.*, ' gives no occasion either for,' etc.]   Only Alc. reads thus.   All the other authorities have : ' gives no light.'
[3] Psalm xxxix, 13 [A.V., xl, 12].
[4] So e.p.   The other authorities have : ' My wickednesses.'
[5] Psalm vi, 4 [A.V., vi, 3].
[6] [*Lit.*, ' the present visage.']   A, B, e.p. have ' object ' for ' visage.'
[7] ' Therein ' is in e.p. only.

3. Desire blinds and darkens the soul ; for desire, as such, is blind, since of itself it has no understanding in itself, the reason being to it always, as it were, a child leading a blind man.[1] And hence it comes to pass that, whensoever the soul is guided by its desire, it becomes blind ; for this is as if one that sees were guided by one that sees not, which is, as it were, for both to be blind. And that which follows from this is that[2] which Our Lord says through S. Matthew : *Si cæcus cæco ducatum præstet, ambo in foveam cadunt.*[3] If the blind lead the blind, both shall fall into the ditch. Of little use are its eyes to a moth, since desire for the beauty of the light dazzles it and leads it into the flame.[4] And even so we may say that one who feeds upon desire is like a fish that is dazzled, upon which the light acts rather as darkness, preventing it from seeing the harm which the fishermen are preparing for it. This is very well explained by David himself, where he says of such persons : *Supercecidit ignis, et non viderunt solem.*[5] Which signifies : There came upon them the fire, which burns with its heat and dazzles with its light.[6] And it is this that desire does to the soul, enkindling its concupiscence and dazzling its understanding so that it cannot see its light. For the cause of its being thus dazzled is that, when another light of a different kind is set before the eye, the visual faculty is attracted by[7] that which is interposed so that it sees not the other ; and, as the desire is set so near to the soul that it is in the soul itself, the soul meets this first light and is attracted by[8] it ; and thus it is unable to see the light of clear understanding, neither will see it until the dazzling power of desire is taken away from it.

4. For this reason one must greatly lament the ignorance of certain men, who burden themselves with extraordinary penances and with many other voluntary practices, and think that this practice or that will suffice to bring them to

---

[1] E.p. has : ' . . . is blind, since of itself it is unreasonable ; and it is reason that always guides and directs the soul rightly in its operations.'

[2] E.p. : ' is exactly that.'

[3] S. Matthew xv, 14.

[4] [*Hoguera.* More exactly : ' fire,' ' bonfire,' ' blaze.']

[5] Psalm lvii, 9 [cf. A.V., lviii, 8].

[6] So Alc. The other MSS. have . ' The light fell upon them and struck their eyes and dazzled them.' E.p. reads : ' The fire came upon them and they saw not the sun.'

[7] Alc. has : ' is blinded by,' probably a copyist's error. [*ciégase* for *cébase*].

[8] Here A and B have *ciégase*, whereas Alc. and e.p. read *cébase.*

the union of Divine Wisdom ; but such is not the case if they endeavour not[1] diligently to mortify their desires. If they were careful to bestow half of that labour on this, they would profit more in a month than they profit by all the other practices in many years. For, just as it is necessary to till the earth if it is to bear fruit, and unless it be tilled it bears naught but weeds, just so mortification of the desires is necessary if the soul is to profit. Without this mortification, I make bold to say, the soul no more achieves progress on the road to perfection and to the knowledge of God and of itself, however many efforts it may make, than the seed grows when it is cast upon[2] untilled ground. Wherefore the darkness and rudeness of the soul will not be taken from it until the desires be quenched. For these desires are like cataracts, or like motes in the eye, which obstruct the sight until they be cast away.

5. And thus David, realizing the blindness of these souls, and the completeness of their exclusion from the light of truth, and the greatness of God's wrath against them, speaks with them, saying : *Priusquam intelligerent spinæ vestræ rhamnum : sicut viventes, sic in ira absorbet eos.*[3] And this is as though He had said : Before your thorns (that is, your desires) hardened and grew, changing from tender thorns into a thick hedge and shutting out the sight of God even as oft-times the living find their thread of life broken in the midst of its course, even so will God swallow them up in His wrath.[4] For the desires that are living in the soul, so that it cannot understand Him, will be absorbed by God by means of chastisement and correction, either in this life or in the next, and this will come to pass through purgation. And He says that He will absorb them in wrath, because that which is suffered in the mortification of the desires is

---

[1] E.p. has : ' who burden themselves with unrestrained [*lit.*, *desordenadas*, disordered, unruly] penances and with many other unrestrained practices—I mean voluntary ones—and place their confidence in these, and think that these alone, without any mortification of their desires in other respects, will be sufficient to lead them to the union of Divine Wisdom ; but this is not the case if they endeavour not,' etc.

[2] E.p. : ' being scattered over.'

[3] Psalm lvii, 10 [A.V., lviii, 9].

[4] [P. Silverio following] Alc. reads : ' Before your thorns (that is, your desires) understood, even as the living, after this manner He will absorb them in His wrath.' All the other MSS., however, and also e.p., read as in the text.

punishment for the ruin which they have wrought in the soul.[1]

6. Oh that men could know how great is the blessing of Divine light whereof they are deprived by this blindness which proceeds from their affections and desires, and into what great hurts and evils these make them to fall day after day, for so long as they mortify them not ! For a man must not rely upon a clear understanding, or upon gifts that he has received from God, and think that he may indulge his affection or desire, and will not be blinded and darkened, and fall gradually into a worse estate. For who would have said that a man so perfect in wisdom and the gifts of God as was Solomon would have been reduced to such blindness and foolishness of the will as to make altars to so many idols and to adore them himself, when he was old ?[2] And no more was needed to bring him to this than the affection which he had for his wives and his neglect to deny his desires and the delights of his heart. For he himself says concerning himself, in Ecclesiastes, that he denied not his heart that which it demanded of him.[3] And this man was capable of being so completely led away by his desires that, although it is true that at the beginning he was cautious, nevertheless, because he denied them not, they gradually blinded and darkened his understanding, so that in the end they succeeded in quenching that great light of wisdom which God had given him, and therefore in his old age he forsook God.

7. And if unmortified desires could do so much in this man who knew so well the distance that lies between good and evil, what will they not be capable of accomplishing by working upon our ignorance ? For we, as God[4] said to the Prophet Jonah concerning the Ninevites, cannot discern between[5] our right hand and our left.[6] At every step we consider evil to be good, and good, evil, and this arises from

---

[1] E.p. reads : ' For God in His wrath will swallow up those whose desires live in the soul and shut out the knowledge of God, either in the next life in the affliction and purgation of purgatory, or in this life with afflictions and trials which He sends to detach them from their desires, or through the mortification of their own desires. This God does that He may remove thereby the false light of desire which is between Himself and us, and which was dazzling us and hindering us from knowing Him ; so that, the sight of the understanding being enlightened, the ruin wrought by the desires may be repaired.'   [2] 3 Kings [A.V., 1 Kings] xi, 4.
[3] Ecclesiastes ii, 10.   [4] E.p. : ' as the Lord.'
[5] [Lit., ' we . . . know not what there is between.']
[6] Jonah iv, 11.

our own nature. What, then, will come to pass if the hindrance of desire[1] is added to our natural darkness ? Naught but that which Isaiah describes thus : *Palpavimus, sicut cœci parietem, et quasi absque oculis attrectavimus : impegimus meridie, quasi in tenebris.*[2] The prophet is speaking with those who love to follow these their desires. It is as if he had said : We have groped for the wall as though we were blind, and we have been groping as though we had no eyes, and our blindness has attained to such a point that we have stumbled at midday as though it were in the darkness.[3] For he that is blinded by desire has this property, that, when he is set in the midst of truth and of that which is good for him, he can no more see it than if he were in darkness.

CHAPTER IX

Wherein is described how the desires defile the soul. This is proved by comparisons and quotations from Holy Scripture.

1. The fourth evil which the desires cause in the soul is that they stain and defile it, as is taught in Ecclesiastes, in these words : *Qui tetigerit picem, inquinabitur ab ea.*[4] This signifies : He that touches pitch shall be defiled therewith. And a man touches pitch when he allows the desire of his will to be satisfied by any creature. Herein it is to be noted that the Wise Man compares the creatures to pitch ; for there is more difference between excellence of soul[5] and the best of the creatures[6] than there is between pure diamond[7], or fine gold, and pitch. And just as gold or diamond, if it were heated and placed upon pitch, would become foul and be stained by it, inasmuch as the heat would have cajoled and allured the pitch, even so the soul that is hot with desire for any creature draws forth[8] foulness from it through the heat of its desire and is stained by it. And there is more

---

[1] [*Lit.*, ' if desire.']   [2] Isaiah lix, 10.
[3] E.p. has slight verbal variations here, the chief being ' as in darkness ' for ' as though we had no eyes,' and ' in obscurity ' for ' in the darkness.'
[4] Ecclesiasticus xiii, 1.
[5] E.p. : ' between the excellence which the soul may have.'
[6] [More literally : ' and all the best that is of the creatures.' ' Best ' is neuter and refers to qualities, appurtenances, etc.]
[7] [*Lit.*, ' bright diamond.']
[8] E.p. : ' even so the soul, in the heat of its desire which it has for any creature, derives,' etc.

difference between the soul and other corporeal creatures
than between a liquid that is highly clarified and mud that
is most foul. Wherefore, even as such a liquid would be
defiled if it were mingled with mud, so is the soul defiled that
clings to creatures, since by doing this it becomes like to the
said creatures. And in the same way that traces of soot
would defile a face that is very lovely and perfect, even in
this way do disordered desires befoul and defile the soul that
has them, the which soul is in itself a most lovely and perfect
image of God.

2. Wherefore Jeremiah, lamenting the ravages of foulness
which these disordered affections cause in the soul, speaks
first of its beauty, and then of its foulness, saying : *Candidiores
sunt Nazaræi ejus nive, nitidiores lacte, rubicundiores ebore antiquo,
sapphiro pulchriores. Denigrata est super carbones facies eorum, et
non sunt cogniti in plateis.*[1] Which signifies : Its hair—that is
to say, that of the soul—is more excellent in whiteness[2]
than the snow, clearer[3] than milk, and ruddier than old
ivory, and lovelier than the sapphire stone. Their face has
now become blacker than coal and they are not known in
the streets.[4] By the hair we here understand the affections
and thoughts of the soul, which, ordered as God orders
them—that is, in God Himself[5]—are whiter than snow, and
clearer[6] than milk, and ruddier than ivory,[7] and lovelier
than the sapphire. By these four things is understood every
kind of beauty and excellence of corporeal creatures, higher
than which, says the writer, are the soul and its operations,
which are the Nazarites or the hair aforementioned ; the
which Nazarites, being disordered[8] and arranged in a way
that God ordered not—that is, being set upon the creatures
—have their face (says Jeremiah) made and turned blacker
than coal.

3. All this harm, and more, is done to the beauty of the
soul by its unruly desires for the things of this world ;[9] so

---

[1] Lamentations iv, 7–8.
[2] A : ' is whiter than whiteness, than the snow.' B : ' is lovelier than
whiteness, than the snow.'
[3] [*Lit., más resplandecientes*, ' more brilliant,' ' more luminous.']
[4] [*Lit., plazas* (derived from the Latin *plateas*), which now, however,
has the meaning of ' squares,' ' (market) places.']
[5] Alc. omits, perhaps by an oversight : ' that . . . Himself.'
[6] Cf. n. 3., above.   [7] E.p. : ' than old ivory.'
[8] [The words translated ' disordered,' ' unruly,' here and elsewhere, and
occasionally ' unrestrained,' are the same in the original : *desordenado*.]
[9] E.p. omits : ' for the things of this world.'

much so that, if we set out to speak of the foul and vile appearance that the desires can give the soul, we should find nothing, however full of cobwebs and worms it might be, not even the corruption of a dead body, nor aught else that is impure and vile, nor aught that can exist and be imagined in this life, to which we could compare it. For, although it is true that the disordered soul, in its natural being,[1] is as perfect as when God created it, yet, in its reasonable being, it is vile, abominable,[2] foul, black and full of all the evils that are here being described, and many more. For, as we shall afterwards say, a single unruly desire, although there be in it no matter of mortal sin, suffices to bring a soul into such bondage, foulness and vileness that it can in no wise come to accord with God in union[3] until the desire be purified. What will be the vileness of the soul that is completely unrestrained with respect to its own passions and given up to its desires, and how far withdrawn will it be from God and from His purity ?

4. It is impossible to explain in words, or to cause to be understood by the understanding, what a variety of impurity is caused in the soul by variety of desire. For, if it could be expressed and understood, it would be a wondrous thing, and one also which would fill us with pity, to see how each desire, in accordance with its quality and degree, be it greater or smaller, leaves in the soul its mark and deposit[4] of impurity and vileness, and how one single disorder of the reason can be the source of innumerable different impurities, some greater, some less, each one after its kind.[5] For even as the soul of the righteous man has in one single perfection, which is the uprightness of the soul, innumerable gifts of great richness, and many virtues of great loveliness, each one full of grace after its kind according to the multitude and difference in the affections of love which it has had in God, even so the disordered soul, according to the variety of the desires which it has for the creatures, has in itself a miserable variety of impurities and meannesses, wherewith it is endowed by the said desires.

---

[1] E.p. : ' natural substance.'   [2] E.p. omits ' abominable.'
[3] E.p. : ' . . . of mortal sin, befouls and stains the soul and renders it unfit to come to accord with God in perfect union.' A, B : ' in any union.' [The Spanish of the text reads literally : ' in a union.']
[4] E.p. : ' . . . how each desire, in agreement with its quality and intention, leaves its mark and deposit,' etc.
[5] E.p. omits : ' and how . . . its kind.'

5. This variety of desire[1] is well described in the book of Ezekiel, where it is written that God showed this prophet, in the interior of the Temple, painted around its walls, all likenesses of creeping things which crawl on the ground, and all the abominations of unclean beasts.[2] And then God said to Ezekiel : Son of man, hast thou not indeed seen the abominations that these do, each one in the secrecy of his chamber ?[3] And God commanded the Prophet to go in farther and he would see greater abominations ; and he says that he there saw women seated, weeping for Adonis, the god of love.[4] And God commanded him to go in farther still, and he would see yet greater abominations, and he says that he saw there five-and-twenty old men whose backs were turned toward the Temple.[5]

6. The diversity of creeping things and unclean beasts that were painted in the first chamber of the Temple are the thoughts and conceptions which the understanding fashions from the lowly things of earth, and from all the creatures, which are painted, just as they are, in the temple of the soul, when the soul[6] embarrasses its understanding with them, which is the soul's first habitation. The women that were farther within, in the second habitation, weeping for the god Adonis, are the desires that are in the second faculty of the soul, which is the will ; the which are, as it were, weeping, inasmuch as they covet that to which the will is affectioned, which are the creeping things painted in the understanding. And the men that were in the third habitation[7] are the images and representations of the creatures, which the third part[8] of the soul,—namely memory—keeps and reflects upon[9] within itself. Of these it is said that their backs are turned toward the Temple because when the soul, according to these three faculties, completely and perfectly embraces anything that is of the earth, it can be said to have its back turned toward the Temple of God, which is the right reason of the soul, which admits within itself nothing that is of creatures.[10]

---

[1] [*Lit.*, ' of desires.']   A, B, e.p. have : ' of impurities.'
[2] Ezekiel viii, 10.   [3] [Ezekiel viii, 12.]
[4] Ezekiel viii, 14.   [5] Ezekiel viii, 16.
[6] E.p. : ' which, being so contrary to things eternal, defile the temple of the soul, and the soul,' etc.
[7] So Alc., e.p.   A, B and some editions have : ' third chamber.'
[8] E.p. : ' third faculty.'
[9] [*Lit.*, ' revolves '—' turns over in its mind ' in our common idiom.]
[10] E.p. : ' admits within itself no created thing that is opposed to God.'

7. And let this now suffice for the understanding of this foul disorder of the soul with respect to its desires. For if we had to treat in detail of the lesser foulness[1] which these imperfections and their variety make and cause in the soul, and that which is caused by venial sins, which is still greater than that of the imperfections, and their great variety, and likewise that which is caused by the desires for mortal sin, which is complete foulness of the soul, and its great variety, according to the variety and multitude of all these three things, we should never end, nor would the understanding of angels suffice to understand it.[2] That which I say, and that which is to the point for my purpose, is that any desire, although it be for but the smallest imperfection, stains and defiles the soul.[3]

CHAPTER X

Wherein is described how the desires weaken the soul in virtue and make it lukewarm.[4]

1. The fifth way in which the desires harm the soul is by making it lukewarm and weak, so that it has no strength to follow after virtue and to persevere therein. For as the strength of the desire, when it is divided, is less than if it were set wholly on one thing alone, and as, the more are the objects whereon it is set, the less of it there is for each one of them, for this cause philosophers say that virtue in union is stronger than if it be dispersed. Wherefore it is clear that, if the desire of the will be dispersed among other things than virtue, it must be weaker as regards virtue. And thus the soul whose will is divided among trifles is like water, which, having an outlet below wherein to empty itself, never rises ; and such a soul has no profit. For this cause the patriarch Jacob compared his son Reuben to water poured out, because in a certain sin he had given rein to his desires. And he said : Thou art poured out like water ; grow thou not.[5] As though he had said : Since thou art poured out like water as to the desires, thou shalt not grow in virtue. And thus, as hot water, when uncovered, readily

---

[1] E.p. : ' of the impediment to this union.'
[2] E.p. shortens : ' and its great diversity, we should never end.'
[3] E.p. omits : ' stains . . . soul,' leaving the sentence incomplete.
[4] E.p. adds : ' This is proved by comparisons and quotations from the Sacred Scripture.'   [5] Genesis xlix, 4.

loses heat, and as aromatic spices, when they are unwrapped,[1] gradually lose the fragrance and strength of their perfume, even so the soul that is not recollected in one single desire for God loses heat and vigour in its virtue. This was well understood by David, when he said, speaking with God : I will keep my strength for Thee.[2] That is, concentrating the strength of my desires[3] upon Thee alone.

2. And the desires weaken the virtue of the soul, because they are to it like the shoots[4] that grow about a tree, and take away its virtue so that it cannot bring forth so much fruit. And of such souls as these says the Lord : *Væ prægnantibus, et nutrientibus in illis diebus.*[5] That is : Woe to them that in those days are with child and to them that give suck. This being with child and giving suck is understood with respect to the desires ; which, if they be not pruned, will ever be taking more virtue from the soul, and will grow to the harm of the soul, like the shoots upon the tree. Wherefore Our Lord counsels us, saying : Have your loins girt about[6]—the loins signifying here the desires. And indeed, they are also like leeches, which are ever sucking the blood from the veins, for thus the Preacher terms them when he says : The leeches are the daughters—that is, the desires— saying ever : *Daca, daca.*[7]

3. From this it is clear that the desires bring no good to the soul but rather take from it that which it has ; and if it mortify them not, they will not cease till they have wrought in it that which the children of the viper are said to work in their mother ; who, as they are growing within her womb, consume her and kill her while they themselves remain alive at her cost. Just so the desires that are not mortified grow to such a point that they kill the soul with respect to God because it has not first killed them. And they alone live in it. Wherefore the Preacher says : *Aufer a me Domine ventris concupiscentias.*[8]

4. And, even though they reach not this point, it is very piteous to consider how the desires that live in this poor soul treat it, how unhappy it is with regard to itself, how dry

---

[1] A, B : ' . . . spices, not being covered.'
[2] Psalm lviii, 10 [A.V., lix, 9].   [3] E.p. : ' my affections.'
[4] A, B, e.p. : ' like the twigs and shoots.'
[5] S. Matthew xxiv, 19.   [6] S. Luke xii, 35.
[7] Proverbs xxx, 15. All the codices have this reading. E.p. reads : ' saying ever : "Give me, give me." '
[8] Ecclesiasticus xxiii, 6. [In the original the last two sentences are transposed.]

with respect to its neighbours, and how weary and slothful with respect to the things of God. For there is no evil humour that makes it as difficult and wearisome for a sick man to walk, or gives him such distaste for eating, as the difficulty and distaste which desire for creatures gives to a soul for following virtue. And thus the reason why many souls have no diligence and eagerness to gain[1] virtue is, as a rule, that they have desires and affections which are not pure and are not fixed upon God.[2]

CHAPTER XI

Wherein it is proved necessary that the soul that would attain to Divine union should be free from desires, howsoever small.[3]

1. I expect that for a long time the reader has been wishing to ask whether it be necessary, in order to attain to this high estate of perfection, to undergo first of all total mortification in all the desires, great and small, or if it will suffice to mortify some of them and to leave others, those at least which seem of little moment. For it appears to be a severe and most difficult thing for the soul to be able to attain to such purity and detachment that it has no will and affection for anything.

2. To this I reply : first, that it is true that all the desires are not equally hurtful, nor do they all equally embarrass the soul[4] (we are speaking of those that are voluntary), for the natural desires hinder the soul little, or not at all, from attaining to union, when they are not consented to nor pass beyond the first movements (that is,[5] all those wherein the rational will has had no part, whether at first or afterward) ; and to take away these—that is, to mortify them wholly in this life—is impossible. And these hinder not the soul in such a way as to prevent attainment to Divine union, even though they be not, as I say, wholly mortified ; for the natural man may well have them, and yet the soul may be

---

[1] A, B : ' to work virtue.' E.p. : ' to work virtues.'

[2] [*Lit.*, ' not pure on God.'] E.p. : ' not pure on God our Lord.'

[3] Alc. differs slightly here, chiefly by using a stronger word for ' small.' We might read : ' how very small soever.'

[4] Alc. omits several lines here, but apparently only through the copyist's negligence.

[5] [The original has no such explanatory phrase.] E.p., however, reads : ' And I mean by " natural " and " first movements " all those. . . . etc.'

quite free from them according to the rational spirit. For it will sometimes come to pass that the soul will be in the full[1] union of the prayer of quiet in the will, while these desires are actually dwelling in the sensual part of the soul,[2] and the higher part, which is in prayer, will have nothing to do with them. Yet the other voluntary desires, whether they be of mortal sin, which are the gravest, or of venial sin, which are less grave, or whether they be only of imperfections, which are the least grave of all, must be driven away every one, and the soul must be free from them all, howsoever small they be, if it is to come to this complete union ; and the reason is that the state of this Divine union consists in the soul's total transformation, according to the will, in the will of God, so that there may be naught in the soul that is contrary to the will of God, but that,[3] in all and through all, its movement may be that of the will of God alone.

3. It is for this reason that we say of this state that it is the making of two wills into one—namely, into the will of God, which will[4] of God is likewise the will of the soul. For if this soul desired any imperfection that God wills not, there would not be made one will of God, since the soul would have a will for that which God had not. It is clear, then, that for the soul to come to unite itself perfectly with God through love and will, it must first be free from all desire of the will, howsoever small. That is, that it must not intentionally and knowingly consent with the will to imperfections, and it must have power and liberty to be able not so to consent intentionally. I say knowingly, because, unintentionally and unknowingly, or without having[5] the power to do otherwise, it may well fall into imperfections and venial sins, and into the natural desires whereof we have spoken ; for of such sins as these which are not voluntary and surreptitious[6] it is written that the just man shall fall seven times in the day and shall rise up again.[7] But of the voluntary desires, which are intentional venial sins, though they be for very small things, as I have said, any one that is not

---

[1] [That is, enjoys all the union that the prayer of quiet gives.] B, e.p. have : ' in high union.'

[2] Thus A, B. The other authorities [and P. Silverio] read : ' of man.'

[3] E.p.: ' [and] so that.'

[4] E.p. : ' the making into one will of God—that is, of my will and the will of God, so that the will,' etc.

[5] E.p. : ' without wholly having.'

[6] These last two words occur in Alc. alone.   [7] Proverbs xxiv, 16.

conquered suffices to impede union.[1] I mean, if this habit
be not mortified ; for sometimes certain acts of different
desires have not as much power when the habits are mortified.[2] Still, the soul will attain to the stage of not having
even these, for they likewise proceed from a habit of imperfection. But some habits of voluntary imperfections,
which are never completely conquered, prevent not only the
attainment of Divine union, but also progress in perfection.

4. These habitual imperfections are, for example, a common custom of much speaking, or some attachment which
we never wish entirely to conquer—such as that to a person,
a garment, a book, a cell, a particular kind of food, tittle-
tattle, fancies for tasting, knowing or hearing certain things,
and suchlike. Any one of these imperfections, if the soul
has become attached and habituated to it, is of as great harm
to its growth and progress in virtue as though it were to fall
daily into many other imperfections and casual venial sins[3]
which proceed not from a common indulgence in any common[4]
and harmful attachment, and will not hinder it so much as
when it has attachment to anything. For while it has this
there is no possibility that it will make progress in perfection,
even though the imperfection[5] be extremely small. For it is
the same thing if a bird be held by a slender cord or by
a stout one ; since, even if it be slender, the bird will be
as well held as though it were stout, for so long as it breaks it not
and flies not away. It is true that the slender one is the easier
to break ; still, easy though it be, the bird will not fly away
if it be not broken. And thus the soul that has attachment
to anything, however much virtue it possess, will not attain
to the liberty of Divine union. For the desire and the attachment of the soul have that power which the sucking-fish[6]
is said to have when it clings to a ship ; for, though but a
very small fish, if it succeed in clinging to the ship, it makes
it impossible for it to reach the port, or to sail onward. It
is sad to see certain souls in this plight ; like rich vessels,

---

[1] [The original omits ' union.'] Only Alc. reads : ' which are intentional
venial sins.' E.p. reads : ' But of desires which are voluntary and quite
intentional, though they be for very small things, as has been said, any one
that is not conquered suffices to impede.'

[2] Alc. only has : ' when . . . mortified.' E.p. substitutes : ' since
they have not become a definite habit.' A, B read similarly, but omit ' not.'

[3] E.p. : ' many other and even greater imperfections.'

[4] E.p. omits this second ' common.'

[5] E.p. : ' that the soul will reach perfection, though the thing,' etc.

[6] [Or ' remora.']

they are laden with wealth and good works and spiritual
exercises, and with the virtues and the favours that God
grants them ; and yet, because they have not the courage
to break with some whim or attachment or affection (which
are all the same), they never make progress or reach the port
of perfection,[1] though they would need to do no more than
make one good flight and thus to snap that cord of desire
right off, or to rid themselves of that sucking-fish of desire
which clings to them.[2]

5. It is greatly to be lamented that, when God has
granted them strength to break the other and stouter cords[3]
of affections for sins and vanities, they should fail to attain[4]
to such blessing because they have not shaken off some
childish thing which God has bidden them conquer[5] for
love of Him, and which is nothing more than a thread or a
hair.[6] And, what is worse, not only do they make no
progress, but because of this attachment they fall back,[7]
lose that[8] which they have gained, and retrace that part of
the road along which they have travelled[9] at the cost of so
much time and labour ; for we know that, on this road, not
to go forward is to turn back, and not to be gaining is to be
losing. This Our Lord desired to teach us when He said :
He that is not with Me is against Me ; and he that gathereth
not with Me scattereth.[10] He that takes not the trouble to
repair the vessel, however slight be the crack in it, is likely
to spill all the liquid that is within it. The Preacher taught
us this clearly when he said : He that contemneth small things
shall fall little by little.[11] For, as he himself says, the fire
is increased by a single spark.[12] And thus one imperfection

---

[1] E.p. : ' neither can attain to the port of perfect union.'
[2] E.p. omits : ' which clings to them.'
[3] [This is a stronger word than that used above, which, if the context
would permit, might better be translated ' string '—its equivalent in
modern speech. Below, this earlier word is translated ' thread.']
[4] E.p. : ' fail to progress and to attain.'
[5] A, B, e.p. : ' God left them to conquer.'
[6] E.p. omits : ' or a hair.' [The word rendered ' thread,' as explained
in n. 3, above, can also be taken in the stronger sense of ' cord.']
[7] E.p. adds : ' in the matter of perfection.'
[8] E.p. : ' losing something of that.'
[9] E.p. omits : ' and retrace . . . travelled.'
[10] S. Matthew xii, 30. E.p. reads : ' For we know that, on this spiritual
road, not to go forward victoriously is to turn back ; and not to be gaining
is to be losing. This Our Lord desired to teach us when He said : He that
gathereth not with Me, scattereth.'
[11] Ecclesiasticus xix, 1. E.p. adds : ' in great things.'
[12] Ecclesiasticus xi, 34 [A.V., xi, 32].

is sufficient to lead to another ; and these lead to yet more ; wherefore you will hardly ever see a soul that is negligent in conquering one desire, and that has not many more arising from the same weakness and imperfection that this desire causes. In this way they are continually falling ; we have seen many persons to whom God has been granting the favour of leading them a long way, into a state of great detachment and liberty, yet who, merely through beginning to indulge some small attachment, under the pretext of being good, or in the guise of conversation and friendship, often lose their spirituality and desire for God and holy solitude, fall from the joy and whole-hearted devotion which they had in their spiritual exercises, and cease not until they have lost everything ; and this because they broke not with that beginning of sensual desire and pleasure and kept not themselves in solitude for God.

6. Upon this road we must ever journey in order to attain our goal ; which means that we must ever be mortifying our desires and not indulging them ; and if they are not all completely mortified we shall not completely attain. For even as a log of wood may fail to be transformed in the fire because a single degree of heat is wanting to it, even so the soul will not be transformed in God if it have but one imperfection, although it be something less than voluntary desire ;[1] for, as we shall say hereafter concerning the night of faith, the soul has only one will, and that will, if it be embarrassed by aught and set upon aught, is not free,[2] solitary and pure, as is necessary for Divine transformation.

7. Of what has been said we have a figure in the Book of Judges, where it is related that the angel came to the children of Israel and said to them that, because they had not destroyed that froward people, but had leagued themselves with some of them, they would therefore be left among them as their enemies, that they might be to them an occasion of stumbling and perdition.[3] And exactly so does God deal with certain souls : though He has taken them out of the world,[4] and slain the giants of their sins, and destroyed the multitude of their enemies, which are the occasions of sin that they had in the world, solely that they may enter this Promised Land of Divine union with greater liberty, yet

[1] E.p. omits : ' although . . . desire.'
[2] A, B, e.p. : ' is not completely free.'   [3] Judges ii, 3.
[4] A, B : ' of the perils of the world.' E.p. : ' of the Egypt of the world.'

they harbour friendship and make alliance with the insig-
nificant peoples[1]—that is, with imperfections—and mortify
them not completely ; therefore Our Lord is angry, and
allows them[2] to fall into their desires and go from bad to
worse.

8. In the Book of Joshua, again, we have a figure of
what has just been said—where we read that God commanded Joshua, at the time that he had to enter into
possession of the Promised Land, to destroy all that were
in the city of Jericho, in such wise as to leave therein nothing
alive, man or woman, young or old, and to slay all the beasts,
and to take naught, neither to covet aught, of the spoils.[3]
This He said that we may understand how, if a man is to
enter this Divine union, all that lives in his soul must die,
both little and much, small and great, and that the soul
must be without desire for all this, and detached from it, even
as though it existed not for the soul, neither the soul for it.
This S. Paul teaches us clearly in his epistle *ad Corinthios*,
saying : This I say to you, brethren, that the time is short ;
it remains, and it behoves you, that they that have wives
should be as though they had none ; and they that weep for
the things of this world, as though they wept not ; and they
that rejoice, as though they rejoiced not ;[4] and they that
buy, as though they possessed not ; and they that use this
world, as though they used it not.[5] This the Apostle says to
us in order to teach us how great must be the detachment
of our soul from all things if it is to journey to God.

CHAPTER XII

*Which treats of the answer to another question,[6] explaining what
the desires are that suffice to cause the evils aforementioned in
the soul.*

1. We might write at greater length upon this matter of
the night of sense, saying all that there is to say concerning

---

[1] [The original phrase (*gente menuda*) means ' little folk.' It is used of
children and sometimes also of insects and other small creatures. There
is a marked antithesis between the ' giants,' or sins, and the ' little folk,'
or imperfections.]

[2] E.p. : ' therefore, since they live negligently and slothfully, His
Majesty is wroth and allows them,' etc. [3] Joshua vi, 21.

[4] E.p. omits this clause. [5] 1 Corinthians vii, 29–31.

[6] E.p. : ' Answers another question.'

the harm which is caused by the desires, not only in the ways aforementioned, but in many others. But for our purpose that which has been said suffices ; for we believe we have made it clear in what way the mortification of these desires is called night, and how it behoves us to enter this night in order to journey to God. The only thing that remains, before we treat of the manner of entrance therein, in order to end this part, is a question concerning what has been said which might occur to the reader.

2. It may first be asked if any desire suffices to work and produce in the soul the two evils aforementioned—namely, the privative, which consists in depriving the soul of the grace of God, and the positive, which consists in causing within it the five serious evils whereof we have spoken.[1] Secondly, it may be asked if any desire, however small it be and of whatever kind, suffices to cause all these together,[2] or if some desires cause some and others cause others. If, for example, some cause torment ; others, weariness ; others, darkness, etc.

3. Answering this, I say, first of all, that with respect to the privative evil—which consists in the soul's being deprived of God, this is wrought wholly,[3] and can only be wrought, by the voluntary desires, which are of the matter of mortal sin ; for they deprive the soul of grace in this life, and of glory, which is the possession of God, in the next. In the second place, I say that both those desires which are of the matter of mortal sin, and the voluntary desires, which are of the matter of venial sin, and those that are of the matter of imperfection, are each sufficient to produce in the soul all these positive evils together ; the which evils, although in a certain way they are privative, we here call positive, since they correspond to a turning towards the creature, even as the privative evils correspond to a turning away from God.[4] But there is this difference, that the desires of mortal sin cause total blindness, torment, impurity, weakness, etc. But those others, which are of the matter of venial sin or imperfection,[5] produce not these evils in a complete and supreme degree, since they deprive not the soul of grace,

[1] E.p. abbreviates : '. . . cause in the soul the two evils, positive and privative, already described.'
[2] So Alc. A, e.p. have : ' all these five evils together.' B : ' all these evils together.'   [3] E.p. omits ' wholly.'
[4] E.p. omits : ' the which . . . from God.'
[5] E.p. : ' or known imperfection.'

whereon depends the possession of them ;[1] since the death of the soul is their life ; but they cause them in the soul remissly, proportionately to the remission of grace which these desires cause in the soul.[2] So that that desire which most weakens grace will cause the most abundant torment, blindness and defilement.[3]

4. But it is to be noted that, although each desire produces all these evils, which we here term positive, there are some which, principally and directly, produce some of them, and others which produce others, and the remainder are produced consequently upon these. For, although it is true that one sensual desire produces all these evils, yet its principal and proper effect is the defilement of the soul and body. And although one avaricious desire likewise produces them all, its principal and direct result is to cause misery. And although similarly one vainglorious desire produces them all, its principal and direct result is to cause darkness and blindness.[4] And although one gluttonous desire produces them all, its principal result is to cause lukewarmness in virtue. And even so with the rest.

5. And the reason why any act of voluntary desire produces in the soul all these effects together lies in the direct contrariety which exists between them and all the acts of virtue which produce the contrary effects in the soul. For, even as an act of virtue produces and begets in the soul sweetness, peace, consolation, light, cleanliness and fortitude all together, even so an unruly desire causes torment, fatigue, weariness, blindness and weakness. All the virtues increase by the practice of any one of them, and all the vices increase by the practice of any one of them likewise, and the remnants[5] of each increase in the soul. And although all these evils are not visible at the moment when the desire is indulged, since the resulting pleasure gives no occasion for them, yet their evil remnants are clearly perceived, whether before or afterwards. This is very well illustrated by that book which the angel commanded S. John to eat, in

---

[1] E.p. : ' . . . of grace, with the which privation goes together the possession of them.'

[2] E.p. : ' But they cause something of these evils, although remissly, proportionately to the lukewarmness and remission which they cause in the soul.'

[3] E.p. : ' will cause more abundantly torment, blindness and non-purity.'   [4] Alc. unintentionally omits this sentence.

[5] E.p. : ' the effects.' [The word translated ' remnants ' also means ' after-taste.']

the Apocalypse, the which book was sweetness to his mouth, and in his belly bitterness.[1] For the desire, when it is sated, is sweet and appears to be good, but its bitter effect is felt afterwards ; the truth of this can be clearly proved by anyone who allows himself to be led away by it. Yet I am not ignorant that there are some men so blind and insensible as not to feel this, for, as they do not walk in God, they are unable to perceive that which hinders them from approaching Him.

6. I am not writing here of the other natural desires which are not voluntary, and of thoughts that go not beyond the first movements, and other temptations to which the soul is not consenting ; for these produce in the soul none of the evils aforementioned. For, although a person who suffers them may believe that the passion and disturbance which they then cause him are defiling and blinding him, it is not so ; rather they are bringing him the opposite advantages.[2] For, in so far as he resists them, he gains fortitude, purity, light and consolation, and many blessings, even as Our Lord said to S. Paul : That virtue was made perfect in weakness.[3] But the voluntary desires work all the evils aforementioned, and more. Wherefore the principal anxiety of spiritual masters is to mortify their disciples immediately of any desire soever, causing them to remain without the objects of their desires, in order to free them from such great misery.

CHAPTER XIII

Wherein is described the way and manner which the soul must observe in order to enter this night of sense.[4]

1. It now remains for me to give certain counsels whereby the soul may know how to enter this night of sense and may be able to enter therein. To this end it must be known that the soul habitually enters this night of sense in two ways : the one is active ; the other passive. The active way consists in what the soul can do of itself, and in what it does,[5]

---

[1] Revelation x, 9. This sentence is omitted by e.p.
[2] E.p. inserts the important modifying adverb ' occasionally.'
[3] 2 Corinthians xii, 9. [' Virtue ' had often, in the author's day, much of the meaning of the modern word ' strength.']
[4] The title in e.p. is : ' Of the way and manner which the soul must observe in order to enter this night of sense through faith.'
[5] The earlier editions add : ' aided by grace.'

in order to enter therein, whereof we shall now treat in the counsels which follow. The passive way is that wherein the soul does nothing,[1] and God works in the soul, and it remains, as it were, patient.[2] Of this we shall treat in the fourth book,[3] where we have to treat of beginners. And because we shall there, with the Divine favour, give many counsels to beginners, according to the many imperfections which they are liable to have on this road, I shall not spend time in giving many here. And this, too, because it belongs not to this place to give them, as at present we are treating only of the reasons for which this journey is called a night, and of what kind it is, and how many parts it has. But, as it seems that it would be incomplete, and less profitable than it should be, if we gave no help or counsel here for walking in this night of the desires, I have thought well to set down briefly here the way which is to be followed : and I shall do the same at the end of each of the next two parts, or causes, of this night, whereof, with the help of the Lord, I have to treat.

2. These counsels for the conquering of the desires, which now follow, albeit brief and few, I believe to be as profitable and efficacious as they are concise ; so that one who sincerely desires to practise them will need no others, but will find them all included in these.

3. First, let him have an habitual desire[4] to imitate Christ in everything that he does, conforming himself to His life ; upon which life he must meditate so that he may know how to imitate it, and to behave in all things as Christ would behave.

4. Secondly, in order that he may be able to do this well, every pleasure that presents itself to the senses, if it be not purely for the honour and glory of God, must be renounced and completely rejected for the love of Jesus Christ, Who in this life had no other pleasure, neither desired such, than to do the will of His Father, which He called His meat and food.[5] I take this example. If there present itself to a man the pleasure of listening to things that tend not to the service

---

[1] The earlier editions add : ' as of itself or by its own effort.'

[2] The earlier editions have : ' but God works it in the soul with more special aids, and the soul is, as it were, patient, consenting thereto freely.'

[3] The earlier editions have : ' in the *Dark Night* ' : it is, of course, that treatise that is referred to.

[4] E.p. has ' care and affection ' for ' desire.' [The word used for desire is *apetito*, which has been used in the past chapters for desires of sense (cf. p. 17, n. 5, above).] [5] [S. John iv, 34.]

and honour of God, let him not desire that pleasure, neither
let him desire to hear them ; and if there present itself
the pleasure of looking at things that help him not Godward,[1] let him not desire the pleasure or look at these things ;
and if in conversation or in aught else soever it present itself,
let him do the same. And similarly with respect to all the
senses, in so far as he can fairly avoid the pleasure in question ; if he cannot, it suffices that although these things
may be present to his senses, he desire not to have this
pleasure. And in this wise he will be able to mortify and
void his senses of such pleasure, and leave them, as it were,
in darkness. And having this care he will soon profit
greatly.

5. For the mortifying and calming of the four natural
passions, which are joy, hope, fear and grief, from the
concord and pacification of which come these blessings, and
others likewise, the counsels which follow are of the greatest
help, and of great merit, and the source of great virtues.

6. Strive always to choose, not that which is easiest, but
that which is most difficult ;

Not that which is most delectable, but that which is most
unpleasing ;

Not that which gives most pleasure, but rather that which
gives least ;[2]

Not that which is restful, but that which is wearisome ;

Not that which gives consolation, but rather that which
makes disconsolate ;

Not that which is greatest, but that which is least ;

Not that which is loftiest, and most precious, but that which
is lowest and most despised ;

Not that which is[3] a desire for anything, but that
which is a desire for nothing ;

Strive not to go about seeking the best of temporal things,
but the worst.

Strive thus to desire to enter into complete detachment
and emptiness and poverty, with respect to that which is in
the world, for Christ's sake.

7. And it is meet that the soul embrace these acts with all
its heart and strive to subject its will thereto. For, if it
perform them with its heart, it will very quickly come to

---

[1] E.p. : ' that lead him not Godward.'
[2] B, e.p. : ' that which gives none.' E.p. omits ' rather.'
[3] [*Lit.*, ' Not that which is to desire anything, etc.']

find in them great delight and consolation, and to act with
order and discretion.

8. These things that have been said, if they be faithfully
put into practice, are quite sufficient for entrance into the
night of sense ; but, for greater completeness, we shall
describe another kind of exercise which teaches us to mortify
the concupiscence of the flesh and the concupiscence of
the eyes, and the pride of life, which, says S. John,[1] are the
things that reign in the world, from which all the other
desires proceed.[2]

9. First, let the soul strive to work in its own despite, and
desire all to do so.[3] Secondly, let it strive to speak in
its own despite and desire all to do so.[4] Third, let it strive
to think humbly of itself, in its own despite, and desire all to
do so.[5]

10. In concluding these counsels and rules, it is well to
set down here those lines which are written in the Ascent of
the Mount,[6] which is the figure that is at the beginning of
this book ; the which lines are instructions for mounting it,
and thus reaching the summit of union. For, although it is
true that that which is there spoken of is spiritual and interior, there is reference likewise to the spirit of imperfection
according to sensual and exterior things, as may be seen by
the two roads which are on either side of the path of perfection. It is in this way and according to this sense that we
shall understand them here ; that is to say, according to that
which is sensual. Afterwards, in the second part of this
night, they will be understood according to that which is
spiritual.[7]

11. The lines are these :

In order to arrive at having[8] pleasure in everything,
Desire to have pleasure in nothing.

---

[1] [1 S. John ii, 16.]

[2] E.p. abbreviates : ' which teaches us to mortify truly the desire for
honour, whence originate many other [desires].'

[3] A, B, e.p. : ' others to do so.' A, B add : ' and this is against the
concupiscence of the flesh.'

[4] A, B add : ' and this is against the concupiscence of the eyes.'

[5] A, B add : ' likewise against it ; and this is against the pride of life.'

[6] A, B, C, D, e.p. have ' figure ' for ' ascent.' The reference is to the
diagram which is reproduced as the frontispiece to this volume. Cf. also
p. xxxiv, above.

[7] The Saint does not, however, allude to these lines again. The order
followed below is that of Alc., which differs somewhat from that followed
in the diagram.   [8] E.p. : ' to have.'

In order to arrive at possessing everything,
Desire to possess nothing.[1]
In order to arrive at being everything,
Desire to be nothing.
In order to arrive at knowing everything,
Desire to know nothing.
In order to arrive at that wherein thou hast no pleasure,
Thou must go by a way wherein thou hast no pleasure.
In order to arrive at that which thou knowest not,
Thou must go by a way that thou knowest not.
In order to arrive at that which thou possessest not,
Thou must go by a way that thou possessest not.
In order to arrive at that which thou art not,
Thou must go through that which thou art not.

THE WAY NOT TO IMPEDE THE ALL

12. When thou thinkest upon anything,
Thou ceasest to cast thyself upon the All.
For, in order to pass from the all to the All,
Thou hast to deny thyself[2] wholly[3] in all.
And, when thou comest to possess it wholly,
Thou must possess it without desiring anything.
For, if thou wilt have anything in all,
Thou hast not thy treasure purely in God.

13. In this detachment the spiritual soul finds its quiet
and repose ; for, since it covets nothing, nothing wearies it
when it is lifted up, and nothing oppresses it when it is cast
down, for it is in the centre of its humility ; since, when it
covets anything, at that very moment it becomes wearied.[4]

CHAPTER XIV

Wherein is expounded the second line of the stanza.[5]

Kindled in love with yearnings.

1. Now that we have expounded the first line of this
stanza, which treats of the night of sense, explaining what

---

[1] [This line, like ll. 6, 8 of the paragraph, reads more literally : ' Desire
not to possess (be, know) anything in anything.' It is more emphatic
than l. 2.]   [2] Thus Alc., A, B, C, D. E.p. repeats : ' cast thyself.'
[3] [There is a repetition here which could only be indicated by translating
' all-ly.' So, too, in the next couplet.]
[4] A, B add : ' and tormented.'
[5] E.p. : ' of the above-mentioned stanza.'

this night of sense is, and why it is called night ; and now that we have likewise described the order and manner which are to be followed for a soul to enter therein actively, the next thing to be treated in due sequence is its properties and effects, which are wonderful, and are described in the next lines of the stanza aforementioned, upon which I will briefly touch for the sake of expounding the said lines,[1] as I promised in the Prologue ;[2] and I will then pass on at once to the second book, treating of the other part of this night, which is the spiritual.

2. The soul, then, says that, ' kindled in love with yearnings,' it passed through this dark night of sense and came out thence to the union of the Beloved. For, in order to conquer all the desires and to deny itself the pleasures which it has in everything, and for which its love and affection are wont to enkindle the will that it may enjoy them, it would be necessary to experience another and a greater enkindling by another and a better love, which is that of its Spouse ; to the end that, having its pleasure set upon Him and deriving from Him its strength, it should have courage and constancy to deny itself all other things with ease. And not only would it be needful, in order to conquer the strength of the desires of sense, to have love for its Spouse but also to be enkindled by love and to have yearnings. For it comes to pass, and so it is, that with such yearnings of desire the sensual nature is moved and attracted to sensual things, so that, if the spiritual part is not enkindled with other and greater yearnings for that which is spiritual, it will be unable to throw off the yoke of nature[3] or to enter this night of sense, neither will it have courage to remain in darkness as to all things, depriving itself of desire for them all.

3. And the nature and different varieties of these yearnings of love which souls have in the early stages of this road to union ; and the diligent means and contrivances which they employ in order to leave their house, which is self-will, during the night of the mortification of their senses ; and how easy, and even sweet and delectable,[4] these yearnings for the Spouse make all the trials and perils of this night to

---

[1] E.p. omits : ' for . . . lines.'

[2] This confirms our point (p. 19, n. 4, above) that the Saint considers the Argument as part of the Prologue. A and B omit the rest of this paragraph.

[3] [*Lit.*, ' to conquer the natural yoke.'] E.p. has : ' the sensual and material yoke.'   [4] E.p. omits : ' and delectable.'

appear to them, this is not the place to say, neither can it be said ; for it is better to know it and meditate upon it than to write of it.   And so we shall pass on to expound the remaining lines in the next chapter.

CHAPTER XV

Wherein are expounded the remaining lines of the aforementioned stanza.[1]

. . . oh, happy chance !—
I went forth without being observed, My house being now at rest.

1. These lines take as a metaphor the miserable state of captivity, a man's deliverance from which, when none of the gaolers[2] hinder his release, is considered a ' happy chance.'   For the soul, on account of[3] original sin, is truly as it were a captive in this mortal body, subject to the passions and desires of nature, from bondage and subjection to which it considers its having gone forth without being observed as a ' happy chance '—having gone forth, that is, without being impeded or apprehended by any of them.

2. For to this end the soul profited by going forth upon a ' dark night '—that is, in the privation of all pleasures and mortification of all desires, after the manner whereof we have spoken.   And by its ' house being now at rest ' is meant the sensual part, which is the house of all the desires, and is now at rest because they have all been overcome and lulled to sleep.   For until the desires are lulled to sleep through the mortification of the sensual nature, and until at last the sensual nature itself is at rest from them, so that they make not war upon the spirit, the soul goes not forth to true liberty and to the fruition of union with its Beloved.

END OF THE FIRST BOOK[4]

---

[1] A has no chapter-heading, considering this chapter as the termination of the last.

[2] A, B have ' gaolers ' ;   Alc., C, D, ' prisoners.'   The first reading is the more apt, though we should not say that the second is inadmissible.

[3] [*Lit.,* ' after.']   [4] So end both the codices and e.p.

BOOK THE SECOND

OF THE 'ASCENT OF MOUNT CARMEL'[1]

Wherein is treated the proximate means of ascending to union with God, which is faith; and wherein is therefore described the second part of this night, which, as we said, belongs to the spirit, and is contained in the second stanza, which is as follows.[2]

STANZA THE SECOND

CHAPTER I[3]

In darkness and secure, By the secret ladder, disguised—oh, happy chance !— In darkness and in concealment, My house being now at rest.

1. In this second stanza the soul sings of the happy chance which it experienced in stripping the spirit of all spiritual imperfections and desires for the possession of spiritual things. This was a much greater happiness to it, by reason of the greater difficulty that there is in putting to rest this house of the spiritual part, and of being able to enter this interior darkness, which is spiritual detachment from all things, whether sensual or spiritual, and a leaning on pure faith[4] alone[5] and an ascent thereby to God. The soul here calls this a 'ladder,' and 'secret,' because all the rungs and parts of it[6] are secret and hidden from all sense and understanding. And thus the soul has remained in darkness as to all light[7] of sense and understanding, going forth beyond all limits of

---

[1] So both codices and e.p.

[2] E.p. abbreviates : ' Treats of the proximate means of attaining to union with God, which is faith, and of the second night of the spirit, contained in the second stanza.' It should be observed that the Saint calls this Second Book ' the second (spiritual) night ' (e.g., on p. 78 below, and elsewhere).

[3] The chapter-headings vary considerably in the codices and editions. B. treats this chapter as an exposition and numbers from the next onward.

[4] E.p. : ' on living faith.'

[5] In parenthesis e.p. adds : ' and of this I am ordinarily speaking because I treat with persons who journey to perfection.'

[6] [*Lit.*, ' all the steps and articles that it has.']

[7] E.p. : ' all natural light.'

66

nature and reason in order to ascend by this Divine ladder
of faith, which attains[1] and penetrates even to the heights[2]
of God.   The soul says that it was travelling ' disguised,'
because it wears its garments and vesture[3] and natural
condition changed into the Divine, as it ascends by
faith.   And this disguise was the cause of its not being
recognized or impeded, either by time or by reason or by
the devil ; for none of these things can harm one that
journeys in faith.   And not only so, but the soul travels in
such wise concealed and hidden and is so far from all the
deceits of the devil that in truth it journeys (as it also says
here) ' in darkness and in concealment '—that is to say,
hidden from the devil, to whom the light of faith is more
than darkness.

2. And thus the soul that journeys through this night,
we may say, journeys in concealment and in hiding from
the devil, as will be more clearly seen hereafter.   Wherefore
the soul says that it went forth ' in darkness and secure ' ;
for one that has such happiness as to be able to journey
through the darkness of faith, taking faith for his guide, like
to one that is blind,[4] and going forth from all phantasms of
nature and reasonings of the spirit, journeys very securely,
as we have said.   And so the soul says furthermore that it
went forth through this spiritual night, its ' house being now
at rest '—that is to say, its spiritual and rational part.
When, therefore, the soul attains to union with God, it has
both its natural faculties at rest, and likewise its impulses and
yearnings of the senses,[5] as to the spiritual part.   For this
cause the soul says not here that it went forth with yearnings,
as in the first night of sense.   For, in order to journey in
the night of sense, and to strip itself of that which is of sense,
it needed yearnings of sense-love so that it might go forth
perfectly ; but, in order to put to rest the house of its spirit,
it needs no more than denial[6] of all faculties and pleasures

---

[1] [Lit., ' climbs ' : the verb (escala) is identical with the noun ' ladder '
(escala).]   [2] [Lit., ' to the depths.']
[3] Only Alc. has : ' vesture.'
[4] [The literal translation is shorter, viz. ' taking faith for a blind man's
guide.']   [5] Alc. omits : ' of the senses.'
[6] [Lit., negation.]   This is the reading of Alc.   ' Affirmation ' is found
in A, B, C, D, e.p.   Though the two words are antithetical, they express
the same underlying concept.   [The affirmation, or establishment, of all
the powers and desires of the spirit upon pure faith, so that they may be
ruled by pure faith alone, is equivalent to the denial, or negation, of those
powers and desires in so far as they are not ruled by pure faith.]

and desires of the spirit in pure faith. This attained, the soul is united with the Beloved in a union of simplicity and purity and love and similitude.

3. And it must be remembered that the first stanza, speaking of the sensual part, says that the soul went forth upon ' a dark night,' while here, speaking of the spiritual part, it says that it went forth ' in darkness.' For the darkness of the spiritual part is by far the greater, even as darkness is a greater obscurity than that of night. For, however dark a night may be, something can always be seen, but in true darkness nothing can be seen ; and thus in the night of sense there still remains some light, for the understanding and reason remain, and are not blinded. But this spiritual night, which is faith, deprives the soul of everything, both as to understanding and as to sense. And for this cause the soul in this night says that it was travelling ' in darkness and secure,' which it said not in the other. For, however little the soul may work with its own ability, it journeys more securely, because it journeys more in faith. And this will be expounded gradually, at length, in this second book, wherein it will be necessary for the devout reader to proceed attentively,[1] because there will be said herein things of great importance to the person that is truly spiritual.[2] And, although they are somewhat obscure, some of them will pave the way to others, so that I believe they will all be quite clearly understood.

CHAPTER II

Which begins to treat of the second part or cause of this night, which is faith. Proves by two arguments how it is darker than the first and than the third.

1. There now follows the treatment of the second part of this night, which is faith ; this is the wondrous means[3] which, as we said, leads to the goal, which is God, Who, as we said, is also to the soul, naturally, the third cause or part of this night. For faith, which is the means, is compared with midnight. And thus we may say that it is darker for the soul either than the first part or, in a way, than the third ;

---

[1] So e.p. The clause ' wherein . . . attentively ' is omitted in A, B, C, D. Alc. reads : ' wherein I request the benevolent attention of the devout reader.'   [2] A, B end the chapter here.
[3] E.p. has ' manner' for ' means.'

for the first part, which is that of sense, is compared to the beginning of night, or the time when sensible objects are no longer visible, and thus it is not so far removed from light as is midnight. The third part, which is the period preceding the dawn, is quite close to the light of day, and it, too, therefore, is not so dark as midnight ; for it is now close to the enlightenment and illumination of the light[1] of day, which is compared with God. For, although it is true, if we speak after a natural manner, that God is as dark a night to the soul as is faith, still, when these three parts of the night are over, which are naturally night to the soul, God begins to illumine the soul by supernatural means with the rays of His Divine light ;[2] which is the beginning of the perfect union that follows, when the third night is past, and it can thus be said to be less dark.[3]

2. It is likewise darker than the first part, for this belongs to the lower part of man, which is the sensual part, and, consequently, the more exterior ; and this second part, which is of faith, belongs to the higher part of man, which is the rational part, and, in consequence, more interior and more obscure, since it deprives it of the light of reason, or, to speak more clearly, blinds it ;[4] and thus it is aptly compared to midnight, which is the depth of night and the darkest part thereof.

[1] So Alc. A, B, e.p. : ' of the brightness.'
[2] E.p. adds these words, which occur in none of the codices : ' and in a loftier, higher and more experimental manner.'
[3] A, B : ' to be dark.'
[4] This was another of the propositions which were cited by those who denounced the writings of S. John of the Cross to the Holy Office. It is interpretable, nevertheless, in a sense that is perfectly true and completely in conformity with Catholic doctrine. The Saint does not, in these words, affirm that faith destroys nature or quenches the light of human reason (S. Thomas, *Summa*, Pt. I, q. 1, a. 8, *et alibi*) ; what he endeavours to show is that the coming of knowledge through faith excludes a simultaneous coming of natural knowledge through reason. It is only in this way that, in the act of faith, the soul is deprived of the light of reason, and left, as it were, in blindness, so that it may be raised to another nobler and sublimer kind of knowledge, which, far from destroying reason, gives it dignity and perfection. Philosophy teaches that the proper and connatural object of the understanding, in this life, is things visible, material and corporeal. By his nature, man inclines to knowledge of this kind, but cannot lay claim to such knowledge as regards the things which belong to faith. For, as S. Paul says in a famous verse : *Fides est sperandarum substantia rerum, argumentum non apparientium* (Hebrews xi, 1). This line of thought is not confined to S. John of the Cross, but is followed by all the mystics and is completely in agreement with theological doctrine. Cf. *Respuesta* [Reply] of P. Basilio Ponce de León and *Dilucidatio*, Pt. II, Chap. ii, and also the following chapter in this present book.

3. We have now to prove how this second part, which is faith, is night to the spirit, even as the first part is night to sense. And we shall then describe also the things that are contrary to it, and how the soul must prepare itself actively to enter therein. For, concerning the passive part, which is that which God works in it, when He brings it into that night, we shall speak in its place, which I intend shall be the third book.[1]

CHAPTER III

How faith is dark night to the soul. This is proved with arguments and quotations and figures from Scripture.[2]

1. Faith, say the theologians, is a habit of the soul, certain and obscure. And the reason for its being an obscure habit is that it makes us believe truths revealed by God Himself, which transcend all natural light, and exceed all human understanding, beyond all proportion.[3] Hence it follows that, for the soul, this excessive light of faith which is given to it is thick darkness, for it overwhelms that which is great and does away with that which is little, even as the light of the sun overwhelms all other lights whatsoever, so that when it shines and disables our powers of vision they appear not to be lights at all. So that it blinds it and deprives it of the sight that has been given to it, inasmuch as its light is great beyond all proportion and surpasses the powers of vision. Even so the light of faith, by its excessive greatness, oppresses and disables that of the understanding ;[4] for the latter, of its own power, extends only to natural knowledge, although it has a faculty[5] for the supernatural, when Our

---

[1] Here end Alc. and e.p. A, B add : ' as we have already spoken and promised to speak of the passive [part] of the first [night] in the second [book].'　　　　[2] A, B omit this sentence.

[3] E.p. omits : ' beyond all proportion.'

[4] E.p. : ' by its excessive greatness and by the way wherein God communicates it, transcends that of our understanding.'

[5] E.p. : ' an obediential faculty ' [*potencia obediencial*] : this phrase is borrowed from the Schoolmen. Among the various divisions of the faculty are two, natural and obediential. The first is that which is directed towards an act within the power of nature ; the second is directed towards an act which exceeds these powers, by God, Who is outside the laws of nature and can therefore work outside the natural domain. This obediential faculty (called also ' receptive ' or ' passive ') frequently figures in mystical theology, since it is this that disposes the faculties of the soul for the supernatural reception of the gifts of grace, all of which exceed natural capacity.

Lord may be pleased to bring it to a supernatural action.

2. Wherefore a man can know nothing by himself, save after a natural manner,[1] which is only that which he attains by means of the senses. For this cause he must have the phantasms and the figures[2] of objects present in themselves and in their resemblances ;[3] otherwise it cannot be, for, as philosophers say : *Ab objeto et potentia paritur notitia.* That is : From the object that is present and from the faculty, knowledge is born in the soul. Wherefore, if one should speak to a man of things which he has never been able to understand, and whose likeness he has never seen, he would have no more illumination from them whatever than if naught had been said of them to him. I take an example. If one should say to a man that on a certain island there is an animal which he has never seen, and give him no idea of the appearance of that animal, that he may compare it with others that he has seen, he will have no more knowledge or imagination of it than he had before, however much is being said to him about it. And this will be better understood by another and a clearer example. If they should describe to a man that was born blind, and has never seen any colour, what is meant by a white colour or by a yellow, he would understand it but indifferently, however much they might describe it to him ; for, as he has never seen such colours or anything like them by which he may judge them, only their names would remain with him ; for these he would be able to comprehend through his hearing, but not their forms or figures, since he has never seen them.

3. Even so[4] is faith with respect to the soul ; it tells us of things which we have never seen or understood, either in themselves, or in aught that resembles them, since they resemble naught at all.[5] And thus we have no light of natural

---

[1] E.p. : ' a natural manner which has its beginning in the senses.' Here the Saint expounds a principle of scholastic philosophy summarized in the axiom : *Nihil est in intellectu quin prius non fuerit in sensu.* This principle, like many other great philosophical questions, has continually been debated. S. John of the Cross will be found as a rule to follow the philosophy most favoured by the Church and is always rigidly orthodox.

[2] E.p. : ' the phantasms and senses.'

[3] E.p. uses *semejanzas*, the abstract noun ; the codices have *semejantes* [a word which can be either abstract or concrete, in the latter case with the sense of ' fellow-creatures '].

[4] E.p. adds in parenthesis : ' though not equivalent in every way.'

[5] E.p. : ' or in aught that resembles them, which might bring us to a knowledge of them without revelation.'

knowledge concerning them, since that which we are told
of them has no relation to any sense of ours ; we know it by
the ear alone, believing that which we are taught, bringing
our natural light into subjection and treating it as if it were
not.[1] For, as S. Paul says, *Fides ex auditu.*[2] As though he
were to say : Faith is not knowledge which enters by any
of the senses, but is only the consent given by the soul to
that which enters[3] through the hearing.

4. And faith greatly surpasses even that which is suggested
by the examples given above. For not only does it give no
knowledge and science,[4] but, as we have said, it deprives us
of all other knowledge and science, and blinds us to them,
so that they cannot judge it well.[5] For other sciences can
be acquired by the light of the understanding ; but the
science that is of faith is acquired without the illumination
of the understanding, which is rejected for faith ; and in
its own light it is lost, if that light be not darkened. Wherefore Isaiah said : *Si non credideritis, non intelligetis.*[6] That is :
If ye believe not, ye shall not understand. It is clear, then,
that faith is dark night for the soul, and it is in this way that
it gives it light ; and the more it is darkened, the greater
light comes to it. For it is by blinding that it gives light,
according to this saying of Isaiah : For if ye believe not,
ye shall not (he says) have light.[7] And thus faith was
foreshadowed by that cloud which divided the children of
Israel and the Egyptians when the former were about to
enter the Red Sea, whereof Scripture says that : *Erat nubes
tenebrosa, et illuminans noctem.*[8] This is to say that that cloud
was full of darkness and gave light by night.

5. A wondrous thing it is that, though it was dark, it
should give light by night. This was in order that faith,
which is a black and dark cloud to the soul (and likewise
is night, since in the presence of faith the soul is deprived of its

---

[1] [*Lit.*, ' submitting and blinding our natural light.']
[2] Romans x, 17.   [3] E.p. : ' but is superior light which enters.'
[4] E.p. : ' no evidence or science.'
[5] E.p. : ' but, as we have said, it surpasses and transcends any other
knowledge and science, so that we may only judge of it in perfect
contemplation.'
[6] Isaiah vii, 9. So Alc. The passage seems to be taken from the
Septuagint.
[7] [*Lit.*, ' If ye believe not, that is, ye shall not have light.'] E.p.
evidently found this not clear, for it expands the sentence thus : For if
ye believe not—that is, if ye blind not yourselves—ye shall not understand
—that is, ye shall not have light and knowledge both lofty and supernatural.'   [8] Exodus xiv, 20.

natural light and is blinded), should with its darkness give
light and illumination to the darkness of the soul, for thus it
was fitting that the disciple should be like the master. For
man, who is in darkness, could not fittingly be enlightened
save by other darkness, even as David teaches us, saying :
Dies diei eructat verbum et nox nocti indicat scientiam.[1] Which
signifies : Day unto day uttereth and aboundeth in speech,
and night unto night showeth knowledge. Which, speaking
more clearly, signifies : The day, which is God in bliss,
where it is day to the blessed angels and souls which are now
day, communicates and reveals[2] the Word, which is His
Son, that they may know Him and rejoice in Him. And the
night, which is faith in the Church Militant, where it is still
night, shows knowledge to the Church, and consequently to
every soul, which knowledge is night to it, since it is deprived
of[3] clear beatific wisdom ; and, in the presence of faith,
it is blind as to this natural light.

6. So that which is to be inferred from this is that
faith, because it is dark night, gives light to the soul, which
is in darkness, that there may come to be fulfilled[4] that which
David likewise says to this purpose, in these words : *Et nox
illuminatio mea in deliciis meis.*[5] Which signifies : The night
will be my illumination in my delights. Which is as much
as to say : In the delights of my pure contemplation and
union with God, the night of faith shall be my guide.
Wherein he gives it clearly to be understood[6] that the soul
must be in darkness in order to have light for this road.[7]

CHAPTER IV

*Treats in general of how the soul likewise must be in darkness, in so
    far as this rests with itself, to the end that it may be effectively
    guided by faith to the highest contemplation.*

1. It is now, I think, becoming clear how faith is dark
night to the soul, and how the soul likewise must be dark,

---

[1] Psalm xviii, 3 [A.V., xix, 2].
[2] Thus e.p. modifies the reading of the codices : ' and pronounces the
Word.'   [3] E.p. : ' since it does not yet enjoy.'
[4] E.p. : ' that there may come and may be fulfilled.'
[5] Psalm cxxxviii, 11 [A.V., cxxxix, 11].
[6] E.p. abbreviates : ' Giving it to be understood.'
[7] E.p. : ' in order to have light and to be able to walk on this road.'

or in darkness as to its own light,[1] so that it may allow itself to be guided by faith to this high goal of union. But, in order that the soul may be able to do this, it will now be well to continue describing, in somewhat greater detail, this darkness which the soul must have, in order that it may enter into this abyss of faith. And thus in this chapter I shall speak of it in a general way ; and hereafter, with the Divine favour, I shall continue to describe more minutely the way in which the soul is to conduct itself that it may neither stray therein nor impede this guide.

2. I say, then, that the soul, in order to be effectively guided to this state by faith, must not only be in darkness with respect to that part that concerns the creatures and temporal things, which is the sensual and the lower part (whereof we have already treated), but that likewise it must be blinded and darkened according to the part which has respect to God and to spiritual things, which is the rational and higher part,[2] whereof we are now treating. For, in order that one may attain supernatural transformation, it is clear that he must be set in darkness and carried far away from all that is contained in his nature,[3] which is sensual and rational. For the word supernatural means that which soars above the natural ; so that the natural self remains beneath. For, although this transformation and union is something that cannot be comprehended by human ability and sense, it must completely and voluntarily void itself of all that can enter into it,[4] whether from above or from below,—I mean according to the affection and will—so far as this rests with itself. For who shall prevent God from doing that which He will in the soul that is resigned, anni-hilated and detached ? But the soul must be voided of all such things as can enter[5] its capacity, so that,[6] however many supernatural things it may have, it will ever remain as it were detached from them and in darkness. It must be like to a blind man, leaning upon dark faith, taking it for guide and light, and leaning upon none of the things that he understands, experiences, feels and imagines. For all these

---

[1] A, e.p. : ' its own natural light.'
[2] Alc. alone reads : ' the reason and the higher part.'
[3] E.p. : ' all that belongs to his nature.'
[4] So Alc. The other authorities have : ' that can be contained in it.' [The difference is slight : caer for caber.]
[5] The variant of the preceding note is repeated here.
[6] E.p. abbreviates : ' But the soul must be voided of all things, so that.'

are darkness, which will cause him to stray ; and faith is above all that he understands and experiences and feels and imagines. And if he be not blinded as to this, and remain not in total darkness,[1] he attains not to that which is greater —namely, that which is taught by faith.

3. A blind man, if he be not quite blind, refuses to be led by a guide ; and, since he sees a little, he thinks it better to go in whatever happens to be the direction which he can distinguish, because he sees none better ; and thus he can lead astray a guide who sees more than he, for after all it is for him to say where he shall go rather than for the guide.[2] In the same way a soul may lean upon any knowledge of its own, or any feeling or experience of God, yet, however great this may be, it is very little and far different from what God is ; and, in going along this road, a soul is easily led astray or forced to halt, because it will not remain in faith like one that is blind, and faith is its true guide.

4. It is this that was meant by S. Paul when he said : *Accedentem ad Deum oportet credere quod est.*[3] Which signifies : He that would journey towards union with God must needs believe in His being. As though he had said : He that would attain to being joined in one union with God must not walk by understanding, neither lean upon experience or feeling or imagination, but he must believe in His Being,[4] which is not perceptible to the understanding, neither to the desire nor to the imagination nor to any other sense, neither can it be known[5] in this life at all. Yea, in this life, the highest thing that can be felt and experienced concerning God is infinitely remote from God and from the pure possession of Him. Isaiah and S. Paul say : *Nec oculus vidit, nec auris audivit, nec in cor hominis ascendit, quæ præparavit Deus iis, qui diligunt illum.*[6] Which signifies : That which God hath prepared for them that love Him neither eye hath seen, nor ear heard, neither hath it entered into the heart or thought of man. . So, however greatly the soul aspires to be perfectly united through grace in this life with that to which it will be united through glory in the next (which, as S. Paul here

---

[1] A, B, e.p. add : ' with respect to it.'

[2] E.p. : ' . . . lead astray his guide, because he acts as if he saw and it is for him to say where he shall go rather than for the guide.'

[3] Hebrews xi, 6.

[4] E.p. : ' but he must believe in the perfection of the Divine Being.'

[5] E.p. : ' known as it is.'

[6] Isaiah lxiv, 4 ; 1 Corinthians ii, 9.

says, eye hath not seen, nor ear heard, neither hath it entered into the heart of man in the flesh[1]) it is clear that, in order perfectly to attain to union in this life through grace and through love, a soul must be in darkness with respect to all that can enter through the eye, and to all that can be received through the ear, and can be imagined with the fancy, and understood with the heart, which here signifies the soul. And thus a soul is greatly impeded from reaching this high estate of union with God when it clings to any understanding or feeling or imagination or appearance or will or manner of its own, or to any other act or to anything of its own, and cannot detach and strip itself of all these. For, as we say, the goal which it seeks is beyond all this, yea, beyond even the highest thing that can be known or experienced ; and thus a soul must pass beyond everything to unknowing.

5. Wherefore, upon this road, to enter upon the road is to leave the road ; or, to express it better, it is to pass on to the goal and to leave one's own way,[2] and to enter upon that which[3] has no way, which is God. For the soul that attains to this state has no longer any ways or methods, still less is it attached to such things or can be attached to them. I mean ways of understanding, or of experience, or of feeling ; although it has within itself all ways, after the way of one that possesses nothing, yet possesses all things. For, if it have courage to pass beyond its natural limitations, both interiorly and exteriorly, it enters within the limits of the supernatural,[4] which has no way, yet in substance[5] has all ways. Hence for the soul to arrive at these limits is for it to leave these limits, in each case going forth out of itself a great way, from this lowly state to that which is high above all others.

6. Wherefore, passing beyond all that can be known and understood, both spiritually and naturally,[6] the soul will desire with all desire to come to that which in this life cannot be known, neither can enter into its heart. And, leaving behind all that it experiences and feels, both temporally and

[1] A, B : ' heart of the flesh.'
[2] [The word translated ' way ' is *modo*, which, in the language of scholastic philosophy, would rather be translated ' mode.']
[3] A, B : ' to enter upon the goal which . . .'
[4] E.p. : ' it enters, without any limit, into the supernatural.'
[5] E.p. has ' eminently ' for ' in substance.'
[6] E.p. : ' and temporally.'

spiritually,[1] and all that it is able to experience and feel in
this life, it will desire with all desire to come to that which
surpasses all feeling and experience. And, in order to be
free and void to that end, it must in no wise lay hold upon
that which it receives, either spiritually or sensually, within
itself[2] (as we shall explain presently, when we treat this
in detail), considering it all to be of much less account. For
the more emphasis the soul lays upon what it understands,
experiences and imagines, and the more it esteems this,
whether it be spiritual or no, the more it loses of the supreme
good, and the more it is hindered from attaining thereto.
And the less it thinks of what it may have, however much
this be, in comparison with the highest good, the more it
dwells upon that good and esteems it, and, consequently,
the more nearly it approaches it. And in this wise the soul
approaches a great way towards union, in darkness, by means
of faith, which is likewise dark, and in this wise faith won-
drously illumines it. It is certain that, if the soul should
desire to see, it would be in darkness much more quickly,[3]
with respect to God, than would one who opens his eyes to
look upon the great brightness of the sun.

7. Wherefore, by being blind in its faculties upon this
road, the soul will see the light, even as the Saviour says in
the Gospel, in this wise : *In judicium veni in hunc mundum : ut
qui non vident, videant, et qui vident, cæci fiant.*[4] That is : I am
come into this world for judgement ; that they which see not
may see, and that they which see may become blind. This,
as it will be supposed, is to be understood of this spiritual
road, where the soul that is in darkness,[5] and is blinded
as to all its natural and proper lights, will see supernaturally ;
and the soul that would depend upon any light of its own
will become the blinder and will halt upon the road to
union.

8. And, that we may proceed with less confusion, I think
it will be necessary to describe, in the following chapter, the
nature of this that we call union of the soul with God ; for,
when this is understood, that which we shall say hereafter

---

[1] Thus Alc. A, B have ' spiritually ' only ; e.p. : ' both spiritually
and sensually.'

[2] [*Lit.*, ' either spiritually or sensually, in its soul.']

[3] A, B : ' it would be in much greater darkness.'

[4] S. John ix, 39.

[5] E.p. omits the quotation and its exposition, abbreviating thus :
' the soul will see the light, so that the soul that is in darkness . . .'

will become much clearer. And so I think the treatment of this union comes well at this point, as in its proper place. For, although the thread of that which we are expounding is interrupted thereby, this is not done without a reason, since it serves to illustrate in this place the very thing that is being described.[1] The chapter which follows, then, will be a parenthetical one, placed, as it were, between the two terms of an enthymeme,[2] since we shall afterwards have to treat in detail of the three faculties of the soul, with respect to the three theological virtues, in relation to this second night.

CHAPTER V

Wherein is described what is meant by union of the soul with God, and a comparison is given.[3]

1. From what has been said above it becomes clear to some extent what we mean by union of the soul with God; what we now say about it, therefore, will be the better understood. It is not my intention here to treat of the

---

[1] A, B end the chapter here. [2] E.p. omits this phrase.

[3] As the Saint has explained above, this is a parenthetical chapter necessary to an understanding of the following chapters on the active purification of the three faculties of the soul; for, in order to make an intelligent use of the means to an end, it is important to know what that end is. S. John of the Cross begins by setting aside the numerous divisions under which the mystics speak of union with God and deals only with that which most usually concerns the soul, namely union which is active, and acquired by our own efforts, together with the habitual aid of grace. This is the kind of union which is most suitably described in this treatise, which deals with the intense activity of the soul with regard to the purgation of the senses and faculties as a necessary means for the loving transformation of the soul in God—the end and goal of all the Saint's writings. In order to forestall any grossly erroneous pantheistic interpretations, we point out, with the author of the *Médula Mística* (Trat. V, Chap. i, No. 2), that by union the Saint understands ' a linking and conjoining of two things which, though united, are still different, each, as S. Thomas teaches (Pt. III, q. 2, a. 1), keeping its own nature, for otherwise there would not be union but identity. Union of the soul with God, therefore, will be a linking and conjoining of the soul with God and of God with the soul, for the one cannot be united with the other if the other be not united with the one, so that the soul is still the soul and God is still God. But just as, when two things are united, the one which has the most power, virtue and activity communicates its properties to the other, just so, since God has greater strength, virtue and activity than the soul, He communicates His properties to it and makes it, as it were, deific, and leaves it, as it were, divinized, to a greater or a lesser degree, corresponding to the greater or the lesser degree of union between the two.' This conception, which is a basic one in Christian mysticism, is that of S. John of

divisions of this union, nor of its parts,[1] for I should never
end if I were to begin now to explain what is the nature of
union of the understanding, and what is that of union
according to the will, and likewise according to the
memory ;   and likewise what is transitory and what
permanent in the union of the said faculties ;   and then
what is meant by total union, transitory and permanent,
with regard to the said faculties all together.   All this we
shall treat gradually in our discourse—speaking first of
one and then of another.   But here this is not to the point
in order to describe what we have to say concerning them ;
it will be explained[2] much more fittingly in its place, when
we shall again be treating the same matter, and shall have
a striking illustration, together with the present explanation,
so that everything will then be considered and explained
and we shall judge of it better.

2. Here I treat only of this permanent and total union
according to the substance of the soul and its faculties with
respect to the obscure habit of union : for with respect to
the act, we shall explain later, with the Divine favour,
how there is no permanent union in the faculties, in this
life, but a transitory union only.

3. In order, then, to understand what is meant by this
union whereof we are treating, it must be known that God
dwells and is present substantially in every soul, even in
that of the greatest sinner in the world.   And this kind of

the Cross.   Had all his commentators understood that fact, some of them
would have been saved from making ridiculous comparisons of him with
Gnostics, Illuminists or even the Eastern seekers after Nirvana.   Actually,
this Saint and Doctor of the Church applies the tenets of Catholic theology
to the union of the soul with God, presenting them in a condensed and
vigorous form and keeping also to strict psychological truth, as in general
do the other Spanish mystics.   This is one of his greatest merits.   In this
chapter he is speaking, not of essential union, which has nothing to do
with his subject, but (presupposing the union worked through sanctifying
grace received in the substance of the soul, which is the source of the
infused virtues, such as faith, hope and charity, and the gifts of the Holy
Spirit) of active actual union, after which we can and should strive, so
that we may will what God wills and abhor what He abhors.   Though not
the only kind of union, it is this which chiefly concerns the soul ;   and,
when once this is attained, God readily grants all other mystical gifts.
Cf. S. Teresa's *Mansions* (Fifth Mansions, Chap. iii).

[1] Only Alc., A, B have : 'nor of its parts.'

[2] E.p. abbreviates : 'And it is not now our intention to explain in
detail what is the union of the understanding, what is that of the will,
and what likewise is that of the memory ;   and what is transitory and
what permanent in the said faculties, for this we shall treat hereafter and
it will be explained . . .'

union[1] is ever wrought between God and all the creatures, for in it He is preserving their being; so that if union of this kind were to fail them, they would at once become annihilated and would cease to be. And so, when we speak of union of the soul with God, we speak not of this substantial union which is continually being wrought,[2] but of the union and transformation of the soul with God,[3] which is not being wrought continually, but only when there exists that likeness that comes from love; we shall therefore term this the union of likeness, even as that other union is called substantial or essential. The former is natural; the latter supernatural. And the latter comes to pass when the two wills—namely that of the soul and that of God—are conformed together in one, and there is naught in the one that is repugnant to the other. And thus, when the soul rids itself totally of that which is repugnant to the Divine will and conforms not with it, it is transformed in God through love.

4. This is to be understood of that which is repugnant, not only in action, but likewise in habit, so that not only do the voluntary acts of imperfection cease, but the habits of those imperfections, whatever they be, are annihilated.[4] And since no creature whatsoever, or any of its actions or abilities, can conform or can attain to that which is God, therefore must the soul be stripped of all things created, and of its own actions and abilities—namely, of its understanding, liking and feeling—so that, when all that is unlike God and unconformed to Him is cast out, the soul may receive the likeness of God; and nothing will then remain in it that is not the will of God and it will thus be transformed in God. Wherefore, although it is true that, as we have said, God is ever in the soul, giving it, and through His presence preserving within it its natural being, yet He does not always communicate supernatural being to it. For this is communicated only by love and grace, which not all souls possess; and all those that possess it have it not in the same degree; for some have attained more degrees of love and others fewer. Wherefore God communicates Himself most to that soul that has progressed farthest in love; namely, that has its will in closest conformity with

---

[1] E.p. adds: 'or presence (which we may call that of the order of nature).'
[2] E.p.: 'we speak not of this presence of God which ever exists in all the creatures.' [3] E.p. adds: 'through love.'
[4] E.p. abbreviates: 'but also the habits.'

the will of God. And the soul that has attained complete
conformity and likeness of will is totally united and transformed in God supernaturally. Wherefore, as has already
been explained, the more completely a soul is wrapped up
in[1] the creatures and in its own abilities, by habit and affection, the less preparation it has for such union ; for it
gives not God a complete opportunity to transform it supernaturally. The soul, then, needs only to strip itself of these
natural dissimilarities and contrarieties, so that God, Who
is communicating Himself naturally to it, according to the
course of nature, may communicate Himself to it supernaturally, by means of grace.[2]

5. And it is this that S. John desired to explain, when he
said : *Qui non ex sanguinibus, neque ex voluntate carnis, neque ex
voluntate viri, sed ex Deo nati sunt.*[3] As though he had said :
He gave power to be sons of God—that is, to be transformed
in God—only to those who are born, not of blood—that is,
not of natural constitution and temperament—neither of
the will of the flesh—that is, of the free will of natural
capacity and ability—still less of the will of man—wherein
is included every way and manner of judging and comprehending with the understanding. He gave power to none
of these to become sons of God, but only to those that are
born of God—that is, to those who being born again through
grace, and dying first of all to everything that is of the old
man, are raised above themselves to the supernatural, and
receive from God this rebirth and adoption, which transcends
all that can be imagined. For, as S. John himself says elsewhere : *Nisi quis renatus fuerit ex aqua, et Spiritu Sancto, non potest
videre regnum Dei.*[4] This signifies : He that is not born again
in the Holy Spirit will not be able to see this kingdom of God,
which is the state of perfection ; and to be born again in the
Holy Spirit[5] in this life[6] is to have a soul most like to God in
purity, having in itself no admixture of imperfection, so that
pure transformation can be wrought in it through participation of union, albeit not essentially.

---

[1] [*Lit.*, ' is clothed with.']
[2] E.p. reads : ' The soul, then, needs to strip itself of these natural
dissimilarities and contrarieties, so that God, Who is naturally present in
it by means of essence, may communicate Himself supernaturally to it by
means of grace, in the transformation of union.'
[3] S. John i, 13.   [4] S. John iii, 5.
[5] E.p. omits the whole of the first part of this paragraph, beginning
thus : ' For the estate of perfection and re-birth in the Holy Spirit . . .'
[6] A, B : ' in this life perfectly.'

6. In order that both these things may be the better understood, let us make a comparison. A ray of sunlight is striking a window. If the window is in any way stained or misty, the sun's ray will be unable to illumine it and transform it into its own light, totally, as it would if it were clean of all these things, and pure ; but it will illumine it to a lesser degree, in proportion as it is less free from those mists and stains ; and will do so to a greater degree, according as it is cleaner from them,[1] and this will not be because of the sun's ray, but because of itself ; so much so that, if it be wholly pure and clean, the ray of sunlight will transform it and illumine it in such wise that it will itself seem to be a ray and will give the same light as the ray. Although in reality the window has a nature distinct from that of the ray itself, however much it may resemble it, yet we may say that that window is a ray of the sun or is light by participation. And the soul is like this window, whereupon is ever beating (or, to express it better, wherein is ever dwelling) this Divine light of the Being of God according to nature, which we have described.

7. In thus allowing God to work in it, the soul (having rid itself of every mist and stain of the creatures, which consists in having its will perfectly united with that of God, for to love is to labour to detach and strip itself for God's sake of all that is not God) is at once illumined and transformed in God, and God communicates to it His supernatural Being, in such wise that it appears to be God Himself, and has all that God Himself has. And this union comes to pass when God grants the soul this supernatural favour,[2] that all the things of God and the soul are one in participant transformation ; and the soul seems to be God rather than a soul, and is indeed God by participation ; although it is true that its natural being, though thus transformed, is as distinct from the Being of God as it was before, even as the window has likewise a nature distinct from that of the ray, though it is illumined by it.

8. This makes it clearer that the preparation of the soul for this union, as we said, is not that it should understand or experience or feel or imagine anything, concerning either God or aught else, but that it should have purity and love—that is, perfect resignation and detachment from everything

---

[1] E.p. omits : ' and will . . . from them.'
[2] A, B, C, e.p. have : ' this sovereign favour.'

for God's sake alone ;[1] and, as there can be no perfect transformation if there be not perfect purity, and as the enlightenment, illumination and union of the soul with God will be
according to the proportion of its purity, in greater or in less
degree ; yet the soul will not be perfect, as I say, if it be
not wholly and perfectly[2] bright and clean.

9. This will likewise be understood by the following
comparison. A picture is most perfect, with many and most
sublime beauties and delicate and subtle brilliance, and
some of its beauties are so fine and subtle that they cannot
be completely realized because of their delicacy and excellence. Less beauty and delicacy will be seen in this picture
by one whose vision is less clear and refined ; and he whose
vision is somewhat more refined will be able to see in it
greater beauties and perfections ; and, if another person
has a vision still more refined, he will see still greater perfection ;[3] and finally, he who has the clearest and purest
faculties will see[4] the greatest beauties and perfections
of all ; for there is so much to see in the image that, however
far one may attain, there will ever remain higher degrees of
attainment.

10. After the same manner we may describe the condition
of the soul with respect to God in this enlightenment or
transformation. For, although it is true that a soul, according to its greater or smaller capacity, may have attained to
union, yet not all do so in the same degree, for this depends
upon what the Lord desires to grant to each one. It is in this
way that souls see God in Heaven ; some more, some less ;[5]
but all see Him, and all are content,[6] for their capacity is
satisfied.

11. Wherefore, although in this life here below we find
certain souls enjoying equal peace and tranquillity in the
state of perfection, and each one of them satisfied, yet some of
them may be many degrees higher than others. All, however, will be equally satisfied, because the capacity of each

---

[1] E.p. modifies : ' that the preparation for this union is purity and
love—that is, perfect resignation and total detachment, for God's sake
alone.'

[2] [*Lit.*, ' wholly perfect and . . .']

[3] E.p. : ' and he whose vision is more refined will be able to see greater
beauties ; and, if another person has a vision still more refined, he will be
able to see still greater perfection.'

[4] E.p. : ' will be able to see.'

[5] E.p. : ' some more perfectly, some less so.'

[6] E.p. : ' content and satisfied.'

one is satisfied.[1] But the soul that attains not to such a measure of purity as is in conformity with its capacity[2] never attains true peace and satisfaction, since it has not attained to the possession of that detachment and emptiness in its faculties which is required for simple union.[3]

CHAPTER VI

Wherein is described how it is the three theological virtues that perfect the three faculties of the soul, and how the said virtues produce emptiness and darkness within them.[4]

1. Having now to endeavour to show how the three faculties of the soul—understanding, memory and will—are brought into this spiritual night, which is the means to Divine union, it is necessary first of all to explain in this chapter how the three theological virtues—faith, hope and charity—which have respect to the three faculties aforesaid as to their proper supernatural objects, and[5] by means whereof the soul is united with God according to its faculties, produce the same emptiness and darkness, each one with regard to its faculty. Faith, in the understanding ; hope, in the memory ; and charity, in the will. And afterwards we shall go on to describe how the understanding is perfected in the darkness of faith ; and the memory in the emptiness of hope ; and likewise how the will must be buried in[6] the withdrawal and detachment of the affection that the soul may journey to God. This done, it will be clearly seen how necessary it is for the soul, if it is to walk securely on this spiritual road, to travel through this dark night, leaning upon these three virtues, which empty it of all things and make it dark with respect to them. For, as we have said, the soul is not united with God in this life through understanding, nor through enjoyment, nor through the imagination, nor through any sense whatsoever ; but only through

---

[1] E.p. : ' equally satisfied, each one according to his preparation and the knowledge that he has of God.'

[2] E.p. : ' to such a measure of purity as seems to be demanded by the enlightenment and vocation [that have been granted it] from God.'

[3] A, B : ' simple union with God.'

[4] E.p. adds : ' To this purpose are quoted two passages, one from S. Luke and the other from Isaiah.'

[5] E.p. omits : ' which have . . . objects, and '.

[6] So Alc., B [' enterrar ']. A, e p. have [' entrar,' which changes the reading to] ' must enter into.'

faith, according to the understanding ; and through hope, according to the memory ; and through love, according to the will.[1]

2. These three virtues, as we have said, all cause emptiness in the faculties : faith, in the understanding, causes an emptiness and darkness with respect to understanding ; hope, in the memory, causes emptiness of all possessions ; and charity causes emptiness in the will and detachment from all affection and from rejoicing in all that is not God. For we see that faith tells us what cannot be understood with the understanding.[2]   Wherefore S. Paul spoke of it *ad Hebræos* after this manner : *Fides est sperandarum substantia rerum, argumentum non apparentium.*[3]   This we interpret as meaning that faith is the substance of things hoped for ; and, although the understanding may be consenting thereto, firmly and certainly, they are not things that are revealed to the understanding ; for, if they were revealed to it, there would be no faith.   So faith, although it brings certainty to the understanding, brings it not clearness, but obscurity.

3. Then, as to hope, there is no doubt but that it renders the memory empty and dark with respect both to things below and to things above.   For hope has always to do with that which is not possessed ; for, if it were possessed, there would be no more hope.   Wherefore S. Paul says *ad Romanos : Spes, quæ videtur, non est spes : nam quod videt quis, quid sperat ?*[4]   That is to say : Hope that is seen is not hope ; for what a man seeth—that is, what a man possesseth—how doth he hope for it ?[5]   This virtue, then, makes emptiness also, for it has to do with that which is not possessed and not with that which is possessed.

4. Similarly, charity causes emptiness in the will with respect to all things, since it obliges us to love God above them all ; which cannot be unless we withdraw our affection from them all in order to set it wholly upon God.   Wherefore Christ[6] says, through S. Luke : *Qui non renuntiat omnibus*

---

[1] E.p. : ' and through hope, which may be attributed to the memory (although it is in the will) with respect to the emptiness and forgetfulness of every other temporal and fleeting thing which it causes, the soul keeping itself entirely for the supreme good for which it hopes ; and through love, according to the will.'

[2] E.p. adds : ' according to its natural light and reason.'

[3] Hebrews xi, 1.   [4] Romans viii, 24.

[5] A, B : ' for if a man possesseth what he seeth, how doth he hope for it ? '

[6] A, B : ' Christ Our Lord,' as in several other places below.

quæ possidet, non potest meus esse discipulus.[1] Which signifies :
He that renounceth not all that he possesseth with the will
cannot be My disciple. And thus all these three virtues set
the soul in obscurity and emptiness with respect to all things.

5. And here we must consider that parable which our
Redeemer taught in the eleventh chapter of S. Luke, wherein He said that a friend had to go out at midnight in order
to ask his friend for three loaves ;[2] the which loaves signify
these three virtues. And he said that he asked for them at
midnight in order to signify that the soul that is in darkness
as to all things must acquire these three virtues[3] according
to its faculties and must perfect itself in them in this night.
In the sixth chapter of Isaiah we read that the two seraphim
whom this Prophet saw on either side of God had each six
wings ; with twain they covered their feet, which signified
the blinding and quenching of the affections of the will with
respect to all things for the sake of God ; and with twain
they covered their face, which signified the darkness of the
understanding in the presence of God ; and with the
other twain they did fly.[4] This is to signify the flight of
hope to the things that are not possessed, when it is raised
above all that it can possess, below or above, apart from
God.

6. To these three virtues, then, we have to lead the three
faculties of the soul, informing each faculty by each one of
them, and stripping it and setting it in darkness[5] as concerning all things save only these three virtues. And this is the
spiritual night which just now we called active ; for the
soul does that which it is able to do in order to enter therein.
And even as, in the night of sense, we described a method of
voiding the faculties of sense of their sensible objects, with
regard to the desire, so that the soul might go forth from
the beginning of its course to the middle, which is faith ;
even so, in this spiritual night, with the favour of God,
we shall describe a method whereby the spiritual faculties
are voided and purified of all that is not God, and are set
in the darkness of these three virtues, which, as we have said,

---

[1] S. Luke xiv, 33
[2] S. Luke xi, 5. E.p. omits : ' his friend.'
[3] E.p. : ' must prepare itself for the perfection of these three virtues.'
[4] Isaiah vi, 2.
[5] E.p. : ' informing the understanding by faith, stripping the memory
of every possession and informing the will by charity, stripping them and
setting them in darkness . . .'

are the means and preparation for the union of the soul
with God.

7. In this method is found all security against the crafts
of the devil and against the efficacy[1] of self-love and its
ramifications, which is wont most subtly to deceive and
hinder spiritual persons on their road, when they know
not how to become detached and to govern themselves
according to these three virtues ; and thus they are never able
to reach the substance and purity of spiritual good, nor do
they journey by so straight and short a road as they might.

8. And it must be noted that I am now speaking particularly to those who have begun to enter the state of contemplation, because as far as this concerns beginners it
must be described somewhat more amply,[2] as we shall note
in the second book, God willing, when we treat of the
properties of these beginners.

CHAPTER VII

*Wherein is described how strait is the way that leads to eternal[3] life
and how completely detached and disencumbered must be those
that will walk in it.   We begin to speak of the detachment of
the understanding.*

1. We have now to describe the detachment and purity of
the three faculties of the soul and for this are necessary a
far greater knowledge and spirituality than mine, in order
to make clear to spiritual persons how strait is this road
which, said Our Saviour, leads to life ; so that they may be
persuaded hereof and not marvel at the emptiness and
detachment to which, in this night, we have to abandon the
faculties of the soul.

2. To this end must be carefully noted the words which
Our Saviour used, in the seventh chapter of S. Matthew,
concerning this road,[4] as follows : *Quam angusta porta, et
arcta via est, quæ ducit ad vitam, et pauci sunt, qui inveniunt eam.*[5]
This signifies : How strait is the gate and how narrow the

---

[1] E.p. reads ' craft ' for ' efficacy.'
[2] So Alc. A, B end the chapter here. E.p. omits the reference to
the ' second book ' as being inexact, and adds simply : ' [more amply]
when we treat of the properties of these beginners.'
[3] E.p. omits ' eternal.'
[4] E.p. adds : ' which [words] we shall now apply to this dark night
and lofty road of perfection.'   [5] S. Matthew vii, 14.

way that leadeth unto life, and few there be that find it !
In this passage we must carefully note the emphasis and
insistence which are contained in that word *Quam*.   For it
is as if He had said : In truth the way is very strait, more so
than you think.   And likewise it is to be noted that He says
first that the gate is strait, to make it clear that, in order
for the soul to enter this gate, which is Christ, and which
comes at the beginning of the road, the will must first be
straitened and detached in all things sensual and temporal,
and God must be loved above them all ; which belongs to
the night of sense, as we have said.

3. He next says that the road is narrow—that is to say,
the road of perfection—in order to make it clear that, to
travel upon the road of perfection, the soul has not only to
enter by the strait gate,[1] emptying itself of things of sense,
but that it has also to constrain[2] itself, freeing and disencumbering itself completely in that which pertains to the
spirit.   And thus we can apply what He says of the strait
gate to the sensual part of man ; and what He says of the
narrow road we can understand of the spiritual or the
rational part ; and, when He says ' Few there be that find
it,' the reason of this must be noted, which is that there are
few who can enter, and desire to enter, into this complete
detachment and emptiness of spirit.   For this path ascending
the high mountain of perfection leads upward, and is narrow,
and therefore requires such travellers as have no burden
weighing upon them with respect to lower things, neither
aught that embarrasses them with respect to higher things :
and as this is a matter wherein we must seek after and
attain to God alone, God alone must be the object of our
search and attainment.

4. Hence it is clearly seen that the soul must not only
be disencumbered from that which belongs to the creatures,
but likewise, as it travels, must be annihilated and detached
from all that belongs to its spirit.   Wherefore Our Lord,
instructing us and leading us into this road, gave, in the eighth
chapter of S. Mark, that wonderful teaching of which I
think it may almost be said that, the more necessary it is for
spiritual persons, the less it is practised by them.[3]   As this
teaching is so important and so much to our purpose, I

---

[1] A alone reads : ' by the road of perfection, that is, by the strait gate.'
[2] [*Lit.*, ' to straiten ' : the Spanish verb is derived from the adjective.]
[3] From this point to the Latin text is omitted by A and B.

shall reproduce it here in full, and expound it according to
its real and spiritual sense. He says, then, thus : *Si quis vult
me sequi, deneget semetipsum : et tollat crucem suam, et sequatur me.
Qui enim voluerit animam suam salvam facere, perdet eam : qui
autem perdiderit animam suam propter me . . . salvam faciet eam.*[1]
This signifies : If any man will follow My road, let him
deny himself and take up his cross and follow Me. For he
that will save his soul shall lose it ; but he that loses it for
My sake, shall gain it.

5. Oh, that one might show us how to understand,
practise and experience what this counsel is which[2] our
Saviour here gives us concerning the denial of ourselves, so
that spiritual persons might see in how different a way they
should[3] conduct themselves upon this road from that which
many of them think proper ! For they believe that any kind
of retirement and reformation of life suffices ; and others
are content with practising the virtues and continuing in
prayer and pursuing mortification ; but they attain not
to detachment and poverty or denial or spiritual purity
(which are all one), which the Lord here commends to us ;
for they prefer feeding and clothing their natural selves with
spiritual feelings and consolations,[4] to stripping themselves
of all things, and denying themselves all things, for God's
sake. For they think that it suffices to deny themselves
worldly things without annihilating and purifying themselves of spiritual attachment. Wherefore it comes to pass
that, when there presents itself to them any of this solid and
perfect[5] spirituality, consisting in the annihilation of all
sweetness in God, in aridity, distaste and trial, which is the
true spiritual cross, and the detachment of the spiritual
poverty of Christ, they flee from it as from death, and seek
only sweetness and delectable communion with God. This
is not self-denial and detachment of spirit, but spiritual
gluttony. Herein they become spiritually enemies of the
cross of Christ ; for true spirituality seeks for God's sake that
which is distasteful rather than that which is delectable ;
and inclines itself rather to suffering than to consolation ;
and desires to go without all blessings for God's sake rather
than to possess them ; and to endure aridities and afflictions
rather than to enjoy sweet communications, knowing that

---

[1] S. Mark viii, 34–5.
[2] E.p. : ' what is contained in this so lofty instruction which . . .'
[3] A, B, e.p. have ' it behoves them to ' for ' they should.'
[4] E.p. : ' with consolations.'   [5] E.p. omits : ' and perfect

this is to follow Christ and to deny oneself, and that the
other is perchance to seek oneself in God, which is clean
contrary to love.[1] For to seek oneself in God is to seek the
favours and refreshments of God ; but to seek God in oneself is not only to desire to be without both of these for God's
sake, but to incline oneself to choose, for Christ's sake,
all that is most distasteful, whether as to God or as to the
world ; and this is love of God.

6. Oh that someone could tell us how far Our Lord
desires this self-denial to be carried ! It must certainly be
like to death and annihilation, temporal, natural and
spiritual, in all things that the will esteems, wherein consists
all self-denial.[2] And it is this that Our Lord meant when He
said : He that will save his life, the same shall lose it. That
is to say : He that will possess anything or seek anything for
himself, the same shall lose it ; and he that loses his soul for
My sake, the same shall gain it. That is to say : He that
for Christ's sake renounces all that his will can desire and
enjoy, and chooses that which is most like to the Cross
(which the Lord Himself, through S. John, describes as
hating his soul),[3] the same shall gain it. And this His
Majesty taught to those two disciples who went and begged
Him for a place on His right hand and on His left ; when,
giving them no reply to their request for such glory, He
offered them the cup which He had to drink, as a thing more
precious and more secure upon this earth than is fruition.[4]

7. This cup is the death of the natural self, which is
attained through the soul's detachment and annihilation, in
order that the soul may travel by this narrow path, with
respect to all that can belong to it according to sense, as we
have said ; and according to the spirit,[5] as we shall now
say ; that is, in its understanding and in its enjoyment and
in its feeling. And, as a result, not only is the soul detached
as to all this, but, having this spiritual help, it is not hindered
upon the narrow road, since there remains to it naught else
than self-denial (as the Saviour explains), and the Cross,
which is the staff whereby one may reach Him,[6] and whereby

---

[1] A, B omit this last clause.
[2] So Alc., A, B, C, D. E.p. has : ' all gain.' The gain, however [says
P. Silverio], is rather a result of the complete self-denial of which the
Saint is here speaking.
[3] S. John xii, 25.   [4] S. Matthew xx, 22.
[5] Thus e.p. Alc., A, B [and P. Silverio] read ' soul ' for ' spirit,'
[6] E.p. : ' the staff whereon to lean.'

the road is greatly lightened and made easy. Wherefore Our
Lord said through S. Matthew : My yoke is easy and My
burden is light ;[1] which burden is the cross. For if a man
resolve to submit himself to carrying this cross—that is to
say, if he resolve to desire in truth to meet trials and to bear
them in all things for God's sake, he will find in them all
great relief and sweetness wherewith he may travel upon
this road, detached from all things and desiring nothing.
Yet, if he desire to possess anything—whether it come from
God or from any other source,—with any feeling of attachment, he is not detached and has not denied himself in all
things ; and thus he will be unable to walk along this
narrow path or to climb upward by it.[2]

8. I would, then, that I could convince spiritual persons
that this road to God consists not in a multiplicity of meditations nor in ways or methods of such, nor in consolations,
although these things may in their own way be necessary to
beginners ; but that it consists only in the one thing that is
needful, which is the ability to deny oneself truly, according
to that which is without and to that which is within, giving
oneself up to suffering for Christ's sake, and to total annihilation. For the soul that thus denies itself will achieve
this suffering and annihilation, and more also, and will
likewise find more than suffering and annihilation therein.
And if a soul be found wanting in this exercise, which is the
sum and root of the virtues, all its other methods are so
much wandering about in a maze, and profiting not at all,
although its meditations and communications may be as
lofty as those of the angels.[3] For progress comes not save
through the imitation of Christ, Who is the Way, the Truth
and the Life, and no man comes to the Father but by Him,
even as He Himself says through S. John.[4] And elsewhere
He says : I am the door ; by Me if any man enter in he shall
be saved.[5] Wherefore, as it seems to me, any spirituality
that would fain walk in sweetness and with ease, and flees
from the imitation of Christ, is worthless.

9. And, as I have said that Christ is the Way, and that
this Way is death to our natural selves, in things both of sense
and of spirit, I will now explain how we are to die, following
the example of Christ, for He is our example and light.

[1] S. Matthew xi, 30.   [2] E.p. omits ' upward.'
[3] E.p. has ' very lofty ' and omits ' as those of the angels,' which is
found, however, in all the codices.
[4] S. John xiv, 6.   [5] S. John x, 9.

10. In the first place, it is certain that He died as to sense, spiritually, in His life ; and also, naturally, at His death. For, as He said, He had not in His life where to lay His head, and, in His death, this was even truer.

11. In the second place, it is certain that, at the moment of His death, He was likewise annihilated[1] in His soul, and was deprived of any relief and consolation, since His Father left Him in[2] the most intense aridity, according to the lower part of His nature.[3] Wherefore He had perforce to cry out, saying : My God ! My God ! Why hast Thou forsaken Me ?[4] This was the greatest desolation, with respect to sense, that He had suffered in His life.[5] And thus He wrought herein[6] the greatest work that He had ever wrought, whether in miracles or in mighty works, during the whole of His life, either upon earth or in Heaven,[7] which was the reconciliation and union of mankind, through grace, with God. And this was, as I say, at the moment and the time when this Lord was most completely annihilated in everything. That is to say, with respect to human reputation ; since, when they saw Him die,[8] they mocked Him rather than esteemed Him ; and also with respect to nature, since His nature was annihilated when He died ; and with respect to the spiritual[9] consolation and protection of the Father, since at that time He forsook Him, that He might pay the whole of man's debt and unite him with God, being thus annihilated and reduced as it were[10] to nothing. Wherefore David says concerning Him : *Ad nihilum redactus sum, et nescivi.*[11] This he said that the truly spiritual man may understand the mystery of the gate and of the way of Christ, in order to be united with God, and may know that, the more completely he is annihilated for God's sake, according to these two parts, the sensual and the spiritual, the more completely is he united to God and the greater is the work which he accomplishes. And when he comes to be reduced to nothing, which will be the greatest extreme of humility, spiritual[12] union will be wrought between the soul and God,

---

[1] E.p. : ' He was likewise forsaken and, as it were, annihilated.'
[2] E.p. : ' left Him without consolation and in.'
[3] E.p. omits : ' according to . . . His nature.'
[4] S. Matthew xxvii, 46.   [5] E.p. omits this sentence.
[6] E.p. has ' then ' for ' herein.'
[7] E.p. omits : ' either upon earth or in Heaven.'
[8] E.p. adds : ' on a tree.'   [9] E.p. omits ' spiritual.'
[10] E.p. : ' and as though reduced, as it were.'
[11] Psalm lxxii, 22 [A.V., lxxiii, 22].   [12] E.p. omits ' spiritual.'

which in this life is the greatest and the highest state attainable. This consists not, then, in refreshment and in consolations and spiritual feelings, but in a living death of the Cross, both as to sense and as to spirit—that is, both inwardly and outwardly.

12. I will not pursue this subject farther, although I have no desire to finish speaking of it, for I see that Christ[1] is known very little by those who consider themselves His friends : we see them seeking their own pleasures and consolations in Him because of their great love for themselves, but not loving His bitter trials and His death because of their great love for Him. I am speaking now of those who consider themselves His friends ; for such as live far away, withdrawn from Him, great men of letters and of influence, and all others who live yonder, with the world, and are eager about their ambitions and their prelacies, may be said not to know Christ ; and their end, however good, will be very bitter. Of such I make no mention in these lines ; but mention will be made of them on the day of judgement, for to them it was necessary to speak first this word of God,[2] as to those whom God set up as guides, by reason of their learning and their high position.

13. But let us now address the understanding of the spiritual man, and particularly that of the man whom God has granted the favour of leading him into the state of contemplation (for, as I have said, I am now speaking to these in particular),[3] and let us say how such a man must direct himself toward God in faith, and purify himself from contrary things, constraining himself[4] that he may enter upon this narrow path of obscure contemplation.

CHAPTER VIII

Which describes in a general way how no creature and no knowledge that can be comprehended by the understanding can serve as a proximate means of Divine union with God.

1. Before we treat of the proper and fitting means of union with God, which is faith, it behoves us to prove how

---

[1] E.p. : ' that Jesus Christ.'
[2] [The reference seems to be to Acts xiii, 46.]
[3] A, B omit the parenthesis.
[4] E.p. has ' girding ' for ' constraining.'

no thing, created or imagined, can serve the understanding
as a proper means of union with God ; and how all that the
understanding can attain serves it rather as an impediment
than as such a means, if it should desire to cling to it.   And
now, in this chapter, we shall prove this in a general way,
and afterwards we shall begin to speak in detail, treating in
turn of all kinds of knowledge that the understanding may
receive from any sense, whether inward or outward, and of
the inconveniences and evils that may result from all these
kinds of inward and outward knowledge,[1] so that it progresses not in dependence upon the proper means, which is
faith.

2. It must be understood, then, that, according to a rule
of philosophy, all means must be proportioned to the end ;
that is to say that they must have some connection and
resemblance with the end, such as is enough and sufficient
that the desired end may be attained through them.   I take
an example.   A man desires to reach a city ; he has of
necessity to travel by the road, which is the means that
brings him to the same city and connects[2] him with it.
Another example.[3]   Fire is to be combined and united with
wood ; it is necessary that heat, which is the means, shall
first prepare the wood, by conveying to it so many degrees
of warmth that it will have great resemblance and proportion
to fire.   Now if one would prepare the wood by any other
than the proper means—namely, with heat—as for example,
with air or water or earth, it would be impossible for the
wood to be united with the fire, just as it would be equally
so to reach the city without going by the road that leads to
it.[4]   Wherefore, in order that the understanding may be
united with God in this life, so far as is possible,[5] it must of
necessity employ that means that unites it with Him and
that bears the greatest resemblance to Him.

3. Here it must be pointed out that, among all the creatures,
the highest or the lowest, there is none that comes near to
God or bears any resemblance to His Being.   For, although
it is true that all creatures have, as theologians say, a certain
relation to God, and bear a Divine impress (some more and
others less, according to what is more or less dominant
in their nature), yet there is no essential resemblance or

---

[1] E.p. : ' kinds of knowledge.'   [2] [Lit., ' unites.']
[3] E.p. adds ' likewise.'   [4] E.p. omits : ' just as . . . leads to it.'
[5] E.p. adds : ' in it ' [i.e., in this life].

connection between them and God,—on the contrary, the distance between their being and His Divine Being is infinite. Wherefore it is impossible for the understanding to attain to God[1] by means of the creatures, whether these be celestial or earthly ; inasmuch as there is no proportion of resemblance between them. Wherefore, when David speaks of the heavenly creatures, he says : There is none among the gods like unto Thee, O Lord ;[2] meaning by the gods the angels[3] and holy souls. And elsewhere : O God, Thy way is in the sanctuary. What God is there so great as our God ?[4] As though he were to say : The way of approach to Thee, O God, is a holy way—that is, the purity of faith. For what God can there be so great ? That is to say : What angel will there be so exalted in his being, and what saint so exalted in glory as to be a proportionate and sufficient road by which a man may come to Thee ? And the same David, speaking likewise of earthly and heavenly things both together, says : The Lord is high and looketh on lowly things, and the high things He knoweth afar off.[5] As though he had said : Lofty in His own Being, He sees that the being of the things here below[6] is very low in comparison with His lofty Being ;[7] and the lofty things, which are the celestial creatures, He sees and knows to be very far from His Being. All the creatures, then, cannot serve as a proportionate means to the understanding whereby it may reach God.[8]

4. Just so all that the imagination can imagine and the understanding can receive and understand in this life is not, nor can it be, a proximate means of union with God. For if we speak of natural things, since understanding can understand naught save that which is contained within, and comes under the category of, forms and imaginings of things that are received through the bodily senses, the which things, we have said, cannot serve as means, it can make no use of natural intelligence. And if we speak of the supernatural (in so far as is possible in this life of our ordinary faculties[9]), the understanding in its bodily prison has no preparation or capacity for receiving the clear knowledge of God ; for

---

[1] E.p. adds ' perfectly.'
[2] Psalm lxxxv, 8 [A.V., lxxxvi, 8].   [3] E.p. : ' the holy angels.'
[4] Psalm lxxvi, 14 [A.V., lxxvii, 13] [lit., ' in the holy '].
[5] Psalm cxxxvii, 6 [A.V., cxxxviii, 6].
[6] E.p. : ' of the things of the earth.'   [7] B omits this sentence.
[8] E.p. : ' . . . means for perfectly reaching God.'
[9] These last four words are found only in Alc.

such knowledge belongs not to this state, and we must either
die or remain without receiving it. Wherefore Moses, when
he entreated God for this clear knowledge, was told that he
could not see Him, in these words[1] : No man shall see Me
and remain alive.[2] Wherefore S. John says : No man hath
seen God at any time,[3] neither aught that is like to Him.
And S. Paul says, with Isaiah : Eye hath not seen Him, nor
hath ear heard Him, neither hath it entered into the heart
of man.[4] And it is for this reason that Moses, in the bush, as
is said in the Acts of the Apostles,[5] ventured not to consider
while God was present ; for he knew that his understanding
could make no such consideration as was fitting concerning
God, corresponding to the sense which he had of God's
presence.[6] And of Elijah, our father,[7] it is said that he
covered his face in the Mount in the presence of God,[8]
which signifies the blinding of his understanding, which he
wrought there, daring not to lay so base a hand upon that
which was so high ; seeing clearly that whatsoever he might
consider, or understand with any precision, would be very
far from God and most unlike Him.

5. Wherefore no supernatural apprehension or knowledge
in this mortal life can serve as a proximate means to the
high union of love with God. For all that can be understood
by the understanding, that can please the will, and that can
be invented by the imagination is most unlike to God and
bears no proportion to Him, as we have said. All this
Isaiah admirably explained in that most noteworthy
passage,[9] where he says : To what thing have ye been able
to liken God ? Or what image will ye make that is like to
Him ? Will the workman in iron perchance be able to make
a graven image ? Or will he that works gold be able to
imitate Him[10] with gold, or the silversmith with plates of
silver ?[11] By the workman in iron is signified the understanding, the office of which is to form intelligences and strip

[1] E.p. abbreviates : '. . . receiving it. Wherefore God said to
Moses : No man . . .'   [2] Exodus xxxiii, 20.
[3] S. John i, 18. E.p. omits 'neither . . . Him,' which is found in all
the codices.
[4] 1 Corinthians ii, 9 ; Isaiah lxiv, 4.   [5] Acts vii, 32.
[6] E.p. : '. . . concerning God, though this sprang from the profound
sense which he had of God['s presence].'
[7] Only Alc., C read : ' our father.'
[8] 3 Kings [A.V., 1 Kings] xix, 13.
[9] Alc. alone has : ' in that most noteworthy passage.'
[10] E.p. : ' to figure Him ' [or ' to form Him ']. A, B : ' to make Him.'
[11] Isaiah xl, 18–19.

them of the iron of species and images. By the workman in
gold is understood the will, which is able to receive the figure
and the form of pleasure, caused by the gold of love.[1] By
the silversmith, who is spoken of as being unable to form[2]
Him with plates of silver, is understood the memory, with
the imagination, whereof it may be said with great propriety
that its knowledge and the imaginings that it can invent[3] and
make are like plates of silver. And thus it is as though he
had said : Neither the understanding with its intelligence
will be able to understand aught that is like Him, nor can
the will taste pleasure and sweetness that bears any resemblance to that which is God, neither can the memory set in
the imagination ideas and images that represent Him. It is
clear, then, that none of these kinds of knowledge can lead
the understanding direct to God ; and that, in order to
reach Him, a soul must rather proceed by not understanding
than by desiring to understand ; and by blinding itself and
setting itself in darkness rather than by opening its eyes in
order the more nearly to approach the ray Divine.

6. And thus it is that contemplation, whereby the understanding has the loftiest knowledge of God,[4] is called mystical
theology, which signifies secret wisdom of God ; for it is
secret to the very understanding that receives it. For this
reason S. Dionysius calls it a ray of darkness. Of this the
prophet Baruch says : There is none that knoweth its way,
nor any that can think of its paths.[5] It is clear, then, that
the understanding must be blind to all the paths to which it
may attain, in order to be united with God. Aristotle says
that, even as are the eyes of the bat with regard to the sun,
which is total darkness to it, even so is our understanding
to that which is greater light in God, which is total darkness
to us. And he says further that, the more profound and
clear are the things of God in themselves, the more completely unknown and obscure are they to us. This likewise
the Apostle affirms, saying : The deepest things of God are
the least known unto men.

7. But we should never end if we continued at this rate
to quote authorities and arguments to prove and make clear

---

[1] A, B, e.p. : ' . . . gold of the love wherewith it loves.'

[2] [All authorities read ' form ' (or ' figure ') here. Cf. p. 96, n. 10, above.]

[3] [This is the word (fingir, ' feign '), translated above as ' imitate.'
Cf. p. 96, n. 10.]

[4] So Alc. All other authorities read : ' . . . the understanding is
enlightened by God.'   [5] Baruch iii, 23.

that among all created things, and things that belong to the understanding, there is no ladder whereby the understanding can attain to this high Lord. Rather it is necessary to know that, if the understanding should seek to profit by all of these things, or by any of them, as a proximate means to such union, they would be not only a hindrance, but even an occasion of·numerous errors and delusions in the ascent of this mount.

CHAPTER IX

How faith is the proximate and proportionate means to the under-standing whereby the soul may attain to the Divine union of love. This is proved by passages and figures from Divine Scripture.[1]

1. From what has been said it is to be inferred that, in order for the understanding to be prepared for this Divine union, it must be pure and void of all that pertains to sense, and detached[2] and freed from all that can clearly be perceived by the understanding, profoundly hushed and put to silence, and leaning upon faith, which alone is the proximate and proportionate means whereby the soul is united with God ; for such is the likeness between itself and God that[3] there is no other difference, save that which exists between seeing God and believing in Him. For, as God is infinite, so faith sets Him before us as infinite ; and as He is Three and One, it sets Him before us as Three and One ; and as God is darkness to our understanding, even so does faith likewise blind and dazzle our understanding.[4] And thus, by this means alone, God manifests Himself to the soul in Divine light, which passes all understanding. And therefore, the greater is the faith of the soul, the more completely is it united with God. It is this that S. Paul meant in the passage which we quoted above, where he says : He that will be united with God must believe.[5] That is, he must walk by faith in his journey to Him, the under-standing being blind and in darkness, walking in faith alone ;[6]

---

[1] This last sentence is found only in Alc. and in e.p.
[2] E.p. omits : ' and detached.'
[3] E.p. omits : ' such is . . . God that,' which is found in all the Codices.
[4] This clause ('and as God . . . our understanding ') is omitted from e.p.   [5] Hebrews xi, 6.
[6] E.p. omits : ' It is this that S. Paul . . . in faith alone.'

for beneath this darkness the understanding is united with God, and beneath it God is hidden, even as David said in these words : Darkness was under His feet. And He rose upon the cherubim, and flew upon the wings of the wind. And He made darkness His hiding-place and the water dark.[1]

2. By his saying that He set darkness beneath His feet, and that He took the darkness for a hiding-place, and that His tabernacle round about Him was in the dark water, is denoted the obscurity of the faith wherein He is concealed. And by his saying that He rose upon the cherubim and flew upon the wings of the winds, is understood His soaring above all understanding. For the cherubim denote those who understand or contemplate. And the wings of the winds signify the subtle and lofty ideas and conceptions of the spirits, above all of which is His Being, and to which none can attain by his own power.

3. This we learn from an illustration in the Scriptures. When Solomon had completed the building of the Temple, God came down in darkness and filled the Temple so that the children of Israel could not see ; whereupon Solomon spoke and said : The Lord hath promised that He will dwell in the thick darkness.[2] Likewise He appeared in darkness to Moses in the Mount, wherein God was concealed. And whensoever God communicated Himself intimately, He appeared in darkness, as may be seen in Job, where the Scripture says that God spoke with him from the air in darkness.[3] All these mentions of darkness signify the obscurity of the faith wherein the Divinity is concealed, when It communicates Itself to the soul ; which will be ended when, as S. Paul says, that which is in part shall be ended,[4] which is this darkness of faith, and that which is perfect shall come, which is the Divine light. Of this we have a good illustration in the army of Gideon, whereof it is said that all the soldiers had lamps in their hands, which they saw not, because they had them concealed in the dark pitchers ; and, when these pitchers were broken, the light was seen.[5] Just so does faith, which is foreshadowed by

---

[1] Psalm xvii, 10 [A.V., xviii, 9–11]. E.p. modifies thus : ' And He made darkness His hiding-place ; round about Him He set His tabernacle, which is dark water, among the clouds of the air.'

[2] 3 Kings [A.V., 1 Kings] viii, 12.

[3] Job xxxviii, 1 ; xl, 1.

[4] 1 Corinthians xiii, 10.   [5] Judges vii, 16.

these pitchers, contain within itself Divine light ;[1] which, when it is ended and broken, at the ending and breaking of this mortal life, will allow the glory and light of the Divinity, which was contained in it,[2] to appear.

4. It is clear, then, that, if the soul in this life is to attain to union with God, and commune directly with Him, it must unite itself with the darkness whereof Solomon spake, wherein God had promised to dwell, and must draw near to the darkness of the air wherein God was pleased to reveal His secrets to Job, and must take in its hands, in darkness, the jars of Gideon, that it may have in its hands (that is, in the works of its will) the light, which is the union of love, though it be in the darkness of faith, so that, when the pitchers of this life are broken, which alone have kept from it the light of faith, it may see God[3] face to face in glory.

5. It now remains to describe in detail all the types of knowledge and the apprehensions which the understanding can receive ; the hindrance and the harm which it can receive upon this road of faith ; and the way wherein the soul must conduct itself so that, whether they proceed from the senses or from the spirit, they may cause it, not harm, but profit.

CHAPTER X

Wherein distinction is made between all apprehensions and types of knowledge which can be comprehended by the understanding.

1. In order to treat in detail of the profit and the harm which may come to the soul, with respect to this means to Divine union which we have described—namely, faith— through the notions and apprehensions of the understanding, it is necessary here to make a distinction between all the apprehensions, whether natural or supernatural, that the soul may receive, so that then, with regard to each of them in order, we may direct the understanding with greater clearness into the night and obscurity of faith. This will be done with all possible brevity.

2. It must be known, then, that the understanding can receive knowledge and intelligence by two channels : the

[1] A, e.p. add : ' that is, the truth of that which God is in Himself.'
[2] E.p. omits : ' which was contained in it.'
[3] E.p. omits ' which . . . of faith ' and inserts ' God,' which word is not found in the Codices.

one natural and the other supernatural. By the natural
channel is meant all that the understanding can understand,
whether by means of the bodily senses or by its own power.[1]
The supernatural channel is all that is given to the understanding over and above its natural ability and capacity.

3. Of these kinds of supernatural knowledge, some are
corporeal and some are spiritual. The corporeal are two
in number : some are received by means of the outward
bodily senses ; others, by means of the inward bodily
senses, wherein is comprehended all that the imagination
can comprehend,[2] form and conceive.

4. The spiritual supernatural knowledge is likewise of
two kinds : that which is distinct and special in its nature,
and that which is confused, general and dark. Of the distinct and special kind there are four manners of apprehension
which are communicated to the spirit without the aid of
any bodily sense : these are visions, revelations, locutions and
spiritual feelings. The obscure and general type of knowledge is of one kind alone, which is contemplation that is
given in faith. To this we have to lead the soul by bringing
it thereto[3] through all these other means, beginning with
the first and detaching it from them.

CHAPTER XI

Of the hindrance and harm that may be caused by apprehensions of
the understanding which proceed from what is supernaturally
represented to the outward bodily senses ; and how the soul
is to conduct itself therein.

1. The first kinds of knowledge whereof we have spoken
in the preceding chapter are those that belong to the understanding and come through natural channels. Of these,
since we have treated them already in the first book, where
we led the soul into the night of sense, we shall here say not a
word, for in that place we gave suitable instruction to the
soul concerning them. What we have to treat, therefore,
in the present chapter, will be solely those kinds of knowledge

---

[1] [*Lit.*, ' by itself.'] E.p. adds : ' after these [senses].' A, B read : ' or
by the channel of itself.'

[2] E.p. : ' can apprehend,' which no doubt more exactly expresses the
Saint's meaning.

[3] Alc. breaks off the chapter here.

and those apprehensions which belong to the understanding
and come supernaturally, by way of the outward bodily
senses—namely, by seeing, hearing, smelling, tasting and
touching. With respect to all these there may come, and
there are wont to come,[1] to spiritual persons representations
and objects of a supernatural kind.[2] With respect to sight,
they are apt to picture figures and forms of persons belonging
to the life to come—the forms of certain saints, and representations of angels, good and evil, and certain lights and
brightnesses of an extraordinary kind. And with the ears
they hear certain extraordinary words, sometimes spoken by
these figures[3] that they see, sometimes without seeing the
person who speaks them. As to the sense of smell, they
sometimes perceive the sweetest perfumes with the senses,
without knowing whence they proceed. Likewise, as to
taste, it comes to pass that they are conscious of the sweetest
savours, and, as to touch, they experience great delight[4]—
sometimes to such a degree that it is as though all the bones
and the marrow rejoice and sing[5] and are bathed in delight ;[6]
this is like that which we call spiritual unction, which in
pure souls[7] proceeds from the spirit and flows into the very
members. And this sensible sweetness is quite an ordinary
thing with[8] spiritual persons, for it comes to them from their
sensible affection and devotion,[9] to a greater or a lesser
degree, to each one after his own manner.

2. And it must be known that, although all these things
may happen to the bodily senses in the way of God, we must
never rely upon them or admit them, but we must always
fly from them, without trying to ascertain whether they
be good or evil ; for, the more completely exterior and
corporeal they are, the less certainly are they of God.[10] For
it is more proper and habitual[11] to God to communicate Himself to the spirit, wherein there is more security and profit
for the soul, than to sense, wherein there is ordinarily much
danger and deception ; for bodily sense judges and makes

---

[1] A, B, e.p. have 'happen' for 'come' both here and in the preceding
clause.
[2] E.p.: 'and objects represented and set before them in a supernatural
way.'   [3] E.p.: 'these persons.'
[4] E.p.: 'and, as to touch, of its own kind of enjoyment and sweetness.'
[5] [*Lit.*, 'and blossom.']   [6] E.p.: 'are bathed therein.'
[7] E.p.: 'in simple souls.'   [8] E.p.: 'is wont to happen to.'
[9] [*Lit.*, 'from the affection and devotion of the sensible spirit.']
[10] E.p.: 'the less certainty is there of their being of God.'
[11] E.p. omits: 'and habitual.'

its estimate of spiritual things by thinking that they are as it feels them to be, whereas they are as different as is the body from the soul and sensuality[1] from reason. For the bodily sense is as ignorant of spiritual things as is a beast of rational things, and even more so.

3. So he that esteems such things errs greatly and places himself in great peril of deception ; and at best will have in himself a complete[2] impediment to the attainment of spirituality. For, as we have said, between spiritual things and all these bodily things there exists no kind of proportion whatever. And thus it may always be supposed that such things as these are more likely to be of the devil than of God ; for the devil has more influence in that which is exterior and corporeal, and can deceive a soul more easily thereby than by that which is more interior and spiritual.

4. And the more exterior are these corporeal forms and objects in themselves, the less do they profit the interior and spiritual nature, because of the great distance and the little proportion existing between the corporeal and the spiritual. For, although they communicate a certain degree of spirituality, as is always the case with things that come from God, there is much less than there would be if the same things were more interior and spiritual. And thus they very easily become the means whereby error and presumption and vanity grow in the soul ; since, as they are so palpable and material, they stir the senses greatly, and it appears to the judgement of the soul that they are of greater importance because they are more readily felt. Thus the soul goes after them, abandoning faith and[3] thinking that the light which it receives from them is the guide and means to its desired goal, which is union with God. But the more attention it pays to such things, the farther it strays from the true way and means, which are faith.

5. And, besides all this, when the soul sees that such extra-ordinary things happen to it, it is often visited, insidiously and secretly, by a certain complacent idea—namely, that it is of some importance in the eyes of God ; which is contrary to humility. The devil, too, knows how to insinuate into the soul a secret satisfaction with itself, which at times becomes very manifest ; wherefore he frequently represents

---

[1] [P. Silverio remarks here that] we must understand [as frequently elsewhere] ' sensibility ' and not sensuality in the grosser sense.
[2] E.p.: ' a great.'   [3] E.p. omits: ' abandoning faith and.'

these objects to the senses, setting before the eyes the figures of saints and most beauteous lights ; and before the ears words well dissembled ; and representing also sweetest perfumes, delicious tastes[1] and things delectable to the touch; to the end that, by producing desires for such things, he may lead the soul into much evil. These representations and feelings, therefore, must always be rejected ; for, even though some of them be of God, He is not offended by their rejection, nor is the effect and fruit which He desires to produce in the soul by means of them any the less surely received because the soul rejects them and desires them not.

6. The reason for this is that corporeal vision, or feeling in respect to any of the other senses, or any other communication of the most interior kind, if it be of God, produces its effect[2] upon the spirit at the very moment when it appears or is felt, without giving the soul time or opportunity to deliberate whether it will accept or reject it.   For, even as God gives these things supernaturally, without effort[3] on the part of the soul, and independently of its capacity, even so likewise, without respect to its effort or capacity, God produces in it the effect that He desires by means of such things ; for this is a thing that is wrought and brought to pass in the spirit passively ;[4] and thus its acceptance or non-acceptance consists not in the acceptance or the rejection of it by the will.   It is as though fire were applied to a person's naked body : it would matter little whether or no he wished to be burned ; the fire would of necessity accomplish its work. Just so is it with visions and representations that are good : even though the soul desire it not,[5] they work their effect upon it, and in the soul chiefly and especially, rather than in the body.   And likewise those that come from the devil (without the consent of the soul) cause it trouble or aridity or vanity or presumption in the spirit. Yet these are not so effective to work evil as are those of God to work good ; for those of the devil can only set in action the first movements of the will,[6] and move it no

---

[1] [Lit., ' and sweetnesses in the mouth.']   [2] E.p. : ' its first effect.'
[3] E.p. : ' For, even as God begins these things supernaturally, without active effort . . .'
[4] The 1630 edition adds : ' without its free consent.'
[5] E.p. omits : ' even . . . not.'
[6] E.p. : ' for those of the devil stop at the first movements and cannot move the will.' This, no doubt, was the Saint's meaning, for the Church teaches that the devil cannot influence the will directly, though indirectly (principally through the senses and the imagination) he may do so.

farther, unless the soul be consenting thereto ; and such
trouble continues not long unless the soul's lack of courage
and prudence be the occasion of its continuance. But the
visions that are of God penetrate the soul and move the will
to love, and produce their effect,[1] which the soul cannot
resist even though it would, any more than the window can
resist the sun's rays when they strike it.

7. The soul, then, must never presume to desire to receive
them, even though, as I say, they be of God ; for if it desire
to receive them, there follow six inconveniences.

The first is that faith[2] grows gradually less ; for things
that are experienced by the senses derogate from faith ;
since faith, as we have said, transcends every sense. And
thus the soul withdraws itself from the means of union
with God when it closes not its eyes to all these things of
sense.

Secondly, they are a hindrance to the spirit, if they be
not denied, for the soul rests in them and its spirit soars not
to the invisible. This was one of the reasons why the Lord
said to His disciples that it was needful for Him to go away
that the Holy Spirit might come ; so, too, He forbade Mary
Magdalene to touch His feet, after His resurrection, that
she might be grounded in faith.

Thirdly, the soul becomes attached to these things and
advances not to true resignation and detachment of spirit.

Fourthly, it begins to lose the effect of them and the inward
spirituality which they cause it, because it sets its eyes upon
their sensual aspect, which is the least important. And
thus it receives not so fully the spirituality which they
cause,[3] which is impressed and preserved more securely
when all things of sense are rejected, since these are very
different from pure spirit.

Fifthly, the soul begins to lose the favours of God, because
it accepts them as though they belonged to it and profits not
by them as it should. And to accept them in this way and
not to profit by them is to seek after them ; but God gives

---

[1] E.p. : ' . . . effect of excitement and overpowering delight, which
makes ready and prepares [the soul] to give its free and loving consent to
good.' It omits the rest of the paragraph as in the text and continues :
' But although these outward visions and feelings be of God, if the soul
make much account of them and endeavour to desire to accept them,
there follow six inconveniences. The first . . .'

[2] E.p. : ' that the perfection of guidance through faith.'

[3] A here repeats the phrase above : ' because it sets . . . least
important.'

them not that the soul may seek after them ;[1] nor should the soul take upon itself to believe that they are of God.[2]

Sixthly, a readiness to accept them opens the door to the devil that he may deceive the soul by other things like to them, which he very well knows how to dissimulate and disguise, so that they may appear to be good ; for, as the Apostle says, he can transform himself into an angel of light.[3] Of this we shall treat hereafter, by the Divine favour, in our third book, in the chapter upon spiritual gluttony.[4]

8. It is always[5] well, then, that the soul should reject these things with closed eyes whencesoever they come. For, unless it does so, it will prepare the way for those things that come from the devil, and will give him such influence that, not only will his visions come in place of God's, but his visions will begin to increase, and those of God to cease, in such manner that the devil will have all the power and God will have none. So it has happened[6] to many uncautious and ignorant souls, who rely on these things to such an extent that many of them have found it hard to return to God in purity of faith ; and many have been unable to return,[7] so securely has the devil rooted himself in them ; for which reason it is well to reject and deny them all.[8] For, by the rejection of evil visions, the errors of the devil are avoided, and by the rejection of good visions no hindrance is offered to faith and the spirit receives the fruit of them. And just as, when the soul allows them entrance, God begins to withhold them because the soul is becoming attached to them and is not profiting by them as it should, while the devil insinuates and increases his own visions, where he finds occasion and cause for them ;[9] just so, when the soul is resigned, or even opposed,[10]

---

[1] E.p. endeavours to bring out the sense more clearly here : ' is to seek after them and to rest in them, and God gives them not for this.'

[2] S. John of the Cross means that the soul should not rely upon its own judgement in such matters but upon some discreet and learned director. [3] 2 Corinthians xi, 14.

[4] Only Alc. and e.p. have this sentence. The ' third book ' must be the *Dark Night* (I, vi). [5] Alc. alone has ' always.'

[6] E.p. abbreviates : ' that his visions will come in place of the others, as has happened . . .'

[7] E.p. : ' have not returned.' This is more exact, since the backslider has always the *power* to return, if he so wills.

[8] E.p. : ' and fear them all.'

[9] A, B, e.p. : ' because the soul gives occasion for them and makes room for them.' [10] E.p. : ' resigned, and has no attachment.'

to them, the devil begins to desist, since he sees that he is working it no harm ; and contrariwise God begins to increase and magnify[1] His favours in a soul that is so humble and detached, making it ruler over[2] many things, even as He made the servant who was faithful in small things.

9. In these favours, if the soul be faithful and humble,[3] the Lord will not cease until He has raised it from one step to another, even to Divine union and transformation. For Our Lord continues to prove the soul and to raise it ever higher, so that He first gives it things that are very unpretentious and exterior and in the order of sense,[4] in conformity with the smallness of its capacity ; to the end that, when it behaves as it should, and receives these first morsels with moderation for its strength and sustenance, He may grant it further and better food. If, then, the soul conquer the devil upon the first step, it will pass to the second ; and if upon the second likewise, it will pass to the third ; and so onward, through all seven mansions,[5] which are the seven steps of love, until the Spouse shall bring it to the cellar of wine of His perfect charity.

10. Happy the soul that can fight against that beast of the Apocalypse,[6] which has seven heads, set over against these seven steps of love, and which makes war therewith against each one, and strives therewith against the soul in each of these mansions, wherein the soul is being exercised and is mounting step by step in the love of God. And undoubtedly if it strive faithfully against each of these heads, and gain the victory, it will deserve to pass from one step to another, and from one mansion to another, even unto the last, leaving the beast vanquished after destroying its seven heads, wherewith it made so furious a war upon it. So furious is this war that S. John says in that place[7] that it was given unto the beast to make war against the saints and to be able to overcome them upon each one of these steps of love, arraying against each one many weapons and munitions of war. And it is therefore greatly to be lamented that many who engage in this spiritual battle against the beast do

---

[1] E.p. omits : ' and magnify.'
[2] [*Lit.*, ' making it over.'] E.p. has : ' setting it and placing it over.'
[3] [*Lit.*, ' and retired.']
[4] E.p. : ' so that He rather visits it first according to sense.'
[5] [The phrase is suggestive of S. Teresa, but the Spanish word is not *moradas*, but *mansiones*.]
[6] [Revelation xiii, 1.]   [7] [*Ibid.*, 7.]

not even destroy its first head by denying themselves the sensual things of the world. And, though some destroy and cut off this head, they destroy not the second head, which is that of the visions of sense whereof we are speaking. But what is most to be lamented is that some, having destroyed not only the first and the second but even the third, which is that of the interior senses,[1] pass out of the state of meditation, and travel still farther onward, and are overcome by this spiritual[2] beast at the moment of their entering into purity of spirit, for he rises up against them once more, and even his first head comes to life again, and the last state of those souls is worse than the first, since, when they fall back, the beast brings with him seven other spirits worse than himself.[3]

11. The spiritual person, then, has to deny himself all the apprehensions, and the temporal delights,[4] that belong to the outward senses, if he will destroy the first and the second head of this beast, and enter into the first chamber of love, and the second, which is of living faith,[5] desiring neither to lay hold upon, nor to be embarrassed by, that which is given to the senses, since it is this that derogates most from faith.[6]

12. It is clear, then, that these sensual apprehensions and visions cannot be a means to union, since they bear no proportion to God ; and this was one of the reasons why Christ desired that the Magdalene and S. Thomas[7] should not touch Him. And so the devil rejoices greatly when a soul desires to receive revelations, and when he sees it inclined to them, for he has then a great occasion and opportunity to insinuate errors and to detract from the faith in so far as he can ; for, as I have said, he renders the soul that desires them very gross, and at times even leads it into many temptations and unseemly ways.

13.[8] I have written at some length of these outward apprehensions in order to give and throw rather more light on the others, whereof we have to treat shortly. There

---

[1] So e.p. The other authorities [and P. Silverio] read : ' the interior sensual senses.'   [2] Only Alc. has ' spiritual.'
[3] [S. Luke xi, 26.]   [4] E.p. : ' and the bodily delights.'
[5] E.p. : ' into the first and the second chamber of love in living faith.'
[6] E.p. : ' . . . this that is the greatest hindrance to this spiritual night of faith.'
[7] E.p. : ' that Mary Magdalene and the apostle S. Thomas.'
[8] This paragraph is not in A or B. It is given as found in Alc. ; C, D, e.p. give it with slight variants.

is so much to say on this part of my subject that I could go on
and never end.   I believe, however, that I am summarizing
it sufficiently by merely saying that the soul must take care
never to receive these apprehensions, save occasionally
on another person's advice, which should very rarely be
given, and even then it must have no desire for them.   I
think that on this part of my subject what I have said is
sufficient.[1]

CHAPTER XII

Which treats of natural imaginary apprehensions.   Describes their
nature and proves that they cannot be a proportionate means of
attainment to union with God.   Shows the harm which results
from inability to detach oneself from them.[2]

1. Before we treat of the imaginary visions which are
wont to occur supernaturally to the interior sense, which is
the imagination and the fancy, it is fitting here, so that we
may proceed in order, to treat of the natural apprehensions of this same interior bodily sense, in order that we
may proceed from the lesser to the greater, and from the
more exterior to the more interior, until we reach the most
interior[3] recollection wherein the soul is united with God ;[4]
this same order we have followed up to this point.   For
we treated first of all the detachment of the exterior senses[5]
from the natural apprehensions of objects,[6] and, in consequence, from the natural power of the desires—this was
contained in the first book, wherein we spoke of the night of
sense.   We then began to detach these same senses from[7]
supernatural exterior apprehensions (which, as we have just
shown in the last chapter, affect the exterior senses), in
order to lead the soul into the night of the spirit.

2. In this second book, the first thing that has now to be
treated is the interior bodily sense—namely, the imagination

---

[1] E.p. has : '. . . never to receive them, save in some rare case and
after close examination by a learned, spiritual and experienced person,
and even then [the soul must receive them] without any desire to do so.'
This is clearly an editorial attempt to clarify [and improve upon] the Saint's
directions.   [2] E.p. adds : ' in time.'
[3] [Or ' the intimate ' ;   but the superlative idea is clearly present.]
Alc. has : ' the last '—probably a copyist's error [' último ' for ' íntimo '].
    [4] A, B omit the rest of this paragraph and the whole of the next.
    [5] E.p. : ' the detachment of the soul.'
    [6] E.p. : ' of exterior objects.'
    [7] E.p. : '. . . began the detachment in particular from . . .

and the fancy; this we must likewise void of all the
imaginary apprehensions and forms that may belong to it
by nature, and we must prove how impossible it is that the
soul should attain to union with God until its operation cease
in them, since they cannot be the proper and proximate
means of this union.

3. It is to be known, then, that the senses whereof we
are here particularly speaking are two interior bodily
senses which are called imagination and fancy, which subserve each other in due order. For the one sense reasons,
as it were, by imagining, and the other forms the imagination, or that which is imagined, by making use of the fancy.[1]
For our purpose the discussion of the one is equivalent to
that of the other, and, for this reason, when we name them
not both, we are to be understood as speaking of either, as
we have here explained.[2] All the things, then, that these
senses can receive and fashion are known as imaginations
and fancies, which are forms that are represented to these
senses by bodily figures and images. This can happen in
two ways. The one way is supernatural, wherein represen-
tation can be made, and is made, to these senses passively,
without any effort of their own; these we call imaginary
visions, wrought after a supernatural manner, and of these
we shall speak hereafter. The other way is natural, wherein,
through the ability of the soul, these things can be actively
produced in it through its operation,[3] beneath forms, figures
and images. And thus to these two faculties belongs meditation, which is a discursive action wrought by means of
images, forms and figures that are produced and imagined by
the said senses, as when we imagine Christ crucified, or bound
to the column, or at another of the stations; or when we
imagine God seated upon a throne with great majesty; or when
we consider and imagine glory to be like a most beauteous
light, etc.; or when we imagine all kinds of other things,
whether Divine or human, that can belong to the imagination. All these imaginings[4] must be cast out from the soul,
which will remain in darkness as far as this sense is concerned,

---

[1] [*Lit.*, 'by fancying.'] E.p.: 'For in the one there is something of
reasoning, though it is imperfect and is [wrought] imperfectly, and the
other forms the image, which is the imagination.'

[2] E.p. adds: 'that what we say of the one is understood likewise of
the other and that we are speaking of both indifferently.'

[3] E.p.: 'The other way is natural, when through its operation these
things can be actively produced.'

[4] A, B: 'All these apprehensions.'

that it may attain to Divine union ; for they can bear no
proportion to proximate means of union with God, any more
than can the bodily imaginings, which serve as object to the
five exterior senses.

4. The reason of this is that the imagination cannot
fashion or imagine anything whatsoever beyond that which
it has experienced through its exterior senses—namely, that
which it has seen with the eyes, or heard with the ears, etc.
At most it can only compose likenesses of those things that it
has seen or heard or felt, which are of no more consequence
than[1] those which have been received by the senses aforementioned, nor are they even of as much consequence. For,
although one imagines palaces of pearls and mountains of
gold, through having seen gold and pearls, all this is in truth
less[2] than the essence of a little gold or of a single pearl,
although in the imagination it be greater in quantity and
beauty.[3] And since no created things, as has already been
said, can bear any proportion to the Being of God, it follows
that nothing that is imagined in their likeness can serve as
proximate means to union with Him, but, as we say, quite
the contrary.[4]

5. Wherefore those that imagine God beneath any of
these figures, or as a great fire or brightness, or in any other
such form, and think that anything like this will be like to
Him, are very far from approaching Him. For, although
these considerations and forms and manners of meditation
are necessary to beginners, in order that they may gradually
feed and enkindle their souls with love by means of sense, as
we shall say hereafter, and although they thus serve them as
remote means to union with God, through which a soul
has commonly to pass in order to reach the goal and abode
of spiritual repose, yet they must merely pass through
them, and not remain ever in them, for in such a manner
they would never reach their goal, which does not resemble
these remote means, neither has aught to do with them.
The stairs of a staircase have naught to do with the top of it
and the room to which it leads, yet are means to the reaching
of both ; and if the climber left not behind the stairs below
him until there were no more to climb, but desired to

---

[1] E.p. : ' which are of no greater excellence than . . .
[2] E.p. has ' no more ' for ' less.'
[3] E.p. : ' although in the imagination it may have the order and trace
of beauty.'   [4] E.p. omits : ' but . . . contrary.'

remain upon any one of them, he would never reach the top of them nor would he mount to the pleasant[1] and peaceful room which is the goal. And just so the soul that is to attain in this life to the union of that supreme repose and blessing, by means of all these stairs of meditations, forms and ideas, must pass through them and have done with them,[2] since they have no resemblance and bear no proportion to the goal to which they lead, which is God.   Wherefore S. Paul says in the Acts of the Apostles : *Non debemus æstimare, auro, vel argento, aut lapidi sculpturæ artis, et cogitationis hominis, divinum esse similem.*[3] Which signifies : We ought not to think of the Godhead by likening Him to gold or to silver, neither to stone that is formed by art, nor to aught that a man can form with his imagination.

6. Great, therefore, is the error of many[4] spiritual persons who have practised approaching God by means of images and forms and meditations, as befits beginners.   God would now lead them on to[5] further spiritual blessings, which are interior and invisible, by taking from them the pleasure and sweetness of discursive meditation ; but they cannot, or dare not, or know not how to detach themselves from those palpable methods to which they have grown accustomed.   They continually labour to retain them, desiring to proceed, as before, by the way of consideration and meditation upon forms, for they think that it must be so with them always.   They labour greatly to this end and find little sweetness or none ; rather the aridity and weariness and disquiet of their souls are increased and grow, in proportion as they labour for that earlier sweetness.   They cannot find this in that earlier manner, for the soul no longer enjoys that food of sense, as we have said ; it needs not this but another food, which is more delicate, more interior and partaking less of the nature of sense ; it consists not in labouring with the imagination, but in setting the soul at rest, and allowing it to remain in its quiet and repose, which is more spiritual.   For, the farther the soul progresses in spirituality, the more it ceases from the operation of the faculties in particular acts, for it becomes more and more occupied in one act that is general and pure ; and thus the faculties

---

[1] [*Lit.*, ' the level '—i.e., by contrast with the steep stairs.]
[2] E.p. omits : ' and have done with them.'
[3] Acts xvii, 29.   [4] E.p. : ' of certain.'
[5] [The verb, *recoger*, of which the derived noun is translated ' recollection,' has more accurately the meaning of ' gather,' ' take inwards.']

that were journeying to a place whither the soul has arrived
cease to work, even as the feet stop and cease to move when
their journey is over. For if all were motion, one would never
arrive, and if all were means, where or when would come
the fruition of the end and goal ?

7. It is piteous, then, to see many a one who,[1] though
his soul would fain tarry in this peace and rest of interior
quiet, where it is filled with the peace and refreshment of
God, takes from it its tranquillity, and leads it away to the
most exterior things, and would make it return and retrace
the ground it has already traversed, to no purpose,[2] and
abandon the end and goal wherein it is already reposing for
the means which led it to that repose,[3] which are meditations.
This comes not to pass without great reluctance and repugnance of the soul, which would fain be in that peace that it
understands not,[4] as in its proper place ; even as one who
has arrived, with great labour, and is now resting, suffers pain
if they make him return to his labour. And, as such souls
know not the mystery of this new experience, the idea comes
to them that they are being idle and doing nothing ; and
thus they allow not themselves to be quiet, but endeavour
to meditate and reason. Hence they are filled[5] with aridity
and affliction, because they seek to find sweetness where it is
no longer to be found ; we may even say of them that the
more they strive the less they profit,[6] for, the more they
persist after this manner, the worse is the state wherein they
find themselves, because their soul is drawn farther away
from spiritual peace ; and this is to leave the greater for
the less, and to retrace the road already traversed, and to
seek to do that which has been done.[7]

8. To such as these the advice must be given to learn to
abide attentively and wait lovingly upon God in that state
of quiet, and to pay no heed either to imagination or to its
working ; for here, as we say, the faculties are at rest, and
are working, not actively, but passively, by receiving that

---

[1] [Lit., ' to see that there are many who.'] E.p. omits ' many who,'
making the subject of the sentence an unspecified ' they.'

[2] E.p. omits : ' to no purpose.'

[3] [P. Silverio prints ' a Él '—' to Him ' ; but he now agrees with me
that ' a él '—' to it,' i.e., the repose just mentioned—is the correct reading.]

[4] E.p. omits : ' that it understands not.'

[5] A, B : ' Hence comes it that they are filled ' [using a stronger word
for ' filled ' with the sense of ' stuffed,' ' swollen '].

[6] E.p. : ' the more they freeze, the more they bind ' [a popular saying].

[7] Alc. omits : ' and to . . . been done,' probably only by an oversight.

which God works in them ; and, if they work at times, it is
not with violence[1] or with carefully elaborated meditation,
but with sweetness of love, moved less by the ability of the
soul itself than by God, as will be explained hereafter. But
let this now suffice to show how fitting and necessary it is for
those who aim at making further progress to be able to
detach themselves from all these methods and manners and
works of the imagination at the time and season when the
profit of the state which they have reached demands and
requires it.

9. And, that it may be understood how this is to be, and
at what season, we shall give in the chapter following[2] certain
signs which the spiritual person will see in himself and
whereby he may know at what time and season he may
freely avail himself of the goal mentioned above, and may
cease from journeying by means of meditation and the work
of the imagination.

CHAPTER XIII

*Wherein are set down the signs which the spiritual person will find
in himself and whereby he may know at what season it behoves
him to leave meditation and reasoning and pass to the state of
contemplation.[3]*

1. In order that there may be no confusion in this instruction it will be meet in this chapter to explain at what
time and season it behoves the spiritual person to lay aside
the task of discursive meditation as carried on through the
imaginations and forms and figures above mentioned, in
order that he may lay them aside neither sooner nor later
than when the Spirit[4] bids him ; for, although it is meet for
him to lay them aside at the proper time in order that he
may journey to God and not be hindered by them, it is no
less needful for him not to lay aside the said imaginative
meditation before the proper time lest he should turn

---

[1] E.p. : ' . . . . and work not, save in that simple and sweet loving
attentiveness ; and if at times they work more [than this] it is not with
violence . . .' The reading in the text is that of Alc.

[2] Only Alc. and e.p. have : ' in the chapter following.'

[3] E.p. : ' Sets down the signs which the spiritual person may recognize
in himself, in order that he may begin to strip the understanding of the
imaginary forms and reasonings of meditation.'

[4] [The MSS. and editions, including P. Silverio, have ' spirit,' but
P. Silverio agrees with me that the correct reading is ' Spirit.']

backward. For, although the apprehensions of these faculties serve not as proximate means of union to the proficient, they serve nevertheless as remote means to beginners in order to dispose and habituate[1] the spirit to spirituality by means of sense, and in order to void the sense, in the meantime, of all the other low forms and images, temporal, worldly and natural. We shall therefore here give certain signs and examples which the spiritual person will find in himself, whereby he may know if it is meet for him to lay them aside or not at this season.[2]

2. The first sign is his realization that he can no longer meditate or reason[3] with his imagination, neither can take pleasure therein as he was wont to do aforetime ; he rather finds aridity in that which aforetime was wont to attract his senses and to bring him sweetness. But, for as long as he finds sweetness in meditation,[4] and is able to reason, he should not abandon this, save when his soul is led into the peace and quietness[5] which is described under the third head.

[1] A, B : ' and habilitate.'
[2] A, B add here : ' The signs which the spiritual person will observe in himself for laying aside discursive meditation are three.' Alc., C, D add none of these words. E.p. adds only : ' which [signs] are three.'
[3] A, e.p. : ' or work.'
[4] Alc. [and P. Silverio] : ' as he extracts sweetness from meditation.'
[5] E.p. omits : ' and quietness.' The Saint's description of this first sign at which a soul should pass from meditation to contemplation was denounced as disagreeing with Catholic doctrine, particularly the phrase : ' that he can no longer meditate or reason with his imagination, neither can take pleasure therein as he was wont to do aforetime.' This language, however, is common to mystics and theologians, not excluding S. Thomas (2ª 2æ, q. 180, a. 6) and Suárez (De Oratione, Bk. II, Chap. x), as is proved, with eloquence and erudition, by P. Basilio Ponce de León and the Elucidatio, in their refutations of the Saint's critics. All agree that, in the act of contemplation of which S. John of the Cross here speaks, the understanding must be stripped of forms and species of the imagination and that the reasonings and reflections of meditation must be set aside. This is to be understood, both of the contemplation that transcends all human methods, and also of that which is practised according to these human methods with the ordinary aid of grace. But there is this important difference, that those who enjoy the first kind of contemplation set aside all intellectual reasoning as well as processes of the fancy and the imagination, whereas, for the second kind, reasoning prior to the act of contemplation is normally necessary, though it ceases at the act of contemplation, and there is then substituted for it simple and loving intuition of eternal truth. It should be clearly understood that this is not of habitual occurrence in the contemplative soul, but occurs only during the act of contemplation, which is commonly of short duration. S. Teresa makes this clear in Chap. xxvii of her Life, and treats this same doctrinal question in many other parts of her works—e.g., Life, Chaps. x, xii ; Way of Perfection, Chap. xxvi ; Mansions, IV, Chap. iii, etc.

3. The second sign is a realization that he has no desire to fix his meditation or his sense upon other particular objects, exterior or interior. I do not mean that the imagination neither comes nor goes (for it is wont to move freely even at times of great recollection), but that the soul has no pleasure in fixing it of set purpose upon other objects.

4. The third and surest sign is that the soul takes pleasure in being alone, and waits with loving attentiveness upon God, without making any particular meditation, in inward peace and quietness and rest, and without acts and exercises of the faculties—memory, understanding and will--at least, without discursive acts, that is, without passing from one thing to another ; the soul is alone, with an attentiveness and a knowledge, general and loving, as we said, but without any particular understanding, and adverting not to what it is contemplating.[1]

5. These three signs, at least, the spiritual person must see in himself, all together, before he can venture with security to abandon the state of meditation and sense,[2] and to enter that of contemplation and spirit.

6. And it suffices not for a man to have the first alone without the second, for it might be that the reason for his being unable to imagine and meditate upon the things of God, as he did aforetime, was his being distracted and careless ;[3] for the which cause he must observe in himself the second likewise, which is the loss of inclination or desire to think upon other things ; for, when the inability to fix the imagination and sense upon the things of God proceeds from distraction or lukewarmness, the soul then has the desire and inclination to fix it upon other and different things, which lead it thence altogether. Neither does it suffice that he should observe in himself the first and second signs, if he observe not likewise, together with these, the third ; for, although he observe his inability to reason and think upon the things of God, and likewise his distaste for thinking upon other and different things, this might proceed from melancholy or from some other kind of humour in the brain or the heart, which

---

[1] Only Alc., B, C, D have : ' and adverting . . . it is contemplating.'

[2] E.p. omits : ' and sense.' Since sense plays so great a part in meditation, S. John of the Cross places it in contradistinction to contemplation, which, the more nearly it attains perfection, becomes the more lofty and spiritual and the more completely freed from the bonds of nature.   Cf. *Elucidatio*, Pt. II, Chap. iii, p. 180.

[3] A, B, C : ' and not recollected.'

habitually produces a certain absorption and suspension of the senses, causing the soul to think not at all, nor to desire or be inclined to think, but rather to remain in that pleasant condition of wonder. Against this must be set the third sign, which is loving attentiveness and knowledge, in peace, etc., as we have said.

7. It is true, however, that, when this condition first begins, this loving knowledge is hardly realized, and that for two reasons. First, this loving knowledge is apt at the beginning to be very subtle and delicate, and almost imperceptible to the senses. Secondly, when the soul has been accustomed to that other exercise of meditation, which is wholly[1] perceptible, it cannot realize, or is hardly conscious of, this other new and imperceptible condition, which is purely spiritual; especially when, not understanding it, the soul allows not itself to rest in it, but strives after the former, which is more readily realized; so that, abundant though the loving interior peace may be, the soul has no opportunity of experiencing and enjoying it. But the more accustomed the soul grows to this,[2] by allowing itself to rest, the more it will grow therein and become conscious of that loving general knowledge of God, in which it has greater enjoyment than in aught else, since this knowledge causes it peace, rest, pleasure and delight without labour.

8. And, to the end that what has been said may be the clearer, we shall give, in this chapter following, the causes and reasons why the three signs aforementioned appear to be necessary for the soul that is journeying to pure spirit.[3]

CHAPTER XIV

Wherein is proved the fitness of these signs, and the reason is given why that which has been said about them is necessary to progress.

1. With respect to the first sign whereof we are speaking —that is to say, that the spiritual person who would enter upon the spiritual road[4] (which is that of contemplation) must leave the way of imagination and of meditation through

---

[1] E.p.: 'which is more.'
[2] A, e.p.: 'becomes prepared for this.'
[3] [*Lit.*, 'appear to be necessary in order to journey to spirit.'] E.p.: 'in order to guide the spirit.' [4] E.p.: 'spiritual life.'

sense, when he takes no more pleasure therein and is unable to reason—there are two reasons why this should be done, which may almost be comprised in one. The first is, that in one way the soul has received all the spiritual good which it would be able to derive from the things of God by the way of meditation and reasoning, the sign whereof is that it can no longer meditate or reason as before,[1] and finds no new sweetness or pleasure therein as it found before, because up to that time it had not progressed[2] as far as the spirituality which was in store for it ; for, as a rule, whensoever the soul receives some spiritual blessing, it receives it with pleasure, at least in spirit, in that means whereby it receives it and profits by it ; otherwise it is astonishing if it profits by it, or finds in the cause of it that help and that sweetness which it finds when it receives it.[3] For this is in agreement with the saying of philosophers, *Quod sapit, nutrit.* That is : That which is palatable nourishes and fattens. Wherefore holy Job said : *Numquid poterit comedi insulsum, quod non est sale conditum ?*[4] Can that which is unsavoury perchance be eaten when it is not seasoned with salt ? It is for this cause that the soul is unable to meditate or reason as before : the little pleasure which the spirit finds therein and the little profit which it gains.

2. The second reason is that the soul at this season has now both the substance and the habit of the spirit of meditation. For it must be known that the end of reasoning and meditation on the things of God is to gain some knowledge and love of God, and each time that the soul gains this through meditation,[5] it is an act ; and just as many acts, of whatever kind, end by forming a habit in the soul, just so, many of these acts of loving knowledge which the soul has been making one after another from time to time come through repetition to be so continuous in it that they become habitual. This end God is wont also to effect in many souls without the intervention of these acts[6] (or at least without many such acts having preceded it), by setting them at once in contemplation.[7] And thus that which aforetime the soul was gaining gradually through its labour of meditation upon particular facts

---

[1] E.p. : ' as it was wont to do before.'
[2] E.p. : ' . . . pleasure therein as before, because before this it had not progressed . . .'   [3] E.p. omits: ' or finds . . . receives it.'
[4] Job vi, 6.   [5] E.p. omits: ' through meditation.'
[6] E.p. : ' This God is wont to do likewise without the intervention of these acts of meditation.'   [7] A adds : ' and love.'

has now through practice, as we have been saying, become
converted and changed into a habit and substance of loving
knowledge, of a general kind, and not distinct or particular
as before.   Wherefore, when it gives itself to prayer, the soul
is now like one to whom water has been brought, so that he
drinks peacefully without labour, and is no longer forced to
draw the water through the aqueducts of past meditations
and forms and figures.[1]   So that, as soon as the soul comes
before God, it makes an act of knowledge, confused, loving,
passive and tranquil, wherein it drinks of wisdom and love
and delight.

3. And it is for this cause that the soul feels great weariness
and distaste, when, although it is in this condition of tranquillity, men try to make it meditate and labour in particular
acts of knowledge.   For it is like a child, which, while receiving the milk that has been collected and brought together
for it in the breast, is taken from the breast and forced to try
to gain and collect food with the diligence of its own squeez-
ing and handling.   Or it is like one who has removed the
rind from a fruit, and is tasting the substance of the fruit, but
is now forced to cease doing this and to try to begin removing
the said[2] rind, which has been removed already.   He finds
no rind to remove, and yet he is unable to enjoy the substance
of the fruit which he already had in his hand ; herein he is
like to one who leaves a prize which he holds for another
which he holds not.

4. And many act thus who begin to enter this state ; they
think that the whole business consists in a continual reasoning
and learning to understand particular things by means of
images and forms, which are to the spirit as rind.   When
they find not these in that substantial and loving quiet
wherein their soul desires to remain, and wherein it understands nothing clearly, they think that they are going astray
and wasting time, and they begin once more to seek the rind
of their imaginings and reasonings,[3] but find it not, because
it has already been removed.   And thus they cannot enjoy
the substance or succeed in their meditation, and they
become troubled by the thought that they are turning backward and are losing themselves.   They are indeed losing
themselves,[4] though not in the way they think, for they

---

[1] [Cf. the simile of the Waters in S. Teresa, *Life*, Chap. xi.]
[2] E.p. : ' the same.'   [3] A : ' the rind of reasoning.'
[4] E.p. : ' And they are indeed doing so.'

are becoming lost to their own senses and to their first manner of perception ;[1] and this means the gain of that spirituality which is being given them. The less they understand, however, the farther they penetrate into the night of the spirit, whereof we are treating in this book, through the which night they must pass in order to be united with God, in a union that transcends all knowledge.

5. With respect to the second sign, there is little to say, for it is clear that at this season the soul cannot possibly take pleasure in other and different objects of the imagination, which are of the world, since, as we have said, and for the reasons already mentioned, it has no pleasure in those which are most like to it—namely, those of God. Only, as has been noted above, the imaginative faculty in this state of recollection is in the habit of coming and going and varying of its own accord ; but neither according to the pleasure nor at the will of the soul, which is troubled thereby, because its peace and joy are disturbed.

6. Nor do I think it necessary to say anything here concerning the fitness and necessity of the third sign whereby the soul may know if it is to leave the meditation aforementioned, which is a knowledge of God or an attentiveness to Him, both general and loving. For something has been said of this in treating of the first sign, and we shall treat of it again hereafter, when we speak in its proper place of this confused and general knowledge, which will come after our discussion of all the particular apprehensions of the understanding. But we will speak[2] of one reason alone by which it may clearly be seen how, when the contemplative has to turn aside from the way of meditation and reasoning, he needs this general and loving attentiveness or knowledge of God. The reason is that, if the soul at that time had not this knowledge of God or this realization of His presence, the result would be that it would do nothing and have nothing ; for, having turned aside from meditation (by means whereof the soul has been reasoning with its faculties of sense), and being still without contemplation, which is the general knowledge whereof we are speaking,[3] wherein the soul has exerted its spiritual faculties[4]—namely, memory, under-

---

[1] A, B, e.p. add : ' and understanding.'
[2] E.p.: ' . . . now speak.'   [3] B: ' whereof we were speaking.'
[4] B: ' . . . the soul has present spiritual faculties.' [The difference in the Spanish between this reading and that of the text is very slight and might be due to a careless copyist.]

standing and will—these being united i
which is already wrought and received i
would of necessity be without any exerci
God, since the soul can neither work nor
has been worked in it, save only by way of these
of faculty,[3] that of sense and that of spirit. For, as we have
said, by means of the faculties of sense it can reason and
search out and gain knowledge of things and by means of
the spiritual faculties it can have fruition of the knowledge[4]
which it has already received in these faculties aforementioned, though the faculties themselves take no part
herein.[5]

7. And thus the difference between the operation of
these two faculties in the soul is like the difference between
working and enjoying the fruit of work which has been done ;
or like that between the labour of journeying and the rest
and quiet which comes from arrival at the goal ; or, again,
like that between preparing a meal and partaking and tasting
of it, when it has been both prepared and masticated, without
having any of the labour of cooking it , or it is like the difference between receiving something and profiting by that
which has been received.[6] Now if the soul be occupied
neither with respect to the operation[7] of the faculties of sense,
which is meditation and reasoning, nor with respect to that
which has already been received and effected in the spiritual
faculties, which is[8] the contemplation and knowledge whereof
we have spoken, it will have no occupation, but will be
wholly idle, and there would be no way in which it could be
said to be employed. This knowledge, then, is needful for
the abandonment of the way of meditation and reasoning.

8. But here it must be made clear that this general knowledge whereof we are speaking is at times so subtle and
delicate, particularly when it is most pure and simple and
perfect, most spiritual and most interior, that, although the

---

[1] E.p. omits : ' the soul ' ; [as a result, the clause may be interpreted
impersonally, but the general sense is the same].
[2] E.p. : ' nor continue in.'   [3] A, B : ' of these two faculties.'
[4] E.p. : ' the object of the knowledge.'
[5] E.p. adds : ' with labour, search or reasoning.'
[6] So Alc., but the other codices and e.p. place this last clause after ' has
been done ' above.
[7] E.p. omits ' and masticated ' and the following clauses, continuing
thus : ' . . . [been prepared]. And if it be not occupied in any kind of
exercise, whether it have respect to the operation . . .'
[8] E.p. omits : ' in the spiritual faculties, which is.'

soul be occupied therein, it can neither realize it nor perceive it. This is most frequently the case when we can say that' it is in itself most clear, perfect and simple ; and this comes to pass when it penetrates a soul that is unusually pure and far removed from other particular kinds of knowledge and intelligence, which the understanding or the senses might fasten upon. Such a soul, since it no longer has those things wherein the understanding and the senses have the habit and custom of occupying themselves, is not conscious of them, inasmuch as it has not its accustomed powers of sense. And it is for this reason that, when this knowledge is purest and simplest and most perfect, the understanding is least conscious of it and thinks of it as most obscure. And similarly, in contrary wise, when it[1] is in itself least pure and simple in the understanding, it seems to the understanding to be clearest and of the greatest importance, since it is clothed in, mingled with or involved in certain intelligible forms which the understanding or the senses[2] may seize upon.

9. This will be clearly understood by the following comparison. If we consider a ray of sunlight which enters through a window, we see that, the more the said ray is charged with atoms and particles of matter, the more palpable, visible and bright it appears to the eye of sense ;[3] yet it is clear that the ray is in itself least pure, clear, simple and perfect at that time, since it is full of so many particles and atoms. And we see likewise that, when it is purest and freest from those particles and atoms, the least palpable and the darkest[4] does it appear to the material eye ; and the purer it is, the darker and less apprehensible it appears to it. And if the ray were completely pure and free from all these atoms and particles, even from the minutest specks of dust, it would appear completely dark and invisible[5] to the eye, since everything that could be seen would be lacking to it—namely, the objects of sight. For the eye would find no objects whereon to rest, since light is no proper[6] object of vision, but the means whereby that which is visible is seen ; so that, if there be no visible objects wherein the sun's ray or any light can

---

[1] E.p.: 'when this knowledge.'   [2] E.p. omits: 'or the senses.'
[3] [Lit., 'to the sight of sense.'] E.p. has : 'to the sense of sight.'
[4] E.p. : 'and the least pure.'
[5] All the MSS. have 'incomprehensible.' E.p. reads 'imperceptible' and [says P. Silverio] rightly so.
[6] A, B : 'no visible.' E.p. : 'since simple and pure light is not as properly an object of sight as a means whereby,' etc.

be reflected, nothing will be seen. Wherefore, if the ray of
light entered by one window and went out by another,
without meeting anything that has material form, it would
not[1] be seen at all ; yet, notwithstanding, that ray of light
would be purer and clearer in itself than when it was more
clearly seen and perceived through being full of visible
objects.

10. The same thing happens in the realm of spiritual light
with respect to the sight of the soul, which is the understanding, and which this general[2] and supernatural knowledge and light whereof we are speaking strikes so purely and
simply. So completely is it detached and removed from all
intelligible forms, which are objects[3] of the understanding,
that it is neither perceived nor observed. Rather, at times
(that is, when it is purest), it becomes darkness, because it
withdraws the understanding from its accustomed lights,
from forms and from fancies, and then the darkness is more
clearly perceived and realized. But, when this Divine light
strikes the soul with less force, it neither perceives darkness
nor observes light, nor apprehends aught that it knows,[4]
from whatever source ; hence at times the soul remains as
it were in a great forgetfulness, so that it knows not where it
has been[5] or what it has done, nor is it aware of the passage
of time. Wherefore it may happen, and does happen, that
many hours are spent in this forgetfulness, and, when the
soul returns to itself, it believes that less than a moment has
passed, or no time at all.[6]

11. The cause of this forgetfulness is the purity and
simplicity of this knowledge which occupies the soul[7] and
simplifies, purifies and cleanses it from all apprehensions
and forms of the senses and of the memory, through which
it acted when it was conscious of time,[8] and thus leaves it in
forgetfulness and without consciousness of time.[9] This
prayer, therefore, seems to the soul extremely brief, although,
as we say,[10] it may last for a long period ; for the soul has

---

[1] E.p. : ' it seems that it would not.'
[2] E.p. omits : ' general and.'
[3] E.p. : ' which are proportionate objects.'
[4] E.p. begins this sentence thus : ' At other times, too, this Divine
light strikes the soul with such force that it neither perceives darkness,
nor observes light, neither does it seem to apprehend aught that it knows.'
[5] A, B : ' has entered.'   [6] E.p. omits : ' or no time at all.'
[7] E.p. adds: ' being itself clear and pure.'   [8] [Lit., ' acted in time.']
[9] [Lit., ' without time.']   E.p. : ' without noticing differences of time.'
[10] E.p. : ' as I have said.'

been united[1] in pure intelligence, which belongs not to time ; and this is the brief prayer which is said to pierce the heavens, because it is brief and because it belongs not to time.[2] And it pierces the heavens, because the soul is united in heavenly intelligence ; and when the soul awakens, this knowledge leaves in it the effects which it created in it without its being conscious of them, which effects are the lifting up of the spirit to the heavenly intelligence, and its withdrawal and abstraction from all things and forms and figures and memories thereof. It is this that David describes as having happened to him when he returned to himself out of this same forgetfulness, saying : *Vigilavi, et factus sum sicut passer solitarius in tecto.*[3] Which signifies : I have watched and I have become like the lonely bird[4] on the house-top. He uses the word ' lonely,' meaning that he was withdrawn and abstracted from all things. And by the house-top he means the elevation of the spirit on high ; and thus the soul remains as though ignorant of all things, for it knows God only, without knowing how. Wherefore the Bride declares in the Songs that among the effects which that sleep and forgetfulness of hers produced was this unknowing. She says that she came down to the garden, saying : *Nescivi.*[5] That is : I knew not whence. Although, as we have said, the soul in this state of knowledge believes itself to be doing nothing, and to be entirely unoccupied, because it is working neither

---

[1] E.p. omits ' united.'

[2] E.p. modifies these lines thus : ' . . . it has been in pure intelligence, which is the brief prayer that is said to pierce the heavens. Because it is brief and because the soul is not conscious or observant of time.' P. José de Jesús María comments thus upon this passage : ' In contemplation the soul withdraws itself from the seashore, and entirely loses sight of land, in order to whelm itself in that vast sea and impenetrable abyss of the Divine Essence ; hiding itself in the region of time, it enters within the most extensive limits of eternity. For the pure and simple intelligence whereinto the soul is brought in this contemplation, as was pointed out by the ancient Dionysius (*Myst. Theol.*, Chap. ii), and by our own Father, is not subject to time. For, as S. Thomas says (Pt. I, q. 118, a. 3, *et alibi*), the soul is a spiritual substance, which is above time and superior to the movements of the heavens, to which it is only subject because of the body. And therefore it seems that, when the soul withdraws from the body, and from all created things, and by means of pure intelligence whelms itself in eternal things, it recovers its natural dominion and rises above time, if not according to substance, at least according to its most perfect being ; for the noblest and most perfect being of the soul resides rather in its acts than in its faculties. Wherefore S. Gregory said (*Morals*, Bk. VIII) : " The Saints enter eternity even in this life, beholding the eternity of God." '   [3] Psalm ci, 8 [A.V., cii, 7].

[4] [The Spanish *pájaro*, ' bird,' is derived from *passer*, ' sparrow.']

[5] Canticles vi, 12.

with the senses nor with the faculties, it should realize that it is not wasting time.[1] For, although the harmony of the faculties of the soul may cease, its intelligence is as we have said. For this cause the Bride, who was wise, answered this question herself in the Songs, saying : *Ego dormio et cor meum vigilat.*[2] As though she were to say : Although I sleep with respect to my natural self, ceasing to labour, my heart waketh, being supernaturally lifted up in supernatural knowledge.[3]

12. But it must be realized that this knowledge is not to be supposed to cause this forgetfulness of necessity, in order for the soul to be in the state that we are here describing ; for this happens only when[4] God suspends in the soul the exercise of all its faculties, both natural and spiritual, which happens very seldom,[5] for this knowledge does not always fill the soul entirely. It is sufficient for the purpose, in the case which we are treating, that the understanding should be withdrawn from all particular knowledge, whether temporal or spiritual, and that the will should not desire to think with respect to either, as we have said, for this is a sign that the soul is occupied.[6] And it must be taken as an indication

---

[1] E.p. adds : ' nor is useless.'   [2] Canticles v, 2.

[3] The words which conclude this paragraph in the edition of 1630 (' The sign by which we may know if the soul is occupied in this secret intelligence is if it is seen to have no pleasure in thinking of aught, whether high or low ') are not found either in the Codices or in e.p. When S. John of the Cross uses the words ' cessation,' ' idleness ' [*ocio.*, Lat. *otium*], ' quiet,' ' annihilation,' ' sleep ' (of the faculties), etc., he does not hold, with the Illuminists, that the understanding and will in the act of contemplation are completely passive, and that the contemplative is therefore impeccable, although he commit the grossest sins. The faculties, according to S. John of the Cross, are active even in the highest contemplation ; the understanding is attentive to God and the will is loving Him. They are not working, it is true, in the way which is usual and natural with them—that is, by reason and imagination—but supernaturally, through the unction of the Holy Spirit, which they receive passively, without any effort of their own. It is in this sense that such words as those quoted above are both expressively and appropriately used by the Saint, for what is done without labour and effort may better be described by images of passivity than by those of activity. Further, the soul is unaware that its faculties are working in this sublime contemplation, though they undoubtedly do work.

S. John of the Cross, philosopher as well as mystic, would not deny the vital and intrinsic activity of the understanding and the will in contemplation. His reasoning is supported by P. José de Jesús María (*Apologia Mística de la Contemplación Divina*, Chap. ix) [quoted at length by P. Silverio, *Obras*, etc., Vol. II, p. 130, note].

[4] E.p. : ' when in a particular way.'

[5] E.p. abbreviates : ' . . . suspends the soul, and this happens very seldom.'   [6] E.p. omits : ' for this . . . occupied.'

that this is so[1] when this knowledge is applied and communicated to the understanding only, which sometimes happens
when the soul is unable to observe it. For, when it is communicated to the will also, which happens almost invariably,
the soul does not cease to understand in the very least degree,
if it will reflect hereon, that it is employed and occupied in
this knowledge, inasmuch as it is conscious of a sweetness of
love therein, without particular knowledge or understanding
of that which it loves. It is for this reason that this knowledge
is described as general and loving ; for, just as it is so in the
understanding, being communicated to it obscurely, even so
is it in the will, sweetness and love being communicated to
it confusedly, so that it cannot have a distinct knowledge of
the object of its love.

13. Let this suffice now to explain how meet it is that the
soul should be occupied in this knowledge, so that it may
turn aside from the way of spiritual[2] meditation, and be sure
that, although it seem to be doing nothing, it is well occupied,
if it discern within itself these signs. It will also be realized,
from the comparison which we have made, that if this light
presents itself to the understanding in a more comprehensible
and palpable manner, as the sun's ray presents itself to the
eye when it is full of particles, the soul must not therefore
consider it purer, brighter and more sublime. It is clear
that, as Aristotle and the theologians say,[3] the higher and
more sublime is the Divine light, the darker is it to our understanding.

14. Of this Divine knowledge there is much to say, concerning both itself and the effects which it produces upon
contemplatives. All this we reserve for its proper place,[4]
for, although we have spoken of it here, there would be no
reason for having done so at such length, save our desire not[5]
to leave this doctrine rather more confused than it is already,
for I confess it is certainly very much so. Not only is it a
matter which is seldom treated in this way, either verbally
or in writing, being in itself so extraordinary and obscure,
but my rude style and lack of knowledge make it more so.
Further, since I have misgivings as to my ability to explain
it, I believe I often write at too great length and go beyond

[1] E.p. : ' it must be taken to show that the soul is in this forgetfulness.'
[2] E.p. omits ' spiritual.'   [3] A, B omit : ' as . . . say.'
[4] In spite of this promise, the Saint does not return to this subject at
such length as his language here would suggest.
[5] Alc., B omit ' not,' which, however, is required by the context.

the limits which are necessary for that part of the doctrine which I am treating.[1] Herein I confess that I sometimes err purposely ; for that which is not explicable by one kind of reason will perhaps be better understood by another, or by others yet ; and I believe, too, that in this way I am shedding more light upon that which is to be said hereafter.

15. Wherefore it seems well to me also, before completing this part of my treatise, to set down a reply[2] to one question which may arise with respect to the continuance of this knowledge, and this shall be briefly treated[3] in the chapter following.

CHAPTER XV

Wherein is explained how it is sometimes well for progressives who are beginning to enter upon this general knowledge of contemplation to profit by natural[4] meditation and the work of the natural faculties.

1. With regard to what has been said, there might be raised one question—if progressives (that is, those whom God is beginning to bring into this supernatural knowledge of contemplation whereof we have spoken) must never again, because of this that they are beginning to experience, return to the way of meditation and argument and natural forms. To this the answer is that it is not to be understood that such as are beginning to experience this loving knowledge must never again, as a general rule, try to return to meditation ;[5] for, when they are first gaining in proficiency, the habit of contemplation is not yet so perfect that whensoever they wish they can give themselves to the act thereof, nor, in the same way, have they reached a point so far beyond meditation that they cannot occasionally meditate and reason in a natural way,[6] as they were wont, using the figures and the steps that they were wont to use,[7] and finding something new in them. Rather, in these early stages, when, by means of the indications already given, they are able to see that the

---

[1] A, B omit the rest of this paragraph.
[2] E.p. : ' not to fail to reply.'
[3] E.p. : ' and this I will do.'   [4] E.p. omits ' natural.'
[5] E.p. : ' this loving and simple knowledge must never meditate again or strive to do so.'
[6] Alc. alone has : ' in a natural way.'
[7] E.p. omits : ' using . . . to use.'

soul is not occupied in that repose and knowledge, they will need to make use of meditation until they come by its means to acquire the habit which we have described and which in some ways is perfect. This will come about when, as soon as they seek to meditate, they experience this knowledge and peace, and find themselves unable to meditate and no longer desirous of doing so, as we have said. For until they reach this stage, which is that of the proficient in this exercise, they use sometimes the one and sometimes the other, at different seasons.[1]

2. The soul, then, will frequently find itself in this loving or peaceful state of waiting upon God[2] without in any way exercising its faculties—that is, with respect to particular acts —and without working actively at all, but only receiving.[3] In order to reach this state, it will frequently need to make use of meditation, quietly and in moderation ; but, when once the soul is brought into this other state,[4] it acts not at all with its faculties,[5] as we have already said. It would be truer to say that understanding and sweetness work in it and are wrought within it, than that the soul itself works at all, save only by waiting upon God and by loving Him without desiring to feel or to see anything.[6] Then God communicates Himself to it passively, even as to one who has his eyes open, so that light is communicated to him passively, without his doing more than keep them open.[7] And this reception of light which is infused supernaturally is passive understanding. We say that the soul works not at all, not because it understands not, but because it understands things not discovered by its own industry and receives only that which is given to it, as comes to pass in the illuminations and enlightenments or inspirations of God.[8]

3. Although in this condition the will freely receives this general and confused knowledge of God, it is needful, in

---

[1] E.p. omits : ' at different seasons.'
[2] [Lit., ' in this loving or peaceful presence,' the original of the latter word having also the sense of ' attendance.']
[3] The words : ' that is . . . only receiving ' occur only in Alc. E.p substitutes : ' as has been explained.'
[4] E.p. : ' when once this [other state] is attained.'
[5] E.p. : ' the soul neither reflects nor labours with its faculties.'
[6] E.p. adds : ' save only to let itself be carried away by God.'
[7] E.p. abbreviates : ' . . . his eyes open, light is communicated.'
[8] This passage (' And this reception . . . inspirations of God ') together with the first clause of the next paragraph (' Although . . . knowledge of God ') is only found in Alc.

order that it may receive this Divine light more simply and
abundantly, only that it should take care not to interpose
other lights which are more palpable, whether forms or ideas
or figures having to do with any kind of meditation ; for
none of these things is similar to that pure and serene light.
Wherefore if at this time the will desires to understand and
consider particular things, however spiritual they be, this
would obstruct the pure and simple general light[1] of the
spirit, by setting those clouds in the way ; even as a man
might set something before his eyes which impeded his vision
and kept from him both the light and the sight of things in
front of him.

4. Hence it clearly follows that, when the soul has completely purified and voided itself of all forms and images that
can be apprehended, it will remain in this pure and simple
light, being transformed therein into a state of perfection.
For, though this light never fails in the soul,[2] it is not infused
into it because of the creature forms and veils wherewith the
soul is veiled and embarrassed ; but if these impediments
and these veils were wholly removed (as will be said hereafter), the soul would then find itself in a condition of pure
detachment and poverty of spirit, and, being simple and
pure, would be transformed into simple and pure Wisdom,
which is the Son of God. For the enamoured soul finds that
that which is natural has failed it, and it is then imbued with
that which is Divine, both naturally and supernaturally,
so that there may be no vacuum in its nature.[3]

5. When the spiritual person cannot meditate, let him
learn to be still in God, fixing his loving attention upon Him,
in the calm of his understanding, although he may think
himself to be doing nothing. For thus, little by little and
very quickly, Divine calm and peace will be infused into his
soul, together with a wondrous and sublime knowledge of
God, enfolded in Divine love. And let him not meddle with
forms, meditations and imaginings, or with any kind of
reflection, lest the soul be disturbed, and brought out of
its contentment and peace, which can only result in its
experiencing distaste and repugnance. And if, as we have

---

[1] E.p. : ' this would obstruct the subtle and simple light.'
[2] E.p. reads : ' For though this light is always made ready to be communicated to the soul.'
[3] C, D : ' for no vacuum occurs in nature.' E.p. : ' it is imbued with
that which is Divine, supernaturally, for God leaves no vacuum without
filling it.'

said, such a person has scruples that he is doing nothing, let him note that he is doing no small thing by pacifying the soul and bringing it into calm and peace, unaccompanied by any act or desire, for it is this that Our Lord asks of us, through David, saying : *Vacate, et videte quoniam ego sum Deus*.[1] As though he had said : Learn to be empty of all things (that is to say, inwardly and outwardly[2]) and you will see[3] that I am God.

CHAPTER XVI

Which treats of the imaginary apprehensions that are supernaturally represented in the fancy. Describes how they cannot serve the soul as a proximate means to union with God.

1. Now that we have treated of the apprehensions which the soul can receive within itself by natural means, and whereon the fancy and the imagination can work by means of reflection,[4] it will be suitable to treat here of the supernatural apprehensions, which are called imaginary visions, which likewise belong to these senses, since they come within the category of images, forms and figures, exactly[5] as do the natural apprehensions.

2. It must be understood that beneath this term ' imaginary vision ' we purpose to include all things which can be represented to the imagination supernaturally by means of any image, form, figure and species.[6] For all the apprehensions and species which, through all the five bodily senses, are represented to the soul, and dwell within it, after a natural manner, may likewise occur in the soul after a supernatural manner, and be represented to it without any assistance of the outward senses. For this sense of fancy, together with memory, is, as it were, an archive and storehouse of the understanding, wherein are received all forms and images that can be understood ; and thus the soul has them within itself as it were in a mirror, having received them by means of the five senses, or, as we say, supernaturally ; and thus it

---

[1] Psalm xlv, 11 [A.V., xlvi, 10].

[2] E.p. omits : ' and outwardly.'   [3] E.p. adds : ' with delight.'

[4] E.p. : ' and whereon it can work by means of the fancy and the imagination.'   [5] E.p. omits ' exactly.'

[6] E.p. here adds a passage which is found in none of the Codices : ' and this with species that are very perfect and that [have power to] make representations and cause influences more vivid and more perfect than [any brought about] through the connatural order of the senses.'

presents them to the understanding, whereupon the understanding considers them and judges them. And not only so,
but the soul can also prepare and imagine others like to those
with which it is acquainted.[1]

3. It must be understood, then, that, even as the five
outward senses represent[2] the images and species of their
objects to these inward senses, even so, supernaturally, as we
say, without using the outward senses, both God and the devil
can represent[3] the same images and species, of much more
beautiful[4] and perfect kinds. Wherefore, beneath these
images, God often represents many things to the soul, and
teaches it much wisdom; this is continually seen in the
Scriptures, as where Isaiah saw God in His glory[5] beneath
the smoke which covered the Temple, and beneath the seraphim who covered their faces and their feet with their
wings;[6] and as Jeremiah saw the wand that was watching,[7]
and Daniel a multitude of visions,[8] etc. And the devil, too,
strives to deceive the soul with his visions, which in appearance are good, as may be seen in the Book of the Kings,
when he deceived all the prophets of Ahab, presenting to
their imaginations the horns wherewith he said the king was
to destroy the Assyrians, which was a lie.[9] Even such were
the visions of Pilate's wife, warning him not to condemn
Christ;[10] and there are many other places where it is seen
how, in this mirror of the fancy and the imagination,[11] these
imaginary visions come more frequently to proficients than
do outward and bodily visions. These, as we say, differ not
in their nature (i.e., as images and species) from those which
enter by the outward senses; but, with respect to the effect
which they produce, and in the degree of their perfection,
there is a great difference; for imaginary visions are subtler
and produce a deeper impression upon the soul, inasmuch as
they are supernatural, and are also more interior than the
exterior supernatural visions. Nevertheless, it is true that
some of these exterior bodily visions may produce a deeper

---

[1] E.p. abbreviates : '. . . and images which it has to make intelligible,
and thus the understanding beholds and judges them.'
[2] E.p. : ' propose and represent.'
[3] E.p. has (for ' both . . . represent ') : ' may be represented.'
[4] E.p. : ' more vivid.'
[5] E.p. : ' as when God showed His glory.'
[6] Isaiah vi, 4.　　　　　[7] Jeremiah i, 11.　　　　[8] Daniel vii, 10.
[9] 3 Kings xxii, 11 [A.V., 1 Kings xxii, 11].
[10] [S. Matthew xxvii, 19.]
[11] E.p. has only : ' and [in] many other places.'

impression ; the communication, after all, is as God wills. We are speaking, however, merely of that which belongs to their nature, as being more spiritual.

4. It is to these senses of imagination and fancy that the devil habitually betakes himself with his wiles—now natural, now supernatural ;[1] for they are the door and entrance to the soul, and here, as we have said,[2] the understanding comes to take up or set down its goods, as it were in a harbour or in a storehouse where it keeps its provisions. And for this reason it is hither that both God and the devil always come with their jewels of supernatural forms and images,[3] to offer them to the understanding ; although God does not make use of this means alone to instruct the soul, but dwells within it in substance, and is able to do this by Himself and by other methods.

5. There is no need for me to stop here in order to give instruction concerning the signs by which it may be known which visions are of God and which not, and which are of one kind and which of another ; for this is not my intention, which is only to instruct the understanding herein, that it may not be hindered or impeded as to union with Divine Wisdom by the good visions, neither may be deceived by those which are false.

6. I say, then, that with regard to all these imaginary visions and apprehensions and to all other forms and species whatsoever, which present themselves beneath some particular kind of knowledge or image or form, whether they be false and come from the devil or are recognized as true and coming from God, the understanding must not be embarrassed by them or feed upon them, neither must the soul desire to receive them or to have them,[4] lest it should no longer be detached, free, pure and simple, without any mode or manner, as is required for union.[5]

7. The reason of this is that all these forms which we have already mentioned are always represented, in the apprehension of the soul, as we have said, beneath certain modes and

---

[1] E.p. omits : ' now natural, now supernatural.' The Saint employs this last word, in this passage, with the sense of ' preternatural.' Only God can surpass the bounds of nature, but the devil can act in such a way that he appears to be doing so, counterfeiting miracles, and so forth.

[2] E.p. omits : ' as we have said.'

[3] E.p. : ' come hither with images and forms.'

[4] E.p. : ' or to set its foot upon them.'

[5] E.p. : ' for Divine union.'

manners which are limited ; and that the Wisdom of God, wherein the understanding is to be united, has no mode or manner, neither is it contained within any particular or distinct kind of intelligence or limit, because it is wholly pure and simple. And as, in order that these two extremes may be united—namely, the soul and Divine Wisdom—it will be necessary for them to attain to agreement, by the mediation of a certain mutual resemblance,[1] hence it follows that the soul must be pure and simple, neither bounded by, nor attached to, any particular kind of intelligence, nor modified by any limitation of form, species and image. As God comes not within[2] any image or form, neither is contained within any particular kind of intelligence, so the soul, in order to reach God,[3] must likewise come within no distinct form or kind of intelligence.

8. And that there is no form or likeness in God is clearly declared by the Holy Spirit in Deuteronomy, where He says ; *Vocem verborum ejus audistis, et formam penitus non vidistis.*[4] Which signifies : Ye heard the voice of His words, and ye saw in God no form whatsoever. But he says that there was darkness there, and clouds and thick darkness, which are the confused and dark knowledge whereof we have spoken, wherein the soul is united with God. And afterwards he says further : *Non vidistis aliquam similitudinem in die, qua locutus est vobis Dominus in Horeb de medio ignis.* That is : Ye saw no likeness in God upon the day when He spoke to you on Mount Horeb, out of the midst of the fire.[5]

9. And that the soul cannot reach the height of God,[6] even as far as is possible in this life, by means of any form and figure, is declared likewise by the same Holy Spirit in Numbers, where God reproves Aaron and Miriam, the brother and sister of Moses, because they murmured against him, and, desiring to convey to them the loftiness of the state of union and friendship with Him wherein He had placed him, said : *Si quis inter vos fuerit Propheta Domini, in visione apparebo ei, vel per somnium loquar ad illum. At non talis servus meus Moyses, qui in omni domo mea fidelissimus est : ore enim ad os loquor ei, et palam, et non per ænigmata, et figuras Dominum videt.*[7]

---

[1] E.p. : ' by a certain manner of resemblance.'
[2] E.p. : ' As God is not contained within.'
[3] [*Lit.*, ' to come within God.'] E.p. : ' to be united with God.'
[4] Deuteronomy iv, 12.   [5] Deuteronomy iv, 15.
[6] E.p. : ' cannot reach the summit of union with God.'
[7] Numbers xii, 6–8.

Which signifies : If there be any prophet of the Lord among you, I will appear to him in some vision or form, or I will speak with him in his dreams ; but there is none like My servant Moses, who is the most faithful in all My house, and I speak with him mouth to mouth, and he sees not God by comparisons, similitudes and figures. Herein He says clearly that, in this lofty state of union whereof we are speaking, God is not communicated to the soul by means of any disguise of imaginary vision or similitude or form, neither can He be so communicated ; but mouth to mouth— that is, in the naked and pure essence of God, which is the mouth of God in love, with the naked and pure essence of the soul,[1] which is the mouth of the soul in love of God.

10. Wherefore, in order to come to this essential union of love in God,[2] the soul must have a care not to lean upon[3] imaginary visions, nor upon forms or figures or particular objects of the understanding ; for these cannot serve it as a proportionate and proximate means to such an end ; rather they would disturb it, and for this reason the soul must renounce them and strive not to have them. For if in any circumstance they were to be received and prized, it would be for the sake of the profit which true visions bring to the soul and the good effect which they produce upon it. But it is not necessary, for this reason, to receive them ;[4] rather, it is well always to reject them for the soul's profit. For these imaginary visions, like the outward bodily visions whereof we have spoken, do the soul good by communicating to it intelligence or love or sweetness. But for this effect to be produced by them in the soul it is not necessary that it should desire to receive them ; for, as has also been said above at this very time[5] when they are present to the imagination, they produce in the soul and infuse into it intelligence and love, or sweetness, or whatever effect God wills them to produce. And not only do they produce this joint effect, but principally, although not simultaneously, they produce

---

[1] The editions of 1630 and later dates add here : ' by means of the will.' But these words are found neither in e.p. nor in the Codices.

[2] E.p. : ' to this so perfect union of God.'

[3] [The progressive form is used in the Spanish : ' not to go (or ' be ') leaning upon.']

[4] A, B : ' but it is necessary, for this reason, not to admit them.' The second part of this sentence shows that the reading of the text, which is that of both Alc. and e.p., is the correct one.

[5] E.p. omits : ' at this very time.'

their effect in the soul passively,[1] without its being able to hinder this effect, even if it so desired,[2] just as it was also powerless to acquire it, although it had been able previously to prepare itself.[3] For, even as the window is powerless[4] to impede the ray of sunlight which strikes it, but, when it is prepared by being cleansed, receives its light passively without any diligence or labour on its own part, even so the soul, although against its will,[5] cannot fail to receive in itself the influences and communications of those figures, however much it may desire to resist them.[6] For the will that is negatively inclined cannot, if coupled with loving and humble resignation, resist supernatural infusions ; it can resist only the impurity and imperfections of the soul,[7] even as the stains upon a window impede the brightness of the sunlight.[8]

11. From this it is clearly seen that, however much the soul may be detached, in its will and affection, from the apprehensions of the stains of those forms, images and figures wherein are clothed[9] the spiritual communications which we have described, not only is it not deprived of these communications and blessings which they cause within it, but it is much better prepared to receive them with greater abundance, clearness, liberty of spirit and simplicity, when all these apprehensions are set on one side, which are, as it were, curtains and veils covering the spiritual thing[10] that is behind them. And thus, if the soul desire to feed upon them, they occupy spirit and sense in such a way that the spirit cannot communicate itself simply and freely ; for, while they are still occupied with the outer rind, it is clear that the understanding is not free to receive the substance.[11] Wherefore, if the soul at that time desires to receive these

[1] E.p. : ' And thus the soul receives their quickening effect passively.'
[2] E.p. omits : ' even though it so desired.'
[3] E.p. substitutes for this last clause : ' notwithstanding its having laboured previously to prepare itself.'
[4] E.p. : ' To some extent it resembles a window, which is powerless . . .'
[5] E.p. omits : ' although against its will.'
[6] E.p. omits : ' however . . . resist them.'
[7] E.p. : ' For the will cannot resist supernatural infusions, although without doubt the impurity and imperfections of the soul are an obstruction.'   [8] [Lit., ' impede the brightness.']
[9] E.p. : ' from the stains of the apprehensions, images and figures wherein are clothed.' A : ' from the apprehensions and the stains of them and the affections wherein are clothed.' B : ' from the apprehensions of the stains of those forms and figures wherein are clothed.'   [10] E.p. : ' the more spiritual thing.'
[11] This is the reading of e.p. A, B [followed by P. Silverio] read : ' to receive those forms.' Alc. reads merely : ' to receive.'

forms and to set store by them, it would be embarrassing
itself, and contenting itself with the least important part of
them—namely, all that it can apprehend and know of them,
which is the form and image and particular object of the
understanding in question.   The most important part of
them, which is the spiritual part that is infused into the soul,
it can neither apprehend nor understand, nor even know what
it is, nor be able to express it, since it is pure spirit.   What it
knows of them, as we say, is only the least part of what is in
them, according to its manner of understanding—namely, the
forms which come through sense.   For this reason I say that
what it cannot understand or imagine is communicated to it by
these visions, passively, without any effort of its own to understand and without its even knowing how to make such an effort.

12. Wherefore the eyes of the soul must ever be withdrawn from all these apprehensions which it can see and
understand distinctly, which are communicated through
sense, and do not produce the sure foundation of faith, and
must be set upon that which it sees not, and which belongs
not to sense, but to spirit, which can be expressed by no
figure of sense ; and it is this which leads the soul to union in
faith, which is the true medium, as has been said.   And thus
these visions will profit the soul substantially, in respect of
faith, when it is able completely to renounce the sensible
and intelligible part[1] of them, and to make good use of the
purpose for which God gives them to the soul, by casting
them aside ; for, as we said of corporeal visions, God
gives them not so that the soul may desire to have them and
to set its affection upon them.

13. But there arises here this question : If it is true that
God gives supernatural visions to the soul, but not so that
it may desire to have them or be attached to them or set
store by them, why does He give them at all, since by their
means the soul may fall into many errors and perils, or at the
least may find in them such hindrances to further progress as are here described, especially since God can come
to the soul, and communicate to it, spiritually and substantially, that which He communicates to it through sense, by
means of the sensible forms and visions aforementioned ?

14. We shall answer this question in the following chapter :[2] it involves an important instruction, most necessary, as

---

[1] E.p. : ' the particular intelligible part.'
[2] The words ' in the following chapter ' occur in Alc. and e.p. only.

I see it, both to spiritual persons and to those who teach them. For herein is taught the way and purpose of God with respect to these visions, which many know not, so that they cannot rule themselves or guide themselves to union, neither can they guide others to union, through these visions. For they think that, just because they know them to be true and to come from God, it is well to receive them and to trust them,[1] not realizing that the soul will become attached to them, cling to them and be hindered by them, as it will by things of the world, if it know not how to renounce these as well as those. And thus they think it well to receive one kind of vision and to reject another, causing themselves, and the souls under their care, great labour and peril in discerning between the truth and the falsehood of these visions. But God commands them not to undertake this labour, nor does He desire that sincere and simple souls should be led into this conflict and danger ; for they have safe and sound instruction, which is that of the faith, wherein they can go forward.

15. This, however, cannot be unless they close their eyes to all that is of particular and clear perception and sense. For, although S. Peter was quite certain of that vision of glory which he saw in Christ at the Transfiguration, yet, after having described it in his second canonical Epistle, he desired not that it should be taken for an important and sure testimony, but rather directed his hearers to faith, saying : *Et habemus firmiorem propheticum sermonem: cui benefacitis attendentes, quasi lucernæ lucenti in caliginoso loco, donec dies elucescat.*[2] Which signifies : And we have a surer testimony than this vision of Tabor—namely, the sayings and words of the prophets who bear testimony to Christ, whereunto ye must indeed cling, as to a candle which gives light in a dark place. If we will think upon this comparison, we shall find therein the instruction which we are giving. For, in telling us to look to the faith whereof the prophets spake, as to a candle that shineth in a dark place, he is bidding us remain in the darkness, with our eyes closed to all these other lights ; and telling us that in this darkness, faith alone, which likewise is dark, will be the light to which we shall cling ; for if we desire to cling to these other bright lights—namely, to distinct objects of the understanding—we cease to cling to that dark light, which is faith, and we no longer have that

---

[1] E.p. : ' it is well to lean on them and cleave to them.'
[2] 2 Peter i, 19.

light in the dark place whereof S. Peter speaks. This place, which here signifies the understanding, which is the candle-stick wherein this candle of faith is set, must be dark until the day when the clear vision of God dawns upon it in the life to come, or, in this life, until the day of transformation and union with God to which the soul is journeying.[1]

CHAPTER XVII

Wherein is described the purpose and manner of God in His com-munication of spiritual blessings to the soul by means of the senses. Herein is answered the question which has been referred to.

1. There is much to be said concerning the purpose of God, and concerning the manner wherein He gives these visions in order to raise up the soul from its lowly estate to His Divine union. All spiritual books deal with this and in this treatise of ours the method which we are pursuing is to explain it ;[2] therefore I shall only say in this chapter as much as is necessary to answer our question, which was as follows : Since in these supernatural visions there is so much hindrance and peril to progress, as we have said, why does God, Who is most wise and desires to remove stumbling-blocks and snares from the soul, offer and communicate them to it ?

2. In order to answer this, it is well first of all to set down three fundamental points.[3] The first is from S. Paul *ad Romanos*, where he says : *Quæ autem sunt, a Deo ordinatæ sunt.*[4] Which signifies : The works that are done are ordained of God. The second is from the Holy Spirit in the Book of Wisdom, where He says : *Disponit omnia suaviter.*[5] And this is as though He had said : The wisdom of God, although it extends from one end to another—that is to say, from one extreme to another—orders all things with sweetness. The third is from the theologians, who say that *Omnia movet secundum modum eorum.* That is, God moves all things accord-ing to their nature.

3. It is clear, then, from these fundamental points, that for God to move the soul and to raise it up from the extreme

---

[1] Alc. ends the chapter with the words : ' transformation and union.' E.p. has ' with Him ' for ' with God.'
 [2] E.p. omits : ' and in this treatise . . . to explain it.'
 [3] E.p. : ' to take for granted three principles.'
 [4] Romans xiii, 1   [5] Wisdom viii, 1.

depth of its lowliness to the extreme height of His loftiness, in Divine union with Him, He must do it with order and sweetness and according to the nature of the soul itself. Then, since the order[1] whereby the soul acquires knowledge is through forms and images of created things, and the natural way wherein it acquires this knowledge and wisdom is through the senses, it follows that, for God to raise up the soul to supreme knowledge, and to do so with sweetness, He must begin to work from the lowest and extreme end of the senses of the soul, in order that He may gradually lead it,[2] according to its own nature, to the other extreme of His spiritual wisdom, which belongs not to sense.   Wherefore He first leads it onward by instructing it through forms, images and ways of sense, according to its own method of understanding, now naturally, now supernaturally, and by means of argument, to this supreme spirit of God.

4. It is for this reason that God gives the soul visions and forms, images and the other kinds of sensible and spiritual[3] intelligible knowledge ; not that God would not give it spiritual wisdom[4] immediately, and all at once, if the two extremes—which are human and Divine, sense and spirit— could in the ordinary way concur and unite in one single act, without the preceding intervention of many other preparatory acts which concur among themselves in order and sweetness, and are a basis and a preparation one for another, like natural agents ; so that the first acts serve the second, the second the third, and so onward, in exactly the same way.[5] And thus God brings man to perfection according to the way of man's own nature, working from what is lowest and most exterior up to what is most interior and highest. First, then, He perfects his bodily senses, impelling him to make use of good things which are natural, perfect and exterior, such as hearing sermons and masses, looking on holy things, mortifying the palate at meals and chastening the sense of touch by penance and holy rigour. And, when these senses are to some extent prepared, He is wont to perfect them still further, by bestowing on them certain supernatural favours and gifts, in order to confirm them the more completely in

---

[1] B : ' since the method and order.' [' Method ' is the *modo* translated above as ' nature.']

. [2] E.p. : ' may gradually raise it.'

[3] E.p. omits ' spiritual.'   [4] E.p. : ' spiritual substance.'

[5] E.p. modifies : ' . . . preparation one for another ; even as with natural agents the first serve the second, the second the third, and so onward.'

that which is good, offering them certain supernatural communications, such as visions of saints and holy things, in corporeal shape, the sweetest perfumes, locutions, and exceeding great delights of touch, wherewith[1] sense is greatly confirmed in virtue and is withdrawn from a desire for evil things. And besides this the interior bodily senses, whereof we are here treating, such as imagination and fancy, He continues at the same time to perfect and habituate[2] to that which is good, by means of considerations, meditations, and reflections of a sacred kind, in all of which He is instructing the spirit. And, when these are prepared by this natural exercise, God is wont to enlighten and spiritualize them still more by means of certain supernatural visions, which are those that we are here calling imaginary ; wherein, as we have said, the spirit, at the same time, profits greatly, for both kinds of vision help to take away its grossness and gradually to reform it. And after this manner God continues to lead the soul from one step to another till it reaches the most interior of all ; not that it is always[3] necessary for Him to observe this order, and to cause the soul to advance exactly in this way, from the first step to the last ; sometimes He allows the soul to attain one stage and not another, or leads it from the more interior to the less, or effects two stages of progress together. This happens when God sees it to be meet for the soul, or when He desires to grant it His favours in this way ;[4] nevertheless His ordinary way agrees with what has been said.

5. It is in this way, then, that God instructs[5] the soul and makes it more spiritual, communicating spirituality to it first of all through outward and palpable things, adapted to sense, on account of the soul's feebleness and incapacity, so that, by means of the outer husk of those things of sense which in themselves are good, the spirit may make[6] particular acts and receive so many morsels of spiritual communication that it may form a habit in things spiritual, and may acquire actual and substantial spirituality,[7] in complete

---

[1] E.p.: locutions, together with pure and singular sweetness, wherewith . . .'   [2] A, B : ' and habilitate.'

[3] E.p. omits ' always.'

[4] E.p.: ' . . . and not another, when He sees that it so befits the soul and desires to grant it favours in this way.'

[5] [The verb is progressive (' is instructing ').] A, B add : ' ordinarily.'

[6] [This verb also is progressive : ' may go (on) making.']

[7] E.p.: ' may acquire the most substantial of the spirit ' [i.e., the most substantial spirituality].

abstraction from every sense. To this, as we have said, the soul cannot attain except very gradually, and in its own way—that is, by means of sense—to which it has ever been attached.[1] And thus, in proportion as the spirit attains more nearly to converse with God, it becomes more completely detached and emptied of the ways of sense, which are those of imaginary meditation and reflection. Wherefore, when the soul attains perfectly to spiritual converse with God, it must of necessity have been voided of all that relates to God and yet comes under the head of sense. Even so, the more closely a thing is attracted to one extreme, the farther it becomes removed and withdrawn[2] from the other; and, when it rests perfectly in the one, it will also have withdrawn itself perfectly from the other. Wherefore there is a commonly quoted spiritual adage which says: *Gustato spiritu, desipit omnis caro.* Which signifies: After the taste and sweetness of the spirit have been received, everything carnal is insipid.[3] That is: No profit or enjoyment is afforded by all the ways of the flesh[4] wherein is included all communication of sense with the spiritual. And this is clear: for, if it is spirit, it has no more to do with sense; and, if sense can comprehend it, it is no longer pure spirit. For, the more that natural apprehension and sense can know of it, the less it has of spirit and of the supernatural, as has been explained above.

6. The spirit[5] that is now perfect, therefore, pays no heed to sense, nor does it receive anything through sense, nor makes any important use of it, neither needs to do so, in its relations with God, as it did aforetime when it had not grown in spirit. It is this that is signified by that passage from S. Paul's Epistle to the Corinthians which says: *Cum essem parvulus, loquebar ut parvulus, sapiebam ut parvulus, cogitabam ut parvulus. Quando autem factus sum vir, evacuavi, quæ erant parvuli.*[6] This signifies: When I was a child, I spake as a child, I knew as a child, I thought as a child; but, when I became a man, I put away[7] childish things. We have already explained how the things of sense, and the knowledge that spirit can derive[8] from them, are the business of a child.

---

[1] A, B add: 'and has come near.'
[2] E.p.: 'and rejected.' [All the verbs in these last two clauses are in the progressive form.]   [3] E.p.: 'is tasteless.'
[4] E.p.: 'all the tastes or roads of sense.'
[5] E.p.: 'the spiritual man.'   [6] 1 Corinthians xiii, 11.
[7] [*Lit.*, 'I emptied.'] A, B, e.p.: 'I voided.'
[8] E.p.: 'that can be derived.'

Thus, if the soul should desire to cling to them for ever, and not to throw them aside, it would never cease to be a child ; it would speak ever of God as a child, and would know of God as a child, and would think of God as a child ;[1] for, clinging to the outer husk of sense, which is the child, it would never attain to the substance of the spirit, which is the perfect man. And thus the soul must not desire to receive the said revelations in order to continue in growth, even though God offer them to it, just as the child must leave the breast in order to accustom its palate to strong meat, which is more substantial.

7. You will say, then, that when the soul is immature, it must take these things, and that, when it is grown, it must abandon them ; even as an infant must take the breast, in order to nourish itself, until it is older and can leave it. I answer that, with respect to meditation and natural reflection by means of which the soul begins to seek God, it is true that it must not leave the breast of sense in order to continue its nourishment until the time and season to leave it have arrived, and this comes when God brings the soul into a more spiritual communion, which is contemplation, concerning which we gave instruction in the eleventh chapter of this book.[2] But, when it is a question of imaginary visions, or other supernatural apprehensions, which can enter the senses without the co-operation of man's free will, I say that at no time and season must it receive them,[3] whether the soul be in the state of perfection, or whether in a state less perfect—not even though they come from God. And this for two reasons. The first is that, as we have said, He produces His effect in the soul,[4] without its being a hindrance to it, although it can and may hinder vision, which comes to pass frequently ;[5] and consequently that effect[6] which was to be produced in the soul is communicated to it much more substantially, although not after that manner. For, as we said likewise, the soul cannot hinder the blessings that God desires to communicate to it, neither is it in the soul to do so,

[1] A, B : ' it would never cease to be a child ; it would ever speak of, know and think of God as a child.'

[2] In reality, this instruction is given in Chap. xiii.

[3] E.p. : ' must it seek them, or remain for long in them.'

[4] So Alc. The other MSS. and e.p. read : ' . . . that, as we have said, they produce their effect passively in the soul.'

[5] E.p. has : ' although it do something to hinder the manner of the vision,' and omits : ' which comes to pass frequently.'

[6] E.p. : ' that second effect.'

save through some imperfection and attachment ; and there is neither imperfection nor attachment in renouncing these things with humility and misgiving.[1] The second reason is that the soul may free itself from the peril and labour inherent in discerning between evil visions and good, and in deciding whether an angel be of light or of darkness. In this labour there is no advantage ; it only wastes the soul's time, and hinders it, and becomes to it an occasion of many imperfections and of failure to make progress. The soul concerns not itself, in such a case, with what is important, nor disencumbers itself of trifles in the shape of apprehensions and perceptions of some particular kind, according as has been said in the discussion of corporeal visions ; and of these more will be said hereafter.

8. And let it be believed that, if Our Lord were not to lead the soul after the soul's own manner, as we say here, He would never communicate to it the abundance of His spirit by these aqueducts, which are so narrow—these forms and figures and particular perceptions—by means whereof He gives the soul enlightenment by crumbs. For this cause David says : *Mittit crystallum suam sicut buccellas.*[2] Which is as much as to say : He sent His wisdom to the souls as in morsels.[3] It is greatly to be lamented that, though the soul has infinite capacity,[4] it should be given its food by morsels of sense, by reason of the small degree of its spirituality and its incapacitation by sense. S. Paul was also grieved by this lack of preparation and this incapability of men for receiving the Spirit, when he wrote to the Corinthians, saying : I, brethren, when I came to you, could not speak to you as to spiritual persons, but as to carnal ; for ye could not receive it, neither can ye now. *Tamquam parvulis in Christo lac potum vobis dedi, non escam.*[5] That is : I have given you milk to drink, as to infants in Christ, and not solid food to eat.[6]

9. It now remains, then, to be pointed out that the soul must not allow its eyes to rest upon that outer husk—namely,

---

[1] E.p. omits the passage : ' For, as we said likewise . . . and attachment,' and substitutes for ' and there . . . misgiving ' : ' For, in renouncing these things with humility and misgiving, there is neither imperfection nor attachment.' The Codices end the sentence at the word ' misgiving,' but e.p. continues : ' but rather disinterestedness and emptiness, which is the best preparation for union with God.'
[2] Psalm cxlvii, 17.   [3] C, D : ' as morsels.'
[4] E.p. : ' has as it were infinite capacity.' All the MSS. have the reading of the text.   [5] 1 Corinthians iii, 1–2.
[6] E.p. omits : ' in Christ ' and ' to eat.'

figures and objects set before it supernaturally.   These may
be presented to the exterior senses, as are locutions and
words audible to the ear ; or, to the eyes, visions of saints,
and of beauteous radiance ; or perfumes to the sense of
smell ; or tastes and sweetnesses to the palate ; or other
delights to the touch, which are wont to proceed from the
spirit, a thing that very commonly happens to spiritual
persons.[1]   Or the soul may have to avert its eyes from
visions of interior sense, such as imaginary[2] visions, all of
which it must renounce entirely.   It must set its eyes only
upon the spirituality which they produce, striving to preserve
it in its good works and to practise that which is for the due[3]
service of God, paying no heed to those representations nor
desiring any pleasure of sense.   And in this way the soul takes
from these things only that which God intends and wills—
namely, the spirit of devotion—for He gives them for no
no other important purpose ; and it casts aside that which
He would not give if these gifts could be received in the
spirit without it,[4] as we have said—namely, the exercise and
apprehension of sense.

CHAPTER XVIII

*Which treats of the harm that certain spiritual masters may do to
souls when they direct them not by a good method with respect to
the visions aforementioned.   Describes also how these visions
may cause deception even though they be of God.*

1. In this matter of visions we cannot be as brief as we
should desire, since there is so much to say about them.
Although in substance we have said what is relevant in order
to explain to the spiritual person how he is to behave with
regard to the visions aforementioned, and to the master who
directs him, the way in which he is to deal with his disciple,[5]
yet it will not be superfluous to go into somewhat greater
detail about this doctrine, and to give more enlightenment
as to the harm which can ensue, either to spiritual souls or to
the masters who direct them, if they are over-credulous
about them, although they be of God.

[1] E.p. omits : ' a thing . . . persons.'
[2] E.p. : ' interior imaginary.'
[3] So Alc., C, D. A, B, e.p. read ' naked ' [i.e., ' pure '] for ' due.'
[4] The remainder of the sentence is omitted in Alc.
[5] A, B, e.p. add : ' concerning them.'

2. The reason which has now moved me to write at length about this is the lack of discretion, as I understand it, which I have observed in certain spiritual masters. Trusting to these supernatural apprehensions, and believing that they are good and come from God, both masters and disciples have fallen into great error and found themselves in dire straits, wherein is fulfilled the saying of Our Lord : *Si cæcus cæco ducatum præstet, ambo in foveam cadunt.*[1] Which signifies : If a blind man lead another blind man, they fall both into the ditch. And He says not ' they shall fall,' but ' they fall.' For they may fall without falling into error, since the very venturing of the one to guide the other is a going astray, and thus, they fall in this respect alone,[2] at the very least. And, first of all, there are some whose way and method with souls that experience these visions cause them to stray, or embarrass them with respect to their visions, or guide them not along the road of humility, but encourage them to fix their eyes upon them in some way (for which reason they remain without the true spirit of faith)[3] and edify them not in faith, but lead them to speak highly of those things.[4] By doing this they make them realize that they themselves set some value upon them, or[5] make great account of them, and, consequently, their disciples do the same. Thus their souls have been set upon these apprehensions, instead of being edified in faith, so that they may be empty and detached and freed from those things and can soar to the heights of dark faith. And all this arises from the terms and language which the soul observes its master to employ with respect to this ; somehow it very easily conceives a satisfaction and an esteem for it, which is not in its own control, and which averts the eyes of the soul from the abyss of faith.

3. And the reason why this is so easy must be that the soul is so greatly occupied therewith that, as these are things of sense, to which it is inclined by nature, and as it is likewise disposed to enjoy the apprehension of those distinct and sensible things, it has only to see in its confessor, or in some other person, a certain esteem and appreciation for them, and not merely will it at once conceive the same itself, but

---

[1] S. Matthew xv, 14. [2] E.p. omits ' alone.'

[3] E.p. : ' for which reason they journey not by way of the pure and perfect spirit of faith.'

[4] E.p. : ' and edify them not, neither fortify them in it [i.e., in faith], making these things of great account.'

[5] E.p. omits : ' set some value upon them, or.'

also, without its realizing the fact, its desire will become allured by them, so that it will feed upon them and will be ever more inclined toward them and will set a certain value[1] upon them. And hence arise mahy imperfections, at the very least ; for the soul is no longer as humble as before, but thinks that all this is of some importance and productive of good, and that it is itself esteemed by God, and that He is pleased and somewhat satisfied with it, which is contrary to humility. And thereupon the devil begins secretly to increase this, without the soul's realizing it, and begins to suggest ideas to it about others, as to whether they have these things or have them not, or are this or are that ; which is contrary to holy simplicity and spiritual solitude.

4. There is much more to be said about these evils, and of how such souls, unless they withdraw themselves, grow not in faith, and also of how there are other evils of the same kind which, although they be not so palpable and recognizable[2] as these, are subtler and more hateful to the Divine eyes, and which result from not living in complete detachment. Let us, however, leave this subject now,[3] until we come to treat of the vice of spiritual gluttony[4] and of the other six vices, whereof, with the help of God,[5] many things will be said, concerning these subtle and delicate stains which adhere to the spirit when its director cannot guide it in detachment.

5. Let us now say something of this manner wherein certain confessors deal with souls, and instruct them ill. And of a truth I could wish that I were able to describe it, for I realize that it is a difficult thing to explain how the spirit of the disciple grows in conformity with that of his spiritual father, in a hidden and secret way ; and this matter is so tedious that it wearies me,[6] for it seems impossible to speak of the one thing without describing the other also, as they are spiritual things, and the one corresponds with the other.

6. But it is sufficient to say here that[7] I believe, if the

---

[1] So all the MSS. E.p. alters to ' much value ' [bringing out the general sense of the passage by the change].

[2] E.p. omits : ' and recognizable.'

[3] E.p. omits ' complete ' and reads : ' We shall leave ' for ' Let us leave.'

[4] A, B omit the remainder of the paragraph.

[5] E.p. has : ' God willing.'

[6] E.p. omits : ' and this . . . wearies me.'

[7] E.p. omits this phrase. A, B have : ' And, treating of that which I promised.'

spiritual father has an inclination toward revelations of such a kind that they mean something to him,[1] or satisfy or delight his soul, it is impossible but that he will impress that delight and that aim[2] upon the spirit of his disciple, even without realizing it, unless the disciple be more advanced than he ; and, even in this case, he may well do him grievous harm if he continue therein.   For, from that inclination of the spiritual father toward such visions, and his pleasure in them, there arises a certain kind of esteem for them, of which, unless he watch it carefully, he cannot fail to communicate some indication or impression to other persons ; and if any other such person is like-minded and has a similar inclination, it is impossible, as I understand, but that there will be communicated from the one to the other a great appreciation of these things and esteem for them.

7. But let us not now go into such detail.   Let us speak of the confessor who, whether or no he be inclined toward these things, has not the prudence that he ought to have in dis-encumbering the soul and detaching the desire of his disciple from them, but begins to speak to him about these visions and devotes the greater part of his spiritual conversation to them, as we have said, giving him signs by which he may distinguish good visions from evil.   Now, although it is well to know this, there is no reason to cause the soul this labour, anxiety and peril.[3]   By paying no heed[4] to visions, and refusing to receive them, all this is prevented, and the soul acts as it should.   Nor is this all, for such confessors, when they see that their penitents are receiving visions from God, beg them to entreat God to reveal them to themselves also, or to say such and such things to them, with respect to themselves or to others, and the foolish souls[5] do so, thinking that it is lawful to desire knowledge by this means.   For they suppose that, because God is pleased to reveal or say something by supernatural means, in His own way or for His own purpose, it is lawful for them to desire Him to reveal it to them, and even to entreat Him to do so.

---

[1] E.p. : ' that they have some weight with him.'
[2] E.p. : ' that same pleasure and esteem.'
[3] E.p. adds : ' save in a case of stringent necessity, as has been said.'
[4] E.p. : ' By paying little heed.'
[5] All the MSS. have this reading, but the editor of e.p. evidently disliked this exact and expressive phrase, for he substituted ' good souls ' for it.

8. And, if it comes to pass that God reveals it at their request, they become more confident, thinking that, because God answers them, it is His will and pleasure to do so ; whereas, in truth, it is neither God's will nor His pleasure. And they frequently act or believe according to that which He has revealed to them, or according to the way wherein He has answered them ; for, as they are attached to that manner of communion with God, their will acquiesces in it and it pleases them greatly. They take a natural pleasure in their own way of thinking and naturally abide by it ; and they frequently go astray.[1] Then they see that something happens not as they had expected ; and they marvel, and then begin to doubt if the thing were of God,[2] since it happens not, and they see it not, after their own manner. At the beginning they thought two things : first, that the vision was of God, since at the beginning it agreed so well with their disposition, and their natural inclination to that kind of thing may well have been the cause of this agreement, as we have said ; and secondly that, being of God, it would turn out as they thought or expected.

9. And herein lies a great delusion, for revelations or locutions which are of God do not always turn out as men expect or as they imagine inwardly. And thus they must never be believed or trusted blindly, even though men know them to be revelations or answers or sayings of God. For, although they may in themselves be certain and true, they are not always so[3] in their causes, and according to our manner of understanding,[4] as we shall prove in the chapter following. And afterwards we shall further say and prove that, although God sometimes gives a supernatural answer to that which is asked of Him, it is not His pleasure to do so, and sometimes, although He answers, He is angered.

---

[1] E.p. abbreviates :   . . . they become more confident about other occasions and think that this manner of communion with God is His pleasure, whereas, in truth, it is neither His pleasure nor His will. And, as they are attached to that manner of communion with God, it pleases them greatly and their will acquiesces naturally in it. For, as it pleases them naturally, they are naturally inclined to their way of thinking, and they frequently go astray in what they say.'

[2] [*Lit.*, 'if it were of God.'] E.p.: 'if they were of God or no.' A: ' if it were of God or were not God [*sic*].' B : ' if it were of God or were not of God.'

[3] E. p. adds : ' of necessity.'   [4] A, B end the chapter here.

CHAPTER XIX

Wherein is expounded and proved how, although visions and locutions which come from God are true,[1] we may be deceived about them. This is proved by quotations from Divine Scripture.[2]

1. For two reasons we have said that, although visions and locutions which come from God are true, and in themselves are always certain, they are not always so with respect to ourselves. One reason is the defective way in which we understand them ; and the other, the variety of their causes.[3] In the first place, it is clear that they are not always as they seem, nor do they turn out as they appear to our manner of thinking. The reason for this is that, since God is vast and boundless, He is wont, in His prophecies, locutions and revelations, to employ ways, concepts and methods of seeing things which differ greatly from such purpose and method as can normally be understood by ourselves ; and these are the truer and the more certain the less they seem so to us. This we constantly see in the Scriptures. To many of the ancients many prophecies and locutions of God came not to pass as they expected, because they understood them after their own manner, in quite a different way, very literally. This will be clearly seen in these passages.

2. In Genesis, God said to Abraham, when He had brought him to the land of the Canaanites : *Tibi dabo terram hanc.*[4] Which signifies, I will give thee this land. And when He had said it to him many times, and Abraham was by now very old, and He had never given it to him, though He had said it to him, Abraham answered God once again and said : *Domine, unde scire possum, quod posesurus sum eam ?* That is : Lord, whereby or by what sign am I to know that I am to possess it ? Then God revealed to him that he was not to possess it in person, but that his sons would do so after four

---

[1] A, B, e.p. add : ' in themselves.'
[2] This sentence is omitted in A, B.
[3] E.p. amplifies thus : ' . . . always certain, they are not always so in our understanding. One reason is the defective way in which we understand them ; and the other is the causes and foundations of them, which are minatory, and, as it were, conditional, depending on the amendment of this or the accomplishment of that, although the locution itself seem to be of an absolute character. These two things we shall prove with a few quotations from Scripture ' [*lit.*, ' from Divine authorities '].
[4] Genesis xv, 7.

hundred years ; and Abraham then understood the promise, which was in itself most true ; for, in giving it to his sons for love of him, God was giving it to himself. And thus Abraham was deceived by the way in which he himself understood the prophecy. If he had then acted according to his own understanding of it, those that saw him die without its having been given to him might have erred greatly ; for they were not to see the time of its fulfilment. And, as they had heard him say that God would give it to him,[1] they would have been confounded and would have believed it to have been false.

3. Likewise to his grandson Jacob, when Joseph his son brought him to Egypt because of the famine in Canaan, and when he was on the road, God appeared and said : *Jacob, Jacob, noli timere, descende in Aegiptum, quia in gentem magnam faciam te ibi. Ego descendam tecum illuc. . . . Et inde adducam te revertentem.*[2] Which signifies : Jacob, fear not ; go down to Egypt, and I will go down there with thee ; and, when thou goest forth thence again, I will bring thee out and guide thee. This, as it would seem according to our own manner of understanding, was not fulfilled, for, as we know, the good old man Jacob died in Egypt and never went out thence alive. The word of God was to be fulfilled in his children, whom He brought out thence after many years, being Himself their guide upon the way. It is clear that anyone who had known of this promise made by God to Jacob would have considered it certain that Jacob, even as he had gone to Egypt alive, in his own person,[3] by the command and favour of God, would of a certainty come out thence, alive and in his own person,[4] in the same form and manner as he went there, since God had promised him a favourable return ; and such a one would have been deceived, and would have marvelled greatly, when he saw him die in Egypt, and the promise, in the sense in which he understood it, unfulfilled. And thus, while the words of God are in themselves most true, it is possible to be greatly mistaken with regard to them.

4. In the Judges, again, we read that, when all the tribes of Israel had come together to make war against the tribe of Benjamin, in order to punish a certain evil to which that tribe had been consenting, they were so certain of victory because God had appointed them a captain for the war, that,

---

[1] E.p. : ' that God had promised it to him.'
[2] Genesis xlvi, 3–4.   [3] E.p. omits : ' in his own person.'
[4] E.p. omits : ' and in his own person.'

when twenty-two thousand of their men were conquered and slain, they marvelled very greatly; and, going into the presence of God, they wept all that day, knowing not the cause of the fall, since they had understood[1] that the victory was to be theirs. And, when they enquired of God if they should give battle again or no, He answered that they should go and fight against them. This time they considered victory to bè theirs, and went out with great boldness,[2] and were conquered likewise the second time, with the loss of eighteen thousand of their men. Hereupon they were in great confusion, and knew not what to do, seeing that God had commanded them to fight and yet each time they were vanquished, though they were superior[3] to their enemies in number and strength, for the men of Benjamin were no more than twenty-five thousand and seven hundred and they were four hundred thousand. And in this way they were mistaken in their manner of understanding the words of God. His words were not deceptive, for He had not told them that they should conquer, but that they should fight; for by these defeats God wished to chastise a certain neglect and presumption of theirs, and thus to humble them. But when in the end He answered that they would conquer it was so, although they conquered only after the greatest stratagem and toil.[4]

5. In this way, and in many other ways, souls are oftentimes deceived with respect to locutions and revelations that come from God, because they interpret them according to their apparent sense[5] and literally; whereas, as has already been explained, the principal intention of God in giving these things is to express and convey the spirit that is contained in them, which is difficult to understand. And the spirit is much more pregnant in meaning than the letter, and is very extraordinary, and goes far beyond its limits. And thus, he that clings to the letter, or to a locution or to the form or figure of a vision, which can be apprehended, will needs go far astray, and will forthwith fall into great confusion and error, because he has guided himself by sense according to these visions, and not allowed the spirit to work in detachment from sense. *Littera enim occidit, spiritus autem*

---

[1] E.p.: 'understood and considered.'
[2] So Alc. A, B: 'with great courage.' E.p.: 'with great daring.'
[3] A, B, e.p.: 'were so greatly superior.'   [4] Judges xx, 12 ff.
[5] [*Lit.*, 'according to the rind.' Cf. p. 119, above.]

vivificat,[1] as S. Paul says.   That is : The letter killeth and the spirit giveth life.[2]   Wherefore in this matter of sense the letter must be set aside, and the soul must remain in darkness, in faith, which is the spirit, and this cannot be comprehended by sense.

6. For which cause, many of the children of Israel, because they understood the sayings and prophecies of the prophets very literally, and these were not fulfilled as they expected, came to make little account of them and believed them not ; so much so, that there grew up a common saying among them—almost a proverb, indeed—which turned prophets into ridicule.[3]   Of this Isaiah complains, speaking and exclaiming in the manner following : *Quem docebit Dominus scientiam ? et quem intelligere faciet auditum ? ablactatos a lacte, avulsos ab uberibus. Quia manda remanda, manda remanda, expecta reexpecta, expecta reexpecta, modicum ibi, modicum ibi. In loquela enim labii, et lingua altera loquetur ad populum istum.*[4]   This signifies : To whom shall God teach knowledge ?   And whom shall He make to understand His word and prophecy ? Only them that are already weaned from the milk and drawn from the breasts.   For all say (that is, concerning the pro-phecies[5]) : Promise and promise again ; wait and wait again ; wait and wait again ;[6] there a little, there a little ; for in the words of His lips and in another tongue will He speak to this people.   Here Isaiah shows quite clearly that these people were turning prophecies into ridicule, and that it was in mockery that they repeated this proverb : ' Wait and then wait again.'   They meant that the prophecies were never fulfilled for them, for they were wedded to the letter, which is the milk of infants, and to their own sense, which is the breasts,[7] both of which contradict the greatness of spiritual knowledge.   Wherefore he says : To whom shall He teach the wisdom of His prophecies ? And whom shall He make to understand His doctrine, save them that are already weaned from the milk of the letter and from the breasts of their own sense ?   For this reason these people understand it not, save

---

[1] 2 Corinthians iii, 6.
[2] A, B : ' The letter surely killeth, but the spirit giveth life.'
[3] Alc. alone has this last clause.
[4] Isaiah xxviii, 9–11.
[5] Only Alc., e.p. have the parenthesis.
[6] [For ' wait,' we may also read ' hope,' Spanish having one word (*esperar*) which expresses both these ideas and which is here used.]
[7] A, B omit : ' which is the breasts.'

according to this milk[1] of the husk and letter, and these
breasts of their own sense, since they say : Promise and
promise again ;[2] wait and wait again, etc.   For it is the
doctrine of the mouth of God, and not their own doctrine,
and it is in another tongue than their own, that God shall
speak to them.

7. And thus, in discussing prophecy, we have not to consider our own sense and language, knowing that the language
of God is very different from ours, and that it is spiritual
language, and very far removed from our understanding and
exceedingly difficult.   So true is this that even Jeremiah,
though a prophet of God, when he sees that the significance
of the words of God is so different from the sense commonly
attributed to them by men, is himself deceived by them and
defends the people, saying : *Heu, heu, heu, Domine Deus,
ergone decepisti populum istum et Jerusalem, dicens : Pax erit vobis ;
et ecce pervenit gladius usque ad animam ?*[3] Which signifies : Ah,
ah, ah, Lord God, hast Thou perchance deceived this people
and Jerusalem, saying ' Peace will come upon you,' and seest
Thou here that the sword reacheth unto their soul ?   For
the peace that God promised them was that which was to be
made between God and man by means of the Messiah Whom
He was to send them, whereas they understood it of temporal
peace ;   and therefore, when they suffered wars and trials,
they thought that God was deceiving them, because there
befell them the contrary of that which they expected.   And
thus they said, as Jeremiah says likewise : *Exspectavimus
pacem, et non erat bonum.*[4]   That is : We have looked for peace
and there is no boon of peace.   And thus it was impossible
for them not to be deceived, since they judged the prophecy
merely by its literal sense.[5]   For who would fail to fall into
confusion and to go astray if he confined himself to a literal
interpretation of that prophecy which David spake concerning Christ, in the seventy-first Psalm, and[6] of all that he says
therein, where he says : *Et dominabitur a mari usque ad mare ;
et a flumine usque ad terminos orbis terrarum.*[7]   That is : He shall
have dominion from one sea even to the other, and from the
river unto the ends of the earth.   And likewise in that which

---

[1] E.p. : ' but follow this milk.' [This involves only the slight variant
of *siguen* for *según*.]   [2] This phrase is repeated in Alc. only.
[3] Jeremiah iv, 10.   [4] Jeremiah viii, 15.
[5] The 1630 edition has : ' literal and grammatical sense.'
[6] E.p. : ' and in particular.'
[7] Psalm lxxi, 8 [A.V., lxxii, 8].

he says in the same place : *Liberabit pauperem a potente, et pauperem, cui non erat adjutor.*[1]   Which signifies : He shall deliver the poor man from the power of the mighty, and the poor man that had no helper.   But later it became known that Christ was born[2] in a low estate and lived in poverty and died in misery ; not only had He no dominion over the earth, in a temporal sense, while He lived, but He was subject to lowly people, until He died under the power of Pontius Pilate.   And not only did He not deliver His disciples, who were poor, from the hands of the mighty, in a temporal sense, but He allowed them to be slain and persecuted for His name's sake.

8. The fact is that these prophecies had to be understood, concerning Christ, spiritually, in which sense they were entirely true.   For Christ was not only Lord of earth alone,[3] but likewise of Heaven, since He was God ; and the poor who were to follow Him He was not only to redeem and free from the power of the devil,[4] that mighty one against whom they had no helper,[5] but He was also to make them heirs of the Kingdom of Heaven.   And thus God was speaking, in the most important sense, of Christ, and of the reward of His followers, which was an eternal kingdom and eternal liberty ; and they understood this, after their own manner, in a secondary sense, of which God takes small account, namely that of temporal dominion and temporal liberty, which in God's eyes is neither kingdom nor liberty at all. Wherefore, being blinded by the insufficiency of the letter, and not understanding its spirit and truth, they took the life of their God and Lord, even as S. Paul said in these words : *Qui enim habitabant Jerusalem, et principes ejus, hunc ignorantes et voces prophetarum, quæ per omne Sabbatum leguntur, judicantes impleverunt.*[6]   Which signifies : They that dwell in Jerusalem, and her rulers, not knowing Who He was, nor understanding the sayings of the prophets, which are read every Sabbath day, have fulfilled them by judging Him.

9. And to such a point did they carry this inability to understand the sayings of God as it behoved them, that even

---

[1] Psalm lxxi, 12 [A.V., lxxii, 12].
[2] [*Lit.,* ' Seeing Him later to be born.']
[3] A, B, e.p. : ' Lord of all the earth.'
[4] E.p. : ' from the hands and the power of the devil.' A, B : ' from the hands of the devil.'
[5] E.p. omits : ' against . . . helper.'   A, B have ' powerful ' for ' mighty.'   [6] Acts xiii, 27.

His own disciples, who had gone about with Him, were
deceived, as were those two who, after His death, were going
to the village of Emmaus, sad and disconsolate, saying :
Nos autem sperabamus quod ipse esset redempturus Israel.[1] That
is : We trusted that He should have redeemed Israel. They,
too, understood that this dominion and redemption were to
be temporal ; but Christ our Redeemer, appearing to them,
reproved them as foolish and heavy and gross[2] of heart as to
their belief in the things that the prophets had spoken.[3] And
even when He was going to Heaven, some of them were still
in that state of grossness, and asked Him, saying : *Domine, si
in tempore hoc restitues Regnum Israel.*[4] That is : Lord, tell us
if Thou wilt restore at this time the kingdom of Israel. The
Holy Spirit causes many things to be said which bear another
sense than that which men understand ; as can be seen in
that which He caused to be said by Caiaphas concerning
Christ : that it was meet that one man should die lest all the
people should perish.[5] This he said not of his own accord ;
and he said it and understood it in one sense, and the Holy
Spirit in another.[6]

10. From this it is clear that, although sayings and revelations may be of God, we cannot always have confidence in
them ; for we can very easily be greatly deceived by them
because of our manner of understanding them. For they are
all[7] an abyss and a depth of the spirit, and to try to limit
them to what we can understand concerning them, and to
what our sense can apprehend, is nothing but to attempt to
grasp the air, and to grasp some particle in it that the hand
touches : the air disappears and nothing remains.

11. The spiritual teacher must therefore strive that the
spirituality of his disciple be not cramped by attempts to
interpret all supernatural apprehensions, which are no more
than spiritual particles, lest he come to retain naught but
these, and have no spirituality at all. But let the teacher
wean his disciple from all visions and locutions, and impress
upon him the necessity of dwelling in the liberty and darkness
of faith, wherein are received spiritual liberty and abundance,[8]
and consequently the wisdom and understanding necessary
to interpret the sayings of God. For it is impossible for a

---

[1] S. Luke xxiv, 21.
[2] So Alc. The other MSS., and e.p., have : ' foolish and hard.'
[3] S. Luke xxiv, 25.   [4] Acts i, 6.   [5] S. John xi, 50.
[6] E.p. adds : ' and a very different one.'
[7] E.p. omits ' all.'   [8] A, B, e.p. : ' abundance of spirit.'

man, if he be not spiritual, to judge of the things of God or understand them in a reasonable way, and he is not spiritual when he judges them according to sense ; and thus, although they come to him beneath the disguise of sense, he understands them not. This S. Paul well expresses in these words : *Animalis autem homo non percipit ea quæ sunt spiritus Dei : stultitia enim est illi, et non potest intelligere : quia de spiritualibus examinatur. Spiritualis autem judicat omnia.*[1] Which signifies : The animal man perceives not the things which are of the Spirit of God, for unto him they are foolishness and he cannot understand them because they are spiritual ; but he that is spiritual judgeth all things. By the animal man is here meant one that uses sense alone ; by the spiritual man, one that is not bound or guided by sense. Wherefore it is temerity to presume to have intercourse with God by way of a supernatural apprehension effected by sense, or to allow anyone else to do so.

12. And that this may be the better understood let us here set down a few examples. Let us suppose that a holy man is greatly afflicted because his enemies persecute him, and that God answers him, saying : I will deliver thee from all thine enemies. This prophecy may be very true, yet, notwithstanding, his enemies may succeed in prevailing, and he may die at their hands. And so if a man should understand this after a temporal manner he would be deceived ; for God might be speaking of the true and principal deliverance and victory, which is salvation, whereby the soul is delivered, freed and made victorious[2] over all its enemies, and much more truly so and in a higher sense than if it were delivered from them here below. And thus, this prophecy would be much more true and comprehensive than the man could understand if he interpreted it only with respect to this life ; for God, in His words, always speaks of, and has regard to, the sense which is most important and profitable, whereas man, according to his own way and purpose, may understand the less important sense, and thus may be deceived. This we see in that prophecy which David makes concerning Christ in the second Psalm, saying : *Reges eos in virga ferrea, et tamquam vas figuli confringes eos.*[3] That is : Thou shalt rule all the people with a rod of iron and thou shalt dash them in

---

[1] 1 Corinthians ii, 14.
[2] [*Lit.*, ' free and victorious.'] So Alc., e.p. A, B have : ' whence the soul remains free and with victory.'   [3] Psalm ii, 9.

pieces like a vessel of clay.   Herein God speaks of the principal and perfect dominion, which is eternal ; and it was in this sense that it was fulfilled, and not in the less important sense, which was temporal, and which was not fulfilled in Christ during any part of His temporal life.   Let us take another example.

13. A soul has great desires to be a martyr. It may happen that God answers him, saying : Thou shalt be a martyr. This will give him inwardly great comfort and confidence that he is to be martyred ; yet notwithstanding it may come to pass that he dies not the death of a martyr, and nevertheless the promise may be true.   Why, then, is it not fulfilled literally ? Because it will be fulfilled, and is capable of being fulfilled,[1] according to the most important and essential sense of that saying—namely, in that God will have given that soul the love and the reward which belong essentially to a martyr ;[2] and thus in truth He gives to the soul that which it formally desired and that which He promised it.   For the formal desire[3] of the soul was, not that particular manner of death, but to do God a martyr's service, and to show its love for Him as a martyr does.   For that manner of death is of no worth in itself without this love, the which love and the showing forth thereof and the reward belonging to the martyr may be given to it more perfectly by other means. So that, though it may not die like a martyr, the soul is well satisfied that it has been given that which it desired.   For such desires (when they are born of living love and other such things), although they be not fulfilled in the way wherein they are described and understood, are fulfilled in another and a better way, and in a way which honours God more greatly than that which they might have asked.   Wherefore David says : *Desiderium pauperum exaudivit Dominus.*[4] That is : The Lord has granted the poor their desire.   And in the Proverbs Divine Wisdom says : *Desiderium suum justis dabitur.*[5] The righteous shall be given their desire.   Hence, then, since we see that many holy men have desired many things in particular for God's sake, and that in this life their desire has not been granted them, it is a matter of faith that,[6] as their

---

[1] E.p. omits : ' and is . . . fulfilled.'
[2] E.p. adds : ' and by His making him a martyr of love, and granting him a prolonged martyrdom in sufferings, the continuance whereof is more painful than death.'
[3] E.p. : ' For the chief desire.'   [4] Psalm ix, 17 [A.V., x, 17].
[5] Proverbs x, 24.   [6] E.p. : ' it is certain that . . .

desire was righteous and true, it has been fulfilled for them perfectly in the next life.   Since this is truth, it would also be truth for God to promise it to them in this life, saying to them : Your desire shall be fulfilled ; and for it not to be fulfilled in the way which they expected.

14. In this and other ways, the words and visions of God may be true and sure and yet we may be deceived by them, through being unable to interpret them in a very high and important sense, which is the purpose and sense wherein God intends them.   And thus it is safest and surest to cause souls to flee prudently from these supernatural things, accustoming them, as we have said, to[1] purity of spirit in dark faith, which is the means of union.

CHAPTER XX

Wherein is proved by passages from Scripture how the sayings and words of God, though always true, do not always rest upon stable causes.

1. We have now to prove the second reason why visions and words which come from God, although in themselves they are always true, are not always stable in their relation to ourselves.   This is because of their causes, whereon[2] they are founded ; for God often makes statements founded upon creatures and the effects of them, which are variable and may fail, for which reason the statements which are founded upon them may also be variable and may fail ; for, when one thing depends on another, if one fails, the other fails likewise. It is as though[3] God should say : In a year's time I shall send upon this kingdom such or such a plague ; and the cause and foundation for this warning is a certain offence which has been committed against God in that kingdom. If the offence should cease or change, the punishment might cease ;[4] yet the warning was true because it was founded upon the fault committed at the time, and, if this had continued, it would have been carried out.[5]

---

[1] A, B : ' bringing them, as we have said, into . . .'
[2] E.p. : ' of the causes whereon . . .'
[3] E.p. abbreviates : ' This is because of the causes and motives whereon they are founded ; and it is to be understood that they will be so for as long as the cause endures which determines God (let us say) to chasten. It is as though . . .'   [4] E.p. : ' cease or change.'
[5] E.p. adds : ' And these warnings or revelations are minatory or conditional.'

2. This, we see, happened in the city of Nineveh, where God said : *Adhuc quadraginta dies, et Ninive subvertetur.*[1] Which signifies : Yet forty days and Nineveh[2] shall be destroyed. This was not fulfilled, because the cause of this warning ceased—namely the sins of the city, for which it did penance —but, if it had not done this, the warning would have been carried into effect. We read likewise in the Third Book of the Kings that, when King Ahab had committed a very great sin, God sent to foretell[3] a great punishment—our father Elijah being the messenger[4]—which should come upon his person, upon his house and upon his kingdom.[5]   And, because Ahab rent his garments with grief and clothed himself in haircloth and fasted, and slept in sackcloth and went about in a humble and contrite manner, God sent again, by the same prophet, to declare to him these words : *Quia igitur humiliatus est mei causa, non inducam malum in diebus ejus, sed in diebus filii sui.*[6] Which signifies : Inasmuch as Ahab has humbled himself for love of Me, I will not send the evil whereof I spake in his days, but in the days of his son. Here we see that, because Ahab changed his spirit and his former affection, God likewise changed his sentence.[7]

3. From this we may deduce, for our purpose, that, although God may have revealed or affirmed something to a soul, whether good or evil, and whether relating to that soul itself or to others, this may, to a greater or a lesser extent, have been changed or altered or withdrawn entirely, according to the change or variation in the affection of this soul, or the cause whereon God passed His judgement,[8] and thus it would not have been fulfilled in the way expected, and oftentimes none would have known why, save only God. For God is wont to declare and teach and promise many things, not that they may be understood or possessed at the time, but that they may be understood at a later time, when it is evident that a soul ought to have light concerning them, or when their effect is attained. This, we see, He did with

---

[1] Jonah iii, 4.

[2] E.p.: '. . . where God sent the prophet Jonah to proclaim this threat from Him in Nineveh : yet forty days and the city of Nineveh . . .'

[3] [*Lit.,* ' to promise.'] A, B : ' God sent to threaten him with.' E.p. : ' God sent him the warning of.'

[4] A, B omit : ' our father . . . messenger.'

[5] 3 Kings [A.V., 1 Kings] xxi, 21.   [6] 3 Kings xxi, 27–9.

[7] E.p. : '. . . because Ahab changed, the warning sentence of God ceased likewise.'

[8] E.p. : ' the cause to which God had regard.'

His disciples, to whom He spake many parables, and gave many judgements, the wisdom whereof[1] they understood not until the time when they had to preach it, which was when the Holy Spirit came upon them, of Whom Christ had said to them that He would declare to them all the things that He had spoken to them in His life. And, when S. John speaks of that entry of Christ into Jerusalem, he says : *Hæc non cognoverunt discipuli ejus primum : sed quando glorificatus est Jesus, tunc recordati sunt quia hæc erant scripta de eo.*[2] And thus there may pass in detail through the soul many things of God which neither the soul nor its director understands until the proper time.

4. Likewise, in the First Book of the Kings, we read that, when God was wroth against Eli, a priest of Israel, for his sins in not chastising his sons, he sent to him by Samuel to say, among other words, these which follow : *Loquens locutus sum, ut domus tua, et domus patris tui, ministraret in conspectu meo, usque in sempiternum. Veruntamen absit hoc a me.* And this is as though He had said :[3] In very truth I said aforetime that thy house and the house of thy father should serve Me continually in the priesthood in My presence for ever, but this purpose is far from Me ; I will not do this thing. For, inasmuch as this office of the priesthood was founded for giving honour and glory to God, and to this end God had promised to give it to the father of Eli for ever if he failed not,[4] when Eli failed in zeal for the honour of God (for, as God Himself complained when He sent to him, he honoured his sons more than God, overlooking their sins so as not to offend them),[5] the promise also failed which would have held good for ever if the good service and zeal of Eli had lasted for ever. And thus, there is no reason to think that, because sayings and revelations[6] come from God, they must invariably come to pass in their apparent sense, especially when[7] they are connected with human causes which may vary, change or alter.

5. And when they are dependent upon these causes[8] God Himself knows, though He does not always declare it, but

---

[1] Thus Alc., e.p.   A, B have : ' the meaning whereof.'
[2] S. John xii, 16.   [3] 1 Kings [A.V., 1 Samuel] ii, 30.
[4] So Alc., which, however, omits : ' if he failed not.'   A, B have : ' and to this end He had promised the priesthood to his father,' etc., B adding : ' [his father] for ever, if for ever good service and zeal continued in them.'   [5] A, B omit the parenthesis.
[6] E.p. adds : ' true in themselves.'
[7] E.p. adds : ' by the command of God Himself.'
[8] E.p. : ' And when this is so.'

pronounces the saying, or makes the revelation, and sometimes says nothing of the condition, as He did to the Ninevites
when He told them definitely that they would be destroyed
after forty days.[1] At other times He lays down the condition,
as He did to Rehoboam, saying to him : If thou wilt keep
My commandments, as did My servant David, I will be
with thee even as I was with him, and will set up thy house
as I did to My servant David.[2] But, whether He declares it or
no, the soul must not have confidence in its own understanding ; for it is impossible to understand the hidden
truths of God which are in His sayings, and the multitude of
their meanings. He is above the heavens, and speaks after
the way of eternity ;[3] we blind souls are upon the earth and
understand only the ways of flesh and time.[4] It was for this
reason, I believe, that the Wise Man said : God is in Heaven,
and thou art upon earth ; wherefore be not thou lengthy or
hasty in speaking.[5]

6. You will perhaps ask me : Why, if we are not to understand these things, or to interfere with them, does God communicate them to us ? I have already said that everything
will be understood in its own time by the command of Him
that declared it, and he whom God wills shall understand it,
and it will be seen that it was fitting ; for God does naught
save with due cause and in truth. Let it be realized, therefore, that there is no complete understanding of the meaning[6]
of the sayings and things of God, and that this meaning cannot be decided by what it seems to be, without great error,
and, in the end, grievous confusion. This was very well
known to the prophets, into whose hands was given the word
of God, and who found it a sore trial to prophesy concerning
the people ; for, as we have said, many of the people saw
that things came not to pass literally, as they were told them,
for which cause they laughed at the prophets and mocked
them greatly ; so much so that Jeremiah went as far as to
say : They mock me all the day long, they scorn and despise
me every one, for I have long been crying against evil and
promising them destruction ; and the word of the Lord has
been made a reproach and a derision to me continually.
And I said, I must not make remembrance of Him, neither

---

[1] Jonah iii, 4.   [2] 3 Kings [A.V., 1 Kings] xi, 38.
[3] [Lit., ' on the road of eternity.']
[4] E.p. : ' . . . earth, so that we cannot attain to His secrets.'
[5] Ecclesiastes v, 1 [A.V., v, 2].   [6] E.p. : ' of the full meaning.'

speak any more in His name.[1] Herein, although the holy prophet was speaking with resignation and in the form of a weak man who cannot endure the ways and workings[2] of God, he clearly indicates the difference between the way wherein the Divine sayings are fulfilled and the ordinary meaning which they appear to have ; for the Divine prophets[3] were treated as mockers, and suffered so much from their prophecy that Jeremiah himself said elsewhere : *Formido et laqueus facta est nobis vaticinatio et contritio.*[4] Which signifies : Prophecy has become to us fear and snares and contradiction of spirit.

7. And the reason why Jonah fled when God sent him to preach the destruction of Nineveh was this, namely, that he knew the different meanings of the sayings of God with respect to the understanding of men and with respect to the causes of the sayings.[5] And thus, lest they should mock him when they saw that his prophecy was not fulfilled, he went away and fled in order not to prophesy ; and thus he remained waiting all the forty days outside the city, to see if his prophecy was fulfilled ; and, when it was not fulfilled, he was greatly afflicted, so much so that he said to God : *Obsecro, Domine, numquid non hoc est verbum meum, cum adhuc essem in terra mea ? propter hoc præoccupavi, ut fugerem in Tharsis.*[6] That is : I pray Thee, O Lord, was not this perchance my saying when I was in my country ? Therefore was I vexed, and fled away to Tarshish. And the saint was wroth and besought God to take away his life.

8. Why, then, must we marvel that God should speak and reveal certain things to souls which come not to pass in the sense wherein they understand them ? For, if God affirms or represents such or such a thing to the soul, whether good or evil, with respect to itself or to another, and if that thing be founded upon a certain affection or service or offence of that soul, or of another, with respect to God, and if the soul persevere therein, it will be fulfilled ; yet even then its fulfilment[7] is not certain, since it is not certain that the soul will persevere. Wherefore, we must have confidence,[8] not in understanding, but in faith.

---

[1] Jeremiah xx, 7–9.   [2] E.p. : ' ways and secrets.'
[3] A, B : ' the sacred prophets.'   [4] Lamentations iii, 47.
[5] E.p. : ' . . . namely, that he understood not the truth of the sayings of God and knew not wholly their meaning.'   [6] Jonah iv, 2.
[7] E.p. adds : ' as it seems ' [i.e., in the sense which it seems to bear].
[8] A, B, e.p. add : ' or security.'

CHAPTER XXI

Wherein is explained how at times, although God answers the prayers that are addressed to Him, He is not pleased that we should use such methods. It is also proved how, although He condescend to us and answer us, He is oftentimes wroth.

1. Certain spiritual men, as we have said, are confident that it is a good thing to display curiosity, as they sometimes do, in striving to know certain things by supernatural methods, thinking that,[1] because God occasionally answers their importunity, this is a good method and pleasing to God. Yet the truth is that, although He may answer them, the method is not good, neither is it pleasing to God, but rather it is displeasing to Him ; and not only so, but oftentimes He is greatly offended and wroth.[2] The reason for this is that it is lawful[3] for no creature to pass beyond the limits that God has ordained for His governance after the order of nature.[4] In His governance of man He has laid down rational and natural limits ;[5] wherefore to desire to pass beyond them is not lawful,[6] and to desire to seek out and attain to anything by supernatural means is to go beyond these natural limits.[7] It is therefore an unlawful thing,[8] and it is therefore not pleasing to God,[9] for He is offended by all that is unlawful. Well knew King Ahab this, since, although Isaiah told him from God to ask for a sign, he would not do it, saying : *Non petam, et non tentabo Dominum.*[10] That is : I will not ask such a thing, neither will I tempt God. For it is tempting God to seek to commune with Him by extraordinary ways, such as those that are supernatural.

2. But why, you will say, if God be displeased, does He sometimes answer ? I reply that it is sometimes the devil who answers. And, when it is God Who answers,[11] I reply that it

---

[1] E.p. : ' Certain spiritual men, as we have said, are confident—not reflecting much upon the curiosity which they sometimes display in striving to know certain things by supernatural means—and think that . . .'
[2] E.p. : ' oftentimes He sorrows greatly for it and is [greatly] wroth.'
[3] E.p. : ' it is fitting.'
[4] E.p. omits : ' after the order of nature.'
[5] E.p. omits : ' and natural.'
[6] E.p. : ' is not fitting.'   [7] E.p. : ' these limits.'
[8] E.p. : ' it is not a holy or a fitting thing.'
[9] E.p. omits the remainder of this paragraph.   [10] Isaiah vii, 12.
[11] Alc. omits : ' I reply that . . . God Who answers,' probably by an oversight.

is because of the weakness of the soul that desires to travel along that road, lest it should be disconsolate and go backward, or lest it should think that God is wroth with it and should be overmuch afflicted ;[1] or for other reasons known to God, founded upon the weakness of that soul, whereby God sees that it is well that He should answer it and deigns to do so by this method. In the same way, too, does He treat many weak and tender souls, granting them favours and sweetness in sensible converse with Himself, as has been said above ; this is not because He desires or is pleased that they should commune with Him after this manner or by these methods ; it is that He gives to each one, as we have said, according to his manner. For God is like a spring, whence everyone draws water according to the vessel which he carries. Sometimes a soul is allowed to draw it by these extraordinary channels ; but it follows not from this that it is lawful to draw water[2] by them, but only that God Himself can permit this, when, how and to whom He wills, and for what reason He wills, without any other party having any right in the matter. And thus, as we say, He sometimes deigns to satisfy the desire and the prayer of certain souls, whom, since they are good and sincere, He wills not to fail to succour, lest He should sadden them, but He wills not this because He is pleased with their methods. This will be the better understood by the following comparison.

3. The father of a family has on his table many and different kinds of food, some of which are better than others. A child is asking him for a certain dish, not the best, but the first that meets its eye, and it asks for this dish because it would rather eat of it than any other ; and as the father sees that, even if he gives it the better food, it will not take it, but will have that which it asks for, since that alone pleases it, he gives it that, regretfully, lest it should take no food at all and be miserable. In just this way, we observe, did God treat the children of Israel when they asked Him for a king : He gave them one, but unwillingly, because it was not good for them. And thus He said to Samuel : *Audi vocem populi in omnibus quæ locuntur tibi : non enim te abjecerunt, sed me.*[3] Which signifies : Hearken unto the voice of this people and grant them the king whom they ask of thee, for they have not

---

[1] E.p. : ' overmuch tempted.'
[2] E.p. : ' that it is fitting to seek to draw water.'
[3] I Kings [A.V., I Samuel] viii, 7.

rejected thee but Me, that I should not reign over them. In this same way God condescends to certain souls, and grants them that which is not best for them, because they will not or cannot walk by any other road. And thus certain souls attain to tenderness and sweetness of spirit or sense ; and God grants them this[1] because they are unable to partake of the stronger and more solid food of the trials of the Cross of His Son, which He would prefer them to take, rather than aught else.

4. I consider, however, that the desire to know things by supernatural means is much worse than the desire for other spiritual favours pertaining to the senses ; for I cannot see how the soul that desires them can fail to commit, at the least, venial sin, however good may be its aims, and however far advanced it may be on the road to perfection ; and he that bids the soul desire them, and consents to it, sins likewise. For there is no necessity for any of these things, since there is a natural reason and an evangelical doctrine and law which are quite sufficient for the soul's guidance, and there is no difficulty or necessity that cannot be solved and reme- died by these means, which are very pleasing to God and of great profit to souls ; and such great use must we make of evangelical doctrine and reason that, if certain things be told us supernaturally, whether we so desire or no, we must only receive that which is in clear conformity with reason and evangelical law. And then we must receive it, not be- cause it is revelation, but because it is reason, setting aside all interest in revelation ; and even then it is well to look at that reason and examine it very much more closely[2] than if there had been no revelation concerning it ; inasmuch as the devil utters many things that are true, and that will come to pass, and that are in conformity with reason, in order that he may deceive.

5. Wherefore, in all our anxieties, trials and difficulties, there remains to us no better and surer means than prayer and hope that God will provide for us, by such means as He wills.[3] This is the advice given to us in the Scriptures, where we read that, when King Jehoshophat was greatly

---

[1] E.p. : ' And if certain souls . . . or sense, God grants them this,' etc.

[2] E.p. abbreviates : ' And then we must receive that which is in con- formity with reason and evangelical law ; and even then it is well to look at it and examine it very much more closely . . .'

[3] A : ' than hope through the means that He wills.'

afflicted and surrounded by enemies, the saintly king gave himself to prayer, saying to God : *Cum ignoremus quid facere debeamus, hoc solum habemus residui, ut oculos nostros dirigamus ad te.*[1] And this is as though he had said : When the means fail and reason is unable to succour us in our necessities, it remains for us only to lift up our eyes to Thee, that Thou mayest succour us as is most pleasing to Thee.

6. And, although this has also been demonstrated, it will be well to prove, from certain passages of Scripture, that, though God may answer such requests, He is none the less sometimes wroth. In the First Book of the Kings it is said that, when King Saul begged[2] that the prophet Samuel, who was already dead, might speak to him, the said prophet appeared to him, and that God was wroth with all this, since Samuel then reproved Saul for having done such a thing, saying : *Quare inquietasti me, ut suscitarer ?*[3] That is : Why hast thou disquieted me, in causing me to arise ? We also know that, in spite of having answered the children of Israel and given them the food that they besought of Him, God was nevertheless greatly incensed against them ; for He sent fire from Heaven upon them as a punishment, as we read in the Pentateuch,[4] and as David relates in these words : *Adhuc escæ eorum erant in ore ipsorum, et ira Dei descendit super eos.*[5] Which signifies : Even as they had the morsels in their mouths, the wrath of God came down upon them. And likewise we read in Numbers that God was greatly wroth[6] with Balaam the prophet, because he went to the Midianites when Balak their king sent for him, although God had bidden him go, because he desired to go and had begged it of God ; and while he was yet in the way there appeared to him an angel with a sword, who desired to slay him, and said to him : *Perversa est via tua, mihique contraria.*[7] Thy way is perverse and contrary to Me ; for which cause he desired to slay him.

7. After this manner and many others God deigns to satisfy the desires of souls though He be wroth with them. Concerning this we have many testimonies in Scripture, and, apart from these, many examples ;[8] but examples are not

[1] 2 Chronicles xx, 12.   [2] E.p. has ' desired ' for ' begged.'
[3] 1 Kings [A.V., 1 Samuel] xxviii, 15.
[4] E.p. is more precise : ' in the Book of Numbers.'
[5] Psalm lxxvii, 30-1 [A.V., lxxviii, 30-1].
[6] E.p. : ' that God was none the less wroth.'
[7] Numbers xxii, 32.
[8] So A, B. E.p. has : ' Concerning this there are many more testimonies in Divine Scripture, and many examples.'

necessary in a thing that is so clear. I only say that it is a most perilous thing, more so than I can express, to desire to commune with God by such means, and that one who is affectioned to such methods will not fail to err greatly and will often find himself in confusion. And anyone who has had experience of this will understand me from his own experience. For over and above the difficulty that there is in being sure that one is not going astray[1] in respect of locutions and visions which are of God, there are ordinarily many of these locutions and visions which are of the devil; for in his converse with the soul the devil habitually wears the same guise as God assumes in His dealings with it, setting before it things that are very like to those which God communicates to it, insinuating himself, like the wolf in sheep's clothing, among the flock, with a success so nearly complete that he can hardly be recognized. For, since he says many things that are true, and in conformity with reason, and things that come to pass as he describes them,[2] it is very easy for the soul to be deceived, and to think that, since these things come to pass as he says, and the future is correctly foretold, this can be the work of none save God; for such souls know not that it is a very easy thing for one that has clear natural light to be acquainted, as to their causes, with things, or with many of them, which have been or shall be.[3] And since the devil has a very clear light of this kind, he can very easily[4] deduce effect from cause, although it may not always turn out as he says, because all causes[5] depend upon the will of God. Let us take an example.

8. The devil knows that the constitution of the earth and the atmosphere, and the laws ruling the sun, are disposed in such manner and in such degree that, when a certain moment has arrived, it will necessarily follow, according to the laws of nature laid down for these elements, that they will infect[6] people with pestilence, and he knows in what places this will be more severe and in what places less so. Here you have a knowledge of pestilence as to its causes. What a wonderful thing it is when the devil reveals this to a soul, saying: 'In a year or in six months from now there

---

[1] So e.p.   The Codices have: 'in going not astray.'
[2] [Lit., 'that come out true.']   E.p.: 'that come out exact.'
[3] E.p. adds: 'and thus [such a] one will predict many things of the future.'
[4] E.p. omits: 'very easily.'   [5] E.p.: 'all things.'
[6] E.p. abbreviates: 'according to their laws, that they will infect.'

will be pestilence,' and it happens as he says ! And yet this
is a prophecy of the devil. In the same way he may have a
knowledge of earthquakes, and, seeing that the bowels of the
earth are filling with air, he will say : ' At such a time there
will be an earthquake.' Yet this is only natural knowledge,[1]
for the possession of which it suffices for the spirit to be free
from the passions of the soul, even as Bœtius says in these
words : *Si vis claro lumine cernere verum, gaudia pelle, timorem,
spemque fugato, nec dolor adsit.*[2] That is : If thou desire to
know truths with the clearness of nature, cast from thee
rejoicing and fear and hope and sorrow.

9. And likewise supernatural events and[3] happenings
may be known, in their causes, in matters concerning
Divine Providence, which deals most justly and surely as is
required by the good or evil causes of the sons of men.[4] For
one may know by natural means[5] that such or such a
person, or such or such a city, or some other thing, is in
such or such necessity, or has reached such or such a point, so
that God, according to His providence and justice, must deal
with such a person or thing in the way required by its cause,
and in the way that is fitting for it, whether by dealing
punishment or reward, or whatsoever it be. And then one
can say : At such a time God will give you this, or will do
this, or that will come to pass, of a surety.[6] It was this that
holy Judith said to Holofernes,[7] when, in order to persuade
him that the children of Israel would without fail be destroyed, she first related to him many of their sins and the evil
deeds that they did. And then she said : *Et, quoniam hæc
faciunt, certum est quod in perditionem dabuntur.* Which signifies :
Since they do these things, it is certain that they will be
destroyed. This is to know the punishment in the cause,[8]

---

[1] E.p. omits the remainder of the paragraph.
[2] The exact reading in Boetius is : ' Tu quoque si vis lumine claro
cernere verum—Tramite recto carpere callem—Gaudia pelle—Pelle
timorem—Spemque fugato—Nec dolor adsit ' (Migne, Vol. LXXV, p. 122).
[3] A, B omit : ' events and.'
[4] E.p. : ' And likewise to some extent particular events and happenings
may be deduced from Divine Providence, which is wont to deal most
justly according to the good and evil [doings] of the sons of men.'
[5] So Alc. E.p. omits : ' by natural means.' A, B : ' one may know
clearly.'
[6] E.p. omits : ' of a surety.'   [7] Judith xi, 12.
[8] E.p. : ' It is this that Achior meant when he said to Holofernes
(Judith v, 18) : *Quotiescumque praeter Deum suum alterum coluerunt, dati
sunt in praedam, et in gladium et in opprobrium.* This is to know the
punishment in the cause.'

which is as much as to say : It is certain that such sins must be the cause of such punishments, at the hand of God Who is most just. And as the Divine Wisdom says : *Per quæ quis peccat, per hæc et torquetur.*[1] With respect to that and for that wherein a man sins, therein is he punished.

10. The devil may have knowledge of this, not only naturally, but also by the experience which he has of having seen God do similar things, and he can foretell it and be correct.[2] Again, holy Tobias was aware of the punishment of the city of Nineveh because of its cause, and he thus admonished his son, saying : Behold, son, in the hour when I and thy mother die, go thou forth from this land, for it will not remain.[3] *Video enim quia iniquitas ejus finem dabit ei.*[4] I see clearly that its own iniquity must be the cause of its punishment, which will be that it shall be ended and destroyed altogether. This might have been known by the devil as well as by Tobias, not only because of the iniquity of the city, but by experience, since they had seen that for the sins of the world God destroyed it in the Flood,[5] and that the Sodomites, too, perished for their sins by fire ; but Tobias knew it also through the Divine Spirit.

11. And the devil may know that one Peter[6] cannot, in the course of nature, live more than so many years, and he may foretell this ; and so with regard to many other things and in many ways that it is impossible to recount fully—nor can one even begin to recount many of them—since they are most intricate and subtle, he insinuates falsehoods ;[7] from which a soul cannot free itself save by fleeing from all revelations and visions and locutions that are supernatural.[8] Wherefore God is justly angered with those that receive them, for He sees that it is temerity on their part to expose themselves to such great peril and presumption and curiosity, and things that spring from pride, and are the root and foundation of vainglory, and of disdain for the things of God, and the beginning of many evils[9] to which many have come.

---

[1] Wisdom xi, 17 [A.V., xi, 16].   [2] E.p. adds : ' at times.'
[3] E.p. has ' city ' for ' land.'   [4] Tobit xiv, 12.
[5] So Alc. E.p. : ' had destroyed men in the Flood.' A, B : ' since they had seen the sins for which God had destroyed the world with the Flood.'
[6] [i.e., any individual.]
[7] E.p. omits : ' he insinuates falsehoods.'
[8] E.p. omits : ' that are supernatural.'
[9] So Alc. A, B : ' and the cause of many evils.' E.p. : ' and many evils.'

Such persons have succeeded in angering God so greatly that He has of set purpose allowed them to go astray and be deceived and to blind their own spirits and to leave the ordered paths of life and give way to their vanities and fancies, according to the word of Isaiah, where he says : *Dominus miscuit in medio ejus spiritum vertiginis.*[1] Which is as much as to say : The Lord hath mingled in the midst thereof the spirit of dissension and confusion. Which in our ordinary vernacular signifies the spirit of misunderstanding. What Isaiah is here very plainly saying is to our point, for he is speaking of those who were endeavouring by supernatural means to know things that were to come to pass. And therefore he says that God mingled in their midst the spirit of misunderstanding ; not that God willed them, in fact, to have the spirit of error, or gave it to them, but that they desired to meddle with that to which by nature they could not attain. Angered by this, God allowed them to act foolishly, giving them no light as to that wherewith He desired not that they should concern themselves. And thus the prophet says that God mingled that spirit in them, privatively.[2] And in this sense God is the cause of such an evil—that is to say, He is the privative cause, which consists in His withdrawal of His light and favour, to such a point that they must needs fall into error.[3]

12. And in this way God gives leave to the devil to blind and deceive many, when their sins and audacities merit it ; and this the devil can do and does successfully, and they give him credence and believe him to be a good spirit ; to such a point that, although they may be quite persuaded that he is not so, they cannot undeceive themselves, since, by the permission of God, there has already been insinuated into them the spirit of perverse understanding, even as we read was the case with the prophets of King Ahab, whom God permitted to be deceived by a lying spirit, giving leave to the devil to do this, and saying : *Decipies, et prævalebis ; egredere, et fac ita.*[4] Which signifies : Thou shalt prevail with thy falsehood and shalt deceive them ; go forth and do so. And so well was he able to work upon the prophets and the king, in order to deceive them, that they would not believe

---

[1] Isaiah xix, 14. [2] E.p. has 'permissively' for 'privatively.'
[3] E.p. : ' . . . and favour, wherefore it follows that they must infallibly fall into error.'
[4] 3 Kings [A.V., 1 Kings] xxii, 22.

the prophet Micaiah, who prophesied the truth to them, saying the exact contrary of that which the others had prophesied, and this came to pass because God permitted them to be blinded, since their affections were attached to that which they desired to happen to them, and God answered them according to their desires and wishes; and this was a most certain preparation and means for their being blinded and deceived, which God allowed of set purpose.

13. Thus, too, did Ezekiel prophesy in the name of God, and, speaking against those who began to desire to have knowledge direct from God, from motives of curiosity, according to the vanity[1] of their spirit, he says : When such a man comes to the prophet to enquire of Me through him, I, the Lord, will answer him by Myself, and I will set My face in anger against that man ; and, as to the prophet, when he has gone astray in that which was asked of him, *Ego Dominus decepi prophetam illum.*[2] That is : I, the Lord, have deceived that prophet. This is to be taken to mean, by not succouring him with His favour so that he might not be deceived ; and this is His meaning when He says : I the Lord will answer him by Myself in anger[3]—that is, God will withdraw His grace and favour from that man. Hence necessarily[4] follows deception by reason of his abandonment by God. And then comes the devil and makes answer according to the pleasure and desire of that man, who, being pleased thereat, since the answers and communications are according to his will,[5] allows himself to be deceived greatly.

14. It may appear that we have to some extent forsaken the purpose that we expressed in the title of this chapter, which was to prove that, although God answers, He sometimes complains. But, if it be carefully considered,[6] all that has been said goes to prove our intention ; for it all shows that God desires not that we should wish for such visions, since He gives cause for us to be deceived by them in so many ways.

---

[1] Alc. has : ' to the variety.'   [2] Ezekiel xiv, 7–9.
[3] [Ezekiel xiv, 7.]   [4] E.p. : ' Hence infallibly.'
[5] E.p. : ' are in conformity with his will.'
[6] The passage from the beginning of the paragraph to this point is found only in Alc. and e.p. The latter reads ' is wroth ' for ' complains.'

CHAPTER XXII

*Wherein is solved¹ a question, namely, why it is not lawful, under
the law of grace,² to ask anything of God by supernatural
means, as it was under the ancient law. This solution is proved
by a passage from S. Paul.³*

1. Questions keep coming to our mind, and thus we
cannot progress with the speed that we should desire. For
as we raise these questions, we are obliged of necessity⁴ to
meet them, that the truth of our teaching may ever be clear
and carry its full force. But there is always⁵ this advantage
in these questions, that, although they somewhat impede
our progress, they serve nevertheless to make our intention
the clearer and more explicit,⁶ as will be the case with the
present question.

2. In the last chapter, we said that it is not the will of
God that souls should desire to receive anything distinctly,
through visions, locutions, etc., by supernatural means.
Further, we saw in the same chapter, and deduced from the
testimonies which were there brought forward from Scripture, that such⁷ communion with God was employed in the
Old Law and was lawful ; and that not only was it lawful,
but God commanded it. And when they used not this
opportunity, God reproved them,⁸ as is to be seen in Isaiah,
where God reproves the children of Israel because they
desired to go down⁹ to Egypt without first enquiring of
Him, saying : *Et os meum non interrogastis.*¹⁰ That is : Ye
asked not first at My own mouth what was fitting. And
likewise we read in Joshua that, when the children of Israel
themselves are deceived by the Gibeonites, the Holy Spirit
reproves them for this fault, saying : *Susceperunt ergo de
cibariis eorum, et os Domini non interrogaverunt.*¹¹ Which signifies : They took of their victuals and they enquired not

---

¹ E.p. : ' is treated.'   ² E.p. : ' under the New Law.'
³ E.p. adds : ' This is somewhat pleasant for an understanding of the
mysteries of our holy faith.'   ⁴ E.p. omits : ' of necessity.'
⁵ Alc. alone has ' always.'
⁶ [*Lit.*, ' they serve nevertheless for the greater doctrine and clearness
of our intention.']
⁷ E.p. abbreviates : ' Further, we know that such . . .'
⁸ E.p. adds : ' for it.'
⁹ A, B, e.p. : ' they thought of going down.'
¹⁰ Isaiah xxx, 2.   ¹¹ Joshua ix, 14.

at the mouth of God. Furthermore we see in the Divine
Scripture that Moses always enquired of God, as did King
David and all the kings of Israel with regard to their wars
and necessities, and the priests and prophets of old, and
God answered and spake with them and was not wroth, and
it was well done ; and if they did it not it was ill done ;
and this is the truth. Why, then, in the new law—the law
of grace—may it not now be as it was aforetime ?

3. To this it must be replied that the principal reason
why in the law of Scripture[1] the enquiries that were made
of God were lawful, and why it was fitting that prophets and
priests should seek visions and revelations of God, was because at that time faith had no firm foundation, neither
was the evangelical law established ; and thus it was needful
that they should enquire of God and that He should speak,
whether by words or by visions and revelations or whether
by figures and similitudes or by many other ways of impressing His meaning. For all that He answered and spake and
revealed belonged to the mysteries of our faith and things
touching it or leading to it. And, since the things of faith
are not of man, but are of the mouth of God Himself, God
Himself reproved them because they enquired not at His
mouth in their affairs, so that He might answer,[2] and might
direct their affairs and happenings toward the faith, of which
at that time they had no knowledge, because it was not yet
founded.[3] But now that the faith is founded in Christ, and,
in this era of grace, the evangelical law has been made manifest, there is no reason to enquire of Him in that manner,
nor for Him to speak or to answer as He did then. For, in
giving us, as He did, His Son, which is His Word—and He
has no other—He spake to us all together, once and for all,
in this single Word, and He has no occasion to speak further.

4. And this is the sense of that passage with which S. Paul
begins, when he tries to persuade the Hebrews that they
should abandon those first manners and ways of converse
with God which are in the law of Moses, and should set
their eyes on Christ alone, saying : *Multifariam multisque
modis olim Deus loquens patribus in Prophetis : novissime autem*

[1] A, B, e.p. : ' why in the Old Law.'
[2] E.p. : ' . . . of God Himself, and by His very mouth were spoken ;
therefore it was needful that, as we have said, they should enquire at the
mouth of God Himself ; wherefore He answered them, when they did it
not, so that He might answer them . . .'
[3] E.p. omits : ' because it was not yet founded.'

diebus istis locutus est nobis in Filio.[1] And this is as though he had said : That which God spake of old in the prophets to our fathers, in sundry ways and divers manners, He has now, at last, in these days, spoken to us once and for all in the Son. Herein the Apostle declares that God has been, as it were, dumb, and has no more to say,[2] since that which He spake aforetime, in part, to the prophets, He has now spoken altogether in Him, giving us the All, which is His Son.

5. Wherefore he that would now enquire of God, or seek any vision or revelation, would not only be acting foolishly, but would be committing an offence against God,[3] by not setting his eyes altogether upon Christ, and seeking no new thing or aught beside. And God might answer him after this manner, saying : If I have spoken all things to thee in My Word, which is My Son, and I have no other word, what answer can I now make to thee, or what can I reveal to thee which is greater than this ?[4] Set thine eyes on Him alone, for in Him I have spoken and revealed to thee all things, and in Him thou shalt find yet more than that which thou askest and desirest. For thou askest locutions and revelations, which are the part ; but if thou set thine eyes upon Him, thou shalt find the whole ; for He is My complete locution and answer, and He is all My vision and all My revelation ; so that I have spoken to thee, answered thee, declared to thee and revealed to thee, in giving Him to thee as thy brother,[5] companion and master, as ransom and as reward. For since that day when I descended upon Him with My Spirit on Mount Tabor, saying : *Hic est filius meus dilectus, in quo mihi bene complacui, ipsum audite*[6] (which is to say : This is My beloved Son, in Whom I am well pleased ; hear ye Him), I have left off all these manners of teaching and answering, and I have entrusted this to Him. Hear Him ; for I have no more faith to reveal, neither have I any more things to declare. For if I spake aforetime,[7] it

---

[1] Hebrews i, 1.
[2] E.p. : ' . . . declares that God has spoken so much already, in this [way], that He has no more to desire.'
[3] E.p. : ' . . . or revelation, would seem to be committing an offence against God.'
[4] E.p. omits : ' and I have . . . greater than this.'
[5] E.p. : ' for He is the Truth, the Guide and the Life, and I have given Him to thee as thy brother,' etc. [6] S. Matthew xvii, 5.
[7] E.p. : ' . . . on Mount Tabor, saying : This is My beloved Son in Whom I am well pleased ; hear ye Him. Thou must seek no new manners of teaching and answering. For if I spake aforetime . . .'

was to promise Christ ; and if they enquired of Me, their enquiries[1] were directed to petitions for Christ and expectancy concerning Him, in Whom they should find every good thing (as is now set forth in all the teaching of the Evangelists and the Apostles) ; but now, any who would enquire of Me after that manner, and desire Me to speak to him or reveal aught to him, would in a sense be asking Me for Christ again, and asking Me for more faith, and be lacking in faith, which has already been given in Christ ; and therefore he would be committing a great offence against My beloved Son, for not only would he be lacking in faith, but he would be obliging Him again first of all to become incarnate and pass through life and death. Thou shalt find[2] naught to ask of Me, or to desire of Me,[3] whether revelations or visions ; consider this well, for thou shalt find that all has been done for thee and all has been given to thee—yea, and much more also—in Him.

6. If thou desirest Me to answer thee with any word of consolation, consider My Son, Who is subject to Me, and bound by love of Me, and afflicted,[4] and thou shalt see how fully He answers thee. If thou desirest Me to expound to thee secret things, or happenings, set thine eyes on Him alone, and thou shalt find the most secret mysteries, and the wisdom and wondrous things of God, which are hidden in Him, even as My Apostle says : *In quo sunt omnes thesauri sapientiae et scientiae Dei absconditi.*[5] That is : In this Son of God are hidden all the treasures of wisdom and knowledge of God. These treasures of wisdom shall be very much loftier and more delectable and more profitable for thee than the things that thou desiredst to know. Herein the same Apostle gloried, saying : That he had not declared to them that he knew anything,[6] save Jesus Christ and Him crucified.[7] And if thou shouldst still desire other Divine or bodily revelations and visions, look also at Him made man, and thou shalt find therein more than thou thinkest, for the Apostle says likewise : *In ipso habitat omnis plenitudo Divinitatis corporaliter.*[8]

[1] Alc. : ' their hopes.'
[2] E.p. abbreviates : ' . . . would in some degree be not content with Christ, and thus he would be committing a great offence against My beloved Son. If thou hast Him, thou shalt find . . .'
[3] E.p. : ' neither to desire.'
[4] E.p. : ' . . . consider My Son, obedient to Me and afflicted for love of Me . . .' [5] Colossians ii, 3.
[6] E.p. : ' . . . saying : That he knew no other thing . . .'
[7] 1 Corinthians ii, 2. [8] Colossians ii, 9.

Which signifies : In Christ dwelleth all the fullness of the Godhead bodily.

7. It is not fitting, then, to enquire of God in any super-natural manner, nor is it now necessary that He should answer ; since all the faith has been given us in Christ, and there is therefore no more of it to be revealed, nor will there ever be.[1] And he that now desires to receive anything in a supernatural manner, as we have said,[2] is, as it were, finding fault with God for not having given us a complete sufficiency in His Son. For, although such a person may be assuming the faith, and believing it, nevertheless he is show-ing a curiosity which belongs to faithlessness. We must not expect, then,[3] to receive instruction, or aught else, in a supernatural manner, For, at the moment when Christ gave up the ghost upon the Cross, saying, *Consummatum est*,[4] which signifies, ' It is finished,' an end was made, not only of all these forms, but also of all those other ceremonies and rites of the Old Law. And so we must now be guided in all things by the law of Christ made man, and by that of His Church, and of His ministers, in a human and a visible manner, and by these means we must remedy our spiritual weaknesses and ignorances, since in these means we shall find abundant medicine for them all. If we leave this path, we are guilty not only of curiosity, but of great audacity : nothing is to be believed in a supernatural way, save only that which is the teaching of Christ made man, as I say, and of His ministers, who are men.[5] So much so that S. Paul says these words : *Quod si Angelus de coelo evangelizaverit, praeterquam quod evangelizavimus vobis, anathema sit.*[6] That is to say : If any angel from Heaven preach any other gospel unto you than that which we men[7] preach unto you, let him be accursed and excommunicate.

8. Wherefore, since it is true that we must ever be guided by that which Christ taught us, and that all things else are

---

[1] E.p. : ' since, having spoken in Christ, He leaves no more to be desired.'

[2] E.p. has : ' in an extraordinary supernatural manner,' and omits : ' as we have said.'

[3] E.p. adds : ' with this curiosity.'   [4] S. John xix, 30.

[5] These two sentences are based on A and B. Alc. omits several lines, apparently by an oversight. E.p. has ' by the doctrine of Christ ' for ' by the law of Christ made man '; omits ' in a human and a visible manner '; and adds ' and withdraw from ' to ' If we leave.'

[6] Galatians i, 8.

[7] E.p. omits ' men,' and also ' who are men ' above.

as nothing, and are not to be believed unless they are in
conformity with it, he acts vainly who still desires to commune with God after the manner of the Old Law. Furthermore, it was not lawful at that time for everyone to enquire
of God, neither did God answer all men, but only the priests
and prophets, from whose mouths it was that the people had
to learn law and doctrine ; and thus, if a man desired to
know anything of God, he enquired of Him through the
prophet or the priest and not of God Himself. And, if
David enquired of God at certain times upon his own
account, this was because he was a prophet, and yet, even
then, he did it not without the priestly vestment, as it is clear
was the case in the First Book of the Kings, where he said
to Abimelech the priest : *Applica ad me Ephod*[1]—which ephod
was one of the chief of the approved priestly vestments,
wherewith he spake with God. But at other times he spake
with God through the prophet Nathan and other prophets.
And by the mouths of these prophets and of the priests men
were to believe that that which was said to them came from
God ; they were not to believe it because of their own
opinions.

9. And thus, men were not authorized or empowered at
that time to give entire credence to what was said by God,
unless it were approved by the mouths of priests and
prophets. For God is so desirous that the government and
direction of every man should be undertaken by another
man like himself,[2] and that every man should be ruled and
governed by natural reason,[3] that He earnestly desires us not
to give entire credence to the things that He communicates
to us supernaturally, nor to consider them as being securely
and completely confirmed until they pass through this human
aqueduct of the mouth of man. And thus, whenever He
says or reveals something to a soul, He gives this same soul
to whom He says it a kind of inclination to tell it to the
person to whom it is fitting that it should be told. Until
this has been done, it gives not entire satisfaction, because
the man has not taken it[4] from another man like himself.[5]

[1] [It was to Abiathar that this was said.] 1 Kings [A.V., 1 Samuel]
xxiii, 9.

[2] [P. Silverio reads : ' like Himself,' but the context seems to require
the interpretation here adopted.]

[3] E.p. omits : ' and that . . . natural reason.'

[4] A, B, e.p. : ' in order that the man may take it.'

[5] E.p. adds : ' whom God has set in His place.'

We see in the book of the Judges that the same thing happened to the captain Gideon, to whom God had said many times that he should conquer the Midianites, yet he was fearful and full of doubts (for God had allowed him to retain that weakness) until he heard from the mouth of men what God had said to him.   And it came to pass that, when God saw that he was weak, He said to him : Rise up and go down to the host. *Et cum audieris quid loquantur, tunc confortabuntur manus tuae, et securior ad hostium castra descendes.*[1]   That is :   When thou hearest what men are saying there, then shalt thou receive strength in that which I have said to thee, and thou shalt go down with greater security to the hosts of the enemy.   And so it came to pass that, having heard a dream related by one of the Midianites to another, wherein the Midianite had dreamed that Gideon should conquer them, he was greatly strengthened, and began to prepare for the battle with great joy.   From this it can be seen that God desired not that he should feel confident, since He gave him not the assurance by supernatural means alone, but caused him first to be strengthened by natural means.[2]

10.   And even more surprising is the thing that happened in this connection to Moses, when God had commanded him, and given him many instructions, which He confirmed with the signs of the wand changed into a serpent and of the leprous hand, enjoining him to go and set free the children of Israel.   So weak was he and so uncertain[3] about this going forth that, although God was angered, he had not the courage to summon up the complete faith necessary for going,[4] until God encouraged him through his brother Aaron, saying : *Aaron frater tuus Levites, scio quod eloquens sit : ecce ipse egredietur in occursum tuum, vidensque te, laetabitur corde. Loquere ad eum, et pone verba mea in ore ejus : et ego ero in ore tuo, et in ore illius,* etc.[5]   Which is as though He had said : I know that thy brother Aaron is an eloquent man : behold,[6] he will come forth to meet thee, and, when he seeth thee, he will be glad in his heart ; speak thou with him and tell him all My words, and I will be in thy mouth and in his

---

[1] Judges vii, 11.
[2] E.p. : 'should feel confident, until he had heard the same thing by the mouth of others.'
[3] [*Lit.*, 'and so dark.'] E.p. : 'and so hesitating and uncertain.'
[4] E.p. has 'strength ' for 'faith.'
[5] Exodus iv, 14–15.   [6] Alc. alone has 'behold.'

mouth, so that each of you shall believe that which is in the mouth of the other.[1]

11. Having heard these words, Moses at once took courage, in the hope of finding consolation in the counsel which his brother was to give him ; for this is a characteristic of the humble soul which dares not to treat with God alone, neither can be completely satisfied without human counsel and guidance. And this is the will of God, for He draws near to those who come together to treat concerning truth, in order to expound and confirm it in them, upon a foundation of natural reason,[2] even as He said that He would do when Moses and Aaron should come together—namely, that He would be in the mouth of the one and in the mouth of the other. Wherefore He said likewise in the Gospel that *Ubi fuerint duo vel tres congregati in nomine meo, ibi sum ego in medio eorum.*[3] That is : Where two or three are met together, in order to consider that which is for the greater honour and glory of My name, there will I be in the midst of them. That is to say, I will make clear and confirm in their hearts the truths of God. And it is to be observed that He said not : Where there is one alone, there will I be ; but : Where there are at least two. In this way He showed that God desires not that any man by himself alone should believe his experiences to be of God,[4] or should act in conformity with them,[5] or trust them, but rather should believe the Church and[6] her ministers, for God will not make clear and confirm the truth in the heart of one who is alone, and thus such a one will be weak and cold.

12. Hence comes that whereon the Preacher insists, where he says : *Vae soli, quia cum ceciderit, non habet sublevantem se. Si dormierint duo, fovebuntur mutuo ; unus quomodo calefiet ? et si quispiam praevaluerit contra unum, duo resistent ei.*[7] Which signifies : Woe to the man that is alone, for when he falleth he hath none to raise him up. If two sleep together, the one shall give warmth to the other (that is to say : with the warmth of God Who is between them[8]) ; but one alone,

---

[1] E.p. omits : ' so that . . . the other.'
[2] E.p. omits : ' upon . . . reason.'   [3] S. Matthew xviii, 20.
[4] [*Lit.*, ' the things which he has to be of God.']
[5] A, e.p. : ' neither should rely upon them.'
[6] [*Lit.*, ' . . . with them, without the Church or . . .'] E.p. has : ' . . . with them, without the counsel and government of the Church or . . .'   [7] Ecclesiastes iv, 10–12.
[8] The parenthetical words are omitted in A and B.

how shall he be warm ? That is to say : How shall he be
other than cold as to the things of God ? And if any man
can fight and prevail against one enemy (that is, the devil,
who can fight and prevail against those that are alone and
desire to have God with them in their acts), two men together will resist him—that is, the disciple and the master[1]
who come together to know and do[2] the truth. And until
this happens such a man is habitually weak and feeble in
the truth, however often he may have heard it from God ;
so much so that, despite the many occasions on which S. Paul
preached the Gospel, which he said that he had heard, not
of men, but of God, he could not do otherwise than go and
consult with S. Peter and the Apostles, saying : *Ne forte in
vacuum currerem, aut cucurrissem.*[3] Which signifies : Perchance
he should run, or had run, in vain,[4] having no assurance of
himself, until man had given him assurance. This seems a
noteworthy thing, O Paul, that He that revealed to thee
this Gospel should be unable likewise to reveal to thee the
assurance of the fault which thou mightest have committed
in preaching the truth concerning Him.[5]

13. Herein it is clearly explained that a man is to place
no confidence in the things that God reveals, save in the
way that we are describing ; for, even in cases where a
person is in possession of such certainty, as S. Paul was
certain of his Gospel (since he had already begun to preach
it), yet, although the revelation be of God, man may still err
with respect to it,[6] or in things relating to it. For, although
God reveals one thing, He reveals not always the other ;
and oftentimes He reveals something without revealing the
way in which it is to be done. For ordinarily He neither
works nor reveals anything that can be accomplished by
human counsel and industry, although He may commune for
a long time very lovingly with the soul. Of this S. Paul was
very well aware, since, as we say, although he knew that
the Gospel was revealed to him by God, he went to take
counsel with S. Peter. And we see this clearly in the Exodus,
where God had communed most familiarly with Moses, yet
had never given him that salutary counsel which was given
him by his father-in-law Jethro—that is to say, that he

---

[1] [i.e., the penitent and the confessor or director.]
[2] E.p. : ' and work.'   [3] Galatians ii, 2.
[4] E.p. omits the rest of this paragraph.
[5] A, B : ' the truth of the Lord.'
[6] E.p. : ' may still err in the execution of it.'

should choose other judges to assist him, so that the people should not be waiting from morning till night.[1] This counsel God approved, though it was not He that had given it to him, for it was a thing that fell within the limits of human judgement and reason. With respect to Divine visions and revelations and locutions, God is not wont to reveal them,[2] for He is ever desirous that men should make such use of their own reason as is possible, and all such things have to be governed by reason,[3] save those that are of faith, which transcend all judgement and reason, although these are not contrary to faith.[4]

14. Wherefore let none think that, because it may be true that God and the saints commune with him familiarly about many things, they will of necessity explain to him the faults that he commits with regard to anything, if it is possible for him to recognize these faults by other means. He can have no assurance about this ; for, as we read came to pass in the Acts of the Apostles, S. Peter, though a prince of the Church, who was taught directly by God, went astray nevertheless with respect to a certain ceremony that was in use among the people, and God was silent. So far did he stray that S. Paul reproved him, as he affirms, saying : *Cum vidissem, quod non recte ad veritatem Evangelii ambularent, dixi coram omnibus : Si tu judaeus cum sis, gentiliter vivis, quomodo Gentes cogis judaizare ?*[5] Which signifies : When I saw (says S. Paul) that the disciples walked not uprightly according to the truth of the Gospel, I said to Peter before them all : If thou, being a Jew, as thou art, livest after the manner of the Gentiles, how feignest thou to force the Gentiles to follow the Jews ? And God reproved not S. Peter Himself for this fault, for that simulation was a thing that had to do with reason, and it was possible for him to know it by rational means.[6]

15. Wherefore on the day of judgement God will punish for their many faults and sins many souls with whom He may quite habitually have held converse here below, and to whom

---

[1] Exodus xviii, 21-2.
[2] E.p. : ' for it was a thing that pertained to human counsel and judgement. And thus God is not wont to reveal all things that may pertain to human counsel and reason with respect to the visions and locutions of God . . .'
[3] E.p. omits : ' and all such . . . by reason.'
[4] A, B, e.p. : ' they are not contrary to reason and judgement.'
[5] Galatians ii, 14.
[6] E.p. : ' for it was a thing that he might know by ordinary means.'

He may have given much light and virtue ; for, as to those things that they have known that they ought to do, they have been neglectful, and have relied upon that converse that they have had with God and upon the virtue that He has given them.[1] And thus, as Christ[2] says in the Gospel, they will marvel at that time, saying : *Domine, Domine, nonne in nomine tuo prophetavimus, et in nomine tuo daemonia ejecimus, et in nomine tuo virtutes multas fecimus ?*[3] That is : Lord, Lord, were the prophecies that Thou spakest to us perchance not prophesied in Thy name ? And in Thy name cast we not out devils ?[4] And in Thy name performed we not many miracles and mighty works ? And the Lord says that He will answer them in these words : *Et tunc confitebor illis, quia numquam novi vos : discedite a me omnes qui operamini iniquitatem.*[5] That is to say : Depart from Me, ye workers of iniquity, for I never knew you. Of the number of these was the prophet Balaam and others like to him, who, though God spake with them and gave them thanks,[6] were sinners. But the Lord will likewise give their proportion of reproof to His friends and chosen ones, with whom He communed familiarly here below, as to the faults and sins of neglect that they may have committed ; whereof there was no need that God should Himself warn them, since He had already warned them through the natural reason and law that He had given to them.

16. In concluding this part of my subject, therefore, I say, and I infer from what has been said, that anything, of whatsoever kind, received by the soul through supernatural means, clearly and plainly, entirely and simply,[7] must at once be communicated to the spiritual director. For although there may seem no reason to speak of it, or to spend time upon it, yet the soul acts safely, as we have said, if it casts it aside and pays no heed to it, neither desires it.[8] Especially is this so when it is a question of visions or revelations or other supernatural communications, which are either quite clear or very nearly so. It is very necessary to give an account of them all, although it may seem to the

---

[1] A, B, e.p. add : ' and on that account being neglectful.'
[2] So Alc. A, B : ' as Christ our Lord.' E.p. : ' as our Lord Jesus.'
[3] S. Matthew vii, 22.
[4] Alc. omits this sentence. E.p. adds : ' Indeed we have cast out devils.' [5] S. Matthew vii, 23.
[6] E.p. omits : ' and gave them thanks.'
[7] E.p. adds : ' with all truth.'
[8] E.p. omits : ' neither desires it.'

soul that there is no reason for so doing. And this for three causes.[1] First, because, as we have said, God communicates many things, the effect, power,[2] light and security whereof He confirms not wholly in the soul, until, as we have said, the soul consults him whom God has given to it as a spiritual judge, which is he that has the power to bind or to loose, and to approve or to blame, as we have shown by means of the passages quoted above ;[3] and we can show it daily by experience, for we see humble souls to whom these things come to pass, and who, after discussing them with fit persons, experience a new satisfaction, power, light and assurance ; so much so that to some it seems that they belong not to them, neither have they possession of them, until they communicate them to the director, and that then they are given to them anew.

17. The second cause is that the soul habitually needs instruction upon the things that come to pass within it, in order to be directed by that means to spiritual poverty and detachment, which is the dark night. For if this instruction is being withheld from it—even when the soul desires not such things—it will gradually, without realizing it, become callous[4] as it treads the spiritual road, and draw near again to the road of sense ; it is partly with respect to this that these distinct things happen.[5]

18. The third cause is that, for the sake of the humility and submission and mortification of the soul, it is well to relate everything to the director, although he make[6] no account of it all and consider it as of no importance. There are some souls who greatly dislike speaking of such things, because they think them to be of no importance. And they know not how the person to whom they are to relate them will receive them ; which is lack of humility, for which reason it is needful to submit themselves and relate these things. And there are others who are very timid in relating them, because they see not why they should have these experiences, which seem to belong to saints, as well as other things which

---

[1] So Alc. B has : ' three reasons ' ; A, e.p. : ' three things.'
[2] A, B : ' the effort, effect . . .'
[3] A, B omit : ' by means of the passages quoted above.'
[4] A, e.p. read ' rude ' for ' callous.' [The change is a slight one : *enrudeciendo* for *endureciendo*.]
[5] E.p. omits : ' it is partly . . . happen.'
[6] [The Spanish phrase equally admits the reading : ' although the soul make.']

they are sorry to have to describe ; for which cause they think there is no reason to speak of them because they make no account of them ; but for this very reason it is well for them to mortify themselves and relate them, until in time they come to speak of them humbly, unaffectedly, submissively and readily, and after this they will always find it easy to do so.

19. But, with respect to what has been said, it must be pointed out that, although we have insisted so much[1] that such things should be set aside, and that confessors should not incite their penitents to discuss them, it is not well that spiritual fathers should show displeasure in regard to them, or should seek to avoid them or despise them, or give their penitents cause to show reserve and not to venture to speak of them, for it would be the means of causing them many inconveniences if the door were closed upon their relating them. For, since this is a means and manner[2] whereby God guides such souls, there is no reason for thinking ill of it or for being alarmed or offended by it ; but rather there is a reason for proceeding[3] very quietly and kindly, for encouraging these souls and for giving them an opportunity to speak of these things ; if necessary, they must be exhorted to speak ; and, in view of the difficulty that some souls experience in describing these things, this is sometimes quite essential. Let confessors direct their penitents in faith, instructing them frankly to turn away their eyes from all such things, teaching them how to void the desire and the spirit of them that they may make progress, and giving them to understand how much more precious in God's sight is one work or act of the will performed in charity than are all the visions and communications[4] that they may receive from Heaven, since these imply neither merit nor demerit.[5] Let them point out, too, that many souls who have known nothing of such things have made incomparably greater progress than others who have received many of them.

---

[1] B : ' so rigorously.'

[2] E.p. : ' For, as we have said, this is a means ; and, since it is a means and manner . . .'

[3] None of the MSS. have ' proceeding,' which e.p. supplies.

[4] E.p. : ' than are all the visions and revelations.' A, B : ' than are all the visions and revelations and communications.'

[5] E.p. omits : ' since these . . . demerit.'

CHAPTER XXIII

Which begins to treat of the apprehensions of the understanding that come in a purely spiritual way, and describes their nature.

1. Although the instruction that we have given with respect to the apprehensions of the understanding which come by means of sense is somewhat brief, in comparison with what might be said about them, I have not desired to write of them at greater length ; I believe, indeed, that I have already been too lengthy for the fulfilment of my present intention, which is to disencumber the understanding of them and direct the soul into the night of faith. Wherefore we shall now begin to treat of those other four apprehensions of the understanding, which, as we said in the tenth chapter,[1] are purely spiritual—namely, visions, revelations, locutions and spiritual feelings. These we call purely spiritual, for they do not (as do those that are corporeal and imaginary) communicate themselves to the understanding by way of the corporeal senses ; but, without the intervention of any inward or outward corporeal sense, they present themselves to the understanding, clearly and distinctly, by supernatural means, passively—that is to say, without the commission of any act or operation on the part of the soul itself, at the least actively.[2]

2. It must be known, then, that, speaking broadly and in general terms, all these four apprehensions may be called visions of the soul ; for we can speak of the understanding of the soul as of its sight. And since all these apprehensions are intelligible to the understanding, they are described, in a spiritual sense, as ' visible.' And thus the kinds of intelligence that are formed in the understanding may be called intellectual visions. Now, since all the objects of the other senses, which are all that can be seen, and all that can be heard, and all that can be smelt and tasted and touched, are objects of the understanding in so far as they fall within the limits of truth or falsehood, it follows that, just as to the eyes of the body all that is visible in a bodily way causes bodily vision, even so, to the spiritual eyes of the soul— namely, the understanding—all that is intelligible causes

---

[1] It is in Chapter x (and not in viii, as is said in A, B and e.p.) that the author treats of these spiritual apprehensions.

[2] E.p. : ' actively and as on its own account.'

spiritual vision ; for, as we have said, for the soul to understand is for it to see. And thus, speaking generally, these
four apprehensions may be called visions. This cannot be
said, however, of the other senses, for no one of them is
capable, as such, of receiving the object of another one.

3. But, since these apprehensions present themselves to
the soul in the same way as they do to the various senses, it
follows that, speaking properly and specifically, we shall
describe that which the understanding receives by means of
sight (because it can see things spiritually, even as the eyes
can see bodily) as a vision ; and that which it receives by
apprehending and understanding new things (as it were
through the hearing, when it hears things that are not
heard[1]) we describe as revelation ; and that which it
receives by means of hearing we call locution ; and that
which it receives through the other senses, such as the perception of sweet spiritual fragrance, and of spiritual taste
and of spiritual delight which the soul may enjoy supernaturally, we call spiritual feelings. From all these the soul
derives spiritual vision or understanding, without any kind
of apprehension concerning form, image or figure of natural
fancy or imagination[2] ; these things are communicated to
the soul directly by supernatural means and a supernatural
process.

4. Of these, likewise (even as we said of the other imaginary corporeal apprehensions), it is well that we should here
disencumber the understanding, leading and directing it by
means of them into the spiritual night of faith, to the Divine
and substantial union of God[3] ; lest, by letting such things
encumber and stultify it, it should be hindered upon the road
to solitude and detachment from all things, which is necessary
to that end. For, although these apprehensions are nobler
and more profitable and much more certain than those which
are corporeal and imaginary, inasmuch as they are interior
and purely spiritual, and are those which the devil is least
able to counterfeit, since they are communicated to the soul
more purely and subtly without any effort of its own or of
the imagination, at least actively,[4] yet not only may the
understanding be encumbered by them upon this road, but

---

[1] E.p. omits the words in parenthesis.
[2] E.p. adds : ' whence it may derive them.'
[3] The 1630 edition emends : ' of the love of God.'
[4] E.p. adds : ' and on its own account,'

it is possible for it to be greatly deceived through its own imprudence.

5. And although, in one sense, we might conclude with these four kinds of apprehension, by treating them all together and giving advice which holds good of them all, as we have given concerning all the others—namely, that they should neither be desired nor aspired to—yet, since we shall presently throw more light upon the way in which this is to be done, and certain things will be said in connection with them, it will be well to treat of each one of them in particular, and thus we shall now speak of the first apprehensions, which are intellectual or spiritual visions.

CHAPTER XXIV

Which treats of two kinds of spiritual vision that come supernaturally.

1. Speaking now strictly of those visions which are spiritual, and are received without the intervention of any bodily sense, I say that there are two kinds of vision that may come to the understanding ; the one kind is of corporeal substances ; the other, of incorporeal or separated substances. The corporeal visions have respect to all material things that are in Heaven and on earth, which the soul is able to see, even while it is still in the body, by the aid of a certain supernatural illumination, derived from God, wherein it is able to see all absent things in Heaven and on earth,[1] even as S. John saw, as we read in the twenty-first chapter of the Apocalypse, where he describes and relates the excellence of the celestial Jerusalem, which he saw in Heaven. Even so, again, we read of S. Benedict that in a spiritual vision he saw the whole world.[2] This vision, says S. Thomas in the first of his Quodlibets, was in the light that is derived from above, as we have said.

2. The other visions, which are of incorporeal substances, cannot be seen by the aid of this derived illumination, whereof we are here speaking, but only by another and a higher illumination which is called the illumination of glory. And thus these visions of incorporeal substances, such as

---

[1] The remainder of this paragraph is omitted by e.p.
[2] S. Gregory : *Dial.*, Bk. II, Chap. xxxv. ' Omnis etiam mundus velut sub uno solis radio collectus, ante oculos eius adductus est.'

angels and souls,[1] are not of this life, neither can they be seen in the mortal body ; for, if God were pleased to communicate them to the soul, in essence as they are, the soul would at once go forth from the flesh and would be loosed from this mortal life. For this reason God said to Moses, when he entreated Him to show him His Essence : *Non videbit me homo, et vivet.*[2] That is : Man shall not see Me and be able to remain alive. Wherefore, when the children of Israel thought that they were to see God, or had seen Him, or some angel, they feared death, as we read in Exodus, where, fearing these things, they said : *Non loquatur nobis Dominus, ne forte moriamur.*[3] As if they had said : Let not God communicate Himself to us openly, lest we die. And likewise in the Judges, Manoah, father of Samson, thought that he and his wife had seen in essence the angel who spake with them (and who had appeared to them in the form of a most beautiful man) and he said to his wife : *Morte moriemur, quia vidimus Dominum.*[4] Which signifies : We shall die, because we have seen the Lord.[5]

3. And thus these visions belong not to this life, save occasionally and fleetingly, when, making an exception to the conditions of our natural life, God so allows it. At such times He totally withdraws the spirit from this life, and the

---

[1] The Toledo edition reads : ' such as the Divine Being, angels, souls.' This is based on an erroneous reading attributed incorrectly to Andrés de la Encarnación, who does not say, in fact, that any MS. so varies the text, but that it *might be* so varied in accordance with the context. No MS. has : ' the Divine Being.'

[2] Exodus xxxiii, 20.　　　[3] Exodus xx, 19.　　　[4] Judges xiii, 22.

[5] E.p. abbreviates this long paragraph thus : ' The other visions, which are of incorporeal substances, demand another and a higher illumination ; and thus these visions of incorporeal substances, such as angels and souls, are not very ordinary, nor proper to this life ; still less is that of the Divine Essence, which is proper to the Blessed in Heaven, save that it may be communicated to a soul fleetingly and as in passing.' The next two paragraphs are omitted from e.p. P. Jerónimo de San José, in the edition of 1630, copies from e.p. the lines given in this note above, and then continues : ' [save when] God so allows, in spite of the condition of our natural life, withdrawing the spirit from it occasionally, as happened to the apostle Saint Paul, when he says that he saw unspeakable secrets in the third heaven.' The adjustments made by P. Salablanca and amplified by P. Jerónimo in the rest of the paragraph [cf. notes below] follow the most usual scholastic doctrine. Among the Discalced Carmelite writers who deal most fully and competently with this doctrine of spiritual visions are the authors of the *Cursus Theologiæ Mysticæ*, Vol. IV, Disp. xx, xxi ; Felipe de la Santísima Trinidad : *Summa Theologiæ Mysticæ*, Pt. II, Tract. III, Disc. iv ; *Médula Mística*, Tract. VI. S. Thomas (I p., q. 88, a. 1) says that we cannot *quidditative* know separated substances.

natural functions of the body are supplied by His favour. This is why, at the time when it is thought that S. Paul saw these (namely, the incorporeal substances in the third heaven) that saint says :[1] *Sive in corpore, nescio, sive extra corpus, nescio, Deus scit.*[2] That is, he was enraptured, and of that which he saw he says that he knows not if it was in the body or out of the body, but that God knows. Herein it is clearly seen that the limits of natural means of communication[3] were passed, and that this was the work of God. Likewise, it is believed that God showed His Essence to Moses, for we read that God said to him that He would set him in the cleft of the rock, and would protect him, by covering him with His right hand, and protecting him so that he should not die when His glory passed ; the which glory passed indeed, and was shown to him fleetingly, and the natural life of Moses was protected by the right hand of God.[4] But these visions that were so substantial—like that of S. Paul and ·Moses, and that of our father[5] Elijah, when he covered his face at the gentle whisper of God—although they are fleeting, occur only very rarely—indeed, hardly ever—and to very few ; for God performs such a thing in those that are spiritually most strong[6] in the Church and the law of God, as were the three men named above.

4. But, although these visions of spiritual substances cannot[7] be unveiled and be clearly seen in this life by the understanding, they can nevertheless be perceived in the substance of the soul, with the sweetest touches and unions, all of which belongs to spiritual feelings, whereof, with the Divine favour, we shall treat presently ; for our pen is being directed and guided to these—namely, to the Divine bond and union of the soul with Divine Substance. We shall speak of this when we treat of the dark and confused mystical understanding which remains to be described, wherein we shall show how, by means of this dark and loving knowledge, God is united with the soul in a lofty and Divine degree ;[8] for, after some manner, this dark and loving knowledge,

---

[1] Alc. omits : 'namely . . . saint says.'   [2] 2 Corinthians xii, 2.
[3] A, B : 'that the limits of life.'   [4] Exodus xxxiii, 22.
[5] Only Alc. and the edition of 1630 have : ' our father.'
[6] The edition of 1630 omits ' most.' A, B [by changing one letter and writing *fuentes* for *fuertes*] read : ' that are spiritual fountains.'
[7] The edition of 1630 adds : ' according to the ordinary law.'
[8] This description the Saint probably accomplished, or intended to accomplish, in his commentaries on the last five stanzas of the *Dark Night,* which have not come down to us.

which is faith, serves as a means to Divine union in this life,
even as, in the next life, the light of glory serves as an intermediary to the clear vision of God.

5. Let us, then, now treat of the visions of corporeal
substances, received spiritually in the soul, which come after
the manner of bodily visions. For, just as the eyes see bodily
visions by means of natural light, even so does the soul,
through the understanding, by means of supernaturally
derived light, as we have said, see those same natural things
inwardly, together with others, as God wills ; the difference
between the two kinds of vision is only in the mode and
manner of them. For spiritual and intellectual visions are
much clearer and subtler than those which pertain to the
body. For, when God is pleased to grant this favour to the
soul, He communicates to it that supernatural light whereof
we speak, wherein the soul sees the things that God wills it
to see, easily and most clearly, whether they be of Heaven or
of earth, and the absence or presence of them is no hindrance
to the vision. And it is at times as though a door were most
clearly opened before it, through which the soul sees a light,
after the manner of a lightning flash, which, on a dark night,
reveals things suddenly, and causes them to be clearly and
distinctly seen, and then leaves them in darkness, although
the forms and figures of them remain in the fancy. This
comes to pass much more perfectly in the soul,[1] because those
things that the spirit has seen in that light remain impressed
upon it in such a way that whensoever it observes[2] them it
sees them in itself as it saw them before ;[3] even as in a mirror
the forms that are in it[4] are seen whensoever a man looks in
it, and in such a way that those forms of the things that he
has seen are never wholly removed from his soul, although
in course of time they become somewhat remote.[5]

6. The effect which these visions produce in the soul is
that of quiet, illumination, joy like that of glory, sweetness,
purity and love, humility and inclination or elevation of
the spirit in God ; sometimes more so, at other times less ;
with sometimes more of one thing, at other times more of
another ; according to the spirit wherein they are received
and according as God wills.

---

[1] E.p. omits the rest of the paragraph.
[2] 'Whensoever, enlightened by God, it observes . . .' reads the edition
of 1630.   [3] A : 'it sees them even as it saw them before.'
[4] Edition of 1630 : 'that are represented in it.'
[5] *Ibid.* : 'more remote.'

7. The devil likewise can cause[1] these visions, by means of a certain natural light,[2] whereby he brings things clearly before the mind, through spiritual suggestion, whether they be present or absent. There is that passage in S. Matthew, which says of the devil and Christ : *Ostendit omnia regna mundi, et gloriam eorum.*[3] That is to say : He showed Him all the kingdoms of the world and the glory of them. Concerning this certain doctors say that he did it by spiritual suggestion,[4] for it was not possible to make Him see so much with the bodily eyes as all the kingdoms of the world and the glory of them. But there is much difference between these visions that are caused by the devil and those that are of God. For the effects produced in the soul by the devil's visions are not like those produced by good visions ; the former cause aridity of spirit as to communion with God and an inclination to esteem oneself highly, and to receive and set store by the visions aforesaid, and in no wise do they cause the gentleness of humility and love of God. Neither do the forms of such visions remain impressed upon the soul with that sweet clearness of the others ; nor do they last, but are quickly effaced from the soul, save when the soul greatly esteems them, in which case its high esteem of itself causes it to recall them naturally, but with great aridity of spirit, and without producing that effect of love and humility which is caused by good visions when the soul recalls them.

8. These visions, inasmuch as they are of creatures, with whom God has no proportion[5] or essential conformity, cannot serve the understanding as a proximate means to union[6] with God. And thus the soul must conduct itself in a purely negative way concerning them, as in the other things that we have described, in order that it may progress by the proximate means—namely, by faith. Wherefore the soul must make no store or treasure of the forms of such visions as remain imprinted upon it, neither must it lean upon them ; for to do this would be to be encumbered with those forms, images and persons which remain inwardly within it, and thus the soul would not progress toward God

---

[1] Edition of 1630 : ' can cause or imitate.'
[2] E.p. adds : ' making use of the fancy.'
[3] S. Matthew iv, 8. Thus the Codices. E.p. omits the Latin text.
[4] E.p. : ' . . . by intelligible spiritual suggestion.' On this passage, cf. Cornelius a Lapide (*Commentaria in Matthæum*, Cap. IV) and S. Thomas (III p., q. 41, ad 3).
[5] A, B : ' no communication.'   [6] A, B : ' to essential union.'

by denying itself all things. For, even if these forms should be permanently set before the soul, they will not greatly hinder this progress, if the soul has no desire to set store by them. For, although it is true that the remembrance of them impels the soul to a certain love of God and contemplation, yet it is impelled and exalted much more by pure faith and dark detachment from them all, without its knowing how or whence they come to it. And thus it will come to pass that the soul will go forward, enkindled with yearnings of purest love for God, without knowing whence they come to it, or on what foundations they have rested. The fact is that, while faith has been acquiring an ever deeper root and foundation in the soul by means of that emptiness and darkness and detachment from all things, or spiritual poverty, all of which may be spoken of as one and the same thing, at the same time the charity of God has become rooted and founded in the soul ever more truly. Wherefore, the more the soul desires obscurity and annihilation with respect to all the outward or inward things that it is capable of receiving, the more deeply founded is it in faith, and, consequently, in love and hope, since these three theological virtues go together in one.[1]

9 But at certain times the soul neither understands this love nor feels it ; for this love has not its basis in sense and in tender feelings, but in the soul, in fortitude and in a courage and daring that are greater than they were before, though sometimes it overflows into sense and produces gentle and tender feelings. Wherefore, in order to attain to that love, joy and delight which such visions produce and cause in the soul, it is fitting that the soul should have fortitude and mortification and love[2] that it may desire to remain in emptiness and darkness as to all things, and to build its love and joy upon that which it neither sees nor feels, neither can see nor feel in this life, which is God, Who is incomprehensible and above all things. It befits us, then, to journey to Him by denying ourselves everything. For otherwise, even if the soul be so wise, humble and strong that the devil cannot deceive it by visions or cause it to fall into some sin of presumption, as he is wont to do, he will not allow it to make progress ; for he sets obstacles in the way of spiritual detachment and poverty of spirit and emptiness in

[1] E.p. omits : ' since . . . in one.'
[2] E.p. omits : ' and love.'

faith, which is the essential condition for union of the soul with God.

10. And as the same teaching that we gave in the nineteenth and twentieth chapters, concerning supernatural apprehensions and visions of sense, holds good for these visions, we shall not spend more time here in describing them.[1]

CHAPTER XXV

Which treats of revelations, describing their nature and making a distinction between them.

1. According to the order which we are here following, we have next to treat of the second kind of spiritual apprehension, which we have described above as revelations, and which properly belongs[2] to the spirit of prophecy. With respect to this, it must first be known that revelation is naught else than the discovery of some hidden truth or the manifestation of some secret or mystery. Thus God may cause the soul to understand something, by making clear to the understanding the truth concerning it, or He may reveal to the soul certain things which He is doing or proposes to do.

2. Accordingly, we may say that there are two kinds of revelation. The first is the revealing to the understanding of truths which are properly called intellectual knowledge or intelligence ; the second is the manifestation of secrets, which are called revelations with more propriety than the others. For the first kind cannot strictly be called revelations, since they consist in this, that God causes the soul to understand naked truths, not only with respect to temporal things, but likewise with respect to spiritual things, revealing them to the soul clearly and openly. These I have desired to treat under the heading of revelations : first, because they have much kinship and similarity with them : secondly, in order not to multiply many distinctive terms.

3. According to this method, then, we shall now be well able to divide revelations into two kinds of apprehension. The one kind we shall call intellectual knowledge, and the other, the manifestation of secrets and hidden mysteries of

---

[1] A, B, e.p. : ' in treating them more extensively.'
[2] E.p. : ' some of which properly belong.'

God. With these we shall conclude in two chapters as briefly as we may, and in this chapter following we shall treat of the first.[1]

CHAPTER XXVI

Which treats of the intuition of naked truths in the understanding, explaining how they are of two kinds and how the soul is to conduct itself with respect to them.

1. In order to speak properly of this intuition of naked truths which is conveyed to the understanding, the writer would need God to take his hand and to guide his pen ; for know, dear reader, that to describe what they are to the soul in themselves surpasses all words. But, since I speak not of them here of set purpose, but only that through them I may instruct the soul and direct it to Divine union, I shall suffer myself to speak of them here in a brief and modified form, as is sufficient for the fulfilment of that intention.

2. This kind of vision (or, to speak more properly, of knowledge of naked truths) is very different from that of which we have just spoken in the twenty-fourth chapter. For it is not like seeing bodily things with the understanding ; it consists rather in comprehending and seeing with the understanding the truths of God, whether of things that are, that have been or that will be, which is in close conformity with the spirit of prophecy, as perchance we shall show hereafter.

3. Here it is to be observed that this kind of knowledge is distinguishable according to two divisions : the one kind comes to the soul with respect to the Creator ; the other with respect to creatures, as we have said. And, although both kinds are very delectable to the soul, yet the delight caused in it by the kind that relates to God is comparable to nothing whatsoever, and there are no words or terms wherein it can be described. This kind of knowledge is of God Himself, and the delight is in God Himself, whereof David says : There is naught soever like to Him. For this kind of knowledge comes to the soul in direct relation to God, when the soul, after a most lofty manner, has a perception of some attribute of God—of His omnipotence, of His might, of His goodness and sweetness, etc. ; and, whensoever it has such a

---

[1] So Alc. A, B omit : ' and in . . . the first.' E.p. has : ' treating, in this first chapter, intellectual knowledge.'

perception, that which is perceived cleaves to the soul.   Inasmuch as this is pure contemplation, the soul clearly sees
that there is no way wherein it can say aught concerning it,
save to speak, in certain general terms, of the abundance of
delight and blessing which it has felt, and this is expressed by
souls that experience it ; but not to the end that what the
soul has experienced and perceived may be wholly apprehended.

4. And thus David, speaking for himself when something
of this kind had happened to him, used only common and
general terms, saying : *Judicia Domini vera, justificata in
semetipsa.   Desiderabilia super aurum et lapidem pretiosum multum ;
et dulciora super mel et favum.*[1]   Which signifies : The judgements of God[2]—that is, the virtues and attributes which we
perceive in God—are in themselves true, justified, more to
be desired than gold and very much more than precious
stones, and sweeter than the honeycomb and the honey.
And concerning Moses we read that, in a most lofty manifestation of knowledge that God gave to him from Himself
on an occasion when He had passed before him, He said
only that which can be expressed in the common terms
above mentioned.   And it was so that, when the Lord passed
before him in that manifestation of knowledge, Moses
quickly prostrated himself upon the ground,[3] saying :
*Dominator Domine Deus, misericors et clemens, patiens, et multæ
miserationis, ac verax.   Qui custodis misericordiam in millia.*[4]
Which signifies : Ruler,[5] Lord, God, merciful and clement,
patient, and of great compassion, and true, that keepest
mercy promised unto thousands.   Here it is seen that Moses
could not express that which he had learned from God in
one single manifestation of knowledge, and therefore he
expressed and gave utterance to it in all these words.   And
although at times, when such knowledge is given to a soul,
words are used, the soul is quite aware that it has expressed
no part of what it has felt ; for it knows that there is no
fit name by which it is able to name it.   And thus S. Paul,
when he was granted that lofty knowledge of God, made no
attempt to describe it, saying only that it was not lawful for
man to speak of it.

---

[1] Psalm xviii, 10–11 [A.V., xix, 9–10].
[2] E.p. : ' That which we judge and perceive concerning God.'
[3] A, B omit ' quickly.'
[4] Exodus xxxiv, 6–7.   [5] [*Lit.*, ' Emperor.']

5. These Divine manifestations of knowledge which have respect to God never relate to particular matters, inasmuch as they concern the Chief Beginning, and therefore can have no particular reference, unless it be a question of some truth concerning a thing less than God, which in some way is seen together with the rest ; but these Divine manifestations themselves—no, in no way whatsoever.[1] And these lofty manifestations of knowledge can only come to the soul that attains to union with God, for they are themselves that union; and to receive them is equivalent to a certain contact with the Divinity[2] which the soul experiences, and thus it is God Himself Who is perceived and tasted therein. And, although He cannot be experienced manifestly and clearly, as in glory, this touch of knowledge and delight is nevertheless so sublime and profound that it penetrates the substance[3] of the soul, and the devil cannot meddle with it or produce any manifestation like to it, for there is no such thing, neither is there aught that compares with it, neither can he infuse pleasure or delight that is like to it ; for such kinds of knowledge savour of the Divine Essence and of eternal life, and the devil cannot counterfeit a thing so lofty.

6. Nevertheless he might make some pretence of imitating it, by representing to the soul certain great things and pregnant matters which can readily be perceived by the senses and endeavouring to persuade the soul that these are God ; but not in such wise that it enters into the substance[4] of the soul and of a sudden[5] renews it and enkindles it with love, as do the manifestations of God. For there are certain kinds of knowledge, and certain of these touches wrought by God in the substance of the soul, which enrich it after such wise that not only does one of them suffice to take from the soul once and for all the whole of the imperfections that it had itself been unable to throw off during its whole life, but it leaves the soul full of virtues and blessings[6] from God.

7. And these touches are so delectable to the soul, and of a delight so intimate, that if it received only one of them it

<hr />

[1] E.p. : ‘ and therefore can have no particular reference, unless this knowledge should be extended to some other truth concerning something less than God which is capable of being described in some way ; but these general manifestations—no.’ [2] E.p. has ‘ Divine Truth ’ for ‘ Divinity.’

[3] E.p. : ‘ the inmost part.’

[4] E.p. : ‘ into the very interior part.’ A : ‘ into the wisdom.’

[5] So Alc., D. A, B, C, P, e.p. have : ‘ and sublimely.’ [The difference is slight : *subidamente* for *súbitamente*.]

[6] A, erroneously, has : ‘ and visions.’

would consider itself well rewarded for all the trials that it had suffered in this life, even had they been innumerable ; and it is so greatly encouraged and given such energy to suffer many things for God's sake that it suffers above all in seeing that it suffers not more.

8. The soul cannot attain to these lofty degrees of knowledge by means of any comparison or imagination of its own, because[1] they are loftier than all these ; and so God works them in the soul without making use of its own capacities. Wherefore, at certain times, when the soul is least thinking of it and least desiring it, God is wont to give it these Divine touches, by causing it certain recollections of Himself. And these are sometimes suddenly caused in the soul by its mere recollection of certain things—sometimes of very small things. And they are so readily perceived[2] that at times they cause not only the soul, but also the body, to tremble. But at other times they come to pass in the spirit when it is very tranquil, without any kind of trembling, but with a sudden[3] sense of delight and spiritual refreshment.

9. At other times, again, they come when the soul repeats or hears some word, from Scripture or possibly from some other source ; but they are not always equally efficacious and sensible, for oftentimes they are extremely faint ; yet, however faint they may be, one of these recollections and touches of God is more profitable to the soul than many other kinds of knowledge or many meditations upon the creatures and the works of God. And, since these manifestations of knowledge come to the soul suddenly,[4] and independently of its own free will, it must neither desire to have them, nor desire not to have them[5] ; but must merely be humble and resigned concerning them, and God will perform His work how and when He wills.

10. And I say not that the soul should behave in the same negative manner with regard to these apprehensions as with regard to the rest, for, as we have said, they are a part of the union, towards which we are directing the soul ; to which end we are teaching it to detach and strip itself of all other apprehensions. And the means by which God will

---

[1] E.p. adds : ' as we have said.'
[2] E.p. : ' And they are so efficacious.'
[3] So Alc. The other authorities read : ' with a sublime ' [*subido* for *súbito*, as above].   [4] E.p. adds : ' as we have said.'
[5] E.p. : ' it must neither strive to have them nor strive not to have them.'

do this must be humility and suffering for love of God with resignation[1] as regards all reward ; for these favours are not granted to the soul which still cherishes attachments, inasmuch as they are granted through a very special love of God toward the soul which loves Him likewise with great detachment. It is to this that the Son of God referred, in S. John, when He said : *Qui autem diligit me, diligetur a Patre meo, et ego diligam eum, et manifestabo ei me ipsum.*[2] Which signifies : He that loves Me shall be loved of My Father, and I will love him and will manifest Myself to him. Herein are included the kinds of knowledge and touches to which we are referring, which God manifests to the soul that truly loves Him.[3]

11. The second kind of knowledge or vision of interior truths[4] is very different from this that we have described, since it is of things lower than God. And herein is included the perception of the truth of things in themselves, and that of the events and happenings which come to pass among men. And this knowledge is of such a kind that, when the soul is taught these truths, they sink into it deeply, without anyone saying aught to it about them, to such an extent that, although they may tell it something else, the soul cannot give its inward assent to this, even though it endeavour to give such assent by making a great effort ; for it is learning something else within the spirit by means of the spirit that teaches it that thing,[5] which is equivalent to seeing it clearly. This pertains[6] to the spirit of prophecy and to the grace which S. Paul calls the gift of the discernment of spirits.[7] Yet, although the soul holds something which it understands to be quite certain and true, as we have said, and although it may be unable to give it that passive interior consent, it must not therefore cease to believe and to give the consent of reason to that which its spiritual director tells it and commands it,[8] even though this may be quite contrary to its own feelings, so that it may be directed in faith to Divine union, to which a soul must journey by believing rather than by understanding.

---

[1] E.p. adds : ' and disinterestedness.'   [2] S. John xiv, 21.
[3] A, B : ' that draws near to Him and truly loves Him.'
[4] A, B : ' or of interior truths.'
[5] E.p. : ' something else in that which has been spiritually represented to it.'
[6] E.p. : ' This may pertain. '   [7] 1 Corinthians xii, 10.
[8] E.p. abbreviates : ' as we have said, it cannot but follow that which its spiritual director commands.'

12. Concerning both these things we have clear testimonies in Scripture. For with respect to the spiritual knowledge[1] of things that may be acquired, the Wise Man says these words : *Ipse dedit mihi horum, quæ sunt, scientiam veram, ut sciam dispositionem orbis terrarum, et virtutes elementorum, initium et consummationem temporum, vicissitudinum permutationes, et con-summationes temporum, et morum mutationes, divisiones temporum, et anni cursus, et stellarum dispositiones, naturas animalium et iras bestiarum, vim ventorum, et cogitationes hominum, differentias vir-gultorum, et virtutes radicum, et quæcumque sunt abscondita, et improvisa didici : omnium enim artifex docuit me sapientia.*[2] Which signifies : God hath given me true knowledge of things, namely : That I should know the disposition of the round world[3] and the virtues of the elements ; the begin-ning, ending and middle of the seasons, the alterations in the changes[4] and the consummations of the seasons, and the changes of customs, the divisions of the seasons,[5] the courses of the year and the dispositions of the stars ; the natures of the animals, and the furies of the beasts, the strength and virtue of the winds, and the thoughts of men ; the diversities in plants and trees and the virtues of roots and all things that are hidden, and those that are not foreseen[6] : all these I learned, for Wisdom, which is the worker of all things, taught me. And although this knowledge which the Wise Man here says that God gave him concerning all things was infused[7] and general, the passage quoted furnishes sufficient evidence for all particular kinds of knowledge which God infuses into souls, by supernatural means, when He wills. And this not that He may give them a general habit of know-ledge as He gave to Solomon in the matters afore-mentioned ; but that He may reveal to them at times certain truths with respect to any of all these things that the Wise Man here enumerates. Although it is true that into many souls Our Lord infuses habits which relate to many things, yet these are never of so general a kind as they were in the case of Solomon. The differences between them are like to those between the gifts distributed by God which are enumerated

---

[1] E.p.: ' to the particular spiritual knowledge.'
[2] Wisdom vii, 17–21. The reading of the Latin text is that of Alc.
[3] [*Lit.*, ' of the roundness of the lands.']
[4] E.p. : ' the changes in events.'
[5] A omits this phrase, and B, this and the phrase preceding.
[6] E.p. omits : ' and . . . foreseen.'
[7] A abbreviates : ' which is the worker of all things, was infused.'

by S. Paul ; among these he sets wisdom, knowledge, faith, prophecy, discernment or knowledge of spirits, understanding of tongues, interpretation of spoken words, etc.[1] All these kinds of knowledge are infused habits,[2] which God gives freely to whom He will, whether naturally or supernaturally ; naturally,[3] as to Balaam, to other idolatrous prophets and to many sybils, to whom He gave the spirit of prophecy ; and supernaturally, as to the holy prophets and apostles and other saints.[4]

13. But over and above these habits or graces[5] freely bestowed,[6] what we say is that persons who are perfect or are making progress in perfection are wont very ordinarily to receive enlightenment and knowledge of things present or absent ; these they know through their spirit,[7] which is already enlightened and purged. We can interpret that passage from the Proverbs in this sense, namely : *Quomodo in aquis resplendent vultus prospicientium sic corda hominum manifesta sunt prudentibus.*[8] Even as there appear in the waters the faces of those that look therein, so the hearts of men are manifest to the prudent. This is understood of those that have the wisdom of saints, which the sacred Scripture calls prudence. And in this way these spirits sometimes learn of other things also, although not whensoever they will ; for this belongs only to those that have the habit, and even to these it belongs not always and with respect to all things, for it depends upon God's will to help them.

14. But it must be known that those whose spirits are purged can learn by natural means with great readiness,[9] and some more readily than others, that which is in the inward spirit or heart, and the inclinations and talents of men, and this by outward indications, albeit very slight ones, as words, movements and other signs. For, even as the devil can do this, since he is spirit, even so likewise can the spiritual man, according to the words of the Apostle, who says : *Spiritualis autem judicat omnia.*[10] He that is spiritual

---

[1] [*Lit.*, ' exposition of words ' ; the reference is clearly to 1 Corinthians xii, 8–10.]
[2] E.p. : ' infused gifts.'   [3] Alc. alone has ' naturally.'
[4] E.p. abbreviates : ' to whom He will, as to the holy prophets and apostles and to other saints.'
[5] E.p. : ' But over and above these graces.'
[6] [The original has *gratis datas*.]
[7] E.p. : ' through the light which they receive in their spirit.'
[8] Proverbs xxvii, 19.
[9] E.p. : ' can learn with greater readiness.'   [10] 1 Corinthians ii, 15.

judgeth all things.   And again he says : *Spiritus enim omnia scrutatur, etiam profunda Dei.*[1]   The spirit searcheth all things, yea, the deep things of God.   Wherefore, although spiritual persons cannot by nature know thoughts, or things that are in the minds of others,[2] they may well interpret them through supernatural enlightenment or by signs.   And, although they may often be deceived in their interpretation of signs, they are more generally correct.   Yet we must trust neither to the one means nor to the other, for the devil meddles herein greatly, and with much subtlety, as we shall afterwards say, and thus we must ever renounce such kinds of knowledge.

15. And that spiritual persons may have knowledge of the deeds and happenings of men, even though they be elsewhere, we have witness and example in the Fourth Book of the Kings, where Gehazi, the servant of our father Elisha,[3] desired to hide from him the money which he had received from Naaman the Syrian, and Elisha said : *Nonne cor meum in præsenti erat, quando reversus est homo de curru suo in occursum tui ?*[4]   Was not my heart perchance present, when Naaman turned again from his chariot and went to meet thee ?   This happens spiritually ; the spirit sees it as though it were happening in its presence.   And the same thing is proved in the same book, where we read likewise of the same Elisha, that, knowing all that the King of Syria did with his princes in his secret place, he told it to the King of Israel, and thus the counsels of the King of Syria were of no effect ; so much so that, when the King of Syria saw that all was known, he said to his people[5] : Wherefore do ye not tell me which of you is betraying me to the King of Israel ?   And then one of his servants said : *Nequaquam, Domine mi Rex, sed Eliseus Propheta, qui est in Israel, indicat Regi Israel omnia verba, quæcumque locutus fueris in conclavi tuo.*[6]   It is not so, my lord, O king, but Elisha, the prophet that is in Israel, telleth the king of Israel all the words that thou speakest in thy bedchamber.

16. Both kinds of this knowledge of things, as well as other kinds of knowledge, come to pass[7] in the soul passively, so

---

[1] 1 Corinthians ii, 10.   [2] [*Lit.*, ' in the interior.']
[3] This phrase is found only in Alc. and e.p.
[4] 4 Kings [A.V., 2 Kings] v, 26.
[5] A, B : ' to his counsellors.'
[6] 4 Kings [A.V., 2 Kings] vi, 12.
[7] E.p. : ' Both kinds of this knowledge of things also come to pass.'

that for its own part it does naught. For it will come to pass that, when a person is inattentive to a matter and it is far from his mind, there will come to him a vivid understanding of what he is hearing or reading, and that much more clearly than it could be conveyed by the sound of the words ; and at times, though he understand not the words, as when they are in Latin and he knows not that tongue, the knowledge of their meaning comes to him, despite his not understanding them.

17. With regard to the deceptions which the devil can bring about, and does bring about, concerning this kind of knowledge and understanding, there is much that might be said, for the deceptions which he effects in this way are very great and very difficult to unmask. Inasmuch as, through suggestion,[1] he can represent to the soul many kinds of intellectual knowledge and implant them so firmly that it appears impossible that they should not be true, he will certainly make the soul to believe innumerable falsehoods if it be not humble and cautious. For suggestion has sometimes great power over the soul, above all when it is to some extent aided by the weakness of sense, causing the knowledge which it conveys to sink into the soul with such great power, persuasiveness and determination that the soul needs to give itself earnestly to prayer and to exert great strength if it is to cast it off. For at times the devil is accustomed to represent to the soul the sins of others, and evil consciences and evil souls,[2] falsely but very vividly, and all this he does to harm the soul, trusting that it may spread abroad his revelations, and that thus more sins may be committed, for which reason he fills the soul with zeal by making it believe that these revelations are granted it so that it may commend the persons concerned to God. Now, though it is true that God sometimes sets before holy souls the necessities of their neighbours, so that they may commend them to God or relieve them, even as we read that He revealed to Jeremiah the weakness of the Prophet Baruch, that he might give him counsel concerning it,[3] yet it is more often the devil who does this, and speaks falsely about it, in order to cause infamy, sin and discouragement, whereof we have very great experience. And at other times he implants other kinds of knowledge

---

[1] E.p. adds : ' making use of the bodily senses.'
[2] A, B : ' and the evil souls of others.'
[3] Jeremiah xlv, 3.

with great assurance, and persuades the soul to believe them.

18. Such knowledge as this, whether it be of God or no, can be of very little assistance to the progress of the soul[1] on its journey to God, if the soul desire it and be attached to it ; on the contrary, if it were not scrupulous in rejecting it, not only would it be hindered on its road, but it would even be greatly harmed and led far astray. For all the perils and inconveniences which, as we have said, may be involved in the supernatural apprehensions whereof we have treated up to this point, may occur here, and more also. I will not, therefore, treat more fully of this matter here, since sufficient instruction has already been given in past chapters ; but I will[2] only say that the soul must always be very scrupulous in rejecting these things, and seek to journey to God by the way of unknowing ; and must ever relate its experiences to its spiritual confessor, and be ever attentive to his counsel. Let the confessor guide the soul past this, as though it were a passing matter, for it is of no kind of importance for[3] the road to union ; for when these things are granted to the soul passively they always leave in it such effect as God wills shall remain, without necessity for the soul to exert any diligence in the matter.[4] And thus it seems to me that there is no reason to describe here either the effect which is produced by true knowledge, or that which comes from false knowledge, for this would be wearisome and never-ending. For the effects of this knowledge cannot all be described in a brief instruction, the knowledge being great and greatly varied, and its effects being so likewise, since good knowledge produces good effects, and evil knowledge, evil effects,[5] etc. In saying that all should be rejected,[6] we have said sufficient for the soul not to go astray.[7]

---

[1] E.p. : ' can bring very little profit to the soul.'
[2] A, B : ' therefore I will . . .'
[3] E.p. : ' . . . passing matter, treating it as of no account for . . .'
[4] E.p. omits : ' without . . . in the matter.'
[5] A, B, e.p. have : ' . . . good effects [leading] to good, and evil knowledge evil effects [leading] to evil.' Alc. ends the chapter here.
[6] E.p. adds : ' and how this is to be done.'
[7] E.p. omits : ' for the soul not to go astray.' We follow A and B in our reading of this last sentence.

CHAPTER XXVII

Which treats of the second kind of revelation, namely, the disclosure of hidden secrets.[1] Describes the way in which these may assist the soul toward union with God, and the way in which they may be a hindrance ; and how the devil may deceive the soul greatly in this matter.

1. We were saying that the second kind of revelation was the manifestation of hidden mysteries and secrets. This may come to pass in two ways. The first with respect to that which God is in Himself, wherein is included the revelation of the mystery of the most holy Trinity and Unity of God. The second is with respect to that which God is in His works, and herein are included the other articles of our Catholic faith,[2] and the propositions deducible from them which may be laid down explicitly as truths. In these are included and comprised a great number of the revelations of the prophets, of promises and threatenings of God, and of other things which have happened and shall happen.[3] Under this second head we may also include many other particular things which God habitually reveals, both concerning the universe in general as also in particular concerning kingdoms, provinces and states and families and particular persons. Of these we have examples in abundance in the Divine writings, both of the one kind and of the other, especially in all the Prophets, wherein are found revelations of all these kinds. As this is a clear and plain fact, I will not here spend time in quoting these examples, but will only say[4] that these revelations do not come to pass by word alone, but that God gives them in many ways and manners, sometimes by word alone, sometimes by signs and figures alone, and by images and similitudes alone, sometimes in more than one way at once, as is likewise to be seen in the Prophets, particularly throughout the Apocalypse, where we find not only all the kinds of revelation which we have described, but likewise the ways and manners to which we are here referring.

---

[1] A, B, e.p. add : ' and mysteries.'
[2] E.p. : ' of our holy Catholic faith.'
[3] The MSS. [and P. Silverio] add : ' with regard to this business of faith.' E.p. omits these words.
[4] A, B : ' . . . I do not speak of them ; I only say . . .'

2. As to these revelations which are included under our second head, God grants them still in our time to whom He will. He is wont, for example, to reveal to some persons how many days they still have to live, or what trials they are to to suffer, or what is to befall such and such a person, or such and such a kingdom, etc. And even as regards the mysteries of our faith, He will reveal and expound to the spirit the truths concerning them,[1] although this is not properly to be termed revelation, for it has already been revealed once, but is more correctly a manifestation or explanation of what has been revealed already.

3. In this kind of revelation[2] the devil may meddle considerably. For, as revelations of this nature come ordinarily through words, figures and similitudes, etc., the devil may very readily counterfeit others like them, much more so than when the revelations are in spirit alone.[3] Wherefore, if with regard to the first and the second kind of revelation which we are here describing, as touching our faith, there be revealed to us anything new, or different, we must in no wise give our consent to it, even though we had evidence that it was spoken by an angel from Heaven.[4] For even so says S. Paul, in these words : *Licet nos, aut Angelus de cœlo evangelizet vobis præterquam quod evangelizavimus vobis, anathema sit.*[5] Which signifies : Even though an angel from Heaven declare or preach unto you aught else than that which we have preached unto you, let him be anathema.

4. Since, then, there are no more articles to be revealed concerning the substance of our faith than those which have already been revealed to the Church, not only must[6] anything which may be revealed anew to the soul concerning this be rejected, but it behoves the soul[7] to be cautious and take no notice of various other things involved therein, and for the sake of the purity of the soul it behoves it to keep the faith, even though the truths already revealed to it be revealed again ; and to believe them, not because they are now revealed anew, but because they have already been sufficiently revealed to the Church ; rather it must close

---

[1] E.p. adds : ' with particular light and impressiveness.'
[2] So the MSS. E.p. reads : ' With regard, then, to what we call revelations (for I speak not now of what has already been revealed, such as the mysteries of the faith) . . .'
[3] E.p. omits : ' much more . . . spirit alone.'
[4] E.p. omits : ' even though . . . from Heaven.'   [5] Galatians i, 8.
[6] E.p. begins the sentence thus : ' And thus, not only must . . .'
[7] E.p. adds : ' apart from this.'

its understanding to them, holding[1] simply to the doctrine of the Church and to its faith, which, as S. Paul says, enters through hearing.[2] And let not its credence and intellectual assent be given to these matters of the faith which have been revealed anew, however fitting and true they may seem to it, if it desire not to be deceived.[3] For, in order to deceive the soul and to instil falsehoods into it, the devil first feeds it with truths and things that are probable in order to give it assurance and afterwards to deceive it.[4] He resembles one that sews leather with a bristle, first piercing the leather with the sharp bristle, after which enters the soft thread ; the thread could not enter unless the bristle guided it.

5. And let this be considered carefully ; for, even were it true that there was no peril in such deception, yet it greatly behoves the soul not to desire to understand clearly things that have respect to the faith,[5] so that it may preserve the merit of faith, in its purity and entirety, and likewise that it may come, in this night of the understanding, to the Divine light of Divine union. And it is equally necessary to consider any new revelation with one's eyes closed, and holding fast the prophecies of old, for the Apostle S. Peter, though he had seen the glory of the Son of God after some manner[6] on Mount Tabor, wrote, in his canonical epistle, these words : *Et habemus firmiorem propheticum sermonem; cui benefacitis attendentes, etc.*[7] Which is as though he had said : Although the vision that we have seen of Christ on the Mount is true, the word of the prophecy that is revealed to us is firmer and surer, and, if ye rest your soul upon it, ye do well.

6. And if it is true that, for the reasons already described, it behoves the soul to close its eyes to the aforementioned revelations which come to it, and which concern the propositions of the faith,[8] how much more necessary will it be neither to receive nor to give credit to other revelations relating to different things, wherein the devil habitually

---

[1] E.p. abbreviates : ' it behoves it to keep the faith, closing its understanding and holding . . .' [2] Romans x, 17.
[3] E.p. has ' be easily given,' and omits ' of the faith ' and ' however fitting and true they may seem to it.'
[4] E.p. omits : ' and afterwards to deceive it.'
[5] E.p. omits : ' that have respect to the faith.'
[6] E.p. omits these three words. [7] 2 S. Peter i, 19.
[8] So Alc. A, B : ' to close its eyes to the things that happen with respect to the propositions or new revelations of the faith.' E.p. : ' not to open its eyes curiously to the new revelations which come to it and which concern the propositions of the faith.'

meddles so greatly that I believe it impossible[1] for a man not
to be deceived in many of them unless he strive to reject
them, such an appearance of truth and security does the
devil give them ? For he brings together so many appear-
ances and probabilities, in order that they may be believed,
and plants them so firmly in the sense and the imagination,
that it seems to the person affected that what he says will
certainly happen ; and in such a way does he cause the soul
to grasp and hold them, that, if it have not humility, it will
hardly be persuaded to reject them and made to believe the
contrary. Wherefore, the soul that is pure, cautious, simple
and humble must resist revelations and other visions with as
much effort and care as though they were very perilous
temptations.[2] For there is no need to desire them ; on the
contrary, there is need not to desire them, if we are to reach
the union of love. For it is this that Solomon meant when
he said : What need has a man to desire and seek the things
that are above his natural capacity ?[3] As though we were
to say : He has[4] no necessity, in order to be perfect, to desire
supernatural things[5] by supernatural means, which are
above his capacity.[6]

7. And as the objections that can be made to this have
already been answered, in the nineteenth and twentieth
chapters of this book, I refer the reader to these, and say
only that the soul must keep itself from all revelations[7] in
order to journey, in purity and without error, in the night
of faith, to union.

CHAPTER XXVIII

*Which treats of interior locutions that may come to the spirit super-
naturally. Says of what kinds they are.*

1. The discreet reader has ever need to bear in mind the
intent and end which I have in this book, which is the

---

[1] E.p. : ' I believe it almost impossible.'
[2] E.p. omits : ' with as . . . temptations.'
[3] Ecclesiastes vii, 1 [Vulgate]. E.p. omits ' natural.'
[4] A, B : ' Man has.'   [5] E.p. : ' supernatural and extraordinary things.'
[6] A, B add : ' for perfection.'
[7] So Alc. A, B read : ' I refer [the reader] to them in that which
touches this matter of revelations ; for it is sufficient to know that it
behoves the soul to keep itself from them all. . . .' E.p. : ' . . . referring
[the reader] to them, I cease as touching this matter of revelations ; for
it is sufficient to know that it behoves the soul to keep itself prudently
from them all. . . .'

direction of the soul, through all its apprehensions, natural and supernatural, without deception or hindrance, in purity of faith, to Divine union with God. If he does this, he will understand that, although with respect to apprehensions of the soul and the doctrine that I am expounding I give not such copious instruction neither do I particularize so much or make so many divisions as the understanding perchance requires, I am not being over-brief in this matter. For with respect to all this I believe that sufficient cautions, explanations and instructions are given for the soul to be enabled to behave prudently in every contingency, outward or inward, so as to make progress. And this is the reason why I have so briefly dismissed the subject of prophetic apprehensions and the other subjects allied to it ; for there is so much more to be said of each of them, according to the differences and the ways and manners[1] that are wont to be observed in each,[2] that I believe one could never know it all perfectly. I am content that, as I believe, the substance and the doctrine thereof have been given, and the soul has been warned of the caution which it behoves it to exercise in this respect, and also concerning all other things of the same kind that may come to pass within it.

2. I will now follow the same course with regard to the third kind of apprehension, which, we said, was that of supernatural locutions,[3] which are apt to come to the spirits of spiritual persons[4] without the intervention of any bodily sense. These, although they are of many kinds, may, I believe, all be reduced to three, namely : successive, formal and substantial. I describe as successive certain words and arguments, which the spirit is wont to form and fashion when it is inwardly recollected. Formal words are certain clear and distinct words[5] which the spirit receives ; not of itself, but from a third person, sometimes when it is recollected and sometimes when it is not. Substantial words are others which also come to the spirit formally, sometimes when it is recollected and sometimes when it is not ; these cause in the substance of the soul[6] that substance and virtue which they signify. All these we shall here proceed to treat in their order.

---

[1] E.p. omits : ' and manners.'   [2] E.p. omits : ' in each.'
[3] E.p. has ' apprehensions ' for ' locutions.'
[4] E.p. omits : ' the spirits of.' A, B have ' may ' for ' are wont to.'
[5] [Lit., ' certain distinct and formal words.']
[6] E.p. : ' in the inmost part of the soul.'

CHAPTER XXIX

Which treats of the first kind of words that the recollected spirit sometimes forms within itself. Describes the cause of these and the profit and the harm which there may be in them.

1. These successive words always come when the spirit is recollected and absorbed very attentively in some meditation ; and, in its reflections upon that same matter whereon it is thinking, it proceeds from one stage to another, forming[1] words and arguments which are greatly to the point, with much facility and distinctness, and by means of its reasoning discovers[2] things which it knew not with respect to the matter of its reflections, so that it believes that it is not doing this itself, but that another person is supplying the reasoning within its mind or answering its questions or teaching it. And in truth it has great cause to think this, for the soul itself is reasoning with itself and answering itself as though it were one person addressing another ; and in some ways this is really so ; for, although it is the spirit itself that works as an instrument,[3] the Holy Spirit oftentimes aids it to produce and form those true reasonings, words and conceptions. And thus it utters them to itself as though to a third person. For, as at that time the understanding is recollected and united with the truth of that whereon it is thinking, and the Divine Spirit is likewise united with it in that truth, as it is always united in all truth,[4] it follows that, when the understanding communicates in this way with the Divine Spirit by means of this truth, it begins to form within itself, successively, those other truths which are connected with that whereon it is thinking, the door being opened to it and illumination being given to it continually by the Holy Spirit Who teaches it. For this is one of the ways wherein the Holy Spirit teaches.

2. And when the understanding is illumined and taught in this way by this master, and comprehends these truths, it begins of its own accord[5] to form the words which relate to the truths that are communicated to it from elsewhere.

---

[1] A, B have ' founding ' for ' forming.'
[2] B has ' reflects upon ' for ' discovers.'
[3] E.p. omits : ' as an instrument.'
[4] E.p. omits : ' in that . . . all truth.'
[5] E.p. omits : ' of its own accord.'

So that we may say that the voice is the voice of Jacob and the hands are the hands of Esau.[1] And one that is in this condition will be unable to believe that this is so, but will think that the sayings and the words come from a third person. For such a one knows not the facility with which the understanding can form words inwardly, as though they come from a third person, and having reference to conceptions and truths which have in fact been communicated to it by a third person.

3. And although it is true that, in this communication and enlightenment of the understanding, no deception is produced in the soul itself, yet deception may, and frequently does occur in the formal words and reasonings which the understanding bases upon it. For, inasmuch as this illumination which it receives is at times very subtle and spiritual, so that the understanding cannot attain to a clear apprehension of it, and it is the understanding that, as we say, forms the reasonings of its own accord, it follows that those which it forms are frequently false, and on other occasions are only apparently true, or are imperfect. For since at the outset the soul began to seize the truth, and then brought into play the skilfulness or the clumsiness of its own lowly understanding, it is natural that it should change its way of thinking in accordance with its intellectual capacity, and continue all the time in the same way, as though a third person were speaking.

4. I knew a person who had these successive locutions, and who among them formed some that were very true and substantial with respect to the most holy Sacrament of the Eucharist; but others were sheer heresy.[2] And I am appalled at what happens in these days—namely, when some soul with the very smallest experience of meditation, if it be conscious of certain locutions of this kind in some state of recollection, at once christens them all as coming from God, and assumes that this is the case, saying : ' God said to me . . .' ; ' God answered me . . .' ; whereas it is not so at all, but, as we have said, it is for the most part they who are saying it to themselves.

5. And, over and above this, the desire which people have for locutions, and the pleasure which comes to their spirits from them, lead them to make answer to themselves

---

[1] Genesis xxvii, 22.
[2] E.p. : ' but others contained much error.'

and then to think that it is God Who is answering them and speaking to them. They therefore commit great blunders if they put not great restraint upon themselves, and if their director obliges them not to abstain from these kinds of reflection. For they are apt to gain from them mere non-sensical talk and impurity of soul rather than humility and mortification of spirit, if they think ' This was indeed a great thing ' and ' God was speaking ' ; whereas it will have been little more than nothing, or nothing at all, or less than nothing. For, if humility and charity be not engendered by such experiences, and mortification and holy simplicity and silence, etc., what can be the value of them ? I say, then, that these things may hinder the soul greatly in its progress to Divine union because, if it pay heed to them, it is led far astray from the abyss of faith, where the understanding must remain in darkness, and must journey in darkness, by love and in faith, and not by much reasoning.

6. And if you ask me why the understanding must be deprived of these truths, since it is illumined through them by the Spirit of God, and that thus they cannot be evil, I say that the Holy Spirit illumines the understanding which is recollected, and illumines it according to the manner of its recollection,[1] and that the understanding cannot find any other and greater recollection than in faith ; and thus the Holy Spirit will illumine it in naught more than in faith. For the purer and the more refined in faith[2] is the soul, the more it has of the infused charity of God ; and the more charity it has, the more is it illumined and the more gifts of the Holy Spirit are communicated to it, for charity is the cause and the means whereby they are communicated to it.[3] And although it is true that, in this illumination of truths, the Holy Spirit communicates a certain light to the soul, this is nevertheless as different in quality from that

---

[1] This profound and important principle, which has often been developed in mystical theology, is well expounded by P. José de Jesús María in a treatise called *Reply to a question* [*Respuesta a una duda*]. Here, among other things, he says : ' As S. Thomas proves (*De Veritate*, q. 12, a. 6), Divine illumination, like every other spiritual form, is communicated to the soul after the manner of the receiver of it, whether according to sense or according to spirit, to the particular or to the universal. And thus, he that receives it must prepare himself for it to be communicated to him further, whether in small measure (as we say) or according to sense, or in large measure intellectually.'

[2] E.p. : ' in perfection of living faith.'

[3] E.p. omits ' of the Holy Spirit ' and ' for charity . . . communicated to it.'

which is in faith, wherein is no clear understanding, as is the most precious gold from the basest metal ; and, with regard to its quantity,[1] the one is as much greater than the other as the sea is greater than a drop of water.   For in the one manner there is communicated to the soul wisdom concerning one or two or three truths, etc., but in the other there is communicated to it all the wisdom of God in general, which is the Son of God, Who communicates Himself to the soul in faith.[2]

7. And if you tell me that this is all good, and that the one impedes not the other, I reply that it impedes it greatly if the soul sets store by it ; for to do this is to busy itself with things which are quite clear and of little importance, yet which are quite sufficient to hinder the communication of the abyss of faith, wherein God supernaturally and secretly instructs the soul, and exalts it in virtues and gifts in a way that it knows not.   And the profit which these successive communications will bring us cannot come by our deliberately applying the understanding to them, for if we do this they will rather lead us astray, even as Wisdom says to the soul in the *Songs* : Turn away thine eyes from me, for they cause me to soar aloft.[3]   That is to say : They make me to soar far away from thee and to set myself higher.   We must therefore not apply the understanding[4] to that which is being supernaturally communicated to it, but simply and sincerely apply the will to God with love,[5] for it is through love that these blessings are communicated and through love they will be communicated in greater abundance than before.   For if the ability of the natural[6] understanding or of other faculties be brought actively to bear upon these things which are communicated supernaturally and passively, its imperfect nature will not reach them, and thus they will perforce be modified according to the capacity of the understanding, and consequently will perforce be changed ; and thus the understanding will necessarily go astray[7] and begin to form reasonings within itself, and there will no longer be anything supernatural or any semblance thereof, but all will be merely natural and most erroneous and unworthy.

[1] E.p. : ' and, as to the abundance of its light.'
[2] E.p. : ' in general, by a simple and universal knowledge which is given to the soul in faith.'   [3] [Canticles vi, 5.]
[4] E.p. : ' the strength of the understanding.'
[5] A, B : ' apply the will to the love of God.'
[6] E.p. omits ' natural.'
[7] E.p. : ' will necessarily be in peril of straying.'

8. But there are certain types of understanding so quick and subtle that, when they become recollected during some meditation, they reason in conceptions, and begin naturally, and with great facility, to form their conceptions into these words and arguments, and think that without doubt they come from God. Yet they come only from the understanding, which, with its natural illumination, being to some extent freed from the operation of the senses, is able to effect all this, and more, without any supernatural aid. This happens very commonly, and such persons are greatly deceived, thinking that they have attained to a high degree of prayer and are receiving communications from God, wherefore they either write this down or cause[1] it to be written. And it turns out[2] to be nothing, and to have the substance of no virtue, and it does them no greater service than to encourage them in vanity.

9. Let these learn to be intent upon naught, save only upon grounding the will in humble love, working diligently, suffering and thus imitating the Son of God in His life and mortifications,[3] for this is the road whereby a man will come to all spiritual good, rather than by much inward reasoning.

10. In this type of locution—namely, in successive interior words—the devil intervenes frequently, especially in the case of such as have some inclination or affection for them. At the time when such persons begin to be recollected, the devil is accustomed to offer them ample material for distractions, forming conceptions or words by suggestion in their understanding, and then corrupting[4] and deceiving it most subtly with things that have great appearance of truth. And this is one of the manners wherein he communicates[5] with those who have made some implicit or expressed compact with him; as with certain heretics, especially with certain heresiarchs, whose understanding he fills with most subtle, false and erroneous conceptions and arguments.

11. From what has been said, it is evident that these successive locutions may proceed in the understanding from three causes, namely : from the Divine Spirit, Who moves and illumines the understanding ; from the natural illumina-

---

[1] E.p. : ' . . . from God, and they write down what happens to them or cause . . .'   [2] E.p. : ' And it all turns out . . .'
[3] E.p. : ' in His life, and mortifying themselves in all things.'
[4] [*Lit.*, ' and then throwing it down.']
[5] E.p. : ' It is in this way that he is wont to communicate . . .'

tion of the same understanding ; and from the devil, who may speak to the soul by suggestion. To describe[1] now the signs and indications by which a man may know when they proceed from one cause and when from another would be somewhat difficult, as also to give examples and indications.[2] It is quite possible, however, to give some general signs, which are these. When in its words and conceptions the soul finds itself loving God and at the same time is conscious not only of love but also of humility and reverence, it is a sign that the Holy Spirit is working within it, for, whensoever He grants favours, He grants them with this accompaniment. When the locutions proceed from the brilliance and illumination of the understanding only, it is the understanding that accomplishes everything, without that operation of the virtues (although the will, in the knowledge and illumination of those truths, may love naturally) ; and, when the meditation is over, the will remains dry, albeit inclined neither to vanity nor to evil, unless the devil should tempt it afresh about this matter. This, however, is not the case when the locutions have been prompted by a good spirit ; for then, as a rule, the will is afterwards affectioned to God and inclined to well-doing. At certain times, nevertheless, it will happen that, although the communication has been the result of a good spirit, the will remains in aridity, since God ordains it so for certain causes which are of assistance to the soul. At other times the soul will not be very conscious of the operations or motions of those virtues, yet that which it has experienced will be good. Wherefore I say that the difference between these locutions is sometimes difficult to recognize, by reason of the varied effects which they produce ; but these which have now been described are the most common, although sometimes they occur in greater abundance and sometimes in less. But those that come from the devil are sometimes difficult to understand and recognize, for, although it is true that as a rule they leave the will in aridity with respect to love of God, and the mind inclined to vanity, self-esteem or complacency, nevertheless they sometimes inspire the soul with a false humility and a fervent affection of the will rooted in self-love, so that at times a person must be extremely spiritually-minded to recognize it. And this the devil does in order the better to

---

[1] E.p. : ' But to describe.'
[2] E.p. : ' examples and signs.'

protect himself; for he knows very well how sometimes[1] to produce tears by the feelings which he inspires in a soul, in order that he may continue to implant in it the affections that he desires. But he always strives to move its will so that it may esteem those interior communications, attach great importance to them, and, as a result, give itself to them and be occupied in that which is not virtue, but is rather the occasion of losing such virtue as the soul may have.

12. Let us remember, then, this necessary caution, both as to the one type of locution and as to the other, so that we may not be deceived or encumbered with them. Let us treasure none of them, but think only of learning to direct our will determinedly to God, fulfilling His law and His holy counsels perfectly, which is the wisdom of the Saints, and contenting ourselves with knowing the mysteries and truths with the simplicity and truth wherewith the Church sets them before us. For this is sufficient to enkindle the will greatly, without our meddling in other deep and curious[2] things wherein it is a wonder if there is no peril. For with respect to this S. Paul says: It is not fitting to know more than it behoves us[3] to know.[4] And let this suffice with respect to this matter of successive words.

CHAPTER XXX

Which treats of the interior words that come to the spirit formally by supernatural means. Warns the reader of the harm which they may do and of the caution that is necessary in order that the soul may not be deceived by them.

1. The interior words belonging to the second type are formal words, which at certain times come to the spirit by supernatural means, without the intervention of any of the senses, sometimes when the spirit is recollected and at other times when it is not. I call them formal because they are communicated to the spirit formally by a third person,[5] the spirit itself playing no part in this. And they are therefore very different from those which we have just described; because

---

[1] E.p. omits 'sometimes.'   [2] A, B omit: 'and curious.'
[3] [The verbs used in the Spanish for 'is fitting' and 'behoves' are the same.]   [4] Romans xii, 3.
[5] A, B: 'because it seems to the spirit that a third person communicates them formally.'

not only have they this difference, that they come without any such intervention of the spirit itself as takes place in the other case ; but also, as I say, they sometimes come when the spirit is not recollected and even when it is far from thinking of the subject of what is being said to it.   This is not so in the first type of locution, which always has some relation to the subject which the soul is considering.

2. These words are sometimes very clearly formed and sometimes less so ; for they are frequently like conceptions in which something is said to the spirit, whether in the form of a reply to it, or in that of another manner of address. Sometimes there is only one word ; sometimes there are two or more ; sometimes the words succeed one another like those already described, for they are wont to be continuous, either instructing the soul or discussing something with it ; and all this comes to pass without any part being played therein by the spirit, for it is just as though one person were speaking with another.   In this way, we read, it came to pass with Daniel, who says that the angel spoke within him.[1] This was a formal and successive discourse within his spirit, which instructed him, even as the angel declared at the time, saying that he had come to instruct him.

3. When these words are no more than formal, the effect which they produce upon the soul is not great.   For ordinarily they serve only to instruct or illuminate with respect to one thing ; and, in order to produce this effect, it is not necessary that they should produce any other effect more efficacious than the purpose to which they are leading.   And when they are of God they invariably work this in the soul ; for they make it ready and quick to do that which it is commanded or instructed to do ; yet at times they take not from it the repugnance or the difficulty which it feels, but are rather wont to increase these, which God does for the better instruction, greater humility and further good of the soul. And this repugnance most commonly occurs when the soul is commanded to do things of a high order, or things of a kind that may exalt it ; when things that make for lowliness and humility are commanded the soul, it responds with greater ease and readiness.   And thus we read in Exodus that, when God commanded Moses to go to Pharaoh and deliver the people, he showed such great repugnance that He had to command him three times to do it and to perform signs for him ;

[1] Daniel ix, 22.

and all this was of no avail until God gave him Aaron for a companion to take part of the honour.[1]

4. On the other hand, when the words and communications are of the devil, it comes to pass that the soul responds with greater ease and readiness to things that are of greater weight,[2] and for lowlier things it conceives repugnance. The fact is that God so greatly abhors seeing souls inclined to high position that, even when He commands and obliges them to accept such position, He desires them not to be ready and anxious to command. It is this readiness which God commonly inspires in the soul, in these formal words, that constitutes one great difference between them and these other successive words : the latter move not the spirit so much, neither do they inspire it with such readiness, since they are less formal, and since the understanding has more to do with them. Nevertheless successive words may sometimes produce a greater effect by reason of the close communication that there is at times between the Divine spirit and the human. It is in the manner of their coming that there is a great difference between the two kinds of locution. With respect to formal words the soul can have no doubt if it is pronouncing them itself, for it sees quite clearly that it is not, especially when it has not been thinking of the subject of that which has been said to it ; and even when it has been so thinking it feels very clearly and distinctly that the words come from elsewhere.

5. The soul must no more attach importance to all these formal words than to the other, or successive, words ; for, apart from the fact that to do so would occupy the spirit with that which is not a legitimate and proximate means to union with God—namely, faith—it might also very easily cause it to be deceived by the devil. For sometimes it is hardly possible to know what words are spoken by a good spirit, and what by an evil spirit. As these produce no great effect, they can hardly be distinguished by their effects ; for sometimes words which come from the devil have more efficacy[3] with imperfect souls than have these others, which come from a good spirit, with souls that are spiritual. The soul, then, must take no account of what these words may express, neither attach any importance to them, whether they come from a

---

[1] Exodus iii, iv.
[2] [Lit., ' greater worth.'] A, B : ' greater truth and worth.'
[3] A, e.p. : ' more sensible efficacy.'

good or from an evil spirit. But the words must be repeated to an experienced confessor, or to a discreet and learned person, that he may give instruction and see what it is well to do, and impart his advice ; and the soul must behave, with regard to them, in a resigned and passive[1] manner. And, if such an expert person cannot be found, it is better to attach no importance to these words[2] and to repeat them to nobody ; for it is easy to find persons who will ruin the soul rather than edify it. Souls must not be given into the charge of any kind of director, since it is a thing of such importance in so grave a matter whether one goes astray or acts rightly.

6. And let it be clearly noted that a soul should never act according to its own opinion or accept anything of what these locutions express, without much reflection and without taking advice of another.[3] For strange and subtle deceptions may arise in this matter ; so much so that I myself believe that the soul that does not set itself against accepting such things cannot fail to be deceived by many of them.[4]

7. And since we have treated of these deceptions and perils, and of the caution to be observed with regard to them, in Chapters seventeen, eighteen, nineteen and twenty of this book, I refer the reader to these and say no more on this matter here ; I only repeat that my chief instruction is that the soul should attach no importance to these things in any way.[5]

CHAPTER XXXI

Which treats of the substantial words that come interiorly to the spirit. Describes the difference between them and formal words, and the profit which they bring and the resignation and respect which the soul must observe with regard to them.[6]

1. The third kind of interior words, we said, is called substantial. These substantial words, although they are

---

[1] [*Lit.*, ' negative.']
[2] E.p. : ' it is better to take the substantial and secure part of what these words bring, and otherwise to attach no importance to them.'
[3] E.p. omits : ' of another.'
[4] A, B, e.p. add : ' either to a small, or to a great extent.'
[5] So Alc. A, B : ' . . . my chief instruction, and the surest, to this end, is that the soul should attach no importance whatever to these things, however highly it may think of them, but should be guided in all things by reason and by what the Church has already taught us and teaches us daily.'
[6] This chapter is notable for the hardly surpassable clarity and precision with which the Saint defines substantial locutions. Some critics, however, have found fault with him for saying that the soul should not fear these

likewise formal, since they are impressed upon the soul with
all formality, differ, nevertheless, in that substantial words
produce vivid and substantial effects upon the soul, whereas
words which are merely formal do not.   So that, although it
is true that every substantial word is formal, every formal
word is not therefore substantial, but only, as we said above,
such a word as impresses substantially[1] on the soul that which
it signifies.   It is as if Our Lord were to say formally to the
soul : ' Be thou good ' ; it would then substantially be good.
Or as if He were to say to it : ' Love thou Me ' ; it would
then have and feel within itself the substance of love for God.[2]
Or as if it feared greatly and He said to it : ' Fear thou not ':
it would at once be conscious of great fortitude and tranquillity.   For the sayings of God, and His words, as the Wise
Man says, are full of power ;[3] and thus that which He says
to the soul He produces substantially within it.   For it is this
that David signified when he said : See, He will give to His
voice a voice of virtue.[4]   And even so with Abraham, when
He said to him : Walk in My presence and be thou perfect :[5]
he was then perfect and walked ever in the fear of God.   And
this is the power of His word in the Gospel, wherewith He
healed the sick, raised the dead, etc., by no more than a
word.   And after this manner He gives certain souls locutions
which are substantial ; and they are of such moment and
price that they are life and virtue and incomparable blessing
to the soul ; for one of these words works[6] a greater blessing
within the soul than all that the soul has itself done
throughout its life.

  2. With respect to these words, the soul should do nothing.
It should neither desire them, nor refrain from desiring

locutions, but accept them humbly and passively, since they depend
wholly on God.   The reply is that, when God favours the soul with these
locutions, its own restless effort can only impede His work in it, as has
already been said.   The soul is truly co-operating with God by preparing
itself with resignation and humble affection to receive His favours : it is
in no sense, as some critics have asserted, completely inactive.   As to the
fear of being deceived by these locutions, both S. Thomas and all the
principal commentators are in conformity with the Saint's teaching.
S. Teresa, too, took the same attitude as S. John of the Cross.   Cf. her
Life, Chap. xxv, and *Mansions*, VI, Chap. iii.
  [1] E.p. : ' impresses truly.'
  [2] E.p. modifies thus : ' Or if He were to say formally to the soul :
Love thou Me : it would then have and feel within itself impulses of love
for God.'   The edition of 1630 has : ' . . . the substance of love—that
is, true love of God,' reading otherwise as in the text.
  [3] Ecclesiastes viii, 4.   [4] Psalm lxvii, 34 [A.V., lxviii, 33].
  [5] Genesis xvii, 1,   [6] E.p. : ' perhaps works.'

them ; it should neither reject them nor fear them. It should do nothing[1] in the way of executing what these words express, for these substantial words are never pronounced by God in order that the soul may translate them into action, but that He may so translate them within the soul ; herein they differ from formal and successive words. And I say that the soul must neither desire nor refrain from desiring, for its desire is unnecessary in order that God may translate these words into effect, nor is it sufficient for the soul to refrain from desiring in order for the said effect not to be produced. Let the soul rather be resigned and humble with respect to them. It should not reject them,[2] since the effect of these words remains substantially within it and is full of the blessing of God. As the soul receives this blessing passively, its action is in no way of any importance. Nor should it fear any deception ; for neither the understanding nor the devil can intervene herein, nor can they succeed[3] in passively producing this substantial effect in the soul, in such a way that the effect and habit of the locution may be impressed upon it, unless the soul should have given itself to the devil by a voluntary compact, and he should have dwelt in it as its master, and impressed upon it these effects, not of good, but of evil.[4] Inasmuch as that soul would be already voluntarily united to him in perversity, the devil might easily impress upon it the effects of his sayings and words with evil intent.[5] For we see by experience that in many things and even upon good souls he works great violence, by means of suggestion, making his suggestions very efficacious ; and if they were evil he might work in them the consummation of these suggestions.[6] But he cannot leave upon a soul effects similar

---

[1] Alc. omits : ' desire nothing . . . should do nothing.'

[2] E.p. abbreviates this paragraph thus : ' With respect to these words, the soul should itself do nothing and desire nothing at the time, but conduct itself with resignation and humility, giving its free consent to God ; neither should it reject anything, nor fear anything. It should not labour in executing what these words express, for by these substantial words God works in the soul ; wherein they differ from formal and successive words. It should not reject them,' etc.

[3] E.p. : ' nor can this evil one succeed . . .'

[4] E.p. has (for ' unless the soul . . . of evil ') : ' although in souls that were given to the devil by a voluntary compact, in whom he dwelt as their master, he could by suggestion impel them to [produce] results of great malignity.'

[5] So A, B. Alc. omits this sentence. E.p. has : ' For, as such souls would already be voluntarily united to him in perversity, the devil could easily impel them thereto.'

[6] E.p. : ' he might impel them more violently still.'

to those of locutions which are good ; for there is no comparison between the locutions of the devil and those of God. The former are all as though they were not, in comparison with the latter, neither do they produce any effect at all compared with the effect of these. For this cause God says through Jeremiah : What has the chaff to do with the wheat ? Are not My words perchance as fire, and as a hammer that breaketh the rock in pieces ?[1] And thus these substantial words are of great service to the union of the soul with God ; and the more interior and the more substantial they are, the greater is the profit that they bring. Happy is the soul to whom God speaks. Speak, Lord, for Thy servant heareth.[2]

CHAPTER XXXII

Which treats of the apprehensions received by the understanding from interior feelings which come supernaturally to the soul. Describes their cause, and the manner wherein the soul must conduct itself so that they may not obstruct its road to union with God.

1. It is now time to treat of the fourth and last kind of intellectual apprehension which we said might come to the understanding through the spiritual feelings which are frequently produced supernaturally in the souls of spiritual persons and which we count amongst the distinct apprehensions of the understanding.

2. These distinct spiritual feelings may be of two kinds. The first kind is in the affection of the will. The second, in the substance of the soul.[3] Each of these may be of many kinds. Those of the will, when they are of God, are most sublime ; but those that are of the substance of the soul are very high and of great good and profit.[4] As to these, neither the soul nor he that treats with it can know or understand the cause whence they proceed, or what are the acts whereby God grants it these favours ; for they depend not upon any good works performed by the soul, nor upon its meditations,

---

[1] Jeremiah xxiii, 28–9. A, B, e.p. read ' stones ' for ' rocks.'
[2] 1 Kings [A.V., 1 Samuel] iii, 10.
[3] E.p. : ' The second, feelings that, though they are also in the will, yet, because they are most intense, sublime, profound and secret, seem not to touch the will, but to be wrought in the substance of the soul.'
[4] E.p. : ' but the second are very high and of great good and profit.'

although both these things are a good preparation for them :
God grants these favours to whom He wills and for what
reason He wills.[1] For it may come to pass that a person will
have performed many good works yet that He will not give
him these touches of His favour ; and another will have
done far fewer good works, yet He will give him them to a
most sublime degree and in great abundance. And thus
it is not needful that the soul should be actually employed
and occupied in spiritual things (although it is much better
that it should be so employed if it is to have these favours) for
God to give it these touches in which the soul experiences the
said feelings ; for in the majority of cases the soul is quite
heedless of them. Of these touches, some are distinct and are
quickly gone ; others are less distinct and last longer.

3. These feelings, inasmuch as they are feelings only,[2]
belong not to the understanding but to the will ; and thus I
refrain, of set purpose, from treating of them here, nor shall
I do so until we treat of the night and purgation of the will
in its affections : this will be in the third book, which
follows this.[3] But since frequently, and even in the majority
of cases, apprehensions and knowledge and intelligence overflow from them into the understanding, it will be well to
make mention of them here, for that reason only. It must
be known, then, that from these feelings, both from those of
the will and from those which are in the substance of the
soul, whether[4] they are caused suddenly by the touches of
God, or are durable and successive, an apprehension of
knowledge or intelligence overflows frequently, as I say, into
the understanding ; and this is normally a most sublime
perception of God, most delectable to the understanding, to
which no name can be given, any more than to the feeling
whence it overflows. And these manifestations of knowledge
are sometimes of one kind and sometimes of another ;
sometimes they are clearer and more lofty, according to the
nature of the touches which come from God and which cause

---

[1] A, B : ' and how He wills.' Note that the Saint does not deprecate
good works, as did the Illuminists (alumbrados), who bade the soul set
them aside for contemplation, even though they were works of obligation.
On the contrary, he asserts that good works have a definite, though a
preparatory part, to play in the life of the contemplative.

[2] E.p. : ' . . . they are feelings only of the kind whereof we here
speak . . .'

[3] Alc. alone has : ' which follows this.' The Saint does not, in fact,
return to this matter, either in the third book or elsewhere.

[4] E.p. : ' that from all these feelings, whether . . .'

the feelings whence they proceed, and according also to their property.[1]

4. It is unnecessary here to spend a great store of words[2] in cautioning and directing the understanding, through these manifestations of knowledge, in faith, to union with God. For albeit the feelings which we have described are produced passively in the soul, without any effective assistance to that end on its own part, even so likewise is the knowledge of them received passively in the understanding, in a way called by the philosophers ' passible,' wherein the understanding plays no part. Wherefore, in order not to go astray on their account nor to impede the profit which comes from them, the understanding must do nothing in connection with these feelings, but conduct itself passively,[3] and not interfere by applying to them its natural capacity. For, as we have said in dealing with successive locutions, the understanding, with its activity, would very easily disturb and ruin the effect of these delicate manifestations of knowledge, which are a delectable supernatural intelligence that human nature cannot reach or apprehend by its own efforts, but only by an attitude of receptivity.[4] And thus the soul must not strive to attain them or desire to receive them,[5] lest the understanding should itself form other manifestations, or the devil should make his entry with still more that are different from them and false. This he may very well do by means[6] of the feelings aforementioned, or of those which he can himself infuse into the soul that gives itself to these kinds of knowledge.[7] Let the soul be resigned, humble and passive herein, for, since it receives this knowledge passively from God, He will communicate it whensoever He is pleased, if He sees the soul to be humble and detached. And in this way the soul will do nothing to counteract the help which these kinds of knowledge give it in its progress toward Divine union, which help is great ; for these touches are all touches of union, which are wrought passively in the soul.[8]

---

[1] E.p.: ' to their capacity.'   [2] E.p.: ' to spend many words.'
[3] E.p. adds here : ' inclining the will to free consent and gratitude.'
[4] [*Lit.*, ' or apprehend by doing, but by receiving.']
[5] E.p. omits : ' or desire to receive them.'
[6] The edition of 1630 has : ' . . . do in the soul, when it gives itself to these kinds of knowledge, by means . . .'
[7] E.p. substitutes for ' or of those . . . kinds of knowledge ' the words : ' making use of the bodily senses.'
[8] Some editions here add a long paragraph, which, however, is the work of P. Jerónimo de S. José, who was responsible for the edition of

5. What has been said concerning this is sufficient, for no matter what may happen to the soul with respect to the understanding, cautions and instructions have been given it in the sections already mentioned.   And although a case may appear to be different and to be in no way included herein, there is none that cannot be reduced to one of these, from which may be deduced the instruction necessary for it.[1]

1630. It appears neither in the MSS. nor in the edition of 1618.   It runs as follows :

All the instruction which has been given in this book on total abstraction and passive contemplation, wherein, oblivious to all created things and detached from images and figures, we allow ourselves to be guided by God, remaining in simple regard of supreme truth, is applicable not only to that act of most perfect contemplation, the lofty and wholly supernatural repose of which is still prevented by the daughters of Jerusalem (namely, good reflections and meditations), if at that time the soul desires them, but also to the whole of the time during which Our Lord communicates the simple, general and loving attentiveness aforementioned, or in which the soul, aided by grace, remains in that state.   For at that time the soul must always strive to keep its understanding in repose, without the intrusion of other forms, figures or particular kinds of knowledge, save to a very slight extent and quite superficially ; and it must have a loving sweetness which will enkindle it ever more.   But, except at this time, in all its exercises, acts and works, the soul must make use of good meditations and remembrances, so as to experience the greater devotion and profit, most of all with respect to the life, passion and death of Our Lord Jesus Christ, so that its actions, practices and life may be made like to His.

[1] Thus Alc.   A, B, e.p. read : ' This suffices to conclude with the supernatural apprehensions of the understanding, so far as concerns the guidance of the understanding, by their means, in faith, to Divine union. And I think that what has been said with regard to this suffices, for, no matter what happens to the soul with respect to the understanding, instructions and cautions concerning it will be found in the sections already mentioned.   And, if something should happen, apparently so different that none of them deals with it (although I think there will be nothing relating to the understanding which cannot be referred to one of the four kinds of distinct knowledge), instructions and cautions concerning it can be deduced from what has been said of others similar to it.   And with this we will pass to the third book, where, with the Divine favour, we shall treat of the interior spiritual purgation of the will with regard to its interior affections which we here call active night.'

C, D have : ' From what has been said may be deduced instructions and cautions for guidance in whatever may happen to the soul with regard to the understanding, even if it seem so different that it includes none of the four distinct kinds, although I think there will be nothing relating to the understanding which cannot be referred to one of them.   And so we will pass to the third book.'

The edition of 1630 follows A, B and e.p., and adds further : ' I therefore beg the discreet reader to read these things in a benevolent and simple spirit ; for, when this spirit is not present, however sublime and perfect be the instruction, it will not yield the profit that it contains, nor will it earn the esteem that it merits.   How much truer is this in the present case, since my style is in so many ways deficient ! '

BOOK THE THIRD

Which treats of the purgation of the active night of the memory and will. Gives instruction how the soul is to behave with respect to the apprehensions of these two faculties, that it may come to union with God, according to the two faculties afore-mentioned, in perfect hope and charity.[1]

CHAPTER I

1. The first faculty of the soul, which is the understanding, has now been instructed, through all its apprehensions, in the first theological virtue, which is faith, to the end that, according to this faculty, the soul may be united with God by means of the purity of faith. It now remains to do likewise with respect to the other two faculties of the soul, which are memory and will, and to purify them likewise with respect to their apprehensions, to the end that, according to these two faculties also, the soul may come to union with God in perfect hope and charity. This will briefly be effected in this third book. We have now concluded our treatment of the understanding, which is the receptacle of all other objects according to its mode of operation;[2] and in treating of this we have gone a great part of the whole way. It is therefore unnecessary for us to write at equal length with respect to these faculties;[3] for it is not possible that, if the spiritual man instructs his understanding in faith according to the doctrine which has been given him, he should not, in so doing, instruct the other two faculties in the other two virtues likewise; for the operations of each faculty depend upon the others.

2. But since, in order to follow our manner of procedure, and in order, too, that we may be the better understood, we must necessarily speak of the proper and determinate

---

[1] So Alc., A, B. This first chapter, in e.p., is called the ' Argument ' of the book, and the numbering of the chapters differs correspondingly from that of the MSS. Cf. the Exposition of Book II (p. 66, above).

[2] E.p.: ' . . . of all the other objects that pass to these faculties.'

[3] E.p. omits the rest of this paragraph.

matter, we shall here be obliged to set down the apprehensions proper to each faculty,[1] and first, those of the memory, making here such distinction between them as suffices for our purpose. This we shall be able to deduce from the distinction between their objects, which are three : natural,[2] imaginary and spiritual ; according to which there are likewise three kinds of knowledge which come from the memory, namely : natural and supernatural,[3] imaginary and spiritual.

3. All these, by the Divine favour, we shall treat here in due course, beginning with natural knowledge, which pertains to the most exterior objects. And we shall then treat of the affections of the will, wherewith we shall conclude this third book of the spiritual active night.

CHAPTER II

Which treats of the natural apprehensions of the memory and describes how the soul must be voided of them in order to be able to attain to union with God according to this faculty.

1. It is necessary that, in each of these books, the reader should bear in mind the purpose of which we are speaking. For otherwise there may arise within him many such questions with respect to what he is reading as might now be arising with respect to what we have said of the understanding, and shall say now of the memory, and afterwards shall say of the will. For, seeing how we annihilate the faculties with respect to their operations, it may perhaps seem to him that we are destroying the road of spiritual practice rather than constructing it ; this would be true if we were seeking here only to instruct beginners, whom it is necessary to prepare through these apprehensible and discursive apprehensions.

2. But, since we are here giving instruction to those who would progress farther in contemplation, even to union with God, to which end all these means and exercises of sense

---

[1] E.p. : ' we shall here have to treat of the acts of each faculty.'

[2] ' Natural and supernatural,' says the edition of 1630, basing its reading upon the similar one two lines below.

[3] It will be seen from what follows that in practice the Saint preserves the strictly tripartite division given in the text above, supernatural knowledge being found in each of the sections.

concerning the faculties must recede into the background, and be put to silence, to the end that God may of His own accord work Divine union in the soul, it is necessary to proceed by this method of disencumbering and emptying the soul, and causing the natural jurisdiction and operations of the faculties to be denied them, so that they may become capable of infusion and illumination from supernatural sources ; for their capacity cannot attain to so lofty an experience, but will rather hinder it, if it be not disregarded.

3. And thus, if it be true, as it is, that the soul must proceed in its growing knowledge of God by learning that which He is not rather than that which He is, in order to come to Him, it must proceed by renouncing and refusing to accept everything in its apprehensions that can be renounced, whether this be natural or supernatural, to the very uttermost. We shall proceed with this end in view with regard to the memory, drawing it out from its natural methods and limitations, and causing it to rise above itself— that is, above all clear knowledge and apprehensible posses-sion—to the supreme hope of God, Who is incomprehensible.

4. Beginning, then, with natural knowledge, I say that natural knowledge in the memory consists of all kinds of knowledge that the memory can form concerning the objects of the five bodily senses—namely : hearing, sight, smell, taste and touch—and all those kinds of knowledge which the soul can form and make after this fashion. Of all these forms and manners of knowledge the soul must strip and void itself, and it must strive to lose the imaginary apprehension of them, so that there may be left in it no kind of impression of knowledge, nor trace of aught soever, but rather the soul must remain barren and bare,[1] as if these forms had never passed through it, and in total oblivion and suspension. And this cannot happen unless the memory be annihilated as to all its forms, if it is to be united with God. For it cannot happen save by total separation from all forms which are not God ; for God comes beneath no definite form or kind of knowledge whatsoever, as we have said in treating of the night of the understanding. And since, as Christ says,[2] no man can serve two masters,[3] and the memory cannot be united[4] both

---

[1] E.p. : '. . . impression of knowledge, but [the soul] must remain as completely detached as it can.'
[2] E.p. : ' as our Redeemer teaches.'
[3] [S. Matthew vi, 24.]   [4] E.p. : ' united in perfection.'

to God and to definite forms and kinds of knowledge ; and, as God has no form or image that can be comprehended by the memory, it follows that, when the memory is united with God (as is seen, too, every day by experience), it remains without form and without figure, its imagination being lost and itself being absorbed in a supreme good, and in a great oblivion, remembering nothing. For that Divine union voids its fancy and clears it[1] of all forms and kinds of knowledge and raises it to the supernatural.

5. Now there sometimes comes to pass here a notable thing ; for occasionally, when God causes these touches of union in the memory, the brain (where memory has its seat), is so perceptibly upset that it seems as if it becomes quite inert, and its judgement and sense are lost. This is sometimes more perceptible and sometimes less so, according to the strength of this touch, and then, by reason of this union, the memory is voided and purged, as I say, of all kinds of knowledge. It remains in oblivion—at times in complete oblivion[2]—so that it has to put forth a great effort and to labour greatly in order to remember anything.

6. And sometimes this oblivion of the memory and suspension of the imagination reach such a point, because of the union of the memory with God, that a long time passes without the soul's perceiving it, or knowing what has taken place during that period. And, as the imaginative faculty is then in suspension, it feels naught that is done to it, not even things that cause pain ; for without imagination there is no feeling, not even coming through thought, since this exists not.[3] And, to the end that God may cause these touches of union, the soul must needs withdraw its memory from all apprehensible kinds of knowledge. And it is to be noted that these suspensions come not to pass in those that are already perfect, since they have attained to perfect union, and these suspensions belong to the beginnings of union.

7. Someone will remark that all this seems very well, but that it leads to the destruction of the natural use and course of the faculties, and reduces man to the state of a beast—a

---

[1] E.p. : ' and seems to clear it.'
[2] So Alc. and P. A : ' It remains in oblivion, and, at times, [is] oblivious to itself.' B : ' It remains transported, and, at times, [is] oblivious to itself.' E.p. omits the whole of the paragraph down to this point, continuing the preceding paragraph, thus : ' . . . raises it to the supernatural, leaving it in such oblivion that it has to put forth . . .'
[3] Alc. ends the sentence at ' feeling.'

state of oblivion and even worse—since he becomes incapable of reasoning or of remembering his natural functions and necessities. It will be argued that God destroys not nature, but rather perfects it ; and that from this teaching there follows necessarily its destruction, when that which pertains to morality and reason is not practised and is forgotten, neither is that which is natural practised ; for (it will be said) none of these things can be remembered, when the soul is deprived of[1] forms and kinds of knowledge which are the means of remembrance.

8. To this I reply that, the more nearly the memory attains to union with God, the more do definite kinds of knowledge become perfected within it, until it loses them entirely— namely, when in perfection it attains to the state of union. And thus, at the beginning, when this is first taking place, the soul cannot but fall into great oblivion with respect to all things, since forms and kinds of knowledge are being erased from it ; and therefore it is guilty of many omissions in its outward behaviour and usage—forgetting to eat or drink, and being uncertain if it has done this or no, if it has seen this or no, if it has said this or no—through the absorption of the memory in God.[2] But when once it attains to the habit of union, which is a supreme blessing, it no longer has these periods of oblivion, after this manner, in that which pertains to natural and moral reason ; actions which are seemly and necessary it performs rather with a much greater degree of perfection, although it performs them no longer by means of forms and manners of knowledge pertaining to the memory. For, when it has the habit of union, which is a supernatural state, memory and the other faculties fail it completely in their natural functions, and pass beyond their natural limitations, even to God, Who is supernatural. And thus, when the memory is transformed in God, it cannot receive impressions of forms or manners of knowledge. Wherefore the functions of the memory and of the other faculties in this state are all Divine ; for, when at last God possesses the faculties and has become the entire master of them, through their transformation into Himself, it is He Himself Who moves and commands them divinely, according

---

[1] E.p. : ' when the soul pays no heed to.'
[2] E.p. abbreviates : ' . . . union with God, the less it heeds definite kinds of knowledge, and this increases in proportion as it draws nearer to the state of union through the absorption of the memory in God.'

to His Divine Spirit and will ;[1] and the result of this is that the operations of the soul are not distinct, but all that it does is of God, and its operations are Divine, so that, even as S. Paul says, he that is joined unto God becomes one spirit with Him.[2]

9. Hence it comes to pass that the operations of the soul in union are of the Divine Spirit and are Divine. And hence it comes that the actions of such souls are only those that are seemly and reasonable, and not those that are ill-beseeming. For the Spirit of God teaches them that which they ought to know, and causes them to be ignorant of that which it behoves them not to know, and to remember that which they have to remember, with or without forms, and to forget that which they should forget ; and it makes them love that which they have to love, and not to love that which is not in God. And thus,[3] all the first motions of the faculties of such souls are Divine and it is not to be wondered at that the motions and operations of these faculties should be Divine, since they are transformed in the Divine Being.[4]

10.[5] Of these operations I will give a few examples : let this be one. A person asks another who is in this state to commend him to God. This person will not remember to do so by means of any form or manner of knowledge that remains in his memory concerning that other person ; and if it is right that he should recommend him to God (which will be if God desires to receive a prayer for that person), He will move his will and give him a desire to pray for him ; and if God desires not such prayer, that other person will not be able nor will desire to pray,[6] though he make great efforts to do so ; and at times God will cause him to pray for others of whom he has no knowledge nor has ever heard. And this is because, as I have said, God alone moves the faculties of

---

[1] E.p. omits the rest of this paragraph and the first sentence of the next.

[2] 1 Corinthians vi, 17.

[3] E.p. substitutes for this sentence : ' For He [i.e., the Spirit of God] specially governs and moves them so that they may perform those actions which are seemly, according to the will and ordinance of God.'

[4] P. José de Jesús María, in his *Vida y excelencias de la Santísima Virgen María* (I, xl), quotes this and part of the last paragraph from what he claims to be an original MS. of S. John of the Cross, but his text varies considerably from that of any MS. now known. [P. Silverio, however (cf. p. 224, above), considers that this and other similar citations are quite untrustworthy.]

[5] E.p. omits paragraphs 10, 11, 12, all of which, however, are restored in the edition of 1630.

[6] Edition of 1630 : ' will not pray nor will desire to pray.'

these souls to do those works which are meet, according to the will and ordinance of God, and they cannot be moved to do others ; and thus the works and prayers of these souls are always effectual.   Such were those of the most glorious Virgin Our Lady, who, being raised to this high estate from the beginning, had never the form of any creature[1] imprinted in her soul, neither was moved by such, but was invariably guided by the Holy Spirit.

11. Another example.   At a certain time a person in this state has to attend to some necessary business.   He will remember it by no kind of form, but, without his knowing how, it will come to his soul,[2] at the time and in the manner that it ought to come, and that without fail.

12. And not only in these things does the Holy Spirit give such persons light, but in many others, relating both to the present and to the future, and, in many cases, even when they are far distant ; and although at times this comes to pass through intellectual forms, it frequently happens without the intervention of any forms that can be apprehended, so that these persons know not how they know.[3]   But this comes to them from the Divine Wisdom ; for, since these souls exercise themselves in knowing and apprehending nothing with the faculties,[4] they come in general, as we have said in the Mount,[5] to know everything, according to that which the Wise Man says :   The worker of all things, who is Wisdom, taught me all things.[6]

13. You will say, perhaps, that the soul will be unable to void and deprive its memory of all forms and fancies to such an extent as to be able to attain to so lofty a state ; for there are two things so difficult that their accomplishment sur-passes human ability and strength, namely, to throw off with one's natural powers that which is natural, which is hard enough,[7] and to attain and be united to the super-

---

[1] Edition of 1630 : 'of any creature that would turn her aside from God.'

[2] Edition of 1630 adds here : 'by the stirring up of his memory described above.'

[3] Edition of 1630 abbreviates : '. . . even when they are distant, so that these persons know not how they know.'

[4] Edition of 1630 : 'and apprehending with the faculties nothing that can impede them.'

[5] The reference is to the drawing of the Mount of Perfection. Cf. p. xxxiv, above.

[6] Wisdom vii, 21.

[7] [Lit., ' which cannot be ' (que no puede ser), but this is a well-known Spanish hyperbole describing what is extremely difficult.]

natural, which is much more difficult—indeed, to speak the truth, is impossible with natural ability alone. The truth, I repeat, is that God must place the soul in this supernatural state ; but the soul, as far as in it lies, must be continually preparing itself ; and this it can do by natural means, especially[1] with the help that God is continually giving it. And thus, as the soul, for its own part, enters into this renunciation and self-emptying of forms, so God begins to give it the possession of union ; and this God works passively in the soul, as we shall say, *Deo dante*, when we treat of the passive night of the soul. And thus, when it shall please God, and according to the manner of the soul's preparation, He will grant it the habit of perfect and Divine union.[2]

14. And the Divine effects which God causes in the soul when He has granted it this habit, both as to the understanding and as to the memory and will, we shall not describe in this account of the soul's active purgation and night, for by this alone the soul does not completely attain Divine union. We shall speak of these effects, however, in treating of the passive night, by means of which is brought about the union of the soul with God.[3] And thus I shall

---

[1] E.p. omits ' especially.'   [2] E.p. omits : ' and Divine.'

[3] E.p. omits all the rest of this paragraph, substituting the following passage, which it introduces in order [says P. Silverio] to describe the scope of the Saint's teaching, and which is copied in the edition of 1630 :

In [treating of] this purgation of the memory, I speak here only of the necessary means whereby the memory may place itself actively in this night and purgation, as far as lies in its power. And these means are that the spiritual man must habitually exercise caution, after this manner. Of all the things that he sees, hears, smells, tastes or touches he must make no particular store in the memory, or pay heed to them, or dwell upon them, but must allow them to pass and must remain in holy oblivion without reflecting upon them, save when necessary for some good reflection or meditation. And this care to forget and set aside knowledge and images is never applicable to Christ and His Humanity. For, although occasionally, at the height of contemplation and simple regard of the Divinity, the soul may not remember this most sacred Humanity, because God, with His own hand, has raised the soul to this, as it were, confused and most supernatural knowledge, yet it is in no wise seemly to study to forget it, since looking and meditating lovingly upon it will aid the soul to [attain] all that is good, and hereby it will most readily rise to the most lofty state of union. And it is clear that, although other bodily and visible things are a hindrance and ought to be forgotten, we must not include among these Him Who became man for our salvation, and Who is the truth, the door, the way and the guide to all good things. This being assumed, let the soul strive after complete abstraction and oblivion, so that, in so far as is possible, there may remain in its memory no knowledge or image of created things, as though they existed not in the world ; and let it leave the memory free and disencumbered for God, and, as it were, lost in holy oblivion.

speak here only of the necessary means whereby the memory may place itself actively in this night and purgation, as far as lies in its power. And these means are that the spiritual man must habitually exercise caution, after this manner. All the things that he hears, sees, smells, tastes or touches, he must be careful not to store up or collect in his memory, but he must allow himself to forget them immediately, and this he must accomplish, if need be, with the same efficacy as that with which others contrive to remember them, so that there remains no knowledge or image of them whatsoever in his memory. It must be with him as if they existed not in the world, and his memory must be left free and disencumbered of them, and be tied to no consideration, whether from above or from below, as if he had no faculty of memory ; he must freely allow everything to fall into oblivion as though all things were a hindrance to him ; and in fact everything that is natural, if one attempt to make use of it in supernatural matters, is a hindrance rather than a help.

15. And if those questions and objections which arose above with respect to the understanding should also arise here (the objections, that is to say, that the soul is doing nothing, is wasting its time and is depriving itself of spiritual blessings which it might well receive through the memory), the answer to this has already been given,[1] and will be given again farther on, in our treatment of the passive night ; wherefore there is no need for us to linger here. It is needful only to observe that, although at certain times the benefit of this suspension of forms and kinds of knowledge may not be realized, the spiritual man must not for that reason grow weary, for God will not fail to succour him in His own time. To attain so great a blessing it behoves the soul to endure much and to suffer with patience and hope.

16. And, although it is true that a soul will hardly be found that is moved by God in all things and at all times, and has such continual union with God that, without the mediation of any form, its faculties[2] are ever moved divinely, there are yet souls who in their operations are very habitually moved by God, and these are not they that move themselves of their own strength, for, as S. Paul says, the sons of God, who are transformed and united in God, are moved by the

---

[1] E.p. : ' . . . through the memory) much has already been said here in reply to them, and there, too, they have been completely answered.'
[2] E.p. omits : ' without the mediation of any form.'

Spirit of God,[1] that is, are moved to Divine actions in their faculties. And it is no marvel that their operations should be Divine, since the union of the soul is Divine.

CHAPTER III

Wherein are described three kinds of evil which come to the soul when it enters not into darkness with respect to knowledge and reflections in the memory. Herein is described the first.

1. To three kinds of evil and inconvenience the spiritual man is subject when he persists in desiring to make use of all natural knowledge and reflections of the memory in order to journey toward God, or for any other purpose : two of these are positive and one is privative. The first comes from things of the world ; the second, from the devil ; the third, which is privative, is the impediment and hindrance to Divine union caused and effected in the soul.

2. The first evil, which comes from the world,[2] consists in the subjection of the soul, through knowledge[3] and reflection, to many kinds of harm, such as falsehoods, imperfections, desires, opinions, loss of time, and many other things which breed many kinds of impurity in the soul. And it is clear that the soul must of necessity fall into many perils of falsehood, when it gives way to knowledge and reasoning ; for oftentimes that which is true must appear false, and that which is certain, doubtful ; and contrariwise ; for there is scarcely a single truth of which we can have complete knowledge. From all these things the soul is free if the memory enters into darkness with respect to every kind of reflection and knowledge.

3. Imperfections meet the soul at every step if it sets its memory upon that which it has heard, seen, touched, smelt and tasted ; for there must then perforce cling to it some affection, whether this be of pain, of fear, of hatred, of vain hope, vain enjoyment, vainglory, etc. ; for all these are, at the least, imperfections, and at times are downright[4] venial sins ; and they leave much impurity most subtly in the soul, even though the reflections and the knowledge have relation

---

[1] Romans viii, 14.　　[2] E.p. : ' from the things of the world.'
[3] A, B : ' through much knowledge.'
[4] [*Lit.*, ' good.'] E.p. reads ' known ' for ' downright.'

to God.[1] And it is also clear that they engender desires within the soul, for these arise naturally from the knowledge and reflections aforementioned, and if one wishes only to have this knowledge and these reflections, even that is a desire. And it is clearly seen that many occasions of judging others will come likewise ; for, in using its memory, the soul cannot fail to come upon that which is good and bad in others, and, in such a case, that which is evil oftentimes seems good, and that which is good, evil. I believe there is none who can completely free himself from all these kinds of evil, save by blinding his memory and leading it into darkness with regard to all these things.

4. And if you tell me that a man is well able to conquer all these things when they come to him, I reply that, if he sets store by knowledge, this is simply and utterly impossible ; for countless imperfections and follies insinuate themselves into such knowledge, some of which are so subtle and minute that, without the soul's realization thereof, they cling to it of their own accord, even as pitch clings to the man that touches it ; so that it is better to conquer once for all by denying the memory completely. You will say likewise that by so doing the soul deprives itself of many good thoughts and meditations upon God, which are of great profit to it and whereby God grants it favours. I reply that to this end purity of soul is of the greatest profit,[2] and this consists in clinging to no creature affection, or temporal affection, or effective advertence ; concerning which I believe that they cannot but cling to the soul because of the imperfection which the faculties have in their own operations. Wherefore it is better to learn to silence the faculties and to cause them to be still, so that God may speak. For, as we have said, in order to attain to this state the natural operations must be lost from sight, and this happens, as the prophet says, when the soul comes into solitude, according to these its faculties, and God speaks to its heart.[3]

5. And if you again reply, saying that the soul will have

[1] So Alc., A, B. E.p. reads : ' . . . venial sins : all of these [being] things which disturb perfect purity and most simple union with God.'
[2] E.p. inserts, after ' grants it favours ' : ' I reply that that which is purely God and assists this simple, pure, universal and confused knowledge is not to be rejected, but that which detains [the memory] in images, forms, figures or similitudes of created things.' It continues : ' And, speaking of this purgation, in order that God may accomplish it, purity of soul is of the greatest profit. . . .' The insertion is also found in the edition of 1630. [3] Hosea ii, 14.

no blessing unless it meditates upon God and allows its memory to reflect upon Him, and that many distractions and negligences will continually enter it, I say that it is impossible, if the memory is recollected with regard both to things of the next life and to things here below, that evils or distractions should enter it, nor other follies or vices (the which things always enter when the memory wanders), since there is no exit or entrance for them. This would come to pass if, when we had shut the door upon considerations and reflections concerning things above, we opened it to things below ; but in this state we shut the door to all things whence distraction may come,[1] causing the memory to be still and dumb, and the ear of the spirit to be attentive, in silence, to God alone, saying with the prophet : Speak, Lord, for Thy servant heareth.[2] It was thus that the Spouse in the Songs said that his Bride should be, in these words : My sister is a garden enclosed and a fountain sealed[3]—that is to say, enclosed and sealed against all things that may enter.

6. Let the soul, then, remain ' enclosed,' without anxieties and troubles, and He that entered in bodily form to His disciples when the doors were shut, and gave them peace,[4] though they neither knew nor thought that this was possible nor knew how it was possible,[5] will enter spiritually into the soul, without its knowing how He does so, when the doors of its faculties—memory, understanding and will—are enclosed against all apprehensions. And He will fill them with peace, coming down upon the soul, as the prophet says, like a river of peace,[6] and taking from it all the misgivings and suspicions, disturbances and darknesses which caused it to fear that it was lost or was on the way to perdition. Let it not lose its anxiety to pray, and let it wait in detachment and emptiness, for its blessing will not tarry.

CHAPTER IV[7]

Which treats of the second kind of evil that may come to the soul from the devil by way of the natural apprehensions of the memory.

1. The second positive evil that may come to the soul by means of the knowledge of the memory proceeds from the

---

[1] [*Lit.,* ' whence that may come.'] E.p. : ' We shut the door to all things which are a hindrance to union, and whence distraction may come.'
[2] 1 Kings [A.V., 1 Samuel] iii, 10.   [3] Canticles iv, 12.
[4] [S. John xx, 19.]   [5] E.p. omits : ' nor knew how it was possible.'
[6] Isaiah xlviii, 18.   [7] P. omits this chapter.

devil, who by this means obtains great influence over the soul. For he can continually bring it new forms, knowledge and reflections, by means whereof he can taint the soul with pride, avarice, wrath, envy, etc., and cause it unjust hatred, or vain love, and deceive it in many ways. And beside this, he is wont to leave impressions,[1] and to implant them in the fancy, in such wise that those that are false appear true, and those that are true, false. And finally all the greatest deceptions which are caused by the devil, and the evils that he brings to the soul, enter by way of knowledge and reflections of the memory. Thus if the memory enter into darkness with respect to them all, and be annihilated in its oblivion to them, it shuts the door altogether upon this evil which proceeds from the devil, and frees itself from all these things, which is a great blessing. For the devil has no power over the soul unless it be through the operations of its faculties, principally by means of knowledge,[2] since upon these depend almost all the other operations of the other faculties. Wherefore, if the memory be annihilated with respect to them, the devil can do naught ; for he finds no foothold, and without a foothold he is powerless.[3]

2. I would that spiritual persons might clearly see how many kinds of harm are wrought by evil spirits in their souls by means of the memory, when they devote themselves frequently to making use of it, and how many kinds of sadness and affliction and vain and evil[4] joys they have, both with respect to their thoughts about God, and also with respect to the things of the world ; and how many impurities are left rooted in their spirits ;[5] and likewise how greatly they are distracted from the highest recollection, which consists in fixing the whole soul, according to all its faculties— upon the one incomprehensible Good, and in withdrawing it from all things that can be apprehended, since these are not incomprehensible Good. This is a great good (although less good results from this emptiness than from the soul's fixing itself upon God), simply because it is the cause which frees the soul from many griefs and afflictions and sorrows, over and above the imperfections and sins from which it is delivered.

---

[1] [Lit., ' to leave things.'] A, B, e.p. : ' to fix things.'
[2] E.p. : ' by means of forms and species.'
[3] [Lit., ' he finds nothing to seize, and with nothing he can do nothing.']
[4] E.p. omits : ' and evil.'
[5] Alc. omits : ' and how many . . . spirits.'

CHAPTER V

Of the third evil which comes to the soul by way of the distinct natural knowledge of the memory.

1. The third evil which comes to the soul through the natural apprehensions of the memory is privative; for these apprehensions can hinder moral good and deprive us of spiritual good. And, in order that first of all we may explain how these apprehensions hinder moral good in the soul, it must be known that moral good consists in the restraining of the passions and the curbing of disorderly desires, from which restraint there come to the soul tranquillity, peace and rest, and moral virtues, all of which things are moral good. This restraining and curbing of the passions cannot be truly accomplished by the soul that forgets not and withdraws not itself from things pertaining to itself, whence arise the affections; and no disturbances ever arise in the soul save through the apprehensions of the memory. For, when all things are forgotten, there is naught that can disturb one's peace or that moves the desires; for, as they say, that which the eye sees not the heart desires not.

2. And this we learn by experience at every moment; for we observe that, whenever the soul begins to think of any matter, it is moved and disturbed, either much or little, with respect to that thing, according to the nature of its apprehension. If it be a troublesome and grievous matter, the soul finds sadness[1] in it; if pleasant, desire and joy,[2] and so forth. Wherefore the result of the changing of that apprehension is necessarily disturbance; and thus the soul is now joyful, now sad; now it hates, now loves; and it cannot continue in one and the same attitude (which is an effect of moral tranquillity), save when it strives to forget all things. It is clear, then, that knowledge greatly hinders the good of the moral virtues in the soul.

3. Again, what has been said clearly proves that an encumbered memory also hinders spiritual good;[3] for the soul that is disturbed, and has no foundation of moral good, is to that extent incapable of spiritual good, which impresses itself only upon souls that are restrained and given to peace. And

---

[1] E.p.: 'sadness or hate.'
[2] E.p.: 'if pleasant, joy and desire.'
[3] The edition of 1630 reads: 'spiritual or mystical good.'

besides this, if the soul pays attention and heed to the apprehensions of the memory—seeing that it can attend to but one thing at a time—if it busies itself with things that can be apprehended, such as the knowledge of the memory, it is not possible for it to be free to attend to the incomprehensible, which is God. For, in order to approach God, the soul must proceed by not comprehending rather than by comprehending ; it must exchange the mutable and comprehensible for the immutable and incomprehensible.

CHAPTER VI

Of the benefits which come to the soul from forgetfulness and emptiness of all thoughts and knowledge which it may have in a natural way with respect to the memory.

1. From the evils which, as we have said, come to the soul through the apprehensions of the memory, we can likewise infer the benefits which are contrary to them and come to the soul as a result of its forgetting them and emptying itself of them. For, as natural philosophers say, the same doctrine which serves for one thing serves likewise for its contrary. In the first place, the soul enjoys tranquillity and peace of mind, since it is freed from the disturbance and the change which arise from thoughts and notions of the memory, and consequently it enjoys purity of conscience and soul, which is more important. And herein the soul has ample preparation for Divine and human wisdom, and for the virtues.

2. In the second place, it is freed from many suggestions, temptations and motions of the devil, which he infuses into the soul by means of thoughts and notions, causing it to fall into many impurities and sins,[1] as David says in these words : They thought and spake wickedness.[2] And thus, when these thoughts have been completely removed, the devil has naught wherewith to assault the soul by natural means.[3]

3. In the third place, the soul has within itself, through this recollection of itself and this forgetfulness as to all things, a preparedness to be moved by the Holy Spirit and taught

---

[1] A, B, e.p. : ' to fall, at the least, into many impurities, and, as we have said, into sins.'

[2] Psalm lxxii, 8 [A.V., lxxiii, 8]. E.p. : ' and found wickedness.'

[3] E.p. omits : ' by natural means.'

by Him, for, as the Wise Man says, He removes Himself
from thoughts which are without understanding.[1] Even if a
man received no other benefit from this forgetfulness and
emptiness of the memory than being freed thereby from
troubles and disturbances, it would be a great gain and
blessing for him.   For the troubles and disturbances which
are bred in the soul by adversity[2] are of no use or profit[3]
for bringing prosperity;[4] indeed, as a rule, they make
things worse and also harm the soul itself.   Wherefore David
said : Of a truth every man is disquieted vainly.[5] For it is
clear that to disquiet oneself is always vain since it brings
profit to none.   And thus, even if everything came to an end
and were destroyed, and if all things went wrong and turned
to adversity, it would be vain to disturb oneself ; for this
hurts a man rather than relieves him.   And to bear everything with equable and peaceful tranquillity not only brings
the soul the profit of many blessings, but likewise causes it,
even in the midst of its adversities, to form a truer judgement
about them and to find them a fitting remedy.

4. For this reason Solomon, being well acquainted both
with the evil and with the benefit of which we are speaking,
said : I knew that there was naught better for man than to
rejoice and to do good in his life.[6] By this he meant that,
in everything that happens to us, howsoever adverse it be,
we should rejoice rather than be troubled, so that we may
not lose a blessing which is greater than any kind of prosperity—namely, tranquillity and peace of mind in all things,
which, whether they bring adversity or prosperity, we must
bear in the same manner.   This a man would never lose if
he were not only to forget all kinds of knowledge and put
aside all thoughts, but would even withdraw himself from
hearing, sight and commerce with others, in so far as was
possible for him.   Our nature is so frail and so easily moved
that, however well it be disciplined, it will hardly fail to
stumble upon the remembrance of things which will disturb
and change a mind that was in peace and tranquillity when
it remembered them not.   For this cause said Jeremiah :
With memory I will remember, and my soul will fail me
for pain.[7]

---

[1] Wisdom i, 5.   [2] [Lit., ' by adverse things and happenings.']
[3] E.p. omits : ' or profit.'
[4] [Lit., ' for the prosperity of the same things and happenings.']
E.p. omits : ' things and.'   [5] Psalm xxxviii, 7 [A.V., xxxix, 6].
[6] Ecclesiastes iii, 12.   [7] Lamentations iii, 20.

CHAPTER VII

Which treats of the second kind of apprehension of the memory— the imaginary—and of supernatural knowledge.

1. Although in writing of natural apprehensions of the first kind we also gave instruction concerning the imaginary, which are likewise natural, it was well to make this division because of the love which the memory preserves for other forms and kinds of knowledge, which are of supernatural things, such as visions, revelations, locutions and feelings which come in a supernatural way. When these things have passed through the soul, there is wont to remain impressed upon it some image, form, figure or notion, whether in the soul or in the memory or fancy, at times very vividly and effectively. Concerning these images it is also needful to give advice, lest the memory be encumbered with them and they be a hindrance to its union with God in perfect and pure hope.

2. And I say that the soul, in order to attain that blessing, must never reflect upon the clear and distinct objects which may have passed through its mind by supernatural means, so as to preserve within it the forms and figures and knowledge of those things. For we must ever bear in mind this principle : the greater heed the soul gives to any clear and distinct apprehensions, whether natural or supernatural, the less capacity and preparation it has for entering into the abyss of faith, wherein are absorbed all things else. For, as has been said, no supernatural forms or knowledge which can be apprehended by the memory are God,[1] and, in order to reach God, the soul must void itself of all that is not God. The memory must also strip itself of all these forms and notions, that it may unite itself with God in hope.[2] For all possession is contrary to hope, which, as S. Paul says, belongs to that which is not possessed.[3] .Wherefore, the more the memory dispossesses itself, the greater is its hope ; and the more it has of hope, the more it has of union with God ; for, with respect to God, the more the soul hopes, the more it attains. And it hopes most when it is most completely

---

[1] E.p. adds : ' nor do they bear any proportion to Him nor can serve as proximate means to union with Him.'
[2] E.p.: ' . . . unite itself with God in a manner of mystical and perfect hope.' [3] Hebrews xi, 1.

dispossessed ; and, when it shall be perfectly dispossessed, it will remain with the perfect possession of God,[1] in Divine union. But there are many who will not deprive themselves of the sweetness and delight which memory finds in those forms and notions, wherefore they attain not to supreme possession and perfect sweetness. For he that renounces not all that he possesses cannot be the disciple of Christ.[2]

CHAPTER VIII

Of the evils which may be caused to the soul by the knowledge of supernatural things, if it reflect upon them. Says how many these evils are.[3]

1. The spiritual man incurs the risk of five kinds of evil if he gives heed to, and reflects upon, these forms and notions which are impressed upon him by the things which pass through his mind in a supernatural way.

2. The first is that he is frequently deceived, and mistakes one thing for another. The second is that he is like to fall, and is exposed to the danger of falling, into some form of presumption or vanity. The third is that the devil has many occasions of deceiving him by means of the apprehensions aforementioned. The fourth is that he is hindered as to union in hope with God. The fifth is that, for the most part, he has a low judgement of God.

3. As to the first evil, it is clear that, if the spiritual man gives heed to these forms and notions, and reflects upon them, he must frequently be deceived in his judgement of them ; for, as no man can have a complete understanding of the things that pass through his imagination naturally, nor a perfect and certain judgement about them, he will be much less able still to have this with respect to supernatural things, which are above our capacity to understand, and occur but rarely. Wherefore he will often think that what comes but from his fancy pertains to God ; and often, too, that what is of God is of the devil, and what is of the devil is of God. And very often there will remain with him deep impressions of forms and notions concerning the good and evil of others, or of himself, together with other figures which

---

[1] E.p. adds : ' in so far as may be in this life.'
[2] S. Luke xiv, 33.
[3] A, B, e.p. add : ' and treats here of the first.'

have been presented to him : these he will consider to be most certain and true, when they will not be so, but very great falsehoods. And others will be true, and he will judge them to be false, although this error I consider safer, as it is apt to arise from humility.

4. And, even if he be not deceived as to their truth, he may well be deceived as to their quantity or quality,[1] thinking that little things are great, and great things, little. And with respect to their quality, he may consider what is in his imagination to be this or that, when it is something quite different ; he may put, as Isaiah says, darkness for light, and light for darkness, and bitter for sweet, and sweet for bitter.[2] And finally, even though he be correct as to one thing, it will be a marvel if he goes not astray with respect to the next ; for, although he may not desire to apply his judgement to the judging of them, yet, if he apply it in paying heed to them, this will be sufficient for some evil to cling to him as a result of it,[3] at least passively ; if not evil of this kind, then of one of the four other kinds of which we shall shortly speak.

5. It behoves the spiritual man, therefore, lest he fall into this evil of being deceived in his judgement, not to desire to apply his judgement in order to know the nature of his own condition or feelings, or the nature of such and such a vision, notion or feeling ; neither should he desire to know it or to give heed[4] to it. This he should only desire in order to speak of it to his spiritual father, who will then teach him how to void his memory of these apprehensions.[5] For, whatever may be their intrinsic nature, they cannot help him to love God as much as the smallest act of living faith and hope performed in the emptiness and renunciation of all things.[6]

CHAPTER IX

Of the second kind of evil, which is the peril of falling into self-esteem and vain presumption.

1. The supernatural apprehensions of the memory already described are also a great occasion to spiritual persons of

---

[1] E.p. : ' quality and value.'   [2] Isaiah v, 20.
[3] The 1630 edition adds : ' and for him to suffer from it.'
[4] E.p. : ' give much heed.'
[5] E.p. adds : ' or [to do] what in his particular case may be most expedient, with this same detachment.'
[6] E.p. : ' in the emptiness of all this.'

falling into some kind of presumption or vanity, if they give heed to them and set store by them. For, even as he who knows nothing of them is quite free from falling into this vice, since he sees in himself no occasion of presumption, even so, in contrary wise, he that has experience of them has close at hand an occasion for thinking himself to be something, since he possesses these supernatural communications. For, although it is true that he may attribute them to God, hold himself[1] to be unworthy of them, and give God the thanks, yet nevertheless he is wont to keep in his spirit a certain secret satisfaction, and a self-esteem and a sense of their value, from which, without his knowledge, there will come to him great spiritual pride.

2. This may be observed very clearly by spiritual men who will consider the dislike and aversion caused them by any who do not praise their spirituality, or esteem the experiences which they enjoy ; and in the mortification which they suffer when they think or are told that others have just those same experiences, or greater ones. All this arises from secret self-esteem and pride, and they cannot manage to understand that they are steeped in pride up to their very eyes. For they think that a certain degree of recognition of their own wretchedness suffices, and, although they have this, they are full of secret self-esteem and satisfaction, taking more delight in their own spirituality and spiritual gifts[2] than in those of others. They are like the Pharisee who gave thanks to God that he was not as other men, and that he practised such and such virtues, whereat he was satisfied with himself and presumed thereon.[3] Such men, although they speak not like the Pharisee in so many words, habitually resemble him in spirit. And some of them even become so proud that they are worse than the devil. For, observing in themselves, as they imagine, certain apprehensions and feelings concerning God which are devout and sweet, they become self-satisfied to such an extent that they believe themselves to be very near God ; and those that are not like themselves they consider very low and despise them after the manner of the Pharisee.[4]

3. In order to flee from this pestilent evil, abhorrent in the eyes of God, they must consider two things. First, that

---

[1] E.p. : ' feel himself.'   [2] E.p. : ' spirituality and gifts.'
[3] S. Luke xviii, 11–12.
[4] A, B : ' and despise them as the Pharisee despised the publican.'

virtue consists not in apprehensions and feelings concerning
God, howsoever sublime they be, nor in anything of this kind
that a man can feel within himself; but, on the contrary,
in that which has nothing to do with feeling—namely, a
great humility and contempt of oneself and of all that pertains to oneself, firmly rooted in the soul and keenly felt by
it; and likewise in being glad that others feel in this very
way concerning oneself and in not wishing to be of any
account in the esteem[1] of others.

4. Secondly, it must be noted that all visions, revelations and feelings coming from Heaven, and any thoughts
that may proceed from these, are of less worth than the least
act of humility; for such an act has the effects of charity.
The humble soul esteems not its own things nor strives to
attain them; nor thinks evil, save of itself; nor thinks any
good thing of itself, but only of others. It is well, therefore,
that these supernatural apprehensions should not attract
men's eyes, but that they should strive to forget them in
order that they may be free.

CHAPTER X

*Of the third evil that may come to the soul from the devil, through
the imaginary apprehensions of the memory.*

1. From all that has been said above it may be clearly
understood and inferred how great is the evil that may come
to the soul from the devil by way of these supernatural
apprehensions. For not only can he represent to the
memory and the fancy many false forms and notions, which
seem true and good, impressing them on spirit and sense
with great effectiveness and certifying them to be true by
means of suggestion (so that it appears to the soul that it
cannot be otherwise, but that everything is even as he represents it; for, as he transfigures himself into an angel of light,
he appears as light to the soul); but he may also tempt the
soul in many ways with respect to true knowledge, which is
of God, moving its desires[2] and affections, whether spiritual
or sensual, in unruly fashion with respect to these; for, if the
soul takes pleasure in such apprehensions, it is very easy for
the devil to cause its desires and affections to grow[3] within it,

---

[1] [*Lit.*, 'in the heart.']   [2] A, B: 'its will and desires.'
[3] A, B and many of the editions (not, however, e.p.) have *creer*
('believe') for *crecer* ('grow'), so that we should have to read: 'to
cause it to believe its desires and affections.'

and to make it fall into spiritual gluttony and other evils.

2. And, in order the better to do this, he is wont to suggest and give pleasure, sweetness and delight to the senses with respect to these same things of God, so that the soul is corrupted and bewildered[1] by that sweetness, and is thus blinded with that pleasure and sets its eyes on pleasure rather than on love (or, at least, very much more than upon love), and gives more heed to the apprehensions than to the detachment and emptiness which are found in faith and hope and love of God. And from this he may go on gradually to deceive the soul and cause it to believe his falsehoods with great facility. For to the soul that is blind falsehood no longer appears to be falsehood, nor does evil appear to be evil, etc. ; for darkness appears to be light, and light, darkness ; and hence that soul comes to commit a thousand foolish errors,[2] whether with respect to natural things, or to moral things, or to spiritual things ; so that that which was wine to it becomes vinegar. All this happens to the soul because it began not, first of all, by denying itself the pleasure of those supernatural things. At first this is a small matter, and not very harmful, and the soul has therefore no misgivings, and allows it to continue, and it grows,[3] like the grain of mustard seed, into a tall tree. For a small error at the beginning, as they say, becomes a great error in the end.

3. Wherefore, in order to flee from this great evil, which comes[4] from the devil, the soul must not desire to have any pleasure in such things, because such pleasure will most surely lead it to become blind and to fall. For of their own nature, and without the help of the devil,[5] pleasure and delight and sweetness blind[6] the soul. And this was the meaning of David when he said : Peradventure darkness shall blind me in my delights and I shall have the night for my light.[7]

---

[1] [The two verbs, in the original, have very definite and concrete meanings, ' sweetened with honey ' and ' dazzled by a lamp ' respectively.]

[2] E.p. adds here : ' so that that which was wine to it becomes vinegar,' omitting this same phrase where it occurs below.

[3] E.p. : ' to continue and grow.'

[4] E.p. : ' which may come.'

[5] E.p. omits : ' and without the help of the devil.'

[6] E.p. : ' dull and blind.'

[7] Psalm cxxxviii, 11 [A.V., cxxxix, 11].

CHAPTER XI

*Of the fourth evil that comes to the soul from the distinct super-
natural apprehensions of the memory, which is the hindrance
that it interposes to union.*

1. Concerning this fourth evil there is not much to be
said, since it has already continually been expounded in this
third book, wherein we have proved how, in order that the
soul may come to union with God in hope, it must renounce
every possession of the memory ; for, in order that its hope
in God may be perfect, it must have naught in the memory
that is not God. And, as we have likewise said, no form or
figure or image or other kind of knowledge that may come
to the memory can be God, neither can be like Him, whether
it be of heaven or of earth,[1] natural or supernatural, even
as David teaches, when he says : Lord, among the gods
there is none like unto Thee.[2]

2. Wherefore, if the memory desires to pay any heed to any
of these things, it hinders the soul from reaching God ; first,
because it encumbers it, and next because, the more the
soul has of possession, the less it has of hope.[3] Wherefore it
is needful for the soul to be stripped of the distinct forms and
notions of supernatural things, and to become oblivious to
them, so that there may be no hindrance to its union with
God according to the memory in perfect hope.

CHAPTER XII

*Of the fifth evil that may come to the soul in supernatural imaginary
forms and apprehensions, which is a low and unseemly judgement
of God.*

1. No less serious is the fifth evil that comes to the soul
from its desire to retain in the memory and imagination the
said forms and images of things that are supernaturally
communicated to it, above all if it desires to take them as a
means to Divine union. For it is a very easy thing to judge
of the Being and greatness of God less worthily and nobly

---

[1] E.p. omits : ' whether it be of heaven or of earth.'
[2] Psalm lxxxv, 8 [A.V., lxxxvi, 8].
[3] E.p. : ' of perfection of hope.'

than befits His incomprehensible nature ; for, although our
reason and judgement may form no express conception that
God is like any one of these things, yet the very consideration
of these apprehensions, if in fact the soul considers them,
makes and causes it not to esteem God,[1] or not to feel concerning Him, as highly as faith teaches, since faith tells us
that He is incomparable, incomprehensible, and so forth.
For, besides the fact that the soul takes from God all that it
gives to the creature, it is natural that, by means of its consideration of these apprehensible things, there should be
formed within it a certain comparison between such things
and God, which prevents it from judging and esteeming God
as highly as it ought.   For the creatures, whether terrestrial
or celestial, and all distinct images and kinds of knowledge,[2]
both natural and supernatural, that can be apprehended
by the faculties of the soul, however lofty they be in this life,
have no comparison or proportion with the Being of God,
since God falls within no genus and no species, as they do,
according as the theologians tell us.[3]   And the soul in this
life is not capable of receiving in a clear and distinct manner
aught save that which falls into a genus and a species.   For
this cause S. John says that no man hath seen God at any
time.[4]   And Isaiah says that it has not entered into the heart
of man what God is like.[5]   And God said to Moses that he
could not see Him in this state of life.[6]   Wherefore, he that
encumbers his memory and the other faculties of the soul
with that which they can comprehend cannot esteem God,
neither feel concerning Him, as he ought.

2. Let us make a comparison on a lower scale.   It is clear
that the more a man fixes his eyes[7] upon the servants of a
king, and the more notice he takes of them, the less notice
does he take of the king himself, and the less does he esteem
him ; for, although this comparison be not formally and
distinctly present in the understanding, it is inherent in the
act, since, the more attention the man gives to the servants,
the more he takes from their lord ; and he cannot have a
very high opinion of the king if the servants appear to him
to be of any importance while they are in the presence of the

---

[1] E.p. abbreviates : ' the very consideration of these apprehensions
makes the soul not to esteem God . . .'
[2] E.p. : ' and all the forms and images.'
[3] E.p. ends this sentence at ' no species.'   [4] S. John i, 18.
[5] Isaiah lxiv, 4.   [6] Exodus xxxiii, 20.
[7] E.p. : ' fixes the eyes of his esteem.'

king, their lord. Even so does the soul treat its God when it pays heed to the creatures[1] aforementioned. This comparison, however, is on a very low scale, for, as we have said, God is of another being than His creatures in that He is at an infinite distance from them all. For this reason they must all be banished from sight, and the soul must withdraw its gaze from them in all their forms, that it may set its gaze on God through faith and hope.[2]

3. Wherefore those who not only pay heed to the imaginary apprehensions aforementioned, but suppose God to be like to some of them, and think that by means of them they will be able to attain to union with God, have already gone far astray and will ever continue to lose the light[3] of faith in the understanding, through which this faculty is united with God ; neither will they grow in the loftiness of hope, by means whereof the memory is united with God in hope,[4] which must be brought about through disunion from all that is of the imagination.

CHAPTER XIII

Of the benefits which the soul receives through banishing from itself the apprehensions of the imagination. This chapter answers a certain objection and describes a difference which exists between apprehensions that are imaginary, natural and supernatural.[5]

1. The benefits that come from voiding the imagination of imaginary forms can be clearly observed in the five evils aforementioned which they inflict upon the soul, if it desires to retain them, even as we also said of the natural forms. But, apart from these, there are other benefits for the spirit —namely, those of great rest and quiet. For, setting aside that natural rest which the soul obtains when it is free from images and forms, it likewise becomes free from anxiety as to whether they are good or evil, and as to how it must behave with respect to the one and to the other. Nor has it to waste the labour and time of its spiritual masters, requiring them to ascertain if these things are good or evil, and if they are of this kind or of another ; for the soul has no need

---

[1] A, B, e.p. : ' to the things.'   [2] E.p. : ' and perfect hope.'
[3] E.p. : ' and profit not greatly by the light.'
[4] E.p. omits : ' in hope.'
[5] So Alc., e.p. The other authorities have the first sentence of the title only.

to desire to know all this if it gives no heed to them.[1]   The
time and energies which it would have wasted in dealing
with these images and forms[2] can be better employed in
another and a more profitable exercise, which is that of the
will with respect to God, and in having a care to seek detachment and poverty of spirit and sense, which consists in
desiring earnestly to be without any support and consolation
that can be apprehended, whether interior or exterior.   This
is well practised when we desire and strive to strip ourselves
of these forms, since from this there will proceed no less a
benefit than that of approach to God (Who has no image,
neither form nor figure) and this will be the greater according
as the soul withdraws itself the more completely from all
forms, images and figures of the imagination.[3]

2.   But perchance you will say : ' Why do many spiritual
persons counsel the soul to strive to profit by the communications and feelings which come from God, and to desire to
receive them from Him, that it may have something to give
Him ; since, if He gives us nothing, we shall give Him
nothing likewise ?   And wherefore does S. Paul say : Quench
not the Spirit ?[4]   And the Spouse to the Bride : Set me as a
seal[5] upon thy heart and as a seal upon thine arm ?[6] This
certainly denotes some kind of apprehension.   And, according to the instruction given above, not only must all this not
be striven after, but, although God sends it, it must be
rejected and cast aside.   But surely it is clear that, since God
gives it, He gives it to a good purpose, and it will have a
good effect.   We must not throw away pearls.   And it is
even a kind of pride to be unwilling to receive the things of
God, as if we could do without them and were self-sufficient.'

3.   In order to meet this objection it is necessary to recall
what we said in the fifteenth and sixteenth chapters[7] of the
second book, where to a great extent this question is answered.
For we said there that the good that overflows in the soul
from supernatural apprehensions, when they come from a
good source, is produced passively in the soul at that very
instant[8] when they are represented to the senses, without

---

[1] E.p. adds : ' but [needs] only to reject them in the sense already
mentioned.'

[2] E.p. abbreviates : ' which would have been wasted upon this.'

[3] E.p. omits : ' of the imagination.'   [4] 1 Thessalonians v, 19.

[5] D, P : ' as a sign.'   [6] Canticles viii, 6.

[7] More correctly, in Chaps. xvi and xvii.

[8] E.p. omits : ' at that very instant.'

the working of any operation of the faculties. Wherefore it is unnecessary for the will to perform the act of receiving them ; for, as we have also said, if at that time the soul should try to labour with its faculties,[1] the effect of its own base and natural operation would be to hinder the supernatural graces[2] which God is even then working in it rather than that, through these apprehensions, God should cause it to derive any benefit from its active exertion. Nay, rather, as the spirituality coming from those imaginary apprehensions is given passively to the soul, even so must the soul conduct itself passively with respect to them, setting no store by its inward or outward actions.[3] To do this is to preserve the feelings that come from God, for in this way they are not lost through the soul's base manner of working. Neither is this to quench the spirit ; for the spirit would be quenched by the soul if it desired to behave in another manner than that whereby God is leading it. And this it would do if, when God had given it spiritual graces[4] passively, as He does in these apprehensions, it should then desire to exert itself actively with respect to them, by labouring[5] with its understanding[6] or by seeking to find something in them. And this is clear because, if the soul desires to labour at that time with its own exertions, its work cannot be more than natural,[7] for of itself it is capable of no more ; for supernaturally[8] it neither moves itself nor can move itself, but it is God that moves the soul and brings it to this state.[9] And thus, if the soul at that time desires to labour with its own exertions (as far as, lies in its power), its active working will hinder the passive work[10] that God is communicating to it, which is that of the Spirit.[11] It will be setting itself to its own work, which is of another and a lowlier kind than that which God

---

[1] A, B : 'labour with the favour of its faculties.' E.p.: 'labour according to the ability of its faculties.'

[2] [*Lit.*, ' the supernatural.']

[3] E.p. adds : ' in the sense mentioned above.'

[4] [*Lit.*, ' had given it spirit ' (or ' spirituality ').]

[5] E.p. inserts : ' of itself.'

[6] E.p. ends the paragraph here, but the 1630 edition adds ' beyond what God gives it ' and continues, with the variants noted below.

[7] The 1630 edition adds : ' or, at most, if it be supernatural, it must be very much inferior to that which God would work in it, for of itself.'

[8] The 1630 edition has : ' for in this most sublime and supernatural way.'

[9] The 1630 edition adds : ' when it gives its consent.'

[10] The 1630 edition has : ' it will, with its working, hinder the work.'

[11] [Or ' that of spirituality.' Cf. n. 4, above.]

communicates to it ; for the work of God is passive and super-natural, and that of the soul is active and natural ;[1] and in this way the soul would therefore be quenching the Spirit.

4. That this activity of the soul is an inferior one is also clear from the fact that the faculties of the soul cannot, of their own power,[2] reflect and act, save upon some form, figure and image, and this is the rind and accident of the substance and spirit which exists below this rind and accident. This substance and spirit unite not with the faculties of the soul in true understanding and love, save when at last the operation of the faculties ceases. For the aim and end of this operation is only that the substance which can be under-stood and loved and which lies beneath these forms may come to be received in the soul. The difference, therefore, be-tween passive and active operation, and the superiority of the former, corresponds to the difference that exists between that which is being done and that which is done already, or between that which a man tries to attain and effect and that which is already effected. Hence it may likewise be inferred that, if the soul desires to employ its faculties actively on these supernatural apprehensions, wherein God, as we have said, bestows the spirit of them passively, it would do nothing less than abandon what it had already done, in order to do it again, neither would it enjoy what it had done, nor could it produce any other result, by these actions of its own, save that of frustrating what has been done already. For, as we say, the faculties cannot of their own power attain to the spirituality which God bestows upon the soul without any operation of their own. And thus the soul would be directly quenching the spirituality[3] which God infuses through these imaginary apprehensions aforementioned if it were to set any store by them ; wherefore it must set them aside, and take up a passive and negative attitude with regard to them.[4] For at that time God is moving the soul to things which are above its own power and knowledge. For this cause the prophet said : I will stand upon my watch and set my step upon my tower, and I will watch to see that which will be said to me.[5] This is as though he were to say : I will stand on guard over

---

[1] The 1630 edition omits : ' for the work . . . active and natural.'
[2] E.p. : ' cannot, according to their natural and ordinary method.'
[3] [Or ' the Spirit.' Cf. p. 251, nn. 4, 11, above.]
[4] E.p. omits ' and negative ' and adds ' as we say.'
[5] Habakuk ii, 1. [The original has ' munition ' for ' tower ' and ' contemplate ' for ' watch to see.']

my faculties and I will take no step forward as to my actions, and thus I shall be able to contemplate that which will be said to me—that is, I shall understand and enjoy that which will be communicated to me supernaturally.

5. And that, too, which is alleged of the Spouse is here understood of the love that He entreats of[1] the Bride, the office of which love between two lovers is to make one like to the other[2] in the principal part of them. Wherefore He tells her to set Him as a seal upon her heart,[3] where all the arrows strike that leave the quiver of love, which arrows are the actions and motives of love. So they will all strike Him Who is there as a mark[4] for them ; and thus all will be for Him, so that the soul will become like Him through the actions and motions of love, until it be transformed in Him. Likewise he bids her set Him as a seal[5] upon her arm, because the arm performs[6] the exercise of love, for by the arm the Beloved is sustained and comforted.

6. Therefore all that the soul has to endeavour to do in all the apprehensions which come to it from above, whether imaginary or of any other kind—it matters not if they be visions, locutions, feelings or revelations—is to make no account of the letter or the rind (that is, of what is signified or represented or given to be understood), but to pay heed only to the possession of the love of God which they cause interiorly within the soul. And in this case the soul will make account, not of feelings of sweetness or delight, nor of figures, but of the feelings of love which they cause it. And with this sole end in view it may at times recall that image and apprehension which caused it to love, in order to place the spirit in the way of love. For, though the effect of that apprehension be not so great afterwards, when it is recalled, as it was on the first occasion when it was communicated, yet, when it is recalled, love is renewed, and the mind is lifted up to God, especially when the recollection is of certain figures, images or feelings which are supernatural, and are wont to be sealed and imprinted upon the soul in such a way that they continue for a long time—some of them, indeed, are never taken from the soul. And those that are thus sealed upon the soul produce in it Divine effects of love, sweetness,

---

[1] A, B : ' that He has to.'
[2] E.p. omits the rest of this sentence.
[3] Canticles viii, 6. A, B : ' as a sign.'
[4] A, e.p. : ' as a sign.'   [5] E.p. : ' as a sign.'
[6] [Lit., ' because in the arm is.']

light and so forth, on almost every occasion when the soul returns to them, sometimes more so and sometimes less ; for it is to this end that they were impressed upon it. And thus this is a great favour for the soul on which God bestows it, for it is as though it had within itself a mine of blessings.

7. The figures which produce effects such as these are deeply implanted in the soul,[1] for they are not like other images and forms that are retained in the fancy. And thus the soul has no need to have recourse to this faculty when it desires to recall them, for it sees that it has them within itself, and that they are as an image seen in the mirror. When it comes to pass that any soul has such figures formally within itself, it will then do well to recall them to the effect of love to which I have referred, for they will be no hindrance to the union of love in faith, since the soul will not desire to be absorbed in the figure, but only to profit by the love ; it will immediately set aside the figure, which will thus rather be a help to it.

8. Only with great difficulty can it be known when these images are imprinted upon the soul, and when they touch but the fancy.[2] For those which touch the fancy are as apt to occur very frequently as are the others ; for certain persons are accustomed habitually to have imaginary visions in their imagination and fancy, which are presented to them in one form with great frequency ; sometimes because the apprehensive power of the organ concerned is very great, and, however little they reflect upon it, that habitual figure is at once presented and outlined in their fancy ; sometimes because it is the work of the devil ; sometimes, again, because it is the work of God ; but the visions are not formally impressed upon the soul. They may be known, however, by their effects. For those that are natural, or that come from the devil, produce no good effect upon the soul, however frequently they be recalled, nor work its spiritual renewal, but the contemplation of them simply produces aridity. Those that are good, however, produce some good effect when they are recalled, like that[3] which was produced in the soul upon the first occasion. But the formal images which

[1] E.p. adds : ' according to its intellectual memory.'
[2] E.p. : ' . . . when these images touch the spiritual part of the soul directly and when they belong to the fancy.'
[3] So e.p. The MSS. [and P. Silverio] read : ' in that.'

are imprinted upon the soul almost invariably produce some effect in it, whensoever they are remembered.

9. He that has experienced these will readily distinguish the one kind from the other, for the great difference[1] between them is very clear to anyone that has experience of them. I will merely say that those which are formally and durably imprinted upon the soul are of very rare occurrence. But, whether they be of this kind or of that, it is good for the soul to desire to understand nothing, save God alone, through faith, in hope. And if anyone makes the objection that to reject these things, if they are good, appears to be pride, I reply that it is not so, but that it is prudent humility to profit by them in the best way, as has been said, and to be guided by that which is safest.

CHAPTER XIV

Which treats of spiritual knowledge in so far as it may concern the memory.

1. We classed spiritual knowledge as the third division of the apprehensions of the memory, not because they belong to the bodily sense of the fancy, as do the rest, for they have no bodily form and image,[2] but because they are likewise apprehensible by spiritual memory and reminiscence. Now, after the soul has had experience of one of these apprehensions, it can recall it whensoever it will ; and this is not by the effigy[3] and image that the apprehension has left in the bodily sense, for, since this is of bodily form, as we say, it has no capacity for spiritual forms ; but because it recalls it, intellectually and spiritually, by means of that form which it has left impressed upon the soul, which is likewise a formal or spiritual form or notion or image, whereby it is recalled, or by means of the effect that it has wrought. It is for this reason that I place these apprehensions among those of the memory, although they belong not to the apprehensions of the fancy.

2. What this knowledge is, and how the soul is to conduct itself with respect to it in order to attain to union with God, are sufficiently described in the twenty-fourth chapter[4] of

---

[1] E.p. : ' the aforementioned difference.'
[2] E.p. omits : ' for they have no bodily form and image.'
[3] E.p. : ' not by the figure.'
[4] Really the chapter is the twenty-sixth.

the second book, where we treated this knowledge as apprehensions of the understanding.   Let this be referred to, for
we there described how it was of two kinds : either uncreated[1]
or of the creatures.   I speak now only of things relating to
my present purpose—namely, how the memory must behave
with respect to them in order to attain to union.   And I say,
as I have just said of formal knowledge in the preceding
chapter (for this, being of created things, is of the same kind),
that these apprehensions may be recalled when they produce
good effects, not that they may be dwelt upon, but that they
may quicken the soul's love and knowledge of God.   But, if
the recollection of them produces not good effects, let the
memory never give them even passing attention.   With
regard to uncreated knowledge,[2] I say that the soul should
try to recall it as often as possible, for it will produce great
effects.   As we said above, it produces touches and impressions of union with God, which is the aim towards which we
are directing the soul.   And by no form, image or figure
which can be impressed upon the soul does the memory
recall these (for these touches and impressions of union with
the Creator[3] have no form), but only by the effects which
they have produced upon it of light, love, joy and renewal of
the spirit, and so forth, some of which are wrought anew in
the soul whensoever they are remembered.

CHAPTER XV

*Which sets down the general method whereby the spiritual person
must govern himself with respect to this sense.*

1. In order to conclude this discussion on the memory, it
will be well at this point to give the spiritual reader an
account of[4] the method which he must observe, and which is
of universal application, in order that he may be united with
God according to this sense.[5]   For, although what has been
said makes the subject quite clear, it will nevertheless be
more easily apprehended if we summarize it here.   To this
end it must be remembered that, since our aim is the union

[1] E.p. : ' either of uncreated perfections.'
[2] E.p. : ' With regard to the knowledge of things uncreated.'
[3] A, B : ' with God.'
[4] Only Alc. and e.p. have : ' an account of.'
[5] E.p. : ' this faculty.'

of the soul with God in hope, according to the memory, and since that which is hoped for is that which is not possessed, and since, the less we possess of other things, the greater scope and the greater capacity we have for hoping, and consequently the greater hope,[1] therefore, the more things we possess, the less scope and capacity there is for hoping, and consequently the less hope[2] have we. Hence, the more the soul dispossesses the memory of forms and things which may be recalled by it, which are not God,[3] the more will it set its memory upon God, and the emptier will its memory become, so that it may hope for Him Who shall fill it. What must be done, then, that the soul may live in the perfect and pure hope of God is that, whensoever these distinct images, forms and notions come to it, it must not rest in them, but must turn immediately to God, voiding the memory of them entirely, with loving affection. It must neither think of these things nor consider them beyond the degree which is necessary for the understanding and performing of its obligations, if they have any concern with these. And this it must do without setting any affection or inclination upon them, so that they may produce no effects[4] in the soul. And thus a man must not fail to think and recall that which he ought to know and do, for, provided he preserves no affection or attachments, this will do him no harm. For this matter the lines of the Mount, which are in the thirteenth chapter[5] of the first book, will be of profit.

3. But here it must be borne in mind that this doctrine of ours does not agree, nor do we desire that it should agree, with the doctrine of those pestilent men, who, inspired by Satanic pride and envy, have desired to remove from the eyes of the faithful the holy and necessary use, and the worthy[6] adoration, of images of God and of the saints. This doctrine of ours is very different from that ; for we say not here, as they do, that images should not exist, and should not be

---

[1] E.p. : ' the greater perfection of hope.'
[2] E.p. : ' the less perfection of hope.'
[3] E.p. : ' which are not Divinity or God made human, the memory of Whom is always a help to that end, since He is the true Way and Guide and Author of all good.' With this addition, cf. that quoted on p. 232, n. 3, above. [4] E.p. : ' no effects or perturbations.'
[5] So e.p. A, B have : ' in the first chapter,' referring apparently to the drawing described above (pp. xxxiv–v). Alc., C, D [followed by P. Silverio] read : ' in the chapter.'
[6] [The Spanish word, *inclita,* is stronger than this, meaning ' distinguished,' ' illustrious.']

adored ; we simply explain the difference between images and God. We exhort men to pass beyond that which is superficial[1] that they may not be hindered from attaining to the living truth beneath it, and to make no more account of the former than suffices for attainment to the spiritual. For means are good and necessary to an end ; and images are means which serve to remind us of God and of the saints. But when we consider and attend to the means more than is necessary for treating them as such, they disturb and hinder us as much, in their own way, as any different thing ;[2] the more so, when we treat of supernatural visions and images,[3] to which I am specially referring, and with respect to which arise many deceptions and perils. For, with respect to the remembrance and adoration and esteem of images, which the Catholic Church sets before us,[4] there can be no deception or peril, because naught is esteemed therein other than that which is represented ;[5] nor does the remembrance of them fail to profit the soul, since they are not preserved in the memory save with love for that which they represent ; and provided the soul pays no more heed to them than is necessary for this purpose,[6] they will ever assist it to union with God, allowing the soul to soar upwards (when God grants it that favour) from the superficial image[7] to the living God, forgetting every creature and everything that belongs to creatures.[8]

CHAPTER XVI

Which begins to treat of the dark night of the will. Makes a division between the affections of the will.[9]

1. We should have accomplished nothing by the purgation of the understanding in order to ground it in the virtue

---

[1] [*Lit.*, ' which is painted.']
[2] E.p. adds : ' disturbs and hinders us.'
[3] E.p. : ' of images and visions that are interior and are formed in the soul.'
[4] B : ' sets corporeally before us ' [P. Silverio, in a note, prefers this reading]. A, Alc. : ' sets naturally before us.' E.p. : ' which our mother the Church sets before us.'
[5] E.p. omits : ' because naught . . . represented.'
[6] E.p. : ' and, provided the soul uses them for this purpose.'
[7] [*Lit.*, ' the painted image.']
[8] A, B have here : ' End of the third book,' the chapters which follow being placed in the fourth book.
[9] A, B omit this second sentence.

of faith, and by the purgation of the memory[1] in order to ground it in hope, if we purged not the will also according to the third virtue, which is charity,[2] whereby the works that are done in faith live and have great merit, and without it are of no worth. For, as S. James says : Without works of charity, faith is dead.[3] And, now that we have to treat of the active detachment and night of this faculty, in order to form it and make it perfect in this virtue of the charity of God, I find no more fitting authority than that which is written in the sixth chapter of Deuteronomy, where Moses says : Thou shalt love the Lord thy God with all thy heart and with all thy soul and with all thy strength.[4] Herein is contained all that the spiritual man ought to do, and all that I have here to teach him, so that he may truly attain to God, through union of the will, by means of charity. For herein man is commanded to employ all the faculties and desires and operations and affections of his soul in God, so that all the ability and strength of his soul may serve for no more than this, according to that which David says, in these words : *Fortitudinem meam ad te custodiam.*[5]

2. The strength of the soul consists in its faculties, passions and desires, all of which are governed by the will. Now when these faculties, passions and desires are directed by the will toward God, and turned away from all that is not God, then the strength of the soul is kept for God, and thus the soul is able to love God with all its strength. And, to the end that the soul may do this, we shall here treat of the purgation from the will of all its unruly affections, whence arise unruly operations, affections and desires,[6] and whence also arises its failure to keep all its strength for God. These affections and passions are four, namely : joy, hope, grief and fear. These passions, when they are controlled by reason with respect to God, so that the soul rejoices only in that which is purely the honour and glory of God, and hopes for naught else, neither grieves save for things that concern this, neither fears aught save God alone, it is clear that the strength and ability of the soul are being directed toward God and kept for Him. For, the more the soul rejoices in any other thing

---

[1] E.p. adds : ' in the sense referred to in the sixth chapter of the second book.'

[2] E.p. : ' if we purged not the will also with respect to charity.'

[3] S. James ii, 20.   [4] Deuteronomy vi, 5.

[5] Psalm lviii, 10 [A.V., lix, 9].

[6] E.p. omits : ' whence arise . . . and desires.'

than God, the less completely will it centre its rejoicing in God ;[1] and the more it hopes in aught else, the less will it hope in God ; and so with the other passions.

3. And in order to give fuller instructions concerning this, we shall treat, in turn and in detail, as is our custom, of each of these four passions and of the desires of the will. For the whole business of attaining to union with God consists in purging the will from its affections and desires ; so that thus it may no longer be a base, human will, but may become a Divine will, being made one[2] with the will of God.

4. These four passions have the greater dominion in the soul and assail it the more vehemently, when the will is less strongly attached to God and more dependent on the creatures. For then it rejoices very readily at things that merit not rejoicing, hopes in that which brings no profit, grieves over that in which perchance it ought to rejoice, and fears where there is no reason for fearing.

5. From these affections, when they are unbridled, arise in the soul all the vices and imperfections which it possesses, and likewise, when they are ordered and composed, all its virtues. And it must be known that, if one of them should become ordered and controlled by reason, the rest will become so likewise ; for these four passions of the soul are so closely and intimately united to one another that the actual direction of one is the virtual direction of the others; and if one be actually recollected the other three will virtually and proportionately be recollected likewise. For, if the will rejoice in anything, it will as a result hope for the same thing to the extent of its rejoicing, and herein are virtually included grief and fear with regard to the same thing ; and, in proportion as desire for these is taken away, fear and grief concerning them are likewise gradually lost, and hope for them is removed.[3] For the will, with these four passions, is denoted by that figure which was seen by Ezekiel, of four beasts with one body, which had four faces ; and the wings of the one were joined to those of the other, and each one went straight before his face, and when they went forward they turned not back.[4] And thus in the same manner the wings of each one of these affections are joined to those of each of the others, so that,

---

[1] [*Lit.*, ' the less strongly its rejoicing will be employed in God.']
[2] [The original is stronger : ' one same thing.']
[3] E.p. adds : ' after the manner (though it is not this that is there meant) of those four beasts that were seen by Ezekiel.'
[4] Ezekiel i, 5–9.

in whichever direction one of them turns—that is, in its operation—the others of necessity go with it virtually also ; and, when one of them descends, as is there said, they must all descend, and, when one is lifted up, they will all be lifted up.   Where thy hope is, thither will go thy joy and fear and grief ; and, if thy hope returns, the others will return, and so of the rest.

6. Wherefore thou must take note[1] that, wheresoever one of these passions is, thither will go likewise the whole soul and the will and the other faculties, and they will all live as captives to this passion, and the other three passions[2] will be living in it also, to afflict the soul with their captivity,[3] and not to allow it to fly upward to the liberty and rest of sweet contemplation and union.   For this cause Boetius told thee that, if thou shouldst desire to understand truth with clear light, thou must cast from thee joys, hope, fear and grief.[4] For, as long as these passions reign, they allow not the soul to remain in the tranquillity and peace which are necessary for the wisdom which, by natural or supernatural means, it is capable of receiving.

CHAPTER XVII

Which begins to treat of the first affection of the will.   Describes the nature of joy and makes a distinction between the things in which the will can rejoice.

1. The first of the passions of the soul and affections of the will is joy, which, in so far as concerns that[5] which we propose to say about it, is naught else than a satisfaction of the will together with esteem for something which it considers desirable ; for the will never rejoices save when an object gives it appreciation and satisfaction.   This has reference to active joy, which arises when the soul clearly and distinctly understands the reason for its rejoicing, and when it is in its own power to rejoice or not.   There is another and a passive joy, a condition in which the will may find itself rejoicing without understanding clearly and distinctly the reason for its rejoicing, and which also occurs at times when

---

[1] A, B, e.p. add : ' O spiritual man.'
[2] A : ' and the other three faculties, or rather passions.'
[3] E.p. omits : ' with their captivity.'
[4] Cf. p. 168, above.   [5] E.p. : ' which, with regard to that.'

it does understand this ; but it is not in the soul's power[1] to rejoice or not. Of this condition we shall speak hereafter. For the present we shall speak of joy when it is active and voluntary and arises from things that are distinct and clear.

2. Joy may arise from six kinds of good things or blessings,[2] namely : temporal, natural, sensual, moral, supernatural and spiritual. Of these we shall speak in their order, controlling the will with regard to them so that it may not be encumbered by them and fail to place the strength of its joy in God. To this end it is well to presuppose one fundamental truth, which will be as a staff whereon we should ever lean as we progress ; and it will be well to have understood it, because it is the light whereby we should be guided and whereby we may understand this doctrine, and direct our rejoicing in all these blessings to God. This truth is that the will must never rejoice save only in that which is to the honour and glory of God ; and that the greatest honour we can show to Him is that of serving Him according to evangelical perfection ; and anything that has naught to do with this is of no value and profit to man.

CHAPTER XVIII

Which treats of joy with respect to temporal blessings. Describes how joy in them must be directed to God.

1. The first kind of blessing of which we have spoken is temporal. And by temporal blessings we here understand riches, rank, office and other things that men desire ; and children, relatives, marriages, etc. : all of which are things wherein the will may rejoice. But it is clear how vain a thing it is for men to rejoice in riches, titles, rank, office and other such things which they are wont to desire ; for, if a man were the better servant of God for being rich, he ought to rejoice in riches ; but in fact they are rather a cause[3] for his giving offence to God, even as the Wise Man teaches, saying : ' Son, if thou be rich, thou shalt not be free from sin.'[4] Although it is true that temporal blessings do not

---

[1] E.p. adds : ' at that time.'
[2] [*Lit.*, ' things or blessings.' The word here translated ' blessings '' is *bienes*, often rendered ' goods.' I use ' blessings ' or ' good things ' in the following chapters, according as best suits the context.]
[3] E.p.: 'but rather they may be a cause.'   [4] Ecclesiasticus xi, 10.

necessarily of themselves cause sin, yet, through the frailty of its affections, the heart of man habitually clings to them and fails God (which is a sin, for to fail God is sin[1]) ; it is for this cause that the Wise Man says : ' Thou shalt not be free from sin.' For this reason the Lord[2] spoke of riches, in the Gospel, as thorns,[3] in order to show that he who touches them[4] with the will shall be wounded by some sin.   And that exclamation which He makes in the Gospel,[5] saying : How hardly shall they that have riches enter the Kingdom of the heavens—that is to say, they that have joy in riches— clearly shows that man must not rejoice in riches, since he exposes himself thereby to such great peril.[6] And David, in order to withdraw us from this peril, said likewise : If riches abound, set not your heart on them.[7] And I will not here quote further testimony on so clear a matter.

2. For in this case I should never cease quoting Scripture, nor should I cease[8] describing the evils which Solomon imputes to riches in Ecclesiastes. Solomon was a man who had possessed great riches, and, knowing well what they were, said : All things that are under the sun are vanity of vanities, vexation of spirit and vain solicitude of the mind.[9] And he that loves riches, he said, shall reap no fruit from them.[10] And he adds that riches are kept to the hurt of their owner,[11] as we see in the Gospel, where it was said from Heaven to the man that rejoiced because he had kept[12] many fruits for many years : Fool, this night shall thy soul be re- quired of thee to give account thereof, and whose shall be that which thou hast gathered ?[13] And finally, David teaches us the same, saying : Let us have no envy when our neighbour becomes rich, for it will profit him nothing in the life to come ;[14] meaning thereby that we might rather have pity on him.

---

[1] E.p. omits : ' for to fail God is sin.'
[2] E.p. : ' For this reason Jesus Christ our Lord.'
[3] S. Matthew xiii, 22 ; S. Luke viii, 14.
[4] [Lit., ' handles them.']
[5] So Alc. A, B : ' which He makes in Saint Luke, and which is so much to be feared.' E.p. : ' which He makes in Saint Matthew and which is so much to be feared.'
[6] S. Matthew xix, 23 ; S. Luke xviii, 24.
[7] Psalm lxi, 11 [A.V., lxii, 10].
[8] E.p. omits : ' quoting Scripture, nor should I cease.'
[9] Ecclesiastes i, 14.   [10] Ecclesiastes v, 9.
[11] Ecclesiastes v, 11.
[12] Alc., erroneously, has : ' he had gained.'   [13] S. Luke xii, 20.
[14] Psalm xlviii, 17–18 [A.V., xlix, 16–17].

3. It follows, then, that a man must neither rejoice in riches when he has them, nor when his brother has them,[1] unless they help them to serve God. For if ever it is allowable to rejoice in them,[2] this will be when they are spent and employed in the service of God, for otherwise no profit will be derived from them. And the same is to be understood of other blessings (titles, offices, etc.) : in all of which it is vain to rejoice if a man feel not that God is the better served because of them and the way to eternal life is made more secure. And as it cannot be clearly known if this is so (if God is better served, etc.), it would be a vain thing to rejoice in these things deliberately, since such a joy[3] cannot be reasonable. For, as the Lord says : If a man gain all the world, he may yet lose his soul.[4] There is naught, then, wherein to rejoice save in the fact that God is better served.

4. Neither is there cause for rejoicing in children, be they many, or rich, or endowed with natural graces and talents and blessings of fortune, but only in that they serve God. For Absalom, the son of David, found neither his beauty nor his riches nor his lineage of any service to him because he served not God.[5] Hence it was a vain thing to have rejoiced in such a son. For this reason it is also vain for men to desire to have children, as do some who trouble and disturb everyone with their desire for them, since they know not if such children will be good and serve God. Nor do they know if their satisfaction in them will be turned into pain ; nor if the comfort and consolation which they should have from them will change to disquiet and trial ; and the honour which they should bring them, into dishonour ; nor if they will cause them to give greater offence to God, as happens to many. Of these Christ says that they encompass sea and land to enrich them and to make them doubly the children of perdition which they are themselves.[6]

5. Wherefore, though all things smile upon a man and all that he does turns out prosperously,[7] he ought to have misgivings rather than to rejoice ; for these things increase

---

[1] E.p.: '. . . rejoice because he has riches, nor because his brother has them.'

[2] A, Alc. [and P. Silverio] add : 'as one will rejoice in riches.'

[3] E.p. : 'such a joy in them.'

[4] S. Matthew xvi, 26. E.p. has : 'If a man gain all the world, it profits him little, if he suffers detriment in his soul.'

[5] 2 Kings [A.V., 2 Samuel] xiv, 25.

[6] S. Matthew xxiii, 15.

[7] E.p. adds : 'and, as they say, [good things] fall into his mouth.'

the occasion and peril of his forgetting God.[1] For this cause
Solomon says, in Ecclesiastes, that he was cautious : Laughter
I counted error and to rejoicing I said, ' Why art thou
vainly deceived ? '[2] Which is as though he had said : When
things smiled upon me I counted it error and deception
to rejoice in them ; for without doubt it is great error and
folly on the part of a man if he rejoice when things are
bright and pleasant for him, knowing not of a certainty that
there will come to him thence some eternal good. The heart
of the fool, says the Wise Man, is where there is gladness,
but that of the wise man is where there is sorrow.[3] For
gladness[4] blinds the heart and allows it not to consider things
and ponder them ; but sadness makes a man open his eyes
and look at the profit and the harm of them. And hence
it is that, as he himself says, anger is better than laughter.[5]
Wherefore it is better to go to the house of mourning than to
the house of a feast ; for in the former is figured the end of
all men,[6] as the Wise Man says likewise.

6. It would therefore be vanity for a woman or her husband to rejoice in their marriage when they know not clearly
that they are serving God better thereby. They ought
rather to feel confounded, since matrimony is a cause, as
S. Paul says, whereby each one sets his heart upon the other
and keeps it not wholly with God. Wherefore he says : If
thou shouldst find thyself free from a wife, desire not to seek
a wife ; while he that has one already should walk with
such freedom of heart as though he had her not.[7] This,
together with what we have said concerning temporal
blessings, he teaches us himself, in these words : This is
certain ; as I say to you, brethren, the time is short ; it
remaineth both that they that have wives be as though they
had none ; and they that weep, as them that weep not ;
and they that rejoice, as them that rejoice not ; and they
that buy, as them that possess not ; and they that use this
world, as them that use it not.[8] All this he says to show us
that we must not set our rejoicing[9] upon any other thing than

---

[1] A, B, e.p. add : ' and of offending Him, as we have said.'
[2] Ecclesiastes ii, 2.   [3] Ecclesiastes vii, 5.
[4] E.p. : ' For vain gladness.'   [5] Ecclesiastes vii, 4.
[6] Ecclesiastes vii, 2.   [7] 1 Corinthians vii, 27.   [8] 1 Corinthians vii, 29–30.
[9] [The original reads : ' to show us that to set,' etc., leaving the sentence
grammatically incomplete. P. Gerardo omits ' since the rest ' and reads :
' to show us that to set . . . service of God is vanity,' etc.]   Alc. omits
all the paragraph down to this point, reading : ' And thus we must not
set our rejoicing . . .'

that which tends to the service of God, since the rest is vanity and that which profits not ; for joy that is not according to God can bring no profit.[1]

CHAPTER XIX

Of the evils that may befall the soul when it sets its rejoicing upon temporal blessings.

1. If we had to describe the evils which environ the soul when it sets the affections of its will upon temporal blessings, neither ink nor paper would suffice us and our time would be too short. For from very small beginnings a man may attain to great evils and destroy great blessings ; even as from a spark of fire, if it be not quenched, may be enkindled great fires which set the world aflame. All these evils have their root and origin in one important evil of a privative kind that is contained in this joy—namely, withdrawal from God. For even as, in the soul that is united with Him by the affection of its will, there are born all blessings, even so, when it withdraws itself from Him because of this creature affection, there beset it all evils and disasters proportionately to the joy and affection wherewith it is united with the creature ; for this is inherent in[2] withdrawal from God. Wherefore a soul may expect the evils which assail it to be greater or less according to the greater or lesser degree of its withdrawal from God. These evils may be extensive or intensive ; for the most part they are both together.

2. This privative evil, whence, we say, arise other privative and positive evils, has four degrees, each one worse than the other. And, when the soul compasses the fourth degree, it will have compassed all the evils and depravities that arise in this connection.[3] These four degrees are well indicated by Moses in Deuteronomy in these words, where he says : The Beloved grew fat and kicked. He grew fat and became swollen and gross.[4] He forsook God his Maker and departed from God his Salvation.[5]

3. This growing fat of the soul, which was loved before it

[1] A, B : ' . . . to God cannot please the soul.' E.p. : ' . . . to God cannot do the soul good.'   [2] [*Lit.*, ' for this is.']
[3] [*Lit.*, ' that can be told in this case.']
[4] E.p. : ' The Beloved became fat and turned ; he became swollen and gross.'   [5] Deuteronomy xxxii, 15.

grew fat,[1] indicates absorption in this joy of creatures. And hence arises the first degree of this evil, namely the going backward ; which is a certain blunting of the mind with regard to God, an obscuring of the blessings of God like the obscuring of the air by mist, so that it cannot be clearly illumined by the light of the sun. For, precisely when the spiritual person sets his rejoicing upon anything, and gives rein to his desire for foolish things, he becomes blind as to God, and the simple intelligence of his judgement becomes clouded, even as the Divine Spirit teaches in the Book of Wisdom, saying : The use and association of vanity[2] and scorn obscureth good things, and inconstancy of desire over-turneth and perverteth the sense and judgement that are without malice.[3] Here the Holy Spirit shows that, although there be no malice[4] conceived in the understanding of the soul, concupiscence and rejoicing in the creatures suffice of themselves to create in the soul the first degree of this evil, which is the blunting of the mind and the darkening of the judgement, by which the truth is understood and each thing honestly judged as it is.

4. Holiness and good judgement suffice not to save a man from falling into this evil, if he gives way to concupiscence or rejoicing in temporal things. For this reason God warned us by uttering these words through Moses : Thou shalt take no gifts, which blind even the prudent.[5] And this was addressed particularly to those who were to be judges ; for these have need to keep their judgement clear and alert, which they will be unable to do if they covet and rejoice in gifts. And for this cause likewise God commanded Moses to make judges of those who abhorred avarice, so that their judgement should not be blunted with the lust of the passions.[6] And thus he says not only that they should not desire it, but that they should abhor it. For, if a man is to be perfectly defended from the affection of love, he must preserve an abhorrence of it, defending himself by means of the one thing against its contrary. The reason why the prophet Samuel, for example, was always so upright and enlightened a judge is that (as he said in the Book of the Kings) he had never received a gift from any man.[7]

---

[1] E.p. : ' This becoming fat of the soul, which previously was loved ...'
[2] E.p. : ' The false appearance of vanity . . .'   [3] Wisdom iv, 12.
[4] E.p. : ' no precedent malice.'   [5] Exodus xxiii, 8.
[6] Exodus xviii, 21-2.   [7] 1 Kings [A.V., 1 Samuel] xii, 3.

5. The second degree of this privative evil arises from the first, which is indicated in the words following the passage already quoted, namely : He grew fat and became swollen and gross.[1] And thus this second degree is dilatation of the will through the acquisition of greater liberty in temporal things ; which consists in no longer attaching so much importance to them, nor troubling oneself about them, nor esteeming so highly the joy and pleasure that come from created blessings. And this will have arisen in the soul from its having in the first place given rein to rejoicing ; for, through giving way to it, the soul has become swollen with it, as is said in that passage, and that fatness of rejoicing and desire has caused it to dilate and extend its will more freely toward the creatures. And from this result great evils. For this second degree causes the soul to withdraw itself from the things of God, and from holy practices, and to find no pleasure in them, because it takes pleasure in other things and devotes itself continually to many imperfections and follies[2] and to joys and vain pleasures.

6. And when this second degree is wholly consummated, it withdraws a man from the practices which he followed continually and makes his whole mind and covetousness to be given to secular things. And those who are affected by this second degree not only have their judgement and understanding darkened so that they cannot recognize truth and justice, like those who are in the first degree, but they are also very weak and lukewarm and careless[3] in acquiring knowledge of, and in practising, truth and justice, even as Isaiah says of them in these words : They all love gifts and allow themselves to be carried away by rewards, and they judge not the orphan, neither doth the cause of the widow come unto them that they may give heed to it.[4] This comes not to pass in them without sin, especially when to do these things is incumbent upon them because of their office. For those who are affected by this degree are not free from malice as are those of the first degree. And thus they withdraw themselves more and more from justice and virtues, since their will reaches out more and more[5] in affection for creatures. Wherefore, the characteristics of those who are

---

[1] Deuteronomy xxxii, 15. E.p. omits : 'grew fat and.'
[2] E.p. : 'and many follies.'
[3] E.p. omits : 'and careless.'   [4] Isaiah i, 23.
[5] A, e.p. : '. . . their will becomes more and more enkindled . . .'
[The change is a slight one : *encendiendo* for *extendiendo*.]

in this second degree are great lukewarmness in spiritual things and failure to do their duty by them ; they practise them from formality or from compulsion or from the habit which they have formed of practising them, rather than because they love them.

7. The third degree of this privative evil is a complete falling away from God, neglect to fulfil His law in order not to lose worldly things and blessings ;[1] and relapse into mortal sin through covetousness. And this third degree is described in the words following the passage quoted above, which says : He forsook God his Maker.[2] In this degree are included all who have the faculties of the soul absorbed in things of the world and in riches and commerce,[3] in such a way that they care nothing for fulfilling the obligations of the law of God. And they are very forgetful and dull with respect to that which touches their salvation, and have a correspondingly greater ardour and ingenuity with respect to things of the world. So much so that in the Gospel Christ calls them children of this world, and says of them that they are more prudent and acute in their affairs than are the children of light in their own.[4] And thus they are as nothing in God's business, whereas in the world's business they are everything. And these are the truly avaricious, who have extended and dispersed their desire and joy on things created, and this with such affection that they cannot be satisfied ; on the contrary, their desire and their thirst grow all the more because they are farther withdrawn from the only source that could satisfy them, which is God. For it is of these that God Himself speaks through Jeremiah, saying : They have forsaken Me, Who am the fountain of living water, and they have hewed them out broken cisterns that can hold no water.[5] And this is the reason why the covetous man finds naught among the creatures wherewith he can quench his thirst, but only that which increases it. These persons are they that fall into countless kinds of sin through love of temporal blessings and the evils which afflict them are innumerable. And of this, David says : *Transierunt in affectum cordis.*[6]

---

[1] E.p.: ' not to lose the trifling things of the world.'
[2] Deuteronomy xxxii, 15.　　　　　[3] E.p. : ' commerce with it.'
[4] S. Luke xvi, 8.　　　　　[5] Jeremiah ii, 13.
[6] Psalm lxxii, 7 [A.V., lxxiii, 7]. Only e.p. has this quotation in its Spanish form. Alc. adds the word *exponat.*

8. The fourth degree of this privative evil is indicated in the last words of our passage, which says : And he departed from God his Salvation.[1] This degree is reached by those of the third degree whereof we have just spoken. For, through not giving heed to setting his heart upon the law of God because of temporal blessings, the soul of the covetous man departs far from God according to his memory, understanding and will, forgetting Him as though He were not his God, which comes to pass because he has made for himself a god of money and of temporal blessings,[2] as S. Paul says when he describes avarice as slavery to idols.[3] For this fourth degree leads a man as far as to forget God, and to set his heart, which he should have set formally upon God, formally upon money, as though he had no god beside.

9. To this fourth degree belong those who hesitate not to subject Divine and supernatural things to temporal things, as to their God, when they ought to do the contrary, and subject temporal things to God, if they considered Him as their God, as would be in accordance with reason.[4] To these belonged the iniquitous[5] Balaam, who sold the grace that God had given to him.[6] And also Simon Magus, who thought to value the grace of God in terms of money, and desired to buy it.[7] In doing this he showed a greater esteem for money ; and he thought there were those who similarly esteemed it, and would give grace for money. In many other ways there are many nowadays who belong to this fourth degree ; their reason is darkened to spiritual things by covetousness ; they serve money and not God, and are influenced by money and not by God, putting first the cost of a thing and not its Divine worth and reward, and in many ways making money their principal god and end, and setting it before the final end, which is God.

10. To this last degree belong also those miserable souls who are so greatly in love with their own goods that they take them for their god, so much so that they scruple not to sacrifice their lives for them, when they see that this god of theirs is receiving some temporal harm. They abandon themselves to despair and commit suicide for miserable ends, showing by their own acts how wretched is the reward which

---

[1] Deuteronomy xxxii, 15.
[2] A, e.p. : '. . . he has made money and temporal blessings a god for himself.'   [3] Colossians iii, 5.
[4] E.p. omits : 'if they considered Him as their God.'
[5] E.p. : 'the impious.'   [6] Numbers xxii, 7.   [7] Acts viii, 18–19.

they receive from a god like their own. For when they can no longer hope for aught from him he bestows on them despair[1] and death ; and those whom he pursues not to this last evil of death he condemns to a dying life[2] in the griefs of anxiety and in many other miseries, allowing no gladness to enter their heart, and no good thing upon earth to enlighten them. They continually pay the tribute of their heart to money by their yearning for it and hoarding of it for the final calamity of their just perdition, as the Wise Man warns them, saying : Riches are kept to the hurt of their owner.[3]

11. And to this fourth degree belong those of whom S. Paul says : *Tradidit illos in reprobum sensum.*[4] For joy, when it strives after possessions as its final goal, drags man down to these evils. But those on whom it inflicts lesser evils are also to be sorely pitied, since, as we have said, their souls are driven far backward upon the way[5] of God. Wherefore, as David says : Be not thou afraid when one is made rich : that is, envy him not, thinking that he outstrips thee, for, when he dieth, he shall carry nothing away, neither shall his glory nor his joy descend with him.[6]

CHAPTER XX

Of the benefits that come to the soul from its withdrawal of joy from temporal things.

1. The spiritual man, then, must see to it carefully that his heart and his rejoicing begin not to lay hold upon temporal things ; he must fear lest from being little it should grow to be great, and should increase from one degree to another. For little things do indeed become great ; and from a small beginning there comes in the end a great matter,[7] even as a spark suffices to set a mountain on fire and to burn up the whole world.[8] And let him never be self-confident because his attachment is small, and fail to uproot it instantly because he thinks that he will do so later. For if,

---

[1] The remainder of this chapter is omitted in Alc.

[2] So e.p. [*lit.*, ' to live dying ']. A : ' to live living '; B : ' to die living.' [3] Ecclesiastes v, 11–12.

[4] Romans i, 28. [5] E.p. : ' upon the road.'

[6] Psalm xlviii, 17–18 [A.V., xlix, 16–17].

[7] Thus the Codices. E.p. alters this to ' a great evil.' [P. Silverio supports the emendation.]

[8] E.p. omits : ' and to burn up the whole world.' [The word rendered ' mountain ' may also mean ' wood.' Cf. S. James iii, 5, Vulgate.]

when it is so small and in its beginnings, he has not the courage to make an end of it, how does he suppose, and presume, that he will be able to do so when it is great and more deeply rooted. The more so since Our Lord said in the Gospel : He that is unfaithful in little will be unfaithful also in much.[1] For he that avoids the small sin will not fall into the great sin ; but great evil is inherent in the small sin,[2] since it has already penetrated within the fence and wall of the heart ; and as the proverb says : Once begun, half done. Wherefore David warns us, saying : Though riches abound, let us not apply our heart to them.[3]

2. Although a man might not do this for the sake of God and of the obligations of Christian perfection, he should nevertheless do it because of the temporal advantages that result from it, to say nothing of the spiritual advantages, and he should free his heart completely from all rejoicing in the things mentioned above. And thus, not only will he free himself from the pestilent evils which we have described in the last chapter, but, besides this, he will withdraw his joy from temporal blessings and acquire the virtue of liberality, which is one of the principal attributes of God,[4] and can in no wise coexist with covetousness. Apart from this, he will acquire liberty of soul, clarity of reason, rest, tranquillity and peaceful confidence in God and a true reverence and worship of God which comes from the will.[5] He will find greater joy and recreation in the creatures through his detachment from them, for he cannot rejoice in them if he look upon them with attachment to them as to his own. Attachment is an anxiety that, like a bond, ties the spirit down to the earth and allows it no enlargement of heart. He will also acquire, in his detachment from things, a clear conception of them, so that he can well understand the truths relating to them, both naturally and supernaturally. He will therefore enjoy them after a very different fashion from that of one who is attached to them, and he will have a great advantage and superiority over such a one. For, while he

---

[1] S. Luke xvi, 10.

[2] [The word ' sin ' is not in the original of this sentence, which reads ' the small . . . the great . . .' etc.]

[3] Psalm lxi, 11 [A.V., lxii, 10]. E.p. : ' let us not attach our heart to them.'

[4] So Alc., e.p. A, B : ' one of the principal virtues of God, or, rather, attributes.'

[5] A, B : ' which comes from liberty.' [The word translated ' reverence ' normally implies respectful acquiescence.]

enjoys them according to their truth, the other enjoys them according to their deceptiveness ;[1] the one appreciates the best side of them and the other the worst ; the one rejoices in their substance ; the other, whose sense is bound to them, in their accident. For sense cannot grasp or attain to more than the accident, but the spirit, purged of the clouds and species of accident, penetrates the truth and worth of things, for this is its object. Wherefore joy, like a cloud, darkens the judgement, since there can be no voluntary joy in creatures without voluntary attachment, even as there can be no joy which is passion when there is no habitual attachment in the heart ;[2] and the renunciation and purgation of such joy leave the judgement clear, even as the mists leave the air clear when they are scattered.

3. This man, then, rejoices in all things—since his joy is dependent upon none of them—as if he had them all ; and this other, through looking upon them with a particular sense of ownership, loses all the pleasure of them in general. This former man, having none of them in his heart, possesses them all, as S. Paul says, in great freedom.[3] This latter man, inasmuch as he has something of them through the attachment of his will, neither has nor possesses anything ; it is rather they that have possessed[4] his heart, and he is, as it were, a sorrowing captive. Wherefore, if he desire to have a certain degree of joy in creatures, he must of necessity have an equal degree of disquietude and grief in his heart, since it is seized and possessed by them. But he that is detached is untroubled by anxieties, whether in prayer or apart from it ; and thus, without losing time, he readily gains great spiritual treasure. But the other man loses everything, running to and fro upon the chain by which his heart is attached and bound ; and with all his diligence he can still hardly free himself for a short time from this bond of thought and rejoicing by which his heart is bound. The spiritual man, then, at the first motion of his heart towards creatures, must restrain it, remembering the truth which we have here laid down, that there is naught wherein a man must rejoice, save in his service of God, and in his striving for His glory and honour in all things, directing all things solely to this end and turning aside from vanity in them, looking in them neither for his own joy nor for his consolation.

---

[1] Alc. omits the rest of this sentence and the whole of the next.
[2] E.p. [for ' when . . . heart '] reads : ' without voluntary attachment.'
[3] 2 Corinthians vi, 10.   [4] A, B : ' they have seized.'

4. There is another very great and important benefit in this detachment of the rejoicing from creatures—namely, that it leaves the heart free for God. This is the dispositive foundation of all the favours which God will grant to the soul, and without this disposition He grants them not. And they are such that, even from the temporal standpoint, for one joy which the soul renounces for love of Him and for the perfection of the Gospel, He will give him a hundred in this life, as His Majesty promises in the same Gospel.[1] But, even were there not so high a rate of interest, the spiritual man should quench these creature joys in his soul because of the displeasure which they give to God. For we see in the Gospel that, simply because that rich man rejoiced at having goods for many years, God was so greatly angered that He told him that his soul would be brought to account on that very night.[2] Therefore, we must believe[3] that, whensoever we rejoice vainly, God is beholding us and preparing some punishment and bitter draught according to our deserts, so that the pain which results from the joy may sometimes be a hundred times greater[4] than the joy. For, although it is true, as S. John says on this matter, in the Apocalypse, concerning Babylon, that as much as she had rejoiced and lived in delights, so much torment and sorrow[5] should be given her, yet this is not to say that the pain will not be greater than the joy, which indeed it will be, since for brief pleasures are given eternal torments. The words mean that there shall be nothing without its particular punishment, for He who will punish the idle word will not pardon vain rejoicing.

CHAPTER XXI

Which describes how it is vanity to set the rejoicing of the will upon the good things of nature, and how the soul must direct itself, by means of them, to God.

1. By natural blessings we here understand beauty, grace, comeliness, bodily constitution and all other bodily endowments ; and likewise, in the soul, good understanding, discretion and other things that pertain to reason. Many a man

---

[1] S. Matthew xix, 29. [2] S. Luke xii, 20.
[3] E.p. : ' Therefore, we may fear.'
[4] E.p. : ' . . . may often be greater.'
[5] Revelation xviii, 7.

sets his rejoicing upon all these gifts, to the end that he himself, or those that belong to him, may possess them, and for no other reason, and gives no thanks to God Who bestows them on him so that He may be the better known and loved by him because of them.   But it is vanity and deception to rejoice for this cause alone, as Solomon says in these words : Deceitful is grace and vain is beauty ; the woman who fears God, she shall be praised.[1]   Here he teaches us that a man ought rather to be fearful because of these natural gifts, since he may easily be distracted[2] by them from the love of God, and, if he be attracted by them, he may fall into vanity and be deceived.   For this reason bodily grace is said to be deceptive because it deceives a man in the way[3] and attracts him to that which beseems him not, through vain joy and complacency, either in himself or in others that have such grace. And it is said that beauty is vain because it causes a man to fall in many ways when he esteems it and rejoices in it, for he should only rejoice if he serves God or others through it.   But he ought rather to fear and harbour misgivings lest perchance his natural graces and gifts should be a cause of his offending God, either by his vain presumption or by the extreme affection[4] with which he regards them.   Wherefore he that has such gifts should be cautious and live carefully, lest, by his vain ostentation, he give cause to any man to withdraw his heart in the smallest degree from God. For these graces and gifts of nature are so full of provocation and occasion of evil, both to him that possesses them and to him that looks upon them, that there is hardly any who entirely escapes from binding and entangling his heart in them.   We have heard that many spiritual persons, who had certain of these gifts, had such fear of this that they prayed God to disfigure them, lest they should be a cause and occasion of any vain joy or affection to themselves or to others, and God granted their prayer.

2. The spiritual man, then, must purge his will, and make it to be blind to this vain rejoicing, bearing in mind that beauty and all other natural gifts are but earth, and that they come from the earth and will return thither ; and that grace and beauty are smoke and vapour of this same earth ; and that they must be held and esteemed as such by a man that desires not to fall into vanity, but will direct his heart to God

---

[1] Proverbs xxxi, 30.
[2] A, B : ' be kept back.'
[3] A, B : ' in the road.'
[4] A, B, e.p. : ' the strange affection.'

in these matters, with rejoicing and gladness, because God is in Himself all these beauties and graces in the most eminent degree, and is infinitely high above all created things. And, as David says, they are all like a garment and shall grow old and pass away, and He alone remains immutable for ever.[1] Wherefore, if in all these matters a man direct not his rejoicing to God, it will ever be false and deceptive. For of such a man is that saying of Solomon to be understood, where he addresses joy in the creatures, saying: To joy I said: ' Wherefore art thou vainly deceived ? '[2] That is, when the heart allows itself to be attracted by the creatures.

CHAPTER XXII

Of the evils which come to the soul when it sets the rejoicing of its will upon the good things of nature.

1. Although many of these evils and benefits that I am describing in treating of these kinds of joy are common to all, yet, because they follow directly from joy and detachment from joy (although comprised under any one of these six divisions which I am treating), therefore I speak under each heading of some evils and benefits which are also found under another, since these, as I say, are connected with that joy which belongs to them all. But my principal intent is to speak of the particular evils and benefits which come to the soul, with respect to each thing, through its rejoicing or not rejoicing in it. These I call particular evils, because they are primarily and immediately caused by one particular kind of rejoicing, and are not, save in a secondary and mediate sense, caused by another. The evil of spiritual lukewarmness, for example, is caused directly by any and every kind of joy, and this evil is therefore common to all these six kinds ; but fornication is a particular evil, which is the direct result only of joy in the good things of nature of which we are speaking.

2. The spiritual and bodily evils, then, which directly and effectively come to the soul when it sets its rejoicing on the good things of nature are reduced to six principal evils. The first is vainglory, presumption, pride and disesteem of our

---

[1] Psalm ci, 27 [A.V., cii, 26–7].   [2] Ecclesiastes ii, 2.

neighbour ; for a man cannot cast[1] eyes of esteem on one thing without taking them from the rest. From this follows, at the least, a real disesteem[2] for everything else ; for naturally, by setting our esteem on one thing, we withdraw our heart from all things else and set it upon the thing esteemed ; and from this real contempt it is very easy to fall into an intentional and voluntary contempt for all these other things, in particular or in general, not only in the heart, but also in speech, when we say that such a thing or[3] such a person is not like such another. The second evil is the moving of the senses to complacency and sensual delight and luxury.[4] The third evil comes from falling into adulation and vain praise, wherein is deception and vanity, as Isaiah says in these words : My people, he that praises thee deceives thee.[5] And the reason is that, although we sometimes speak the truth when we praise grace and beauty, yet it will be a marvel if there is not some evil enwrapped therein or if the person praised is not plunged into vain complacency and rejoicing, or his imperfect intentions and affections are not directed thereto. The fourth evil is of a general kind : it is a serious[6] blunting of the reason and the spiritual sense, such as is effected by rejoicing in temporal good things. In one way indeed it is much worse. For as the good things of nature are more closely connected with man than are temporal good things, the joy which they give leaves an impression and effect and trace upon the senses more readily and more effectively, and deadens them more completely. And thus reason and judgement are not free, but are clouded with that affection of joy which is very closely connected with them ; and from this arises the fifth evil, which is distraction of the mind by created things. And hence arise and follow luke-warmness and weakness of spirit, which is the sixth evil, and is likewise of a general kind ; this is apt to reach such a pitch that a man may find the things of God very tedious and troublesome, until at last he comes to abhor them. In this rejoicing purity of spirit, at least, is invariably lost first of all. For if any spirituality is discerned, it will be of such a gross and sensual kind that it is hardly spiritual or interior or recollected at all, since it will consist rather in pleasure of

---

[1] E.p. : ' cannot excessively cast.'
[2] E.p. : ' a real and, as it were, negative disesteem.'
[3] E.p. omits : ' such a thing or.' [4] E.p. omits : ' and luxury.'
[5] Isaiah iii, 12. [6] [Lit., ' the great.']

sense than in strength of spirit. Since, then, the spirituality of the soul is of so low and weak a character at that time as not to quench the habit of this rejoicing (for this habit alone suffices to destroy pure spirituality, even when the soul is not consenting to the acts of rejoicing), the soul must be living, so to say, in the weakness of sense rather than in the strength of the spirit. Otherwise,[1] it will be seen in the perfection and fortitude which the soul will have when the occasion demands it. Although I deny not that many virtues may exist together with serious imperfections, no pure or delectable inward spirituality can exist while these joys are not quenched ; for the flesh reigns[2] within, warring against the spirit, and, although the spirit may be unconscious of the evil, yet at the least it causes it hidden distraction.

3. Returning now to speak of that second evil, which contains innumerable evils within itself, it is impossible to describe with the pen or to express in words the lengths to which it can go, neither is this unknown or hidden,[3] nor the extent of the misery that arises from the setting of our rejoicing on natural beauty and graces. For every day we hear of numerous deaths, the loss by many of their honour, the commission of many insults, the dissipation of much wealth, numerous cases of emulation and strife, of adultery, rape and fornication,[4] and of the fall[5] of many holy men, comparable in number to that third part of the stars of Heaven which was swept down by the tail of the serpent on earth.[6] All these disasters come from that cause. The fine gold has lost its brilliance and lustre and is become mire ; and the notable and noble men of Sion, who were clothed in finest gold, are counted as earthen pitchers, that are broken and have become potsherds.[7] How far does the poison of this evil not penetrate ?

4. And who drinks not, either much or little, from this golden chalice of the Babylonian woman of the Apocalypse ?[8] She seated herself on that great beast, that had seven heads

---

[1] E.p. omits ' otherwise.'
[2] E.p. : ' the flesh almost reigns here.'
[3] E.p. omits : ' neither . . . hidden.'
[4] E.p. : ' of adultery and rape.'
[5] The Codices [followed by P. Silverio] have ' of the fall to the ground ' which e.p. abbreviates [as in the text].
[6] Revelation xii, 4.   [7] Lamentations iv, 1–2.
[8] Revelation xvii, 4. Here eleven pages are missing from Alc., which P. Andrés de la Encarnación supplies, taking them from the old MS. which in his time was preserved at Duruelo.

and ten crowns, signifying that there is scarce any man, whether high or low, saint or sinner, who comes not to drink of her wine, to some extent enslaving his heart thereby, for, as is said of her in that place, all the kings of the earth have become drunken with the wine of her prostitution. And she seizes upon all estates of men, even upon the highest and noblest estate—the service of the sanctuary and the Divine priesthood—setting her abominable cup, as Daniel says, in the holy place,[1] and leaving scarcely a single strong man without making him to drink, either little or much, from the wine of this chalice, which is vain rejoicing. For this reason it is said that all the kings of the earth have become drunken with this wine, for very few will be found, however holy they may have been, that have not been to some extent stupefied and bewildered by this draught of the joy and pleasure of natural graces and beauty.

5. This phrase ' they have become drunken ' should be noted. For, however little a man may drink of the wine of this rejoicing, it at once takes hold upon the heart, and stupefies it and works the evil of darkening the reason, as does wine to those who have been corrupted by it. So that, if some antidote be not at once taken against this poison, whereby it may be quickly expelled, the life of the soul is endangered. Spiritual weakness will increase, bringing it down to such great evil that it will be like Samson, when his eyes[2] were put out and the hair of his first strength was cut off, and like Samson it will see itself grinding in the mills, a captive among its enemies ;[3] and afterwards, peradventure, it will die the second death among its enemies, even as did he,[4] since the drinking of this rejoicing will produce spiritually in them all those evils that were produced in him physically, and does in fact produce them in many persons to this day. Let his enemies come and say to him afterwards, to his great confusion : Art thou he that broke the knotted cords,[5] that tore asunder the lions, slew the thousand Philistines, broke down the gates and freed himself from all his enemies ?

6. Let us conclude, then, by giving the instruction necessary to counteract this poison. And let it be this : As soon

---

[1] Daniel ix, 27.

[2] The Codices have : ' when the eyes of his sight . . .' This reading [adopted by P. Silverio] is shortened by e.p., as being pleonastic, to ' when his eyes . . .'   [3] Judges xvi.

[4] The 1630 edition reads : ' even as he died the first [death].'

[5] E.p. : ' the three knotted cords.'

as thy heart feels moved by this vain joy in the good things of nature, let it remember how vain a thing it is to rejoice in aught save the service of God, how perilous and how pernicious. Let it consider how great an evil it was for the angels to rejoice and take pleasure in their natural endowments and beauty, since it was this that plunged them into the depths of shame.[1] Let them think, too, how many evils come to men daily through this same vanity, and let them therefore resolve in good time to employ the remedy which the poet counsels to those who begin to grow affectioned to such things. ' Make haste now,' he says, ' to use the remedy at the beginning ; for when evil things have had time to grow in the heart, remedy and medicine come late.'[2] Look not upon the wine, as the Wise Man says, when its colour is red and when it shines in the glass ; it enters pleasantly and bites like a viper and sheds abroad poison like a basilisk.[3]

CHAPTER XXIII

Of the benefits which the soul receives from not setting its rejoicing upon the good things of nature.

1. Many are the benefits which come to the soul through the withdrawal of its heart from this rejoicing ; for, besides preparing itself for the love of God and the other virtues, it makes a direct way for its own humility, and for a general charity toward its neighbours. For, as it is not led by the apparent[4] good things of nature, which are deceitful, into affection for anyone, the soul remains free and able[5] to love them all rationally and spiritually, as God wills them to be loved. Here it must be understood that none deserves to be loved, save for the virtue that is in him. And, when we love in this way, it is very pleasing to the will of God, and this love also brings great liberty ; and if there be attachment in it, there is greater attachment to God. For, in that case, the more this love grows, the more grows our love toward God ; and, the more grows our love toward God, the greater be-

---

[1] [*Lit.*, ' since through this they fell into the vile abysses.']
[2] So Alc. The other authorities have only : ' medicine comes late.'
[3] Proverbs xxiii, 31–2. Only Alc. and e.p. have : ' and sheds abroad poison [really ' poisons '] like a basilisk.' A, B have ' its poison ' and use the word *basilisco*, where Alc., e.p. have *régulo*, with the same meaning.
[4] E.p. omits ' apparent.'   [5] [*Lit.*, ' free and clear.']

comes our love for our neighbour. For, when love is grow
in God, the reason for all love is one and the same an
cause of all love is one and the same also.

2. Another excellent benefit results to the soul from its
renunciation of this kind of rejoicing,[1] which is that it fulfils
and keeps[2] the counsel of Our Saviour which He gives us
through S. Matthew. Let him that will follow Me, He says,
deny himself.[3] This the soul could in no wise do if it were to
set its rejoicing upon the good things[4] of nature ; for he that
attaches any importance to himself neither denies himself nor
follows Christ.

3. There is another great benefit in the renunciation of
this kind of rejoicing, which is that it produces great tranquillity in the soul, empties it of distractions and brings
recollection to the senses, especially to the eyes. For the
soul that desires not to rejoice in these things desires neither
to look at them nor to attach the other senses to them, lest
it should be attracted or entangled by them.[5] Neither will it
spend time or thought upon them, being like the prudent
serpent, which stops its ears that it may not hear the charmers[6]
lest they make some impression upon it.[7] For, by guarding
its doors, which are the senses, the soul guards itself safely
and increases its tranquillity and purity.

4. There is another benefit of no less importance to those
that have become proficient in the mortification of this kind
of rejoicing, which is that evil things and the knowledge of
them neither make an impression upon them nor stain them
as they do those to whom they still give any delight. Wherefore the renunciation and mortification of this rejoicing result
in spiritual cleanness of soul and body ; that is, of spirit and
sense ; and the soul comes to have an angelical conformity
with God, and becomes, both in spirit and in body, a worthy
temple of the Holy Spirit. This cannot come to pass if the
heart rejoices in natural graces and good things.[8] For this
reason it is not necessary to have given consent to any evil
thing, or to have remembrance of such ;[9] for that rejoicing

---

[1] ' From . . . rejoicing ' are words found in Alc. only.
[2] E.p. adds : ' with perfection.'
[3] S. Matthew xvi, 24. [4] A, B, e.p. read : ' the gifts.'
[5] E.p. omits : ' or entangled by them.'
[6] So Alc. A, B : ' incantations.' E.p. : ' charms.'
[7] Psalm lvii, 5 [A.V., lviii, 4–5].
[8] E.p. : ' if the heart allows itself to be to any extent carried away by
rejoicing in natural graces and good things.'
[9] E.p. omits : ' or to have remembrance of such.'

suffices to stain the soul and the senses with impurity by means of the knowledge of evil ;[1] for, as the Wise Man says, the Holy Spirit will remove Himself from thoughts that are without understanding—that is, without the higher reason that has respect to God.[2]

5. Another benefit of a general kind follows, which is that, besides freeing ourselves from the evils and dangers afore-mentioned, we are delivered also from countless vanities, and from many other evils, both spiritual and temporal ; and especially from falling into the small esteem in which are held all those that are seen to glory or rejoice in the said natural gifts, whether in their own or in those of others. And thus these souls are held and esteemed as wise and prudent, as indeed are all those who take no account of these things, but only of that which pleases God.

6. From these said benefits follows the last, which is a generosity of the soul, as necessary to the service of God as is liberty of spirit, whereby temptations are easily vanquished and trials faithfully endured, and whereby, too, the virtues[3] grow and become prosperous.

CHAPTER XXIV

Which treats of the third kind of good thing whereon the will may set the affection of rejoicing, which kind pertains to sense. Indicates what these good things are and of how many kinds, and how the will has to be directed to God and purged of this rejoicing.

1. We have next to treat of rejoicing with respect to the good things of sense, which is the third kind of good thing wherein we said that the will may rejoice. And it is to be noted that by the good things of sense we here understand everything in this life that can be apprehended by the senses of sight, hearing, smell, taste or touch, and by the interior fashioning of imaginary reflections, all of which things belong to the bodily senses, interior and exterior.

2. And, in order to darken the will and purge it of rejoicing with respect to these sensible objects, and direct it

---

[1] E.p. concludes this paragraph here, but the 1630 edition continues, as in the Codices, which we here follow.
[2] Wisdom i, 5.   [3] A, B : ' the virtues of the soul.'

to God by means of them, it is necessary to assume one truth, which is that, as we have frequently said, the sense of the lower part of man, which is that whereof we are treating, is not, neither can be, capable of knowing or understanding God as God is.   So that the eye cannot see Him, or aught that is like Him ; neither can the ear hear His voice, or any sound that resembles it ; neither can the sense of smell perceive a perfume so sweet as He ; neither can the taste detect a savour so sublime and delectable ; neither can the touch feel a movement so delicate and full of delight, nor aught like to it ; neither can His form or any figure that represents Him enter into the thought or imagination.   Even so says Isaiah : Eye hath not seen Him, nor hath ear heard Him, neither hath it entered into the heart of man.[1]

3. And here it must be noted that the senses may receive pleasure and delight, either from the spirit, by means of some communication that it receives from God interiorly, or from outward things communicated to them.   And, as has been said, neither by way of the spirit nor by that of sense can the sensual part of the soul know God.   For, since it has no capacity for attaining to such a point, it receives in the senses both that which is of the spirit and that which is of sense,[2] and receives them in no other way.   Wherefore it would be at the least but vanity to set the rejoicing of the will upon pleasure caused by any of these apprehensions, and it would be hindering the power of the will from occupying itself with God and from centring its rejoicing in Him alone.   This the soul cannot perfectly accomplish, save by purging itself and remaining in darkness as to rejoicing of this kind, as also with respect to other things.

4. I said advisedly that if the rejoicing of the will were set upon any of these things it would be vanity.   But, when it is not set upon them, and when, as soon as the will finds pleasure in that which it hears, sees and does, it soars upward to rejoice in God—to which end its pleasure furnishes a motive and provides strength—this is very good.   In such a case not only need the said motions not be shunned when they cause this devotion and prayer, but the soul may profit by them, and indeed should so profit, to the end that it may accomplish this holy exercise.   For there are souls who

---

[1] Isaiah lxiv, 4 ; 1 Corinthians ii, 9.
[2] E.p. : ' and that which is of the intellect.'

are greatly moved by objects of sense to seek God. But much caution must be observed herein and the resulting effects must be considered ; for oftentimes many spiritual persons indulge in the recreations of sense aforementioned under the pretext of offering prayer and devotion to God ; and they do this in a way which must be called recreation rather than prayer, and which gives more pleasure to themselves than to God. And, although[1] the intention that they have is toward God, the effect which they produce[2] is that of recreation of sense, wherein they find weakness and imperfection, rather than revival of the will and surrender thereof to God.

5. I wish, therefore, to propose a test here whereby it may be seen when these delights of the senses aforementioned are profitable and when they are not. And it is that, whensoever a person hears music and other things, and sees pleasant things,[3] and is conscious of sweet perfumes, or tastes things that are delicious or feels soft touches, if his thought and the affection of his will are at once centred upon God and if that thought of God gives him more pleasure than the movement of sense which causes it, and save for that he finds no pleasure in the said movement, this is a sign that he is receiving benefit therefrom, and that this thing of sense is a help to his spirit. In this way such things may be used, for then such things of sense subserve the end for which God created and gave them, which is that He should be the better loved and known because of them. And it must be known, furthermore, that one upon whom these things of sense cause the pure spiritual effect which I describe has no desire for them, and makes hardly any account of them, though they cause him great pleasure when they are offered to him, because of the pleasure which, as I have said, they cause him in God. He is not, however, solicitous for them, and when they are offered to him, as I say, his will passes from them at once and he abandons it to God and sets it upon Him.

6. The reason why he cares little for these motives, although they help him on his journey to God, is that the spirit which is so ready to go by every means and in every way to God is so completely nourished and prepared and satisfied by the spirit of God that it lacks nothing and desires nothing ; or, if it desires anything to that end, the desire

---

[1] E.p. : ' although it seems that.'   [2] E.p. : ' which they cause.'
[3] A, e.p. : ' hears music or other pleasant things.'

at once passes and is forgotten, and the soul makes no account of it. But one that feels not this liberty of spirit in these things and pleasures of sense, but whose will rests in these pleasures and feeds upon them, is greatly harmed by them and should withdraw himself from the use of them. For, although his reason may desire to employ them to journey toward God, yet, inasmuch as his desire finds pleasure in them which is according to sense, and their effect is ever dependent upon the pleasure which they give, he is certain to find hindrance rather than help in them, and harm rather than profit. And, when he sees that the desire[1] for such recreation reigns in him, he must mortify it ; for, the stronger it becomes, the more imperfection he will have and the greater will be his weakness.

7. Whatsoever pleasure, then, presents itself to the spiritual person from sense, and whether it come to him by chance or by design, he must make use of it only as a means to God, lifting up to Him the rejoicing of his soul so that his rejoicing may be useful and profitable[2] and perfect ; realizing that all rejoicing which implies not renunciation[3] and annihilation of every other kind of rejoicing, although it be with respect to something apparently very lofty, is vain and profits not, but is a hindrance towards the union of the will in God.

CHAPTER XXV

Which treats of the evils that afflict the soul when it desires to set the rejoicing of its will upon the good things of sense.

1. In the first place, if the soul does not darken and quench the joy which may arise within it from the things of sense, and direct its rejoicing to God, all the general kinds of evil which we have described as arising from every other kind of rejoicing follow from this joy in the things of sense : such evils are darkness in the reason, lukewarmness, spiritual weariness, etc. But, to come to particulars, many are the evils, spiritual, bodily and sensual, into which the soul may fall through this rejoicing.

2. First of all, from joy in visible things, when the soul denies not itself in order to reach God, there may come to it,

---

[1] E.p. : ' that the spirit.' [2] Alc. alone has : ' and profitable.'
[3] [*Lit.*, ' that is not in renunciation . . .']

directly, vanity of spirit and distraction of the mind, unruly covetousness, immodesty, outward and inward unseemliness, impurity of thought, and envy.

3. From joy in hearing useless things there may directly arise distraction of the imagination, gossiping, envy, rash judgements and vacillating thoughts ; and from these arise many other and pernicious evils.

4. From joy in sweet perfumes, there arise loathing of the poor, which is contrary to the teaching of Christ, dislike of serving others, unruliness of heart in humble things, and spiritual insensibility, at least to a degree proportionate with its desire for this joy.

5. From joy in the savour of meat and drink, there arise directly such gluttony and drunkenness, wrath, discord and want of charity with one's neighbours and with the poor, as had that Epulon,[1] who fared sumptuously every day, with Lazarus.[2] Hence arise bodily disorders, infirmities and evil motions, because the incentives to luxury become greater. Directly, too, there arises great spiritual torpor, and the desire for spiritual things is corrupted, so that the soul cannot taste any of them, neither endure them nor treat of them. From this joy is likewise born distraction of the other senses and of the heart, and discontent with respect to many things.

6. From joy in the touch of soft things arise many more evils and more pernicious ones, which more quickly cause sense to overflow into spirit,[3] and quench all spiritual strength and vigour. Hence arises the abominable vice of effeminacy, or the incentives thereto, according to the proportion of joy of this kind which is experienced. Hence luxury increases, the mind becomes effeminate and timid, and the senses grow soft and delicate and are predisposed to sin and evil. Vain gladness and joy are infused into the heart ; the tongue takes to itself licence and the eyes roam unrestrainedly ; and the remaining senses are blunted and deadened, according to the measure[4] of this desire. The judgement is confounded, being nourished by spiritual folly and insipidity ; moral cowardice and inconstancy increase ; and, by the darkness of the soul and the weakness of the heart, fear is begotten even where no fear is. At times, again, this joy begets a spirit of confusion, and insensibility

---

[1] E.p. : ' as had that rich eater.'   [2] S. Luke xvi, 19.
[3] E.p. : ' which more quickly hurt the spirit.'
[4] [Lit., ' to the quantity.'] E.p. : ' to the degree.'

with respect to conscience and spirit ; wherefore the reason is greatly enfeebled, and is affected in such a way that it can neither take nor give good counsel, and remains incapable of moral and spiritual blessings and becomes as useless as a broken vessel.

7. All these evils are caused by this kind of rejoicing—in some more intensely,[1] according to the intensity of their rejoicing, and also according to the complacency or weakness or variableness of the person who yields to it.   For there are natures that will receive greater detriment from a small occasion of sin than will others from a great one.

8. Finally, from joy of this kind in touch, a person may fall into as many evils and perils as those which we have described as concerning the good things of nature ; and, since these have already been described, I do not detail them here ; neither do I describe many other evils wrought thus, such as diminution of spiritual exercises and bodily penance and lukewarmness and lack of devotion in the use of the sacraments of penance and of the Eucharist.

CHAPTER XXVI

Of the benefits that come to the soul from self-denial in rejoicing as to things of sense, which benefits are spiritual and temporal.

1. Marvellous are the benefits that the soul derives from self-denial in this rejoicing : some of these are spiritual and some temporal.

2. The first is that the soul, by restraining its rejoicing as to things of sense, is restored from the distraction into which it has fallen through excessive exercise of the senses, and is recollected in God.   The spirituality and the virtues that it has acquired are preserved ; nay, they are increased and increase continually.[2]

3. The second spiritual benefit which comes from self-denial in rejoicing as to things of sense is exceeding great. We may say with truth that that which was sensual becomes spiritual, and that which was bestial becomes rational ; and even that the soul is journeying from a human life to a

---

[1] E.p. : ' in some more, in others less, more or less intensely . . .'
[2] [*Lit.*, ' and gain continually.'] So Alc. A, B add ' anew.' E.p. omits : ' and increase continually.'

portion which is angelical ; and that, instead of being temporal and human, it becomes celestial and divine. For, even as a man who seeks the pleasure of things of sense and sets his rejoicing upon them neither merits nor deserves any other name than those which we have given him—that is, sensual, bestial, temporal, etc.—even so, when he exalts his rejoicing above these things of sense, he merits all those other names—to wit, spiritual, celestial, etc.

4. And it is clear that this is true ; for, although the exercise of the senses and the power of sensuality are contrary, as the Apostle says, to the power and the exercises of spirituality,[1] it follows that, when the one kind of power is diminished and brought to an end, the other contrary kinds, the growth of which was hindered by the first kinds, are increased. And thus, when the spirit is perfected, (which is the higher part of the soul and the part that has relations with God and receives His communications), it merits all these attributes aforementioned, since it is perfected in the heavenly and spiritual gifts and blessings of God. Both these things are proved by S. Paul, who calls the sensual man (namely, the man that directs the exercise of his will solely to sense) the animal man, who perceives not[2] the things of God. But this other man, who lifts up his will to God, he calls the spiritual man, saying that this man penetrates and judges all things, even the deep things of God.[3] Therefore the soul gains herein the marvellous[4] benefit of a disposition well able to receive the blessings and spiritual gifts of God.

5. The third benefit is that the pleasures and the rejoicing of the will in temporal matters are very greatly increased ; for, as the Saviour says, they shall receive an hundredfold in this life.[5] So that, if thou deniest thyself one joy, the Lord will give thee an hundredfold in this life, both spiritually and temporally ; and likewise, for one joy that thou hast in these things of sense, thou shalt have an hundredfold of affliction and misery. For, through the eye that is purged from the joys of sight, there comes to the soul a spiritual joy, directed to God in all things that are seen, whether Divine or profane.[6] Through the ear that is purged from the joy of hearing, there

---

[1] Galatians v, 17.   [2] A, B : ' who is he that perceives not . . .'
[3] 1 Corinthians ii, 9, 10, 14.
[4] Here P. Juan Evangelista's copy recommences (cf. p. 278, n. 8, above).
[5] S. Matthew xix, 29.   [6] E.p. : ' or human.'

comes to the soul joy most spiritual an hundredfold, directed
to God in all that it hears, be it Divine or profane.[1] Even so
is it with the other senses when they are purged. For, even
as in the state of innocence all that our first parents saw and
said and ate in Paradise furnished them with greater sweetness of contemplation, so that the sensual part of their nature
might be duly subjected to, and ordered by, reason ; even
so the man whose sense is purged from all things of sense and
made subject to the spirit, receives, in his very first motion,
the delight of delectable knowledge and contemplation of
God.

6. Wherefore, to him that is pure, all things, whether high
or low, are an occasion of greater good and further purity ;
even as the man that is impure is apt to derive evil from things
both high and low, because of his impurity. But he that
conquers not the joy of desire will not enjoy the serenity of
habitual rejoicing in God through His creatures and works.
In the man that lives no more according to sense, all the
operations of the senses and faculties are directed to Divine
contemplation. For, as it is true in good philosophy that
each thing operates according to its being, and to the life that
it lives, so it is clear, beyond contradiction, that, if the soul
lives a spiritual life, the animal life[2] being mortified, it must
be journeying straight to God, since all its spiritual actions
and motions pertain to the life of the spirit. Hence it follows
that such a man, being pure in heart, finds in all things a
knowledge of God which is joyful and pleasant, chaste, pure,
spiritual, glad and loving.

7. From what has been said I deduce the following
doctrine—namely that, until a man has succeeded in so
habituating his senses to the purgation of the joys of sense
that from his first motion[3] he is gaining the benefit aforementioned of directing all his powers to God, he must needs
deny himself joy and pleasure with respect to these powers,
so that he may withdraw his soul from the life of sense. He
must fear that, since he is not yet spiritual, he may perchance
derive from the practice of these things a pleasure and an
energy which is of sense rather than of spirit ; that the
energy which is of sense may predominate in all his actions ;

---

[1] E.p. : ' or human.'
[2] E.p. : ' . . . that according to the being which everything has is the
life that it lives, therefore, in a soul [*lit.*, ' in him '] that has a spiritual
being, the animal life . . .'
[3] E.p. omits : ' from his first motion.'

and that this may lead to an increase of sensuality and may sustain and nurture it. For, as Our Saviour says, that which is born of the flesh is flesh, and that which is born of the Spirit is spirit.[1] Let this be closely considered, for it is the truth. And let not him that has not yet mortified his pleasure in things of sense dare to make great use of the power and operation of sense with respect to them, thinking that they will help him to become more spiritual ; for the powers of the soul will increase the more without the intervention of these things of sense—that is, if it quench the joy and desire for them rather than make any use of it.

8. There is no need to speak of the blessings of glory that, in the life to come, result from the renunciation of these joys. For, apart from the fact that the bodily gifts of the life of glory, such as agility and clarity, will be much more excellent than in those souls who have not denied themselves, there will be an increase in the essential glory of the soul corresponding to its love of God, for Whose sake it has renounced the things of sense aforementioned. For every momentary, fleeting joy that has been renounced, as S. Paul says, there shall be laid up an exceeding weight of glory eternally.[2] And I will not here recount the other benefits, whether moral, temporal or spiritual, which result from this night of rejoicing ; for they are all those that have already been described, and to a more eminent degree ; since these joys that are renounced are more closely linked to the natural man, and therefore he that renounces them acquires thereby a more intimate purity.

CHAPTER XXVII

Which begins to treat of the fourth kind of good—namely, the moral. Describes wherein this consists, and in what manner joy of the will therein is lawful.

1. The fourth kind of good wherein the will may rejoice is moral. By this we here understand the virtues, and the habits of the virtues, in so far as these are moral, and the practice of any virtue, and the practice of works of mercy, the keeping of the law of God, and of that of the common-

---

[1] S. John iii, 6.   [2] 2 Corinthians iv, 17.

weal,[1] and the putting into practice of all good intentions and inclinations.

2. These kinds of moral good, when they are possessed and practised, deserve perhaps more than any of the other kinds aforementioned that the will should rejoice in them. For a man may rejoice in his own affairs for one of two reasons, or for both reasons together—namely, for that which they are in themselves, or for the good which they imply and bring with them as a means and instrument. We shall find that the possession of the three kinds of good already mentioned merits no rejoicing of the will. For, as has been said, they do no good to man of themselves, nor have they any good in themselves, since they are so fleeting and frail ; rather, as we have likewise said, they cause and bring him trouble and grief and affliction of spirit. Now, although they might merit that man should rejoice in them for the second reason—which is that he may profit by them for journeying to God—this is so uncertain that, as we commonly see, they more often harm man than bring him profit. But moral goods merit a certain degree of rejoicing in him that possesses them, and this for the first reason—namely, for their intrinsic nature and worth. For they bring with them peace and tranquillity, and a right and ordered use of the reason and actions that are consistent therewith, so that a man cannot, humanly speaking, have anything better in this life.

3. Thus, since these virtues deserve to be loved and esteemed, humanly speaking, for their own sakes, a man may well rejoice in the possession of them, and may practise them for that which they are in themselves, and for the blessing which they bring to man in human and temporal form. In this way and for this reason[2] philosophers and wise men and princes of old esteemed and praised them, and endeavoured to possess and practise them ; and, although they were heathen, and regarded them only in a temporal manner, merely considering the blessings which they knew would result from them—temporal, corporal and natural—they not only obtained by means of them the temporal renown and benefits which they sought, but, apart from this, God, Who

---

[1] [Lit., *política*, which I take as an adjective qualifying *ley* ('law') in the sense of 'law of the commonweal.' P. Silverio seems to consider it to be a noun, and glosses it as meaning 'good government in the commonweal, courtesy and other social virtues.'] A, B read *plática* ['conversation'], thereby entirely altering the sense.

[2] E.p. omits : 'and for this reason.'

loves all that is good (even in barbarians and heathen) and, as the Wise Man says, hinders naught that is good,[1] gave them longer life, greater honour, dominion and peace (as He did for example to the Romans), because they followed just laws ; for He subjected nearly the whole world to them, and gave rewards of a temporal kind for their good customs to those who because of their unbelief were incapable of eternal reward. For God loves moral good so much that, merely because Solomon asked wisdom of Him that he might teach his people, govern them justly and bring them up in good customs, God Himself was greatly pleased with him, and told him that, because he had asked for wisdom to that end, this should be given him, and there should also be given him that which he had not asked, namely, riches and honour, so that no king, either in the past or in the future, should be like him.[2]

4. But, although the Christian should rejoice in this first way in the moral good that he possesses and in the good works of a temporal kind which he does, since they lead to the temporal blessings which we have described, he must not allow his joy to stop at this first stage (as we have said the heathen did, because their spiritual sight extended not beyond the things of this mortal life) ; but, since he has the light of faith, wherein he hopes for eternal life, without which nothing that belongs to this life and the next will be of any value to him, he must rejoice principally and solely in the possession and employment of these moral goods after the second manner—namely, in that by doing these works for the love of God he will gain eternal life. And thus he should set his eyes and his rejoicing solely on serving and honouring God with his good customs and virtues. For without this intention the virtues are of no worth in the sight of God, as is seen in the ten virgins of the Gospel, who had all kept their virginity and done good works ; and yet, because the joy of five of them was not of the second kind (that is, because they had not directed their joy to God), but was rather after the first and vain kind, for they rejoiced[3] in the possession of their good works, they were cast out from Heaven with no acknowledgement or reward from the Bridegroom. And likewise many persons of old had many virtues[4] and practised

---

[1] Wisdom vii, 22.
[2] 3 Kings [A.V., 1 Kings] iii, 11–13.
[3] A, B, e.p. add : ' and boasted.'   [4] E.p. : ' certain virtues.'

good works, and many Christians have them[1] nowadays and accomplish great acts, which will profit them nothing for eternal life, because they have not sought in them the glory and honour which belong to God alone.[2] The Christian, then, must rejoice, not in the performing of good works and the following of good customs, but in doing them for the love of God alone, without respect to aught else soever. For, inasmuch as good works that are done to serve God alone will have the greater reward in glory, the greater will be the confusion in the presence of God of those who have done them for other reasons.

5. The Christian, then, if he will direct his rejoicing to God with regard to moral good, must realize that the value of his good works, fasts, alms, penances, etc., is not based upon the number or the quality of them, but upon the love of God which inspires him to do them ; and that they are the more excellent when they are performed with a purer and sincerer love of God, and when there is less in them of self-interest, joy, pleasure, consolation and praise, whether with reference to this world or to the next. Wherefore the heart must not be set upon pleasure, consolation and delight, and the other interests which good works and practices commonly bring with them, but it must concentrate its rejoicing upon God. It must desire to serve Him in its good works, and purge itself from this other rejoicing, remaining in darkness with respect to it and desiring that God alone shall have joy in its good works and shall take secret pleasure therein, without any other intention and delight than those relating to the honour and glory of God. And thus, with respect to this moral good, the soul will concentrate all the strength of its will upon God.

CHAPTER XXVIII

Of seven evils into which a man may fall if he set the rejoicing of his will upon moral good.

1. The principal evils into which a man may fall through vain rejoicing in his good works and habits I find to be seven ; and they are very hurtful because they are spiritual.[3]

---

[1] E.p. : ' have and practise them.'
[2] E.p. adds : ' and His love above all things.'
[3] A, B, e.p. add : ' These I shall here briefly describe.'

2. The first evil is vanity, pride, vainglory and presumption ; for a man cannot rejoice in his works without esteeming them. And hence arise boasting and like things, as is said of the Pharisee in the Gospel, who prayed and congratulated himself before God,[1] boasting that he fasted and did other good works.

3. The second evil is usually linked with this : it is our judging others, by means of comparisons, as wicked and imperfect, when it seems to us that their acts and good works are inferior to our own ; we esteem them the less highly in our hearts, and at times in our speech. And this evil was likewise that of the Pharisee, for in his prayer he said : I thank Thee that[2] I am not as other men are : robbers, unjust and adulterers.[3] So that by one single act he fell into these two evils, esteeming himself and despising others, as do many nowadays, saying : I am not like such a man, nor do I do this and that, as does such or such a man. And many of these are even worse than the Pharisee. He, it is true, not only despised others, but also pointed to an individual, saying : Nor am I like this publican. But they, not satisfied with either of these things, go so far as to be angry and envious when they see that others are praised, or do more, or are of greater use, than themselves.

4. The third evil is that, as they look for pleasure in their good works, they usually perform them only when they see that some pleasure and praise will result from them. And thus, as Christ says, they do everything *ut videantur ab hominibus*,[4] and work not for the love of[5] God alone.

5. The fourth evil follows from this. It is that they will have no reward from God, since they have desired in this life to have joy or consolation or honour or some other kind of interest as a result of their good works : of such the Saviour says that herein they have received their reward.[6] And thus they have had[7] naught but the labour of their work and are confounded, and receive no reward. There is so much misery among the sons of men which has to do with this evil that I myself believe that the greater number of good works which they perform in public are either vicious or will be of no value to them, or are imperfect[8] in the sight of God, since

---

[1] S. Luke xviii, 11–12.   [2] E.p. omits : ' I thank Thee that.'
[3] S. Luke xviii, 11.   [4] S. Matthew xxiii, 5.
[5] A, B, e.p. omit : ' the love of.'
[6] S. Matthew vi, 2.   [7] E.p. : ' And thus they will have.'
[8] A, e.p. : ' or are imperfect and defective.'

they are not detached from these human intentions and interests. For what other judgement can be formed of some
of the actions which certain men perform, and of the
memorials which they set up, when they will not perform
these actions at all unless they are surrounded by human
respect and honour, which are the vanity of life, or unless
they can perpetuate in these memorials their name, lineage
or authority, until they set up their emblems[1] and escut-
cheons in the very churches, as if they wished to set themselves, in the stead of images, in places where all bend the
knee ? In these good works which some men perform, may
it not be said that they are worshipping[2] themselves more
than God ? This is certainly true if they perform them for
the reason described and otherwise would not perform them
at all.[3] But leaving aside these, which are the worst cases,
how many are there who fall into these evils in their good
works in many ways ? Some wish to be praised, others to be
thanked, others enumerate their good works and desire that
this person and that shall know of them, and indeed the
whole world ; and sometimes they wish an intermediary to
present their alms, or to carry out other charitable deeds,[4] so
that more may be known of them ; and some desire all
these things.   This is the sounding of the trumpet, which,
says the Saviour in the Gospel, vain men do, for which
reason they shall have no reward for their works from God.[5]

6. These persons, then, in order to flee from this evil, must
hide their good works so that God alone may see them, and
must not desire anyone to take notice of them.   And they
must hide them, not only from others, but even from themselves. That is to say that they must find no satisfaction in
them, nor esteem them as if they were of some worth, nor
derive pleasure from them at all. It is this that is spiritually
indicated in those words of Our Lord : Let not thy left hand
know what thy right hand doeth.[6] Which is as much as to
say : Esteem not with thy carnal and temporal eye the work
that thou doest spiritually. And in this way the strength of
the will is concentrated upon God, and a good deed bears
fruit in His sight ; so that not only will it not be lost, but it

[1] A, B : ' their names.'
[2] [*Lit.*, ' are adoring.'] E.p. : ' are esteeming.'
[3] E.p. omits this entire sentence.
[4] [*Lit.*, ' to present their alms or that which they do.']
[5] S. Matthew vi, 2.
[6] S. Matthew vi, 3.

will be of great merit.[1] And in this sense must be understood
that passage from Job : If I have kissed my hand with my
mouth, which is a great sin and iniquity, and my heart hath
rejoiced in secret.[2] Here by the hand is understood good
works, and by the mouth is understood the will which finds
satisfaction in them. And since this is, as we say, finding
satisfaction in oneself, he says : If my heart hath rejoiced in
secret ; which is a great iniquity and a denial of God. And
this is as though he were to say that he had no satisfaction,
neither did his heart rejoice in secret.[3]

7. The fifth of these evils is that such persons make no
progress on the road of perfection. For, since they are
attached to the pleasure and consolation which they find in
their good works, it follows that, when they find no such
pleasure and consolation in their good works and exercises,
which is ordinarily when God desires to lead them on, by
giving them the dry bread of the perfect and taking from
them the milk of babes, in order to prove their strength and
to purge their delicate appetites so that they may be able to
enjoy the food of grown men, they commonly faint and cease
to persevere, because their good works give them no pleasure.
In this way may be spiritually understood these words of the
Wise Man : Dying flies spoil the sweetness of ointment.[4]
For, when any mortification comes to these persons, they die
to their good works and cease to practise them ; and thus
they lose their perseverance, wherein are found sweetness of
spirit and interior consolation.

8. The sixth of these evils is that such persons commonly
deceive themselves, thinking that the things and good works
which give them pleasure must be better than those that give
them none. They praise and esteem the one kind and
depreciate the other ;[5] yet as a rule those works whereby a
man is most greatly mortified (especially when he is not proficient in perfection) are more acceptable and precious in
the sight of God, by reason of the self-denial which a man

---

[1] So Alc. A, B, e.p. read : 'where not only will it be lost [sic. Read :
' where otherwise '], but oftentimes, through inward vanity and boasting,
the soul will sin greatly before God.'   [2] Job xxxi, 27-8.
    [3] So Alc. A, B and (with slight variations) e.p. add : 'For to assign
and attribute good works to oneself is to deny them to God, to Whom
belongs every good work ; this Lucifer did, rejoicing in himself and
denying to God that which was His, and exalting himself because of it,
which was the cause of his perdition.'   [4] Ecclesiastes x, 1.
    [5] So Alc. A, B : 'and reprehend and despise the other.' E.p. : ' and
condemn and despise the other.'

must observe in performing them, than are those wherein he finds consolation and which may very easily be an occasion of self-seeking. And in this way Micah says of them : *Malum manuum suarum dicunt bonum.*[1] That is : That which is bad in their works they call good. This comes to them because of the pleasure which they take in their good works, instead of thinking only of giving pleasure to God. The extent to which this evil predominates, whether in spiritual men or in ordinary persons, would take too long to describe, for hardly anyone can be found who is moved to do such works simply for God's sake, without the attraction of some advantage of consolation or pleasure, or some other consideration.

9. The seventh evil is that, in so far as a man stifles not vain rejoicing in moral works, he is to that extent incapable of receiving reasonable counsel and instruction with regard to good works that he should perform. For he is fettered by the habit of weakness that he has acquired through performing good works with attachment to vain rejoicing ; so that he cannot consider the counsel of others as best, or, even if he considers it to be so, he cannot follow it, through not having the necessary strength of mind. Such persons as this are greatly weakened in charity toward God and their neighbour ; for self-love, in which they indulge with respect to their good works, causes their charity to grow cold.

CHAPTER XXIX

Of the benefits which come to the soul through the withdrawal of its rejoicing from moral good.

1. Very great are the benefits which come to the soul when it desires not to set the vain rejoicing of its will on this kind of good. For, in the first place, it is freed from falling into many temptations and deceits of the devil, which are involved in rejoicing in these good works, as we may understand by that which is said in Job, namely : He sleepeth under the shadow, in the covert of the reed[2] and in moist places.[3] This he applies to the devil, who deceives the soul in the moisture of rejoicing and in the vanity of the reed—that is, in vain

---

[1] Micah vii, 3.
[2] This is the emendation of e.p. The Codices [followed by P. Silverio] have : ' of the feather,' as also below.   [3] Job xl, 16 [A.V., xl, 21].

works. And it is no wonder if the soul is secretly deceived by the devil in this rejoicing ; for, apart altogether from his suggestions, vain rejoicing is itself deception. This is especially true when there is any boasting of heart concerning these good works, as Jeremiah well says in these words : *Arrogantia tua decepit te.*[1] For what greater deception is there than boasting ? And from this the soul that purges itself from this rejoicing is freed.

2. The second benefit is that the soul performs its good works more deliberately and more perfectly, which is impossible if there be in them the passion of joy and pleasure. For, because of this passion of joy, the passions of wrath and concupiscence are so strong that they will not submit to reason,[2] but ordinarily cause a man to be inconsistent in his actions and purposes, so that he abandons some and takes up others, and begins a thing only to abandon it without completing any part of it. For, since he acts under the influence of pleasure, and since pleasure is variable, being much stronger in some natures than in others, it follows that, when this pleasure ceases, both the action and its purpose cease, even though they may be important. To such persons the joy which they have in their work is the soul and the strength thereof ; and, when the joy is quenched,[3] the work ceases and perishes, and they persevere therein no longer. It is of such persons that Christ says : They receive the word with joy, and then the devil taketh it away from them, lest they should persevere.[4] And this is because they have no strength and no roots save in the joy aforementioned. To take and to withdraw their will, therefore, from this rejoicing is the cause of their perseverance and success.[5] This benefit, then, is a great one, even as the contrary evil is great likewise. The wise man sets his eyes upon the substance and benefit of his work, not upon the pleasure and delight which it gives him ; and so he is not beating the air, but derives from his work a stable joy, without any meed of bitterness.[6]

[1] Jeremiah xlix, 16. E.p. adds the translation : ' Thy arrogance hath deceived thee.'

[2] [*Lit.*, ' will not give place to the weight of reason.']

[3] A, B : ' when the joy ceases.'   [4] S. Luke viii, 12.

[5] E.p. : ' . . . is an excellent preparation for perseverance and success.'

[6] E.p. : ' without demanding any meed of pleasure.' [The word translated ' bitterness ' in the text is *sinsabor*, the contrary of *sabor*, which is translated above ' pleasure.' The chief idea beneath *sinsabor* is that of insipidity and boredom.]

3. The third benefit is divine. It is that, when vain joy in these good works is quenched, the soul becomes poor in spirit, which is one of the blessings spoken of by the Son of God when He says : Blessed are the poor in spirit, for theirs is the Kingdom of Heaven.[1]

4. The fourth benefit is that he that denies himself this joy will be meek, humble and prudent in his actions. For he will not act impetuously and rapidly, through being impelled[2] by the wrath and concupiscence which belong to joy ; neither presumptuously, through being affected by the esteem of his own work which he cherishes because of the joy that he has in it ; neither incautiously, through being blinded by joy.[3]

5. The fifth benefit is that he becomes pleasing to God and man, and is freed from spiritual sloth, gluttony and avarice, and from spiritual envy and from a thousand other vices.

CHAPTER XXX

Which begins to treat of the fifth kind of good thing wherein the will may rejoice, which is the supernatural. Describes the nature of these supernatural good things, and how they are distinguished from the spiritual, and how joy in them is to be directed to God.

1. It now behoves us to treat of the fifth kind of good thing wherein the soul may rejoice, which is the supernatural. By this term we here understand all the gifts and graces given by God which transcend natural virtue and capacity and are called *gratis datæ*. Such as these are the gifts of wisdom and knowledge which God gave to Solomon, and the graces whereof S. Paul speaks[4]—namely, faith, gifts of healing, the working of miracles, prophecy, knowledge and discernment of spirits, interpretation of words and likewise the gift of tongues.

2. These good things, it is true, are also spiritual, like those of the same kind of which we have to speak presently ; yet, since the two are so different, I have thought well to make a distinction between them. The practice of these has an intimate relation with the profit of man, and it is with a view to this profit and to this end that God gives them, as

---

[1] S. Matthew v, 3.
[2] E.p. : ' being carried away.'
[3] Alc. omits : ' neither . . . by joy.'
[4] I Corinthians xii, 9-10.

S. Paul says : The spirit is given to none save for the profit of the rest ;[1] and this is understood of these graces. But the use and practice of spiritual graces has to do with the soul and God alone, and with God and the soul, in the communion of understanding and will, etc., as we shall say hereafter. And thus there is a difference in their object, since spiritual graces have to do only with the Creator and the soul ;[2] whereas supernatural graces have to do with the creature, and furthermore they differ[3] in substance, and therefore differ in their operation, and thus of necessity the instruction which we give concerning them differs also.

3. Speaking now of supernatural graces and gifts as we here understand them, I say that, in order to purge ourselves of vain joy in them, it is well here to notice two benefits which are comprised in this kind of gift—namely, temporal and spiritual. The temporal benefits are the healing of infirmities, the receiving of their sight by the blind, the raising of the dead, the casting out of devils, prophesying concerning the future so that men may take heed to themselves, and other things of this kind. The spiritual and eternal benefit is that God is known and served through these good works by him that performs them, or by those in whom and in whose presence they are performed.

4. With respect to the first kind of benefit—namely, the temporal—supernatural works and miracles merit little or no rejoicing on the part of the soul ; for, without the second kind of benefit, they are of little or no importance to man, since they are not in themselves a means for uniting the soul with God, as charity is. And these supernatural works and graces may be practised by those who are not in a state of grace and charity, whether they truly give thanks and attribute their gifts to God,[4] as did the wicked prophet Balaam, and Solomon, or whether they perform them falsely, by means of the devil, as did Simon Magus, or by other secrets of nature. These works and marvels, if any of them were to be of any profit to him that worked them, would be true works given by God. And S. Paul teaches us what these are worth[5] without the second benefit, saying :

---

[1] i Corinthians xii, 7.

[2] E.p. : ' spiritual graces are between God and the soul.'

[3] E.p. : ' but the other supernatural graces of which we were speaking have relation to other creatures and are for their profit. And furthermore they differ.'

[4] [Lit., ' give thanks and gifts to God.']   [5] A, B omit ' worth.'

Though I speak with the tongues of men and of angels, and have not charity, I am become as a sounding bell or metal. And though I have prophecy and know all mysteries and all knowledge ; and though I have all faith, even as much as may remove mountains, and have not charity, I am nothing, etc.[1] Wherefore Christ will refuse the requests of many who have esteemed their good works in this way, when they beg Him for glory because of them, saying[2] : Lord, have we not prophesied in Thy name and worked many miracles ? Then Christ will say to them : Depart from Me, workers of iniquity.[3]

5. A man, then, should rejoice, not when he has such graces and practises them, but when he reaps from them the second spiritual fruit, namely that of serving God in them with true charity, for herein is the fruit of eternal life. For this cause Our Saviour reproved the disciples who were rejoicing because they cast out devils, saying : Desire not to rejoice in this, that devils are subject to you, but rather because your names are written in the book of life.[4] This, according to good theology, is as much as to say : Rejoice if your names are written in the book of life. By this it is understood that a man should not rejoice save when he is walking in the way of life, which he may do by performing good works in charity ; for where is the profit and what is the worth in the sight of God of aught that is not love of God ? And this love is not perfect if it be not strong and discreet in purging the will of joy in all things, and if it be not set upon doing the will of God alone. And in this manner the will is united with God through these good things which are supernatural.

CHAPTER XXXI

Of the evils which come to the soul when it sets the rejoicing of the will upon this kind of good.

1. Three principal evils, it seems to me, may come to the soul when it sets its rejoicing[5] upon supernatural good. These are : that it may deceive and be deceived ; that it

---

[1] 1 Corinthians xiii, 1–2.
[2] A, B : ' and say to Him.' The other authorities omit ' saying.'
[3] S. Matthew vii, 22–3.   [4] S. Luke x, 20.
[5] E.p. : ' may come to man when he sets his rejoicing.'

may fall away from the faith ; and that it may indulge in vainglory or some other such vanity.

2. As to the first of these, it is a very easy thing to deceive others, and to deceive oneself, by rejoicing in this kind of operation. And the reason is that, in order to know which of these works are false and which are true, and how and at what time they should be practised, much counsel and much light from God are needful, and both these are greatly impeded by joy in these operations and esteem for them. And this for two reasons : first, because joy deadens and darkens judgement ; second, because, when a man has joy in these things, not only does he the more quickly become eager to obtain them, but he is also the more impelled[1] to work them out of the proper season. And supposing even that the virtues and operations which are practised are genuine, these two defects suffice for us to be frequently deceived in them, either through not understanding them as they should be understood, or through not profiting by them and using them at the times and in the ways that are most meet. For, although it is true that, when God gives these gifts and graces, He gives light by which to see them, and the impulse whereby a man may know at what times and in what ways to use them ; yet these souls, through the attachment and imperfection which they may have with regard to them, may greatly err, not using them with the perfection that God desires of them therein, and in the way and at the time that He wills. We read that Balaam desired to do this, when, against the will of God, he determined to go[2] and curse the children of Israel, for which reason God was wroth and purposed to slay him.[3] And S. James and S. John[4] desired to call down fire from Heaven upon the Samaritans because they gave not lodging to Our Saviour, and for this He reproved them.[5]

3. Here it is evident that these persons[6] were led to determine to perform these works, when it was not meet to do so, by a certain imperfect passion, which was inherent in their joy in them and esteem for them. For, when no such imperfection exists, the soul is moved and determined to perform these virtues only in the manner wherein God so

---

[1] E.p. : ' the more inclined.'   [2] E.p. : ' he dared to go.'
[3] Numbers xxii, 22–3.   [4] E.p. adds : ' carried away by zeal.'
[5] S. Luke ix, 54–5.
[6] E.p. : ' that these imperfect persons of whom we are speaking.'

impels it, and at His time, and until then it is not right that they should be performed. It was for this reason that God complained of certain prophets, through Jeremiah, saying : I have not sent the prophets, and they ran ; I have not spoken to them, and they prophesied.[1] And later He says : They deceived My people by their lying and their miracles, when I had not commanded them, neither had I sent them.[2] And in that place He says of them likewise : They see the visions of their heart, and speak of them[3] ; which would not happen if they had not this abominable attachment to these works.

4. From these passages it is to be understood that the evil of this rejoicing not only leads men to make wicked and perverse use of these graces given by God, as did Balaam and those of whom the prophet here says that they worked miracles whereby they deceived the people, but it even leads them to use these graces without having been given them by God, like those who prophesied their own fancies and published the visions which they invented or which the devil represented to them. For, when the devil sees them affectioned to these things, he opens a large field to them, gives them abundant material and interferes with them in many ways ; whereupon they spread their sails and become shamelessly audacious, devoting themselves freely to these prodigious works.

5. Nor does the evil stop here. To such a point does their joy in these works and their eagerness for them extend that, if before they had a secret compact with the devil (and many of them do in fact perform these works by such secret compacts), it now makes them bold enough to work with him by an explicit and manifest compact, submitting themselves to him, by agreement, as his disciples and allies. Hence we have wizards, enchanters, magicians, fortune-tellers and sorcerers. And so far does the joy of these persons in their works carry them that, not only do they seek to purchase gifts and graces with money, as did Simon Magus, in order to serve the devil ; but they even strive to obtain sacred things, and (which cannot be said without trembling) Divine things,[4] for even the very Body[5] of our Lord Jesus Christ has been seen to be usurped for the use of their wicked deeds

---

[1] Jeremiah xxiii, 21. [2] Jeremiah xxiii, 32.
[3] Jeremiah xxiii, 26.
[4] The remainder of this sentence is omitted from e.p.
[5] [Lit., ' the awful Body.']

and abominations. May God here extend and show to them His great mercy !

6. Everyone will clearly understand how pernicious are such persons to themselves and how prejudicial to Christianity.[1] It may be noted here that all those magicians and fortune-tellers who lived among the children of Israel, whom Saul destroyed out of the land, because they desired to imitate the true prophets of God, had fallen into such abominations and deceits.

7. He, then, that has supernatural gifts and graces ought to withdraw himself from desiring to practise them, and from joy in so doing, nor ought he to care to exercise them ;[2] for God, Who gives Himself to such persons, by supernatural means, for the profit of His Church and of its members, will move them likewise supernaturally[3] in such a manner and at such time as He desires. As He commanded His faithful ones[4] to take no thought as to what they were to say, or as to how they were to say it, since this is the supernatural business of faith, it will likewise be His will (as these operations are no less a supernatural matter) that a man should wait and allow God to work, by moving his heart, since in the virtue of this working will be wrought all virtue. The disciples (so we read in the Acts of the Apostles), although these graces and gifts had been infused within them, prayed to God, beseeching Him to be pleased to stretch forth His hand in making signs and performing works of healing through them, that they might introduce the faith of our Lord Jesus Christ into the hearts of men.[5]

8. From this first evil may proceed the second, which is a falling away from the faith ; this can come to pass after two manners. The first has respect to others ; for, when a man sets out, unseasonably and needlessly, to perform a marvel or a mighty work, apart from the fact that this is tempting God, which is a great sin, it may be that he will not succeed, and will engender in the hearts of men discredit and contempt for the faith. For, although at times such persons may succeed because for other reasons and purposes God so wills it, as in the case of Saul's witch[6] (if it is true that it was indeed Samuel who appeared on that occasion), they will not always

---

[1] A, B, e.p. : ' to the Christian commonweal.'
[2] A : ' to name them.'   E.p. omits : ' nor ought he to care to exercise them.'   [3] E.p. adds : ' to exercise them.'
[4] E.p. : ' His disciples.'   [5] Acts iv, 29–30.
[6] i Kings [A.V., i Samuel] xxviii, 7, ff.

so succeed ; and, when they do so, they go astray none the less and are blameworthy for having used these graces when it was not fitting to do so. The second manner in which we may fall away is in ourselves[1] and has respect to the merit of faith ; for, if a man make much account of these miracles, he ceases to lean upon the substantial practice of faith, which is an obscure habit ; and thus, where signs and witnesses abound, there is less merit in believing. In this way S. Gregory says that faith has no merit when human reason supplies experience.[2] And thus these marvels are never worked by God save when they are really necessary for belief.[3] Therefore, to the end that His disciples should not be without merit, though they had experience of His resurrection, He did many things before He showed Himself to them, so that they should believe Him without seeing Him. To Mary Magdalene, first of all, He showed the empty tomb, and afterwards bade the angels speak to her ;[4] for, as S. Paul says, faith comes by hearing ;[5] and, having heard, she believed before she saw. And, although she saw Him, it was as an ordinary man,[6] that, by the warmth of His presence, He might completely instruct her in the belief in which she was wanting. And He first sent to tell His disciples, with the women, and afterwards they went to see the tomb. And, as to those who went to Emmaus, He first of all enkindled their hearts in faith so that they might see Him, dissembling with them as He walked.[7] And finally He reproved them all because they had not believed those who had announced to them His resurrection.[8] And He reproved S. Thomas because he desired to have the witness of His wounds, by telling him that they who saw Him not and yet believed Him were blessed.[9]

9. And thus it is not the will of God that miracles should be wrought, for, as men say, when He works them, He does so only because He cannot do otherwise.[10] And for this cause He reproved the Pharisees because they believed not save

---

[1] Alc. has ' in like manner ' [asimismo] for ' in ourselves ' [en sí mismo].
[2] ' Nec fides habet meritum cui humana ratio praebet experimentum.' S. Gregory, Hom. 26 in Evang. (Migne, Vol. LXXVI, p. 1137). The translation in the text is that of Alc. A, B, e.p. have : ' . . . supplies experience of a human and palpable kind.'
[3] E.p. adds : ' and for other ends concerning His glory and His saints.'
[4] [S. Luke xxiv, 6 ; S. John xx, 2.]   [5] [Romans x, 17.]
[6] E.p. : ' as a gardener ' [S. John xx, 15].   [7] S. Luke xxiv, 15.
[8] [S. Luke xxiv, 25–6.]   [9] S. John xx, 29.
[10] E.p. omits : ' for, as . . . do otherwise.'

through signs, saying : Unless ye see marvels and signs, ye believe not.[1] Those, then, who love to rejoice in these supernatural works, lose much in the matter of faith.

10. The third evil is that, because of their joy in these works, men commonly fall into vainglory or some other vanity. For even their joy in these wonders, when it is not, as we have said, purely in God and for God, is vanity ; which is evident in the reproof given by Our Lord to the disciples because they had rejoiced that devils were subject to them ;[2] for which joy, if it had not been vain, He would not have reproved them.

CHAPTER XXXII

Of two benefits which are derived from the renunciation of rejoicing in the matter of the supernatural graces.

1. Besides the benefits which the soul gains by being delivered from the three evils aforementioned through its renunciation of this joy, it acquires two excellent benefits. The first is that it magnifies and exalts God : the second is that it exalts itself. For God is exalted in the soul after two manners : first, by the withdrawal of the heart and the joy of the will from all that is not God, in order to set them upon Him alone. This David signified in the verse[3] which we quoted when we began to speak of the night of this faculty ; namely : Man shall attain to a lofty heart, and God shall be exalted.[4] For, when the heart is raised above all things, the soul is exalted above them all.

2. And, because in this way the soul centres itself in God alone, God is exalted and magnified, when He reveals to the soul His excellence and greatness ; for, in this elevation of joy, God bears witness of Himself, Who He is. This cannot be done save if the will be voided of joy and consolation with respect to all things, even as David said also, in these words : Be still and see that I am God.[5] And again he says : In a desert land, dry and pathless, have I appeared before Thee, to see Thy power and Thy glory.[6] And, since it is true that God is exalted by the fixing of the soul's rejoicing

---

[1] S. John iv, 48.
[2] S. Luke x, 20.
[3] E.p. : 'in the place.'
[4] Psalm lxiii, 7 [A.V., lxiv, 6–7].
[5] Psalm xlv, 11 [A.V., xlvi, 10].
[6] Psalm lxii, 3 [A.V., lxiii, 1–2].

upon detachment from all things, He is much more highly exalted when the soul withdraws itself from the most wondrous of these things in order to fix its rejoicing on Him alone. For these, being supernatural, are of a higher nature ; and thus for the soul to cast them aside, in order to set its rejoicing upon God alone, is to attribute greater glory and excellence to God than to them. For, the more and the greater things a man despises for the sake of another, the more does he esteem and exalt that other.

3. Furthermore, God is exalted after the second manner when the will is withdrawn from this kind of operation ; for, the more God is believed and served without testimonies and signs, the more He is exalted by the soul, for it believes more concerning God than signs and miracles can demonstrate.

4. The second benefit wherein the soul is exalted consists in this, that, withdrawing the will from all desire for apparent[1] signs and testimonies, it is exalted in purest faith, which God increases and infuses within it much more intensely. And, together with this, He increases in it the other two theological virtues, which are charity and hope, wherein the soul enjoys the highest Divine knowledge by means of the obscure and detached habit of faith ; and it enjoys great delight of love by means of charity, whereby the will rejoices in naught else than in the living God ; and likewise it enjoys satisfaction in the memory[2] by means of hope. All this is a wondrous benefit, which leads essentially and directly to the perfect union of the soul with God.

CHAPTER XXXIII

Which begins to treat of the sixth kind of good wherein the soul may rejoice. Describes its nature and makes the first division under this head.[3]

1. Since the intention of this work of ours is to lead the spirit through these good things of the spirit even to the Divine union of the soul with God, it will now behove both myself and the reader to give our consideration to this matter with particular care. For, in speaking of this sixth

[1] [*i.e.*, that are perceived by the faculties of the soul in other ways than by pure faith.] [2] A, B, e.p. : ' in the will.'
[3] This last sentence is found in A, B and e.p. only.

kind of good, we have to treat of the good things of the spirit, which are those that are of the greatest service to this end. For it is quite certain, and quite an ordinary occurrence,[1] that some persons, because of their lack of knowledge, make use of spiritual things with respect only to sense, and leave the spirit empty. There will scarcely be anyone whose spirit is not to a considerable degree corrupted by sweetness of sense ; since, if the water be drunk up before it reaches the spirit, the latter becomes dry and barren.

2. Coming to this matter, then, I say that by good things of the spirit I understand all those that influence and aid the soul in Divine things and in its intercourse with God, and the communications of God to the soul.

3. Beginning by making a division between these supreme kinds of good, I say that good things of the spirit are of two kinds : the one kind is delectable and the other painful. And each of these kinds is likewise of two manners ; for the delectable kind consists of clear things that are distinctly understood, and also of things that are not understood clearly or distinctly. The painful kind, likewise, may be of clear and distinct things, or of things dark and confused.

4. Between all these we may likewise make distinctions with respect to the faculties of the soul. For some kinds of spiritual good, being of knowledge, pertain to the understanding ; others, being of affection, pertain to the will ; and others, inasmuch as they are imaginary, pertain to the memory.

5. We shall leave for later consideration those good things that are painful, since[2] they pertain to the passive night, in treating of which we shall have to speak of them ; and likewise the delectable blessings which we described as being of things confused and not distinct, of which we shall treat hereafter, since they pertain to that general, confused and loving knowledge wherein is effected the union of the soul with God, and which we passed over in the second book, deferring it so that we might treat of it later[3] when we should make a division between the apprehensions of the understanding.[4] We shall speak here and now of those delectable blessings which are of things clear and distinct.

---

[1] [*Lit.*, ' thing.'] E.p. : ' For it is quite a certain thing . . .'
[2] E.p. : ' inasmuch as.'   [3] Cf. p. 126, n. 4, above.
[4] Alc. omits : ' when we should . . . understanding.' E.p. adds to this last phrase : ' and this we shall duly do in the book of the *Dark Night*.'

CHAPTER XXXIV

Of those good things of the spirit which can be distinctly apprehended by the understanding and the memory. Describes how the will is to behave in the matter of rejoicing in them.

1. We might spend much time here upon the multitude of the apprehensions of the memory and the understanding, teaching how the will is to conduct itself with regard to the joy that it may have in them, had we not treated of this at length in the second and the third book. But, since we there spoke of the manner wherein it behoves these two faculties to act with respect to them, in order that they may take the road to Divine union, and since it behoves the will to conduct itself likewise as regards rejoicing in them, it is unnecessary to go over this here ; for it suffices to say that wheresoever we there said that those faculties should void themselves of this or that apprehension, it is to be understood also that the will should likewise be voided of joy in them. And in the way wherein it is said that memory and understanding should conduct themselves with regard to all these apprehensions, the will must conduct itself likewise ; for, since the understanding and the other faculties cannot admit or reject anything unless the will intervene therein, it is clear that the same teaching that serves for the one will serve also for the other.

2. It may there be seen, then, what is requisite in this case, for the soul will fall into all the evils and perils to which we there referred if it cannot direct the rejoicing of the will to God in all those apprehensions.[1]

CHAPTER XXXV

Of the delectable spiritual good things which can be distinctly apprehended by the will. Describes the kinds of these.

1. We can reduce all the kinds of good which can distinctly cause joy to the will to four : namely, motive, provocative, directive and perfective. Of these we shall speak in turn, each in its order ; and first, of the motive kind

---

[1] Alc. abbreviates : ' It may there be seen what is requisite herein, for the soul will fall into all those evils if it cannot direct itself to God.'

—namely, images and portraits of saints, oratories and ceremonies.

2. As touching images and portraits, there may be much vanity and vain rejoicing in these. For, though they are most important for Divine worship and most necessary to move the will to devotion, as is shown by the approval given to them and the use made of them by our Mother Church (for which reason it is always well that we should employ them, in order to awaken our lukewarmness), there are many persons who rejoice rather in the painting and decoration of them than in what they represent.

3. The use of images has been ordained by the Church for two principal ends—namely, that we may reverence the Saints in them, and that the will may be moved and devotion to the Saints awakened by them. When they serve this purpose they are beneficial and the use of them is necessary ; and therefore we must choose those that are most true and lifelike, and that most move the will to devotion, and our eyes must ever be fixed upon this motive rather than upon the value and cunning of their workmanship and decoration. For, as I say, there are some who pay more attention to the cunning with which an image is made, and to its value, than to what it represents ; and that interior devotion which they ought to direct spiritually to the saint whom they see not, forgetting the image at once, since it serves only as a motive,[1] they squander upon the cunning and the decoration of its outward workmanship. In this way sense is pleased and delighted, and the love and rejoicing of the will remain there. This is a complete hindrance to true spirituality, which demands annihilation of the affections as to all particular things.

4. This will become quite clear from the detestable custom which certain persons observe with regard to images in these our days. Holding not in abhorrence the vain trappings of the world, they adorn images with the garments which from time to time vain persons invent in order to satisfy their own pleasures and vanities.[2] They clothe images with these garments which are reprehensible even in themselves, a kind of vanity which was, and is still, abhorrent to the saints whom the images represent. Herein, with their help, the devil succeeds in canonizing his vanities,

---

[1] E.p. omits the phrase : ' forgetting . . . as a motive.'
[2] A, B, e.p. have ' frivolities ' for ' vanities.'

by clothing the saints with them, not without causing them great displeasure. And in this way the honest and grave devotion of the soul, which rejects and spurns all vanity and every trace of it, is reduced in them to little more than a dressing of dolls ; some persons use images merely as idols upon which they have set their rejoicing.[1] And thus you will see certain persons who are never tired of adding one image to another, and wish them to be of this or that kind and workmanship, and to be placed in this or that manner, so as to be pleasing to sense ; and they make little account of the devotion of the heart. They are as much attached to them as was Micah to his idols,[2] or as was Laban ;[3] for the one ran out of his house crying aloud because they were being taken from him ; and the other, having made a long journey and been very wroth because of them, disturbed all the household stuff of Jacob, in searching for them.

5. The person who is truly[4] devout sets his devotion principally upon that which is invisible ; he needs few images and uses few, and chooses those that harmonize with the Divine rather than with the human, clothing them, and with them himself, in the garments of the world to come, and following its fashions rather than those of this world. For not only does an image belonging to this world in no way influence his desire ; it does not even lead him to think of this world, in spite of his having before his eyes something worldly, akin to the world's interests. Nor is his heart attached to the images that he uses ; if they are taken from him, he grieves very little, for he seeks within himself the living image, which is Christ crucified, for Whose sake he rather desires that all should be taken from him and he should have nothing. Even when the motives and means which lead him closest to God[5] are taken from him, he remains in tranquillity. For the soul is nearer perfection when it is tranquil and joyous, though it be deprived of these motives, than if it has possession of them together with desire and attachment. For, although it is good to be pleased to have such images as assist the soul to greater devotion (for which reason it is those which move it most

---

[1] E.p. abbreviates : ‘. . . to little more than curiosity and vanity.’
[2] Judges xviii, 22–4.   [3] Genesis xxxi, 34–7.
[4] Alc. alone has ‘ truly.’
[5] E.p. : ‘ Even when the means that seemed to be leading him closest to God . . .’

that must always be chosen), yet it is something far removed from perfection to be so greatly attached to them as to possess them with attachment, so that, if they are taken away from the soul, it becomes sad.

6. Let the soul be sure that, the more closely it is attached to an image or a motive,[1] the less will its devotion and prayer mount to God. For, although it is true that, since some are more appropriate than others, and excite devotion more than others, it is well, for this reason alone, to be affectioned to some rather than to others, as I have just now said,[2] yet there must be none of the attachment and affection which I have described. Otherwise, that which has to sustain the spirit in its flight to God, in total forgetfulness, will be wholly occupied by sense, and the soul will be completely immersed in a delight afforded it by what are but instruments. These instruments I have to use solely in order to assist me in devotion ; yet, on account of my imperfection, they may well serve me as a hindrance, no less so than may affection and attachment to anything else.[3]

7.[4] But, though perhaps in this matter of images you may think that there is something to be said on the other side, if you have not clearly understood the detachment and poverty of spirit which is required by perfection, at least you cannot excuse the imperfection which is commonly indulged with regard to rosaries ; for you will hardly find anyone who has not some weakness with regard to these, desiring them to be of this workmanship rather than of that,[5] or of this colour or metal rather than of that, or decorated in some one style or in some other. Yet no one style is better than another for the hearing of a prayer by God, for this depends upon the simple and true heart,[6] which looks at no more than pleasing God, and, apart from the question of indulgences, cares no more for one rosary than for another.

8. Our vain concupiscence is of such a nature and quality that it tries to cling to everything ; and it is like the worm which destroys healthy wood, and works upon things both good and evil. For what else is your desire to have a rosary of

---

[1] E.p. : ' or a motive of sense.'
[2] Alc. omits : ' as-I have just now said.'
[3] E.p. omits : ' no less . . . anything else.'
[4] [In this and the next paragraph the Saint is more than usually personal in his approach to the reader. The word *tú* (you) is repeated many times, and placed in emphatic positions, in a way which cannot be exactly reproduced in English.]
[5] E.p. : ' than of the other.'   [6] E.p. : ' and upright heart.'

cunning workmanship, and your wish that it shall be of one kind rather than of another, but the fixing of your rejoicing upon the instrument ? It is like desiring to choose one image rather than another, and considering, not if it will better awaken Divine love within you, but only if it is more precious and more cunningly made. If you employed your desire and rejoicing solely in the love of God, you would care nothing for any of these considerations. It is most vexatious to see certain spiritual persons so greatly attached to the manner and workmanship of these instruments and motives, and to the curiosity and vain pleasure which they find in them ; for you will never see them satisfied, but they will be continually leaving one thing for another, and forgetting and forsaking spiritual devotion for these visible things, to which they have affection and attachment, frequently of just the same kind as that which a man has to temporal things ; and from this they receive no small harm.[1]

CHAPTER XXXVI

Which continues to treat of images, and describes the ignorance which certain persons have with respect to them.

1. There is much that might be said of the stupidity which many persons display with regard to images ; their foolishness reaches such a point that some of them place more confidence in one kind of image than in another, believing that God will hear them more readily because of these than because of those, even when both represent the same thing, as when there are two of Christ or two of Our Lady. And this happens because they have more affection for the one kind of workmanship than for the other ; which implies the crudest ideas concerning intercourse with God and the veneration and honour that are owed to Him, which has solely to do with the faith and the purity of heart of him that prays.[2] For if God sometimes grants more favours by

[1] Alc. abbreviates the last sentence thus : ' And it is a pity to see certain spiritual persons so greatly attached to the manner and workmanship of these instruments, and having the [same] affection and attachment to them as to other temporal things.' C, D also abbreviate, but resemble the other authorities rather than Alc.

[2] E.p. reads : ' . . . in one kind of image than in another, being influenced herein solely by the affection which they have for one figure rather than for another. This implies the crudest and meanest ideas concerning intercourse with God and the veneration and honour that are owed to Him, which has principally to do with the faith and the purity of heart of him that prays.'

means of one image rather than by another of the same kind, it is not because there is more virtue to this effect in one than in another (however much difference there may be in their workmanship), but because some persons better awaken their own devotion by one than by another. If they had the same devotion for the one as for the other (or even without the use of either), they would receive the same favours from God.[1]

2. Hence the reason for which God works[2] miracles and grants favours by means of one kind of image rather than by another is not that these should be esteemed more than those, but to the end that, by means of the wonder that they cause, there may be awakened sleeping devotion and the affection of the faithful for prayer. And hence it comes that, as the contemplation of the image at that time enkindles devotion and makes us to continue in prayer (both these being means whereby God hears and grants that which is asked of Him), therefore, at that time and by means of that same image, God continues to work favours and miracles because of the prayer and affection which are then shown; for it is certain that God does it not because of the image, which in itself is no more than a painted thing, but because of the devotion and faith which the person has toward the saint whom it represents. And so, if you had the same devotion and faith in Our Lady before one image representing her as before another, since the person represented is the same (and even, as we have said, if you had no such image at all), you would receive the same favours. For it is clear from experience that, when God grants certain favours and works miracles, He does so as a rule by means of certain images which are not well carved or cunningly formed or painted, so that the faithful may attribute nothing to the figure or the painting.[3]

3. Furthermore, Our Lord is frequently wont to grant these favours by means of those images that are most remote and solitary. One reason for this is that the effort necessary to journey to them causes the affections to be increased and makes the act of prayer more earnest. Another reason is that we may withdraw ourselves from noise and from people, so

---

[1] E.p. : ' . . . of the same kind, it is (although there may be much difference in their workmanship) to the end that people may awaken their own devotion better by means of one than by means of another.' This concludes the paragraph, the last sentence being omitted.

[2] [*Lit.*, ' awakens.' Cf. the use of the same metaphor below.]

[3] A, B, e.p. : ' to the painting or the workmanship.'

that we may pray, even as did the Lord.   Wherefore he that makes a pilgrimage does well if he makes it at a time when no others are doing so, even though the time be unusual. When a great multitude is making a pilgrimage, I should never advise him to do so ; for, as a rule, people return on these occasions in a state of greater distraction than when they went.   And many set out and make these pilgrimages for recreation rather than for devotion.   When there is devotion and faith, then, any image will suffice ; but, if there is none, none will suffice.[1]   Our Saviour was a very living image in the world ; and yet those that had no faith, even though they went about with Him and saw His wondrous works, derived no benefit from them.   And this was the reason why, as the Evangelist says, He did few mighty works in His own country.[2]

4.   I desire also to speak here of certain supernatural effects which are sometimes caused by certain images in particular persons.   The effect is that God gives to certain images a particular spiritual influence upon them, so that the figure of the image and the devotion caused by it remain fixed in the mind, and the person has them ever present before him ; and so, when he suddenly thinks of the image, the spiritual influence which works upon him is of the same kind as when he saw it—sometimes it is less but sometimes it is even greater —yet, from another inage, although it be of the most perfect workmanship, he will not obtain the same spiritual effect.

5.   Many persons, too, have devotion to one kind of workmanship rather than to another, and to some they will have no more than a natural inclination and affection, just as we prefer seeing one person's face to another's.   And they will naturally become more attracted to a particular image, and will keep it more vividly in their imagination,[3] even though it be not as beautiful as others, just because their nature is attracted to that kind of form and figure which it represents. And some persons will think that the affection which they have to such or such an image is devotion, whereas it will perhaps be no more than natural inclination and affection. Again, it may happen that, when they look at an image, they

---

[1] E.p.: 'When there is no devotion and faith, then, no image will suffice.'

[2] S. Luke iv, 24.   [Rather S. Matthew xiii, 58; S. Mark vi, 5.]

[3] A : '. . . and will keep it more vividly, because it is a natural thing and (sic) to have it ever in the memory.'

will see it move, or make signs and gestures and indications, or speak. This, and the variety of supernatural effects caused by images of which we have here been speaking, are,[1] it is true, quite frequently good and true effects, produced by God either to increase the devotion or so that the soul may have some support on which to lean, because it is somewhat weak, and so that it may be not distracted. Yet frequently, again, they are produced by the devil[2] in order to cause deception and harm. We shall therefore give instruction concerning this in the chapter following.

CHAPTER XXXVII

Of how the rejoicing of the will must be directed, by way of the images, to God, so that the soul may not go astray because of them or be hindered by them.

1. Just as images are of great benefit for remembering God and the saints, and for moving the will to devotion when they are used in the ordinary way,[3] as is fitting, so they will lead to great error if, when supernatural happenings come to pass in connection with them, the soul should not be able to conduct itself as is fitting for its journey to God. For one of the means by which the devil lays hold on uncautious souls, with great ease, and obstructs the way of spiritual truth for them, is the use of extraordinary and supernatural[4] happenings, of which he gives examples by means of images, both the material and corporeal images used by the Church, and also those which he is wont to fix in the fancy in relation to such or such a saint, or an image of him, transforming himself into an angel of light that he may deceive. For in those very means which we possess for our relief and help the astute devil contrives to hide himself in order to catch us when we are least prepared. Wherefore it is concerning good things that the soul that is good must ever have the greatest misgivings, for evil things bear their own testimony with them.

---

[1] A: '. . . or speak in this manner or in another. But concerning the supernatural effects, etc, . . . they are.'
[2] E.p.: 'Yet at other times they are not true [effects] and are apt to be produced by the devil.'   [3] Alc. omits: 'in the ordinary way.'
[4] E.p.: 'and rare.' Cf. p. 132, n. 1, above.

2. Hence, in order to avoid all the evils which may happen to the soul in this connection, which are its being hindered from soaring upward to God, or its using images in an unworthy and ignorant manner, or its being deceived by them through natural or supernatural means,[1] all of which are things that we have touched upon above ; and in order likewise to purify the rejoicing of the will in them and to direct the soul by means of them to God, for which reason the Church recommends their use, I desire here to set down only one warning, which will suffice for everything, and this is that, since images serve us as a motive for invisible things, we must strive to set the motive and the affection and the rejoicing of our will only upon that which in fact they represent. Let the faithful soul, then, be careful that, when he sees the image, he desire not that his senses should be absorbed by it, whether the image be corporeal or imaginary, whether beautifully made or richly adorned, whether the devotion that it causes be of sense or of spirit, whether it give supernatural manifestations or no. The soul must on no account set store by these accidents, nor even regard them, but[2] must raise up its mind from the image to that which it represents, centring the sweetness and rejoicing of its will, together with the prayer and devotion of its spirit, upon God or upon the saint who is being invoked ; for that which belongs to the living reality and to the spirit should not be usurped by sense and by the painted object. If the soul pays heed to this, it will not be deceived, for it will set no store by anything that the image may say to it, nor will it occupy its sense or its spirit in such a way that they cannot travel freely to God, nor will it place more confidence in one image than in another. And an image which would cause the soul devotion by supernatural means will now do so more abundantly, since the soul will now go with its affections directly to God. For, whensoever God grants these and other favours, He does so by inclining the affection of the joy of the will to that which is invisible, and this He wishes us also to do, by annihilating the power and sweetness of the faculties with respect to these visible things of sense.

---

[1] E.p. omits : ' through natural or supernatural means.'
[2] E.p. here interpolates : ' having paid to the image the adoration which the Church commands.'

CHAPTER XXXVIII

Continues to describe motive good. Speaks of oratories and places dedicated to prayer.

1. I think it has now been explained how the spiritual person may find as great imperfection in the accidents of images, by setting his pleasure and rejoicing[1] upon them, as in other corporal and temporal things, and perchance imperfection more perilous still. And I say that the imperfection may perchance be more perilous, because, when a person says that the objects of this rejoicing are holy, he becomes more secure, and fears not to become naturally affectioned and attached to them. And thus such a person is sometimes greatly deceived, thinking himself to be full of devotion because he perceives that he takes pleasure in these holy things, when, perchance, this is due only to his natural desire and temperament, which lead him to this just as they lead him to other things.

2. Hence it arises (for we are now beginning to treat of oratories) that there are some persons who never tire of adding images of one kind or another to their oratories, and take pleasure in the order and arrangement in which they place them, so that their oratories may be well adorned and pleasing to behold. Yet they love not God more when their oratories are arranged in the one way than in the other—indeed they love Him less, since the pleasure which they set upon their painted adornments is taken, as we have said, from the living reality. It is true that all the adornment and embellishment and respect that can be lavished upon images amounts to a very small thing, and that therefore those who have images and treat them with little decency and respect are worthy of severe reproof, as are those who have images so ill-carved that they take away devotion rather than produce it, for which reason some image-makers who are very defective and unskilled in this art should be forbidden to practise it. This is true, but what has it to do with the attachment and affection and desire which you have[2] for these outward adornments and decorations, when your senses are absorbed by them in such a way that your heart is

---

[1] E.p. omits : ' and rejoicing.'
[2] [Again the Saint begins, repeatedly and emphatically, to employ the pronoun *tú*. Cf. p. 312, n. 4, above.]

hindered from journeying to God, and from loving Him and
forgetting all things for love of Him ? If you fail in the latter
aim for the sake of the former, not only will God not esteem
you for it, but He will even chasten you for not having
sought His pleasure in all things rather than your own.
This you may clearly gather from the description of that
feast which they made for His Majesty when He entered
Jerusalem. They received Him with songs and with
branches, and the Lord wept ;[1] for they kept their hearts
very far removed from Him and paid Him reverence only by
outward adornments and signs. We may say of them that
they were making a festival for themselves rather than for
God ; and this is done nowadays by many, who, when there
is some solemn festival,[2] are apt to rejoice because of the
pleasure which they themselves will find in it—whether in
seeing or in being seen, or whether in eating or in some other
way—rather than to rejoice at being acceptable to God.
By these inclinations and intentions they are giving no
pleasure to God. Especially is this so when those who
celebrate festivals invent ridiculous and undevout things to
intersperse in them, so that they may incite people to
laughter, which causes them greater distraction. And other
persons invent things which simply please people rather than
move them to devotion.

3. And what shall I say of persons who celebrate festivals
for reasons connected with their own interests ? They alone,
and God Who sees them, know if their regard and desire are
set upon such interests rather than upon the service of God.
Let them realize, when they act in any of these ways, that
they are making festivals in their own honour rather than
in that of God. For that which they do for their own
pleasure or for the pleasure of men, God will not account as
done for Himself. Yea, many who take part in God's
festivals will be enjoying themselves even while God will
be growing wroth with them, as He was with the children
of Israel when they made a festival, and sang and danced
before their idol, thinking that they were keeping a festival
in honour of God ; of whom He slew many thousands.[3] Or
again, as He was with the priests Nadab and Abihu, sons of
Aaron, whom He slew with the censers in their hands,

---

[1] S. Matthew xxi, 9. [Cf. S. Luke xix, 41.]
[2] E.p. : ' when there is a solemnity anywhere.'
[3] Exodus xxxii, 7–28.

because they offered strange fire.[1] Or as with the man that
entered the wedding feast ill-adorned[2] and ill-garbed, whom
the king commanded to be thrown into outer darkness,
bound hand and foot.[3] By this it may be known how ill God
suffers these irreverences in assemblies that are held for His
service. For how many festivals, O my God, are made Thee
by the sons of men in which the devil gains more than Thou !
The devil takes a delight in them, because such gatherings
bring him business, as to a trader. And how often wilt Thou
say concerning them : This people honoureth Me with their
lips alone, but their heart is far from Me, for they serve Me
from a wrong cause.[4] For the sole cause[5] for which God
must be served is that He is Who He is, and not for any
other mediate ends. And thus to serve Him for other reasons
than solely that He is Who He is, is to serve Him without
considering this final end.[6]

4. Returning now to oratories, I say that some persons
deck them out for their own pleasure rather than for the
pleasure of God ; and some persons set so little account by
the devotion which they arouse that they think no more of
them than of their own secular antechambers ; some,
indeed, think even less of them, for they take more pleasure
in the profane than in the Divine.

5. But let us cease speaking of this and speak only of
those who are more particular[7]—that is to say, of those who
consider themselves devout persons. Many of these centre
their desire and pleasure upon their oratory and its adornments, to such an extent that they squander on them all the
time that they should be employing in prayer to God and
interior recollection. They cannot see that, by not arranging
their oratory with a view to the interior recollection and
peace of the soul, they are as much distracted by it as by
anything else, and the pleasure which they take in it will be
a continual distraction to them, and more so still if anyone
endeavours to take it from them.

---

[1] Leviticus x, 1-2.
[2] E.p. : ' ill-clad.'
[3] S. Matthew xxii, 12-13.
[4] S. Matthew xv, 8. [Lit., ' they serve Me without cause.']
[5] E.p. : ' For the principal cause.'
[6] This last sentence is omitted in e.p.
[7] [Lit., ' that spin more finely '—a common Spanish metaphor.]

CHAPTER XXXIX

Of the way in which oratories and churches should be used, in order to direct the spirit to God.

1. With regard to the direction of the spirit to God through this kind of good, it is well to point out that it is certainly lawful, and even expedient, for beginners to find some sensible sweetness and pleasure in images, oratories and other visible objects of devotion, since they have not yet weaned or detached their desire from things of the world, so that they can leave the one pleasure for the other. They are like a child holding something in one of its hands ; to make it loosen its hold upon it we give it something else to hold in the other hand lest it should cry because both its hands are empty. But the spiritual person that would make progress must strip himself of all those pleasures and desires wherein the will may rejoice, for pure spirituality is bound very little to any of those objects, but only to interior recollection and mental converse with God. So, although he may make use of images and oratories, this will be only for a time ; his spirit will soon come to rest in God and he will forget all things of sense.

2. Wherefore, although it is best to pray where there is most decency, yet notwithstanding one should choose the place where sense and spirit are least hindered from journeying to God. Here we should consider that answer made by Our Saviour to the Samaritan woman, when she asked Him which was the more fitting place wherein to pray, the temple or the mountain, and He answered her[1] that true prayer was not connected with the mountain or with the temple,[2] but that those who adored the Father and were pleasing to Him were those that adored Him in spirit and in truth.[3] Wherefore, although churches and pleasant places are[4] set apart and furnished for prayer (for a church must not be used for aught else), yet, for a matter as intimate[5] as converse held with God, one should choose that place which gives sense the least occupation and the least encouragement. And thus it must not be a place that is pleasant and delectable

---

[1] E.p. omits : ' and He answered her.'
[2] E.p. omits : ' or with the temple.'
[3] S. John iv, 23–4.   [4] E.p. has ' may be ' for ' are.'
[5] A, B : ' as important and intimate.'

to sense (like the places that some habitually contrive to find), for otherwise, instead of the recollection of the spirit in God, naught will be achieved save recreation and pleasure and delight of sense. Wherefore it is good to choose a place that is solitary, and even wild, so that the spirit may wholly and directly soar upward to God, and be not hindered or detained by visible things; for, although these sometimes help to raise up the spirit, it is better to forget them at once and to rest in God. For this reason Our Saviour used to choose solitary places for prayer, and such as occupied the senses but little, in order to give us an example. He chose places that lifted up the soul to God, such as mountains,[1] which are lifted up above the earth, and are ordinarily bare, thus offering no occasion for recreation of the senses.

3. The truly spiritual man, then, is never bound to a place of prayer which is in any way convenient, nor does he even consider this, for that would be to remain bound to sense. But, to the end that he may attain interior recollection, and forget everything, he chooses[2] the places most free from sensible objects and attractions, withdrawing his attention from all these, that he may be able to rejoice in his God and be far removed from all things created. But it is a remarkable thing to see some spiritual persons, who waste all their time in setting up oratories and furnishing places which please their temperaments or inclinations, yet make little account of interior recollection, which is the most important thing, but of which they have very little. If they had more of it, they would be incapable of taking pleasure in those methods and manners of devotion, which would simply weary them.

CHAPTER XL

Which continues to direct the spirit to interior recollection with reference to what has been said.

1. The reason, then, why some spiritual persons never enter perfectly into the true joys of the spirit is that they never succeed in raising their desire for rejoicing above these

---

[1] Alc. ends the paragraph here.
[2] E.p. abbreviates, from the beginning of the paragraph: 'Wherefore the truly spiritual man, considering only interior recollecting and forgetting everything, chooses.'

things that are outward and visible. Let such take note that, although the visible oratory and temple is a decent place set apart for prayer, and an image is a motive to prayer, the sweetness and delight of the soul must not be set upon the motive and visible temple, lest the soul should forget to pray in the living temple, which is the interior recollection of the soul. The Apostle, to remind us of this, said : See that your bodies are living temples of the Holy Spirit, Who dwelleth in you.[1] And this thought is suggested by the words of Christ which we have quoted, namely that they who truly adore God must needs adore Him in spirit and in truth.[2] For God takes little heed of your oratories and your places set apart for prayer if your desire and pleasure are bound to them, and thus you have little interior detachment, which is spiritual poverty and renunciation of all things that you may possess.

2. In order, then, to purge the will from vain desire and rejoicing in this matter, and to direct it to God in your prayer, you must see only to this, that your conscience is pure, and your will perfect with God, and your spirit truly set upon Him. Then, as I have said, you should choose the place that is the farthest withdrawn and the most solitary that you can find, and devote all the rejoicing of the will to calling upon God and glorifying Him ; and you should take no account of those whims about outward things, but rather strive to renounce them. For, if the soul be attached to the delight of sensible devotion, it will never succeed in passing onward to the power of spiritual delight, which is found in spiritual detachment coming through interior recollection.

CHAPTER XLI

Of certain evils into which those persons fall who give themselves to pleasure in sensible objects and who frequent places of devotion in the way that has been described.

1. Many evils, both interior and exterior, come to the spiritual person when he desires to follow after sweetness of sense in these matters aforementioned. For, with regard to

---

[1] i Corinthians iii, 16. E.p. adds : ' And Christ said through Luke : The kingdom of God is within you ' (S. Luke xvii, 21).
[2] S. John iv, 24.

the spirit, he will never attain to interior spiritual recollection, which consists in neglecting all such things, and in causing the soul to forget all this sensible sweetness, and to enter into true recollection, and to acquire the virtues by dint of effort. With regard to exterior things, he will become unable to dispose himself for prayer in all places, but will be confined to those places that are to his taste ; and thus he will often fail in prayer, because, as the saying runs, he knows no other book than that of his own village.

2. Furthermore, this desire leads such persons into great inconstancy. Some of them never continue in one place nor sometimes in one state : now they will be seen in one place, now in another ; now they will go to one hermitage, now to another ; now they will set up this oratory, now that.[1] Some of them, again, wear out their lives in changing from one state or manner of life to another. For, as they possess only the sensible fervour and joy which they find in spiritual things, and have never had the strength to attain to spiritual recollection by the renunciation of their own will, and submitting to suffering inconveniences, whenever they see a place which they think well suited for devotion, or any kind of life or state well adapted to their temperament and inclination, they at once go after it and leave the condition or state in which they were before. And, as they have come under the influence of that sensible pleasure, it follows that they soon seek something new, for sensible pleasure is not constant, since it very quickly fails.[2]

CHAPTER XLII

Of three different kinds of place of devotion and of how the will should conduct itself with regard to them.

1. I can think of three kinds of place by means of which God is wont to move the will to devotion. The first consists in certain dispositions of the ground and situation, which, by means of a pleasing effect of variety, whether obtained by the arrangement of the ground or of trees, or by means of quiet solitude, naturally awaken devotion. These places it is beneficial to use, if they at once lead the will to God and

---

[1] Alc. omits : ' now they . . . now that.'
[2] E.p. : ' and very quickly fails.'

cause it to forget the places themselves, even as, in order to reach one's journey's end, it is advisable not to pause and consider the means and motive of the journey more than is necessary. For those who strive to refresh their desires and to gain sensible sweetness will rather find spiritual aridity and distraction ; for spiritual sweetness and satisfaction are not found save in interior recollection.

2. When they are in such a place, therefore, they should forget it and strive to be inwardly with God, as though they were not in that place at all. For, if they be attached to the pleasure and delight of the place, as we have said, they are seeking refreshment of sense and instability of spirit rather than spiritual tranquillity. The anchorites and other holy hermits, who in the most vast and pleasing wildernesses selected the smallest places that sufficed for them, built there the smallest cells and caves, in which to imprison themselves. S. Benedict was in such a place for three years, and another —namely, S. Simon[1]—bound himself with a cord that he might have no more liberty nor go any farther than to places within its reach ; and even so did many who are too numerous ever to be counted. Those saints understood very clearly that, if they quenched not the desire and eagerness for spiritual sweetness and pleasure, they could not attain to spirituality.

3. The second kind is of a more special nature, for it relates to certain places (whether deserts or any other places whatsoever), where God is accustomed to grant to certain particular persons certain very delectable spiritual favours ; ordinarily, such a place attracts the heart of the person who has received a favour there, and sometimes gives him great desires and yearnings to return to it ; although, when he goes there, what happened to him before is not repeated, since this is not within his power. For God grants these favours[2] when and how and where He pleases, without being tied to any place or time, nor to the free-will of the person to whom He grants them. Yet it is good to go and pray in such places at times if the desire is free from attachment ; and this for three reasons. First, because although, as we said, God is not bound to any place, it would seem that He

---

[1] E.p. omits : 'namely S. Simon.' The allusion is, of course, to S. Simon Stylites.

[2] A, B : 'since it is not within his power to receive those favours ; God grants them . . .'

has willed to be praised by a soul in the place where He has granted it a favour. Secondly, because in that place the soul is more mindful to give thanks to God for that which it has received there. Thirdly, because, by remembering this, the soul's devotion is the more keenly awakened.

4. It is for these reasons that a man should go to such places, and not because he thinks that God is bound to grant him favours there, in such a way as to be unable to grant them wheresoever He wills, for the soul is a fitter and more comely place for God than any physical place. Thus we read in Holy Scripture that Abraham built an altar in the same place at which God appeared to him, and invoked His holy name there, and that afterwards, coming from Egypt, he returned by the same road where God had appeared to him, and called upon God there once more at the same altar which he had built.[1] Jacob, too, marked the place where God had appeared to him, leaning upon a ladder, by raising there a stone which he anointed with oil.[2] And Hagar gave a name to the place where the angel had appeared to her, and prized it highly, saying : Of a truth I have here seen the back of Him that seeth me.[3]

5. The third kind consists of certain special places which God chooses that He may be called upon and served there, such as Mount Sinai, where He gave the law to Moses.[4] And the place that He showed Abraham, that he might sacrifice his son there. [5] And likewise Mount Horeb, where He appeared to our father Elijah.[6]

6. The reason for which God chooses these places rather than others, that He may be praised there, is known to Himself alone. What it behoves us to know is that all is for our advantage, and that He will hear our prayers there, and also in any place where we pray to Him with perfect faith ; although there is much greater occasion for us to be heard in places that are dedicated to His service, since the Church has appointed and dedicated those places to that end.

---

[1] Genesis xii, 8 ; xiii, 4.   [2] Genesis xxviii, 13–19.
[3] Genesis xvi, 13.   [4] Exodus xxiv, 12.   [5] Genesis xxii, 2.
[6] 3 Kings [A.V., 1 Kings] xix, 8. A, B, e.p. amplify, thus : ' And likewise Mount Horeb, whither God sent for our father Elijah to come, that He might show Himself to him there. And the place which S. Michael set apart for his service, namely Mount Garganus, when he appeared to the bishop of Siponto, and said that he was the guardian of that place and that an oratory should be dedicated to God in memory of the angels. And the glorious Virgin chose (by the remarkable sign of snow) a place for the church, to be named after her, which she desired Patricius to build.'

CHAPTER XLIII

*Which treats of other motives for prayer that many persons use—
namely, a great variety of ceremonies.*

1. The useless joys and the imperfect attachment which
many persons have to the things which we have described
are perhaps to some extent excusable, since these persons
act more or less innocently with regard to them. But[1] the
great reliance which some persons place in many kinds of
ceremonies introduced by uninstructed persons who lack the
simplicity of faith is intolerable. Let us here disregard those
which bear certain extraordinary names or are described in
terms that signify nothing, and other things that are not
sacred which persons who are foolish and gross and naturally
suspicious of soul are wont to interpolate in their prayers.
For these are clearly evil, and contain sin, and many of them
imply a secret compact with the devil ; by such means these
persons provoke God to wrath and not to mercy, wherefore
I treat them not here.

2. I wish to speak solely of those ceremonies into which
enters nothing of a suspicious nature, and of which many
people make use nowadays with indiscreet devotion, attribut-
ing such efficacy and faith to these ways and manners wherein they desire to perform their devotions and prayers, that
they believe that, if they fail to the very slightest extent in
them, or go beyond their limits, God will not be served by
them nor will He hear them. They place more reliance upon
these methods and kinds of ceremony than upon the reality
of their prayer, and herein they greatly offend and displease
God. I refer, for example, to a Mass which is said with so
many candles, neither more nor fewer ; which is said by the
priest in such or such a way ; and must be at such or such
an hour, and neither sooner nor later ; and must be after a
certain day, and neither sooner nor later ; and the prayers
and stations must be made at such and such times, with such
and such ceremonies, and neither sooner nor later nor in
any other manner ; and the person who makes them must
have such or such qualities or qualifications. And there are
those who think that if any of these details which they have
laid down be wanting, nothing is accomplished.[2]

[1] E.p. alone has ' but.'

[2] A, B add : ' and [there are] a thousand other things that are offered
and used.' So e.p., but omitting : ' offered and.'

3. And, what is worse, and indeed intolerable, is that certain persons desire to feel some effect in themselves, or to have their petitions fulfilled, or to know that the purpose of these ceremonious prayers of theirs will be accomplished. This is nothing less than to tempt God and to offend Him greatly, so much so that He sometimes gives leave to the devil to deceive them, making them feel and understand things that are far removed from the benefit of their soul, which they deserve because of the attachment which they have in their prayers, not desiring God's will to be done therein more than their own desires ; and thus, because they set not all their confidence in God, nothing goes well with them.[1]

CHAPTER XLIV

Of the manner wherein the rejoicing and strength of the will must be directed to God through these devotions.

1. Let these persons, then, know that, the more reliance they place on these things and ceremonies,[2] the less confidence they have in God, and that they will not obtain of God that which they desire. There are certain persons who pray[3] because of their own desire rather than for the honour of God. Although they suppose that a thing will be done' if it be for the service of God, and not otherwise, yet, because of their attachment to it and the vain rejoicing which they have in it, they multiply a large number of petitions for a thing, when it would be better for them to change these petitions into others of greater importance to them, such as for the true cleansing of their consciences, and for a real application to things concerning their own salvation, leaving to a much later season all those other petitions of theirs which are not of this kind. And in this way they would attain that which is of the greatest importance to them, and at the same time all the other things that are good for them (although they might not have prayed for them), much better and much earlier than if they had expended all their energy

---

[1] With the last word of this chapter, which is also the last word of the page in Alc., the copy of P. Juan Evangelista comes to an end. The remainder of Alc. comes from another very early copy which, in the time of P. Andrés, existed at Duruelo (cf. p. xxvi, above).

[2] B : ' the more they rely on their ceremonies.' E.p. : ' the more they lean on these their ceremonies.'

[3] A, e.p. : ' who work ' [*obran* for *oran*].

on those things. For this the Lord promised, through the Evangelist, saying : Seek ye first and principally the King-dom of God and His righteousness, and all these other things shall be added unto you.[1]

2. This is the seeking and the asking that is most pleasing to God, and, in order to obtain the fulfilment of the petitions which we have in our hearts, there is no better way than to direct the energy of our prayer to the thing that most pleases God. For then not only will He give that which we ask of Him, which is salvation, but also that which He sees to be fitting and good for us, although we pray not for it. This David makes clear in a psalm where he says : The Lord is nigh unto those that call upon Him in truth,[2] that beg Him[3] for the things that are in the highest degree true, such as salvation ; for of these he then says : He will fulfil the will of them that fear Him, and will hear their cries, and will save them. For God is the guardian of those that truly love Him.[4] And thus, this nearness to God of which David here speaks is naught else than His being ready to satisfy them and grant them even that which it has not passed through their minds to ask. Even so we read that, because Solomon did well in asking God for a thing that was pleasing to Him—namely, wisdom to lead and rule his people righteously—God answered him, saying : Because more than aught else thou didst desire wisdom, and askedst not victory over thine enemies, with their deaths, neither riches nor long life, I will not only give thee the wisdom that thou askedst to rule My people righteously, but I will likewise give thee that which thou hast not asked—namely, riches and substance and glory—so that neither before thee nor after thee shall there be any king like unto thee.[5] And this He did, giving him peace also from his enemies, so that all around him paid tribute to him and troubled him not. We read of a similar incident in Genesis, where God promised Abraham to increase the generation of his lawful sons, like the stars of Heaven, even as he had asked of Him, and said to him : Likewise I will increase the children of the bondwoman, for they are thy children.[6]

---

[1] S. Matthew vi, 33.   [2] Psalm cxliv, 18 [A.V., cxlv, 18].
[3] E.p., keeping near the Latin text of the psalm, has : '. . . that call upon Him, to those that call upon Him in truth. And those that call upon Him in truth are such as beg Him.'
[4] Psalm cxliv, 19 [A.V., cxlv, 19–20].
[5] 2 Paralipomenon [A.V., 2 Chronicles] i, 11–12.   [6] Genesis xxi, 13.

3. In this way, then, the strength of the will and its rejoicing must be directed to God in our petitions, and we must not be anxious to cling to ceremonial inventions which are not used or approved by the Catholic Church. We must leave the method and manner of saying Mass to the priest, whom the Church sets there in her place, giving him her orders as to how he is to do it. And let not such persons use new methods, as if they knew more than the Holy Spirit and His Church. If, when they pray in their simplicity, God hears them not, let them not think that He will hear them any the more however many may be their inventions. For God is of such a kind that, if they behave towards Him as they should, and conformably to His nature, they will do with Him as much as they will ; but, if they act from selfish ends, they cannot speak with Him.[1]

4. With regard to further ceremonies connected with prayer and other devotions, let not the will be set upon other ceremonies and forms of prayer than those which Christ[2] taught us.[3] For it is clear that, when His disciples besought Him that He would teach them to pray, He would tell them all that is necessary in order that the Eternal Father may hear us, as He knew His nature so well. Yet all that He taught them was the Pater Noster, with its seven petitions, wherein are included all our needs, both spiritual and temporal ;[4] and He taught them not many other kinds of prayer, either in words or in ceremonies. On the contrary, He told them that when they prayed they ought not to desire to speak much, since our heavenly Father knows well what is meet for us.[5] He charged them only, but with great insistence, that they should persevere in prayer (that is, in the prayer of the Pater Noster), saying elsewhere : It behoves us always to pray and never to fail.[6] But He taught not a variety of petitions, but rather that our petitions should be repeated frequently and with fervour and care. For, as I say, in them is contained all that is the will of God and all that is meet for us. Wherefore, when His Majesty drew near three times to the Eternal Father, He prayed all these three times using those very words of the Pater Noster, as the Evangelist tells us, saying : Father, if it cannot be but that I must drink this cup, Thy will be done.[7] And the ceremonies

---

[1] So Alc. E.p. omits the sentence : ' For God . . . speak with Him.'
[2] E.p. : ' Christ and His Church.'   [3] S. Luke xi, 1-4.
[4] A, B : ' both corporal and spiritual.'   [5] S. Matthew vi, 7-8.
[6] S. Luke xviii, 1.   [7] S. Matthew xxvi, 39.

which He taught us to use in our prayers are only two. Either we are to pray in the secret place of our chamber, where without noise and without paying heed to any we can pray with the most perfect and pure heart, as He said in these words : When thou prayest, enter into thy closet and shut the door and pray.[1] Or else He taught us to go to a solitary and desert place, as He Himself did, and at the best and quietest time of night. And thus there is no reason to fix any limit of time, or any appointed days, or to set apart one time more than another for our devotions, neither is there any reason to use[2] other forms, in our words and prayers, nor phrases with double meanings, but only those which the Church uses and in the manner wherein she uses them ; for all are reduced to those which we have described—namely, the Pater Noster.

5. I do not for this reason condemn—nay, I rather approve—the fixing of days on which certain persons sometimes arrange to make their devotions, such as novenas,[3] or other such things. I condemn only their conduct as concerns the fixity of their methods and the ceremonies with which they practise them. Even so did Judith rebuke and reprove the people of Bethulia because they had limited God as to the time wherein they hoped for His mercy,[4] saying : Do ye set God a time for His mercies ? This, she says, is not to move God to clemency, but to awaken His wrath.[5]

CHAPTER XLV

Which treats of the second kind of distinct good, wherein the will may rejoice vainly.

1. The second kind of distinct and delectable good wherein the will may rejoice vainly is that which provokes or persuades us to serve God and which we have called provocative. This belongs to preachers, and we might speak of it in two ways, namely, as affecting the preachers themselves and as affecting their hearers. For, as regards both, we

[1] S. Matthew vi, 6.
[2] E.p. abbreviates : ' And thus there is no reason to fix times or fixed [*sic*] days, nor is there any reason to use.'
[3] So A, B. The other authorities [and P. Silverio] read : ' such as to fast.'
[4] A, B : ' for mercy from His hand.'
[5] Judith viii, 11–12.

must not fail to observe that both must direct the rejoicing of their will to God, with respect to this exercise.

2. In the first place, it must be pointed out to the preacher, if he is to cause his people profit and not to embarrass himself[1] with vain joy and presumption, that the exercise of preaching is spiritual rather than vocal. For, although it be practised by means of outward words, its power and efficacy reside not in these but in the inward spirit. Wherefore, however lofty be the doctrine that is preached, and however choice the rhetoric and sublime the style wherein it is clothed, it brings as a rule no more benefit than is present in the spirit of the preacher. For, although it is true that the word of God is of itself efficacious, according to those words of David, ' He will give to His voice a voice of virtue,'[2] yet fire, which has also a virtue—that of burning—will not burn when the material is not prepared.

3. To the end that the force of the preacher's instruction may take hold upon the hearer, there must be two kinds of preparation : that of the preacher and that of the hearer ; for as a rule the benefit derived from a sermon depends upon the preparation of the teacher. For this reason it is said that, as is the master, so is wont to be the disciple. For, when in the Acts of the Apostles those seven sons of that chief priest of the Jews[3] were wont to cast out devils in the same form as S. Paul, the devil rose up against them, saying : Jesus I confess and Paul I know, but you, who are ye ?[4] And then, attacking them, he stripped and wounded them. This was only because they had not the fitting preparation, and not because Christ willed not that they should not do this in His name. For the Apostles once found a man, who was not a disciple, casting out a devil in the name of Christ, and they forbade him, and the Lord reproved them for it, saying : Forbid him not, for no man that has done any mighty works in My name shall be able to speak evil of Me after a brief space of time.[5] But He is angry with those who, though teaching the law of God, keep it not, and, while preaching spirituality, possess it not. For this reason God says, through S. Paul : Thou teachest others and teachest not thyself. Thou who preachest that men should not steal, stealest.[6]

---

[1] E.p. : ' and not to become vain.'
[2] Psalm lxvii, 34 [A.V., lxviii, 33].
[3] E.p. : ' those seven sons of Sceva.'   [4] Acts xix, 15.
[5] S. Mark ix, 38–9.   [6] Romans ii, 21.

And through David the Holy Spirit says : To the sinner, God said : ' Why speakest thou of My righteousness and takest My law in thy mouth, when thou hast hated discipline and hast cast My words behind thee ? '[1] Here it is made plain that He will give them no spirituality whereby they may bear fruit.

4. It is a common matter of observation that, so far as we can judge here below, the better is the life of the preacher, the greater is the fruit that he produces, however undistinguished his style may be, however small his rhetoric and however ordinary his instruction. For warmth that comes from the living spirit clings ; whereas the other kind of preacher will produce very little profit, however sublime be his style and his instruction. For, although it is true that a good style and gestures and sublime instruction and eloquent language influence men and produce much effect when accompanied by true spirituality, yet without this, although a sermon give[2] pleasure and delight to the sense and the understanding, very little or nothing of its sweetness remains in the will. As a rule, in this case, the will remains as weak and remiss with regard to good works as it was before. Although marvellous things may have been marvellously said by the preacher, they serve only to delight the ear, like a concert of music or a peal of bells ; the spirit, as I say, goes no farther from its habits than before, since the voice has no virtue to raise one that is dead from his grave.

5. Little does it matter that one kind of music should sound better than another if the better kind move me not more than the other to do good works. For, although marvellous things may have been said, they are at once forgotten if they have not fired the will. For, not only do they of themselves bear little fruit, but the fastening of the sense upon the pleasure that it finds in that sort of instruction hinders the instruction from passing to the spirit, so that only the method and the accidents of what has been said are appreciated, and the preacher is praised for this characteristic or for that, and followed from such motives as these rather than because of the purpose of amendment of life which he has inspired. This doctrine is well explained by S. Paul to the Corinthians, where he says : I, brethren, when I came to you, came not

---

[1] Psalm xlix, 16–17 [A.V., l, 16–17].
[2] So Alc. The other authorities have : ' although it give . . .'

preaching Christ with loftiness of doctrine and of wisdom, and my words and my preaching consisted not in the rhetoric of human wisdom, but in the showing forth of the spirit and of the truth.[1]

6. Although the intention of the Apostle here, like my own intention, is not to condemn good style and rhetoric and phraseology, for, on the contrary, these are of great importance to the preacher, as in everything else, since good phraseology and style raise up and restore things that are fallen and ruined, even as bad phraseology ruins and destroys good things. . . .[2]

---

[1] 1 Corinthians ii, 1–4. B, e.p. : ' and of virtue.'

[2] E.p. adds : ' End of the *Ascent of Mount Carmel*.' The treatise thus remains incomplete, the chapter on the preacher being unfinished and no part of any chapter upon the hearer having come down to us. Further, the last two divisions of the four mentioned in Chap. xxxv, § 1 are not treated in any of the MSS. or early editions.

The fragments which P. Gerardo added to the *Ascent*, forming two chapters, cannot be considered as a continuation of this book. They are in reality a long and admirable letter, written to a religious, who was one of the Saint's spiritual sons, and copied by P. Jerónimo de San José in his *History of S. John of the Cross* (Bk. VI, Chap. vii). There is not the slightest doubt that the letter, which was written at Segovia, and is fully dated, is a genuine letter, and not an editor's maltreatment of part of a treatise. Only the similarity of its subject with that of these last chapters is responsible for its having been added to the *Ascent*. It is hard to see how P. Gerardo could have been misled about a matter which is so clear.